CHURCHES AND CHURCHMEN IN
MEDIEVAL EUROPE

Churches and Churchmen in Medieval Europe

Christopher N. L. Brooke

THE HAMBLEDON PRESS

London and Rio Grande

Published by The Hambledon Press, 1999

102 Gloucester Avenue, London NW1 8HX (UK)
Po Box 162, Rio Grande, Ohio 45674 (USA)

ISBN 1 85285 183 X

A description of this book is available from the
British Library and from the Library of Congress

Typeset by Carnegie Publishing, Lancaster
Printed on acid-free paper and bound in the UK
by Cambridge University Press

Contents

Illustrations

For Rosalind Brooke

co-author of this book
and
collaborator in many other adventures

Preface

The essays in this volume spring from a lifetime spent in the central middle ages. Some range widely in time, but most have more than a foothold in the eleventh, twelfth or thirteenth centuries. I have attempted in them to penetrate to the heart of a number of problems in understanding and interpreting the medieval church. They were written at various times over the last thirty years; but they all represent living interests and commitments and convictions.

They all have (I hope) something to contribute to current study and debate. For this reason I have revised them with a light hand, correcting my errors, revealing where I have changed my mind, introducing some of the more recent literature – but not attempting a radical revision or full bibliography of every theme. By the same token I have pruned overlaps and repetitions, but sparingly, so as to avoid drastic surgery on the original papers.

It is frequently alleged that British historians are lone workers and eschew collaboration; and that they are wholly empirical and avoid any brush with scientific theory. Both notions are misleading if not wholly false.

All the essays in this book reflect my interest in working with others, and two were written in collaboration. In 1950–51 Dr Rosalind Clark – from 1951 Dr Rosalind Brooke – worked on the sources for the history of the Anglo-Norman Church in Normandy and Paris. This was to provide new foundations for our common interest in the impact of the Norman Conquest on the English church, which has borne fruit in many regions of my own work; in particular, we presented Chapter 6, the fruit of detailed prosopographical study of the Anglo-Norman bishops, to the *La Mendola* conference of 1974 held in Milan, in Italian dress. She herself has long held a leading international role among Franciscan scholars, and I have often played the part of her research assistant. Together we offered Chapter 15, on St Clare, to Professor Rosalind Hill as part of the volume on *Medieval Women* which formed her Festschrift in 1978. The closest collaboration of my life has influenced many of the studies in and out of this book, and Rosalind Brooke is indeed its part-author.

In the 1940s I served an apprenticeship with my father, Professor
Z. N. Brooke, cut short all too soon by his death in 1946. We worked on
the letters of Gilbert Foliot, bishop of Hereford (1148–63) and London
(1163–87) – and we produced a first study of the dignitaries and archdeacons
of Hereford Cathedral in 1944.[1] I continued his work on Gilbert Foliot's
letters with Dom Adrian Morey, and the outcome came in two books
published in 1965 and 1967.[2] My early interest in Hereford is reflected in a
wide-ranging study of the see in Chapter 2, and my early devotion to
archdeacons in Chapter 7. Hereford was one of several sees I have studied,
and I surveyed the wider structure of the English church, from diocese to
parish, in a European setting at Spoleto in 1980 – hence Chapter 1.

After my father, the chief inspiration of my earliest studies was Dom
David Knowles, and the medieval religious orders play a role in many of
the chapters of this book. It was often observed that his *Monastic Order in
England* (1940) lacked any serious enquiry into monastic patronage, and a
part of this gap I attempted to fill in the study of Anglo-Norman and
Scottish kings in Chapters 8 and 9. In Chapter 11 I wrote of St Bernard, a
central figure in Dom David's own studies. Monastic studies – especially
the much debated question of the relation of different types of religious,
above all of monk and canon, form the theme of Chapters 12 and 13.

Already in the 1940s my father had ambitious schemes for studies of the
prosopography of the twelfth-century English church, and David Knowles
had laid foundations for lists of monastic superiors. They agreed on collaboration in 1942, and this issued thirty years later in *Heads of Religious Houses:
England and Wales, 940–1216*, by David Knowles, Christopher Brooke and
Vera London – one of the books most often cited in this volume.[3] The
interest of the Brookes, father and son, in archdeacons and the like was
later absorbed, to my great delight, in the new Le Neve in the Institute of
Historical Research; and Professor Diana Greenway's work for Le Neve's
Fasti, 1066–1300 has not only provided new foundations for my study of
archdeacons in Chapter 7 but has caused me to revise some of my cherished
theories about the origins of Norman Chapters, reflected especially in my
account of York Minster in Chapter 3. She has added to my many debts
to her by rereading Chapter 7 and helping me in its revision.

When I moved from Liverpool to London in 1967, I hoped to play a part
in reviving interest in medieval London. This has indeed been accomplished

[1] Z. N. and C. N. L. Brooke, 'Hereford Cathedral Dignitaries in the Twelfth Century', *Cambridge Historical Journal*, 8 (1944–46), pp. 1–21, with supplement in 8 (1944–46), pp. 179–85.

[2] *GF* and *GFL*.

[3] As *Heads* – soon to be renamed *Heads* i, since D. M. Smith and V. C. M. London, *Heads
of Religious Houses: England and Wales*, ii, 1216–1377, is nearing completion.

beyond my dreams under the leadership of Caroline Barron and Derek Keene – and of many others, including the archaeologists in the Museum of London. My own role was to join with the Reverend Gillian Keir in writing a volume on *London, 800–1216* (1975). We received generous support from the City of London through its Library Committee and their interest is reflected in ample chapters on early sheriffs and mayors. In this field, as in much of our work, we were greatly encouraged and inspired by the generous help of Susan Reynolds; and we benefited in all manner of ways from the chance to see the Winchester Research Unit at work, and from many conversations with Martin Biddle and Derek Keene – who has since carried his special expertise in urban history to London, to its very great benefit. The most original part of our own contribution lay in three approaches to urban history. First of all, we attempted to break through the parochialism of many studies of English towns by wide-ranging comparative study, especially with Italian cities of the early and mid middle ages. Secondly, we brought our own perception of the vital importance of the church – both in forming medieval cities and in providing the bulk of the evidence about them. And thirdly, we tried to bring into the open the fundamental, yet deeply puzzling, topographical evidence of the city itself – its streets and wards and above all its parishes.[4]

My aim here is not to defend the doctrines propounded in the book, but rather to indicate that they formed part of a developing field of research, and so have their place in its study still. Research into urban parishes has flourished since we wrote, most notably in Derek Keene's studies in Winchester and London, and in the very recent volume *The Church in the Medieval Town*, edited by T. R. Slater and Gervase Rosser (Aldershot, 1998), which came too late to influence the revision of my chapters. Though most of its thrust is in the late middle ages, when evidence becomes more copious,

---

[4] Topographical study has since been put on new foundations by the *British Atlas of Historic Towns*, iii, *The City of London from Prehistoric Times to c. 1520*, ed. M. D. Lobel (Oxford, 1989), to which I contributed a chapter on the period 800–1270 which was in effect a summary of our book; and Gillian Keir contributed detailed notes on the city churches, which were incorporated into the gazetteer edited by Martha Carlin and Victor Belcher. Among the more fundamental studies of early city topography, particular mention should be made of Tim Tatton-Brown, 'The Topography of Anglo-Saxon London', *Antiquity*, 60 (1986), pp. 21–28 (including conjectures on some early churches); V. Horsman, C. Milnes and G. Milne, *Aspects of Saxon-Norman London*, i, *Building and Street Development near Billingsgate and Cheapside*, London and Middlesex Archaeological Society Special Paper, 11 (1988), pp. 112–16. I find less convincing Jeremy Haslam's attempt to rewrite the history of ward and parish in eastern London, and his reconstruction of a hypothetical hierarchy of minsters, in 'Parishes, Churches, Wards and Gates in Eastern London', in *Minsters and Parish Churches*, ed. J. Blair (Oxford, 1988), pp. 35–43.

it affects the themes of Chapters 4 and 5 at several points, most notably in the study of 'The Origins of Urban Parish Boundaries' by Nigel Baker and Richard Holt. They show from evidence in Worcester and Gloucester the development of parish boundaries under the varying pressures of a long period from the tenth to the thirteenth centuries. This fits well the perceptions in Chapters 4 and 5 below, while adding a dimension to the later period when parish boundaries became fossilised. The authors try to drive a wedge between Brooke and Keir, who allegedly made tithe allocation the basis of the formation of city parishes, and Keene, who found in late medieval evidence at Winchester that at that date the defining factor of allegiance to a parish was the distance of a house from a church.[5] What I have tried to expound in Chapters 4 and 5 – as Gillian Keir and I did in our book – was indeed a palimpsest of the differing influences of different periods, in which the evidence from the tenth to twelfth centuries must not be confused with evidence from the fifteenth. In the early period what above all needs to be explained is the formation of the vast number of parishes in some English towns. The problem is not – 'how was a parish defined?' – but who took the initiative in building so many tiny churches and forming so many tiny parishes? The answer must lie, not in legal definitions – important though they come to be later on – but in the common action of groups of neighbours. That is a crucial element in the palimpsest, though there are indeed many others.

Collaborative work is most necessary in the editing of historical sources, and it is in this field that most of mine has lain, as editor and general editor. As one of a group of general editors of Nelson's and Oxford Medieval Texts, from 1959 to 1987, I helped to see well over forty volumes into print; and as David Smith's assistant as General Editor of the British Academy's *English Episcopal Acta* I have had a hand in seeing twenty more to press. In some of these volumes my share has been large, in some small; but all reflect my fundamental concern to improve the foundations of our science. My own work as editor is reflected most obviously here by a general account of John of Salisbury (Chapter 14), which in a measure summed up many years of studying, editing and interpreting the letters of a major figure of the twelfth-century renaissance who yields his message only on the closest scrutiny.

[5] N. Baker and R. Holt, 'The Origins of Urban Parish Boundaries', esp. pp. 211–12. For the study of early urban parishes Tim Tatton-Brown's paper on 'Medieval Parishes and Parish Churches in Canterbury', also in *The Church in the Medieval Town*, pp. 236–71, is of outstanding importance – though his conclusion that the immediate post-conquest period is seminal for the growth of numerous tiny parishes raises a puzzle: for this was the era of Lanfranc, the most authoritarian of archbishops (1070–89).

John of Salisbury spans historical and literary studies; and on this border-line I have often dwelt. I am convinced that it is on the frontiers of what is sometimes quaintly called straight history and its neighbours that new perspectives are most readily to be observed. I have often attempted a like study of vernacular literature: Chrétien of Troyes, Wolfram von Eschenbach, Chaucer and Shakespeare fill many pages of my *Medieval Idea of Marriage* (Oxford, 1989) – and I return to Chaucer in Chapter 16, in company with Edmund Gonville, founder of Gonville and Caius College – and sole representative of a major interest in more recent years in academic history.

The other borders which I have explored have been those of history and archaeology, and history and the history of art and architecture. Chapter 10 is a pioneer essay written many years ago; architectural historians have studied Anglo-Norman cathedrals in much greater detail and depth; but the principles I enunciated are still worth meditating. By the same token, the relation of St Bernard to monastic art and planning has been the theme of a copious literature; but Chapter 11 still states succinctly the excitement, the paradoxes and the problems of relating the great puritan to the environment he did so much to create.

Without more ado, let us open the workshop and display its wares.

Acknowledgements

For the illustrations, I am greatly indebted to the generous kindness of Dr John Crook, who provided Figs. 5–8. Figs 1–4 are reproduced, with permission, from the Council of British Archaeology's volume, *European Towns: Their Archaeology and Early History*, ed. Maurice Barley (1977).

For permission and approval for the reprinting of the chapters in this volume, I am very grateful to: The Director, Prof. Stefano Brufani, and the Centro Italiano di Studi sull'Alto Medioevo, Spoleto, for Chapter 1. The Honorary Secretary, Mr J. W. Tonkin, and the Woolhope Naturalists' Field Club, for Chapter 2. The Reverend the Chancellor and the Dean and Chapter of York Minster, and the Oxford University Press, for Chapter 3 – and also for the kind approval of the editor, Professor Gerald Aylmer. The editor, Dr Robert Swanson, and the Ecclesiastical History Society, for Chapters 4, 12–15 (in which copyright remains with the society). The Deputy Director and the Council for British Archaeology for Chapter 5. Professor Dom Giorgio Picasso, OSB, and the Centro di Studi Medioevali of the Università Cattolica del Sacro Cuore, Milan, for Chapters 6 and 8. The Permissions Controller and the Cambridge University Press for Chapters 7, 11, and also for Chapter 4. Professor Coloman Viola and the Service Juridique et Auteurs of Fleurus – Mame for Chapter 9. The General Secretary and the Friends of Winchester Cathedral, for Chapter 10. Professor David Smith, Director of the Borthwick Institute, University of York, for Chapter 16.

My thanks to some of those who helped me in the preparation and correction of these papers have been recorded in the Preface; more are given in the notes to the chapters below. For the chapters which were originally conference papers, I offer renewed thanks to successive Presidenti and Direttori of the Settimane at Spoleto (Chapter 1) and La Mendola (Chapters 6, 8) for their kind invitations and generous hospitality. In addition, I recall the generous help I received from Dr Dorothy Owen, Professor David Smith, and Dr Michael Franklin in Chapter 1.

In revising several of the chapters I have had invaluable help from Professor Simon Keynes. Chapter 2 was originally written as a tribute to Miss Penelope

Morgan – and given in the series of Lectures in honour of her father, F. C. Morgan; and when I delivered the lecture I recalled the many kindnesses I had received from Penelope Morgan when she was Hereford Cathedral Librarian. Chapter 3 as first published included a warm appreciation to the late Canon Reginald Cant, to Professors Gerald Aylmer, Barrie Dobson and David Smith; to the late Mrs Norah Gurney, Professor C. R. Dodwell, Drs Eric Gee and John Harvey and Mr John Beckwith; to Dr Marie Lovatt, Miss Katharine Longley and Mr Bernard Barr. For Chapter 8, I was especially indebted to Dr Martin Brett, Professor Brian Kemp and Sir Richard Southern.

Three chapters were originally contributions to Festschriften, and it is a special pleasure to record the approval of Dr Marjorie Chibnall and Professor Raymonde Foreville for the reprinting of Chapters 7 and 9 – sadly Professor Rosalind Hill died too soon to give a similar blessing to Chapter 15.

These essays have been written over a period of thirty years, and there will be other generous scholars who have helped and advised me, whose names I have failed to record: I offer my thanks and my apologies to them all – and my warmest thanks to Martin Sheppard of the Hambledon Press for undertaking the publication of the book, and for all the trouble he has taken with it.

Abbreviations

Councils and Synods	*Councils and Synods: With Other Documents Relating to the English Church*, i, 871–1204, ed. D. Whitelock, M. Brett and C. N. L. Brooke, 2 parts (Oxford, 1981)
EHR	*English Historical Review*
English Episcopal Acta	*English Episcopal Acta*, 1–17 (so far; 18–20 in the press), ed. D. M. Smith et al., British Academy (London, 1980–98)
Fasti	J. Le Neve, *Fasti Ecclesiae Anglicanae, 1066–1300*, ed. D. E. Greenway, 6 vols to date (London, 1968–99)
Fasti, 1300–1541	J. Le Neve, *Fasti ecclesiae anglicanae, 1300–1541*, ed. H. P. F. King, J. M. Horn and B. Jones, 12 vols (London, 1962–67)
GF	A. Morey and C. N. L. Brooke, *Gilbert Foliot and his Letters* (Cambridge, 1965)
GFL	*The Letters and Charters of Gilbert Foliot*, ed. A. Morey and C. N. L. Brooke (Cambridge, 1967)
Heads	D. Knowles, C. N. L. Brooke and V. C. M. London, *The Heads of Religious Houses: England and Wales, 940–1216* (Cambridge, 1972)
John of Salisbury, Letters	*The Letters of John of Salisbury*, i, ed. W. J. Millor, H. E. Butler and C. N. L. Brooke, NMT (Edinburgh, 1955; corrected reprint, Oxford, 1986); ii, ed. W. J. Millor and C. N. L. Brooke, OMT (Oxford, 1979)
Knowles, *Monastic Order*	D. Knowles, *The Monastic Order in England* (Cambridge, 1940; 2nd edn, 1963, pagination unaltered)
Mendola, 1–8	*Atti della prima-ottava settimana internazionale di studio Mendola*, Miscellanea del centro di studi medioevali (Università Cattolica del Sacro Cuore), 3–10 (Milan, 1959–80)
NMT	Nelson's Medieval Texts
OMT	Oxford Medieval texts

Orderic	*The Ecclesiastical History of Orderic Vitalis*, ed. and trans. M. Chibnall, 6 vols, OMT (Oxford, 1968–80)
PL	*Patrologiae cursus completus, series latina*, ed. J. P. Migne, 221 vols (Paris, 1844–64)
RS	The Rolls Series: Chronicles and Memorials of Great Britain and Ireland during the Middle Ages
VCH	*The Victoria Histories of the Counties of England*

Rural Ecclesiastical Institutions in England: The Search for their Origins

It is commonly said, and it is broadly true, that the provinces of Britain formed the only major part of the Roman Empire in the west in which the ancient structures of Christendom were totally destroyed in the early middle ages. In the land of the Angles, England, pagan German-speaking rulers and settlers obliterated the language and most of the culture of Roman Britain. Like every great historical generalisation, this has been much criticised, and recent research, as we shall see, has found serious qualifications. But in a measure it is obviously true; and let us start with some examples which reveal how deep a cleavage the Anglo-Saxon conquest made in English ecclesiastical institutions.[1]

The conversion of England and the creation of the English church as we know it began with the mission sent by Pope Gregory the Great in 596–97; and however deeply the medieval church in England was influenced by the British, Celtic, Christian missionaries who lived in the west and north of

First printed in *Settimane di studio del Centro italiano di studi sull'alto medioevo*, 28 (1982), pp. 685–711.

[1] There is a general discussion of ecclesiastical structures in the eleventh century in F. Barlow, *The English Church, 1000–1066*, 2nd edn (London, 1979), pp. 159–231, on the dioceses see esp. ibid., pp. 162ff.; H. Mayr-Harting, *The Coming of Christianity to Anglo-Saxon England* (London, 1972; 3rd edn, 1991); J. Campbell, 'The Church in Anglo-Saxon Towns', *Studies in Church History*, 16 (1979), pp. 119–35, esp. 119–20, 132–34. Campbell's essay has much that is relevant to countryside as well as town; and on country parishes see Barlow; and literature cited, esp. R. Lennard, *Rural England, 1086–1135* (Oxford, 1959), pp. 288–338; valuable brief introductions to their subject are G. W. O. Addleshaw, *The Beginnings of the Parochial System: The Development of the Parochial System ... [768–1099]*; *Rectors, Vicars and Patrons in Twelfth- and Early Thirteenth-Century Canon Law*, St Anthony's Hall publications (Borthwick Institute of Historical Research), nos. 3, 6, 9 (3rd edn, York, 1970; 2nd edn 1970; 1956). There is a useful general survey in John Godfrey, *The English Parish, 600–1300* (London, 1969). For churches in the time of Domesday Book (1086) see the evidence laid out in H. C. Darby, *Domesday Geography of England*, ed. H. C. Darby, 7 vols (Cambridge, 1952–77). But the interpretation of Domesday's evidence on churches is obscure, if not, as some scholars think, haphazard.

the island already in the sixth century, and penetrated into many parts of England in the seventh and eighth centuries, the framework and the organisation of the English church kept the shape and orientation given by the Roman missionaries, especially by St Augustine of Canterbury and Archbishop Theodore, two generations later.[2] Pope Gregory himself thought of Britain as a lost Roman province and devised a scheme little related to current geography: for two provinces based on London and York.[3] In the event the see of the southern province has been not in London but in Canterbury from that day to this, where St Augustine, the first archbishop, set it, in the territory of the first major, Christian king to be converted by the Roman missionaries; and it was only after a false start and some vicissitudes that the northern province was established in York in the eighth century.[4] It is true that in the twelfth century a bishop of London was to flirt with the idea of fulfilling Gregory's sketch or plan, and moving the centre of the archbishopric there; and that since the late twelfth century, in fact, the chief home of the archbishops of Canterbury has been in Lambeth Palace in London.[5] But the medieval dioceses, in varying degrees, reflected the political geography of seventh century England. In the sixth and seventh centuries the kaleidoscope of minor confederacies and shifting settlements and frontiers of the invading peoples was beginning to turn and to clarify:[6]

[2] There is an admirable survey in H. Mayr-Harting, *Coming of Christianity* (n. 1); and for Gregory's mission strategy see esp. R. A. Markus, 'Gregory the Great and a Papal Missionary Strategy', *Studies in Church History*, 6 (1970), pp. 29–38. The chief evidence is in Bede's *Historia ecclesiastica*, on whose context see esp. *Famulus Christi*, ed. G. Bonner (London, 1976); P. Hunter Blair, *The World of Bede* (London, 1970); G. Musca, *Il venerabile Beda, storico dell'alto medioevo* (Bari, 1973). See now J. M. Wallace-Hadrill, *Bede's Ecclesiastical History of the English People: A Historical Commentary*, OMT (Oxford, 1988), with bibliography. If Augustine first attached bishops' sees to tribal leaders and centres, it was Theodore (669–90) who carried this out on a much more systematic scale. For Roman influence in England see esp. J. M. Wallace-Hadrill, 'Rome and the Early English Church: Some Problems of Transmission', *Settimane di studio del centro italiano di studi sull'alto medioevo*, 7, ii, (1960), pp. 519–48.

[3] Bede, *Historia ecclesiastica*, i, p. 29, ed. B. Colgrave and R. A. B. Mynors, OMT (Oxford, 1969), pp. 104–7.

[4] See R. M. T. Hill, *A History of York Minster*, ed. G. E. Aylmer and R. Cant (Oxford, 1977), pp. 4ff; H. Mayr-Harting, 'Paulinus of York', *Studies in Church History*, 4 (1967), pp. 15–21; P. Hunter Blair, 'The Letters of Pope Boniface V and the Mission of Paulinus to Northumbria', in *England before the Conquest: Studies in Primary Sources Presented to Dorothy Whitelock*, ed. P. Clemoes and K. Hughes (Cambridge, 1971), pp. 5–13.

[5] *GF*, pp. 151–62; C. N. L. Brooke and G. Keir, *London, 800–1216* (London, 1975), p. 364; D. Gardiner, *The Story of Lambeth Palace* (London, 1930).

[6] The phrase derives from the penetrating study of H. E. Walker, 'Bede and the Gewissae: The Political Evolution of the Heptarchy and its Nomenclature', *Cambridge Historical Journal*, 12 (1956), pp. 174–86. The fundamental account is in F. M. Stenton, *Anglo-Saxon England* (3rd edn, Oxford, 1971).

by the late seventh and eighth centuries the main kingdoms which were to dominate later Saxon history – Northumbria, in the north, Mercia in the centre and west, and Wessex in the south – were coming to be recognised, and spreading their shadow over earlier flourishing kingdoms, St Augustine's Kent, East Anglia and Essex, and several others. In the centre of England the kingdom of Mercia came to embrace a span of territory across the midlands and the west, absorbing what to us are the shadowy kingdoms of the Magonsaetan and the Hwicce, which had formed the English advance guard on the borders of Wales.[7] These peoples, and the shape of their provinces or kingdoms, would be very misty to us, but for the fact that the sees established for them in the late 670s survived to the end of the middle ages, and with modifications to this day. There are still bishops at Hereford and at Worcester; and down to the Reformation the boundaries of their sees – which are not precisely those of the ancient shires of those regions – preserved the line of the boundaries of the forgotten kingdoms of the Magonsaetan and the Hwicce.[8] This is an extreme case; but not isolated. Rather commoner are the cases of the southern sees, of Winchester, Salisbury and Exeter, which divided Wessex between them – though Exeter in the extreme south west represented in a sense the area where British and Romano-British populations survived latest, and least anglicised, in the south of England. In the midlands, Mercia was divided in the long run by Archbishop Theodore,[9] between the main Mercian diocese with its centre usually in Lichfield, and the diocese which sprawled from Oxfordshire to Lincoln, which eventually became the see of Lincoln, and was almost as large as the Alpine diocese of Chur or some of the missionary dioceses in central Europe. But for the rest, the southern dioceses reflected the early kingdoms: East Anglia, Essex (the see of London till very recent times was the only witness of the original extent of Essex),[10] Sussex and Kent, where two bishops reigned at Canterbury and Rochester. Further north, after some changes of shape and fortune, two sees were established, representing the

---

[7] On the Hwicce, Magonsaetan and their sees of Worcester and Hereford, see below, ch. 2, esp. p. 22 and nn.

[8] See below, p. 22, and article by J. Hillaby cited; p. 19n. P. Sims-Williams, *Religion and Literature in Western England* (Cambridge, 1990), chs 2–4.

[9] H. Mayr-Harting, *Coming of Christianity*, pp. 130–32; also references in n. 7 above.

[10] Brooke and Keir, *London, 800–1246* (n. 5), pp. 16–17; but see D. Whitelock, *Some Anglo-Saxon Bishops of London*, Chambers Memorial Lecture, University College London (London, 1974), p. 4. There is, however, a qualification to be made: there are undoubtedly later influences esp. on the north-western boundary of the medieval diocese of London; see F. Neininger in *English Episcopal Acta*, 15 (London, 1999), p. xxxix and n. 1, citing esp. the work of P. Taylor, 'The Endowment and Military Obligations of the See of London', *Anglo-Norman Studies*, 14 (1992), pp. 287–312, at pp. 296–97.

two ancient parts of Northumbria, one with its centre in York, the other with its centre in the island cathedral at Lindisfarne – home of St Aidan and St Cuthbert, whose cathedral and shrine were later moved to Durham.[11] In the Viking period, in the ninth and tenth centuries, much of northern England was resettled by pagans and became a no man's land of diocesan organisation; and when Christianity revived and the old organisation reasserted itself in the tenth century, we find the see of York spreading right across the island to the north west, forming a frontier along the watershed at the heart of what we now call the English Lake District with the kingdom of the Scots. The history of this part of the see of York is obscure;[12] doubtless it is closely related to the history of Northumbria in some sense; but how, we cannot tell, for the shape of the see first emerges into the light of day when Northumbria itself had crumbled and decayed, to be overtaken, first by Viking invaders, then by the larger kingdom of England. These are the major units of the medieval English church, representing for the most part, with varying degrees of fidelity, the political geography of seventh or eighth century England. Later in the middle ages new sees were formed; but the essential continuity and extraordinary conservatism of English ecclesiastical geography after the upheavals of the early middle ages are reflected in the modesty of these later changes. The see of Ely was formed in 1109 by taking what was approximately a single shire out of the see of Lincoln; and Carlisle was formed, originally from lands conquered from the Scots in the late eleventh and twelfth centuries, in the northern parts of Cumbria.[13]

These are the basic facts of the larger-scale geography; but if we want to check them in detail, and to compare them to the smaller units, to the country parishes which are the main theme of this chapter, we have to turn from the political world of the seventh and eighth centuries to the assessments for papal taxation of the thirteenth. Two major assessments were made for papal taxes in thirteenth century England, in 1254 (the so-called Valuation of Norwich) and 1291 (the 'Taxation of Pope

[11] See esp. *The Relics of St Cuthbert*, ed. C. F. Battiscombe (Oxford, 1956). For what follows see esp. D. Whitelock, 'The Conversion of the Eastern Danelaw', *Saga Book of the Viking Society* 12 (1941), pp. 159–76.

[12] It may well have some connexion with King Athelstan's reestablishment of English royal authority in Northumbria. Athelstan granted Amounderness (Lancashire, north of the river Ribble) as an estate to the archbishop of York: their title in it did not survive, but Amounderness continued to form the nucleus of their jurisdiction in this area. On the grant see D. Whitelock, *English Historical Documents* (2nd edn, London, 1979), p. 48.

[13] M. Brett, *The English Church under Henry I* (Oxford, 1975), pp. 57–58; *Fasti*, ii, pp. 19, 45. The eastern frontiers of the diocese of Ely and of Cambridgeshire were not and are not identical, however, since the diocese respects the more ancient frontier of the kingdom of East Anglia (I owe this point to the kindness of Dr D. Owen).

Nicholas'); and although recent study has shown that the facts and documents are more complex than was once supposed, the records of these
valuations between them provide us with the earliest lists of parishes anything like complete.[14] By plotting these parishes on the map, ecclesiastical
geographers can show how complete was the geography of English country
parishes in the mid thirteenth century, how little it altered from then until
the mid nineteenth century; and also, how precisely the macro-units, the
dioceses, conform to the pattern I have already sketched. In other words,
if we wish to study the history of English rural parishes, to penetrate back
to their origins, it is with these comprehensive thirteenth-century lists that
we must start, and from them work backwards towards the origins of the
parishes.

By the mid or late thirteenth century (outside the towns, which form no
part of our story),[15] the pattern of English parishes was firmly established;
and a very common situation in many parts of the country was for a village
community to be identical with a parish; in thousands of English villages
today one can still see a medieval church at the heart of the village – or at
least a church built on medieval foundations. Parish, village – and in many
cases also an ancient estate – are identical.[16] But there are also many
exceptions. Characteristic of one kind of exception is the tiny village in
Cornwall in the far south west of England, St Just in Roseland: here there
is a beautiful medieval church sitting on its own by the side of a natural

[14] The statements in the text are somewhat simplified, for even the papal taxation assessments are incomplete, and can only be turned into a complete record by comparison with
much earlier and later evidence, of the kind undertaken by Dr Hase and Dr Michael Franklin
(n. 21). For this Domesday Book (1086) is too haphazard in recording churches to be really
helpful; of greater value are the sixteenth-century records such as the *Valor ecclesiasticus*.
The *Taxatio ecclesiastica ... P. Nicholai IV, circa AD 1291*, and the *Valor ecclesiasticus* were
published by the Record Commission (London, 1802; 1810–34); the *Valuation of Norwich*
(1254), was ed. W. E. Lunt (Oxford, 1926). Lunt's introduction and his *Financial Relations of
the Papacy with England to 1327* (Cambridge, Mass., 1939) are the fundamental studies for the
history of papal taxation; on 1291 see also R. Graham, *English Ecclesiastical Studies* (London,
1929), pp. 271–301; and the studies of B. Mains, 'The Beneficed Clergy of the diocese of
Canterbury, 1279–1313' (unpublished D.Phil. thesis, University of Oxford, 1976). A major study
of the 1291 Taxation records is being prepared under the direction of Professor Jeffrey Denton.
See also M. J. Franklin, 'The Assessment of Benefices for Taxation in Thirteenth-Century
England', *Nottingham Medieval Studies*, 29 (1985), pp. 73–98.

[15] Although very important for a full understanding of the history of English parishes,
needless to say: see J. Campbell, 'The Church in Anglo-Saxon Times', *Studies in Church History*,
16 (1979), pp. 119–35; below, chs. 4–5; Brooke and Keir, *London, 800–1216* (n. 5), ch. 6.

[16] This comes out most clearly in the parish histories in many volumes of the *VCH*.

small harbour – an inlet of the sea, sheltered from wind and tide.[17] But the village lies on the top of the hill, out of sight, more than half a mile away. Cornwall is one of many parts of Britain where large village centres, the traditional 'nucleated' villages of central England, are relatively scarce. Sometimes a church is left on its own in a corner of a village away from houses because settlement has moved on; but in these scattered villages it may have been sited for quite a different reason, in a centre of communications which was never actually a centre of housing. St Just in Roseland is an extreme case of this: it sits by the water, which evidently in early times formed the main centre of communication; if one is a little romantic, one may imagine the early Celtic or British missionary who brought Christianity to Roseland landing here; more prosaically, St Just served a community of peasants and boatmen, and lies midway between land and water.

Between the diffuse community of the parish of St Just and the nucleated village-parish so characteristic of the rich arable lands of the midlands and many parts of eastern England there are all manner of varieties; and to some of these we shall return anon. For the moment, all these are in some measure examples of the small country parish: the parish which is at least no larger than a single fair-sized village and its appurtenant lands for arable and pasture and woods. But the map of thirteenth-century England deduced from the taxation returns and the other material geographical, archaeological and historical, which help us to interpret them, shows a number of parishes, and whole areas of the kingdom, where the pattern is quite different. In the north and west a much larger parish, comprising several villages or a wide stretch of country of scattered hamlets and farmsteads, is common. At Bunbury in Cheshire is a fine church which stood at the centre of a parish of twenty-four small villages; on the coast not too far to the north west, at the end of the Wirral peninsula, stretched the great parishes of West Kirby and Bebington, which between them accounted for another twenty villages.[18] Further north, in Cumbria, lies the Furness peninsula, and here one finds still more spectacular parishes. At Kirkby Ireleth, near the sea, the parish church lay in a small village; but the parish stretched

---

[17] N. Pevsner, *The Buildings of England: Cornwall*, edited by E. Radcliffe (2nd edn, Harmondsworth, 1970), pp. 183–4 and plate 11. Of the saint little seems to be known: presumably the same saint, St Just, is patron of St Just in Penwith, Cornwall. The most likely candidate is St Just of Beauvais and Auxerre. See Paul A. Hayward, 'The Idea of Innocent Martyrdom in Medieval England *ca.* 700 to 1150 A.D.' (unpublished Ph.D. thesis, University of Cambridge, 1995), pp. 71–88, esp. p. 86.

[18] G. Ormerod, *The History of the County Palatine and City of Chester*, ed. T. Helsby, 3 vols (2nd edn, London, 1875–82), ii, pp. 485–500, 520–32; cf. Brooke and Keir, *London, 800–1216* (n. 5), pp. 139–40 (acknowledging the help of P. Hodges).

nearly fifteen miles inland to the top of the valley of the River Duddon, to the summit of Wrynose Pass.[19] Variations in parish size occur all over the country; but the most substantial lie in the north west: here one finds relatively small and enormous parishes side by side.

The explanation of these large parishes, and of the many anomalies on the parish map, seems to lie in many different elements and stages of the history of English parishes, some peculiar to England, some part of the story of medieval Christendom as a whole; there are currently large gaps in our knowledge, and there always will be; but it is possible to see some relationship between the major stages in the development of English parishes and the present state of the map, even if many of the connexions in detail are very conjectural. I am codifying, and simplifying, the work of a large number of scholars, ranging from Dr Dorothy Owen, who has worked extensively in this field herself, especially in the diocese of Lincoln, and perhaps commands the widest view of any living scholar of the whole field of parochial history in England, to the groups of local historians and archaeologists, who are identifying on the ground, by field surveys and field archaeology, the ancient parish boundaries of Dorset and parts of Yorkshire.[20]

Broadly speaking, the accepted story is as follows.[21] In the wake of the missionary enterprises of the seventh and eighth centuries, and especially after the fairly stable formation of episcopal sees by Archbishop Theodore, a number of centres were established within each see, much larger than most of the later parishes, but still viable working units from which priests

[19] *VCH Lancashire*, vii, ed. W. Farrer and J. Brownbill (London, 1914), pp. 387–91; H. V. Koop, *Broughton in Furness: A History* (repr. Beckermet, 1975), pp. 4ff, 30ff. On the other side of the river Duddon lay the old parish of Millom, which also stretched from a village (now town) near the coast through a very long, narrow strip of land into the hills.

[20] See esp. D. Owen, *Church and Society in Medieval Lincolnshire* (Lincoln, 1961). See also esp. R. Morris, *Churches in the Landscape* (London, 1989).

[21] For the detailed work on which the following pages are based, I owe much to the work of Paul Hodges – see Brooke and Keir, *London, 800–1216* (n. 5), pp. 138–40, esp. p. 138 n. 4; of Michael Franklin, see below, and 'Minsters and Parishes: Northamptonshire Studies' (unpublished Ph.D. thesis, University of Cambridge, 1982); of Frank Barlow, n. 1; of Brian Kemp, below nn. 39, 44; M. Brett, *The English Church under Henry I* (Oxford, 1975), esp. chap. 7; P. H. Hase, 'The Development of the Parish in Hampshire, Particularly in the Eleventh and Twelfth Centuries' (unpublished Ph.D. Thesis, University of Cambridge, 1976). For archaeological evidence, see below, esp. for the work of Dr Harold Taylor, esp. H. M. and J. Taylor, *Anglo-Saxon Architecture*, 3 vols (Cambridge, 1965–78). Of fundamental importance are *Minsters and Parish Churches: The Local Church in Transition, 950–1200*, ed. J. Blair (Oxford, 1988), with studies by Blair, Hase, Kemp, Franklin and others; and R. Morris, *Churches in the Landscape* (London, 1989).

could tour the local villages, and to which the local folk could come to their 'mother church'. In due course there came to be quite a hierarchy of these minster churches or mother churches. Thus the centre of the diocese of York lay in the cathedral in York itself; but the archbishop also came to preside in the large minster churches at Ripon, Southwell and Beverley, which were almost secondary cathedrals. Such minsters came to be a feature of sees quite a bit smaller than York: for much of the middle ages Lichfield served in this way for Coventry and Wells for Bath; and sometimes a great abbey church, like Eynsham in Oxfordshire, served as a local centre for the pentecostal processions and provision of chrism and other cathedral functions in the later middle ages.[22] Below this level of the great minsters there grew up a network of lesser minsters serving ten or twenty villages. This development took place fundamentally in the seventh and eighth centuries. In the ninth and tenth centuries the north and east, and parts of the north west, were subjected to the Viking invasions; large areas of northern England became pagan for a time again, the work of the missionaries began once more, and a new pattern of Christian organisation was imposed, which revived some but far from all the elements of the eighth century English church.[23] In most of the midlands and the south the Viking conquests hardly impinged on the organisation of the church, though they may have done something to speed the breakdown of the old minsters. However that may be, the formation of the village parishes is first clearly discernible in the tenth century; and so far as we know at present the network of medieval parishes was essentially the creation of the period between the tenth and the twelfth centuries, between the first substantial break up of the old minster and mother churches and their areas of jurisdiction in the tenth century, and the establishment of the rule of classical canon law, and the effective dominance of canon law courts in disputes on parish boundaries and tithe, which one may associate with the age of Gratian and Pope Alexander III in the twelfth century in many parts of western Europe.[24] This made the alteration of parish rights and parish boundaries much more difficult; it fossilised a system and a network, in

[22] For pentecostal processions and chrism payments, see esp. M. Brett, *The English Church under Henry I*, pp. 162–66 and ch. 10 below; for Beverley, Ripon and Southwell, Lichfield and Wells, see also D. Knowles and R. N. Hadcock, *Medieval Religious Houses: England and Wales* (2nd edn, London, 1971), pp. 421, 429, 435, 439, 442; J. Armitage Robinson, *Somerset Historical Essays* (London, 1921), esp. ch. 3.

[23] See esp. D. Whitelock, 'The Conversion of the Eastern Danelaw'.

[24] Below, pp. 10, 12–13, and literature there cited; and on tithes esp. G. Constable, *Monastic Tithes from their Origins to the Twelfth Century* (Cambridge, 1964) and copious literature there cited. For the general context, there are several important *relazioni* in *Mendola*, 6 (1977).

effect, which was to last – totally unaffected at the parish level by the Reformation – into the nineteenth century. Obviously this gives too simple a picture, and some of the qualifications must be stated at once. Village churches were common before the tenth century, tiny oratories and private chapels of every kind broke the symmetry of the pattern in every epoch; arguments about the status of parochial chapels, manorial chapels and what have you were the stuff of episcopal court litigation in the late middle ages. Nor did the minsters surrender their rights without a struggle: they decayed at very various speeds, so that some were still almost intact at the time of the Norman Conquest in 1066 – had it not been so, we should hardly be able to penetrate their history.[25] But at the very centre of our story lie two concepts of marvellous ambiguity: minster and parish. The word minster (*mynster* in Old English, and very similar in other Germanic languages) is simply a loan word from the Latin *monasterium*, and there is no kind of religious community, or church bereft of a religious community, which was not at one time or another called a *monasterium*.[26] The confusion is compounded by our ignorance of the nature of the communities or groups of clergy who served the majority of the minster churches for most of the period between 600 and 1100 – but this is a problem universal in western Christendom. Some minster churches were served by monks, some by canons following a rule, some by canons following no particular rule, some even by communities of nuns;[27] the word itself reminds us of the fundamental ambiguity in the relation between monastic communities and pastoral work which is so characteristic of the tenth and eleventh centuries.[28] Similarly *parochia* notoriously continued to be used throughout the middle ages for any area of ecclesiastical jurisdiction, from a diocese like York or Lincoln or Konstanz or Krakow – which covered half a kingdom – to the tiny city parishes so

[25] For examples, see below, pp. 29–30. Dr Michael Franklin has drawn my attention to an excellent example of the fairly late formation of parochial chapels: in 1366 the bishop of Lincoln had to deal with the *querela* of the parishioners of Uppingham 'about the obligations of the dependent chapels of Ridlington, Wing and Marsthorpe to assist in providing for the reconciliation of the churchyard of the mother church' (Lincoln Archives Office, Register XII, fol. 38).

[26] For a brief conspectus, see J. F. Niermeyer and C. van de Kieft, *Mediae latinitatis lexicon minus* (Leiden, 1976), pp. 702–3.

[27] Examples are Berkeley, Leominster and Withington (below, nn. 39, 44, 53).

[28] See esp. Constable, *Settimane di studio del centro italiano di studi sull'alto medioevo*, 28 (1982), pp. 349–89, and *Monastic Tithes* (n. 24). Constable's admirable *relazione* has set the old problem of monks and pastoral work on a new and more secure foundation.

characteristic of English towns, sometimes no more than two or three acres in extent.[29]

For our purpose the word minster must serve for any large church originally, or vestigially, serving an area wider than a village; and a parish is the ultimate, small unit of ecclesiastical jurisdiction which is the essential theme of this essay. The renaissance of canon law in the twelfth century established the rights to tithes, to burials and to baptism; and it is these which constituted the hard core of parish rights whose defence made later changes in parish structure more and more difficult.[30] Anyone who has studied the history of parishes and of canon law knows that these are superficial statements; that they cover an immense variety of different situations and problems; but yet there is a broad measure of truth in them essential to grasp if we are to make any sense of our data. The parish churches (where we have evidence) were often in origin *Eigenkirchen*, proprietary churches built by the lords; but we may suspect that often many others than the lords had a hand in them; that they became early, in country villages as well as in towns (where the fact is more certain) symbols and centres of local loyalty, village halls as well as places of worship; and that the role of the parish church as the centre of a worshipping community and a social community counted more than baptism or burial, more even than tithes, in determining the establishment of a parish church.[31] In England the system of tithes first acquired full legal force by royal legislation in the tenth century – it came somewhat later than on the adjacent parts of the Continent, though everywhere there was a long prehistory, needless to say, older than the Christian Church.[32] In the tenth century tithes were paid to the mother churches, which meant at that time, in general terms, the old minster churches of the neighbourhood. But only in general terms, for the decay of the minsters was already under way. It is a desperately obscure process, but we have numerous indications of this decay at work. The process can only be brought down from the very general to the concrete and actual by taking a series of examples, which will illustrate both the variety of the problems, and also the fascinating variety of evidence which scholars working in this field have to handle.

[29] Niermeyer and van de Kieft, *Lexicon Minus* (n. 26), pp. 764–65; for the extensive *paruchia* in the Irish church, see esp. K. Hughes, *The Church in Early Irish Society* (London, 1966), pp. 50–53, 65–78.

[30] Cf. n. 24; and below, p. 32.

[31] Ibid.; Brooke and Keir, *London, 800–1216* (n. 5), chap. 6. Baptism and burial were not indeed universal parochial rights: see e.g. D. Keene, *Survey of Medieval Winchester* (n. 33), i, p. 107.

[32] Cf. n. 24; for tenth century English legislation, see *Councils and Synods* i, 2, pp. 1143–44, Index s. v. 'tithes'.

First of all, the archaeological evidence. In the past there was a tendency for architectural historians, studying the standing structures of medieval churches, to deduce a history of the building, which explained what we now see, based on the minimum of structural changes needed to make sense of it; whereas the archaeological study of churches was inclined to suggest more complex histories, with more frequent changes over the centuries.[33] In more recent years the two approaches have come together, and in the 1970s the late Dr Harold Taylor worked closely with archaeologists in his study of Anglo-Saxon churches, especially at Deerhurst and Repton.[34] Outstanding examples of Anglo-Saxon minster churches of which the main part of the structure still survives are Deerhurst in Gloucestershire, where Dr Taylor himself led a team of investigators, and Brixworth in Northamptonshire, most recently expounded to us by Dr David Parsons.[35] In both cases a complex building history emerges. From about the eighth century they were comparatively large – not large by Romanesque standards, but very much larger than the tiny churches which did duty for the famous monastic communities in which the Venerable Bede lived at Monkwearmouth and Jarrow.[36] Both Deerhurst and Brixworth underwent much alteration and rebuilding; in both, monastic communities probably served at one time and another; in both, it is extremely unlikely that the monastic community served continuously. After the Norman Conquest Brixworth had subsided into being a parish church, and active building work in the twelfth century actually reduced its size; Deerhurst remained a monastic dependency, but a parish church too, never serving a community of any

[33] Good examples of the older approach are in early volumes of the Royal Commission on Historical Monuments (England) – more recent volumes show a sophisticated understanding of the problem. For the archaeologist's approach, see an excellent example in the Winchester churches discussed by M. Biddle in *Antiquaries Journal*, esp. 48 (1968), pp. 263–65; 50 (1970), 302–5, 309–10; 52 (1972), 104–7, 111–15; 55 (1975), 308, 312–13, 318–20; and more recently by Derek Keene, *Survey of Medieval Winchester, Winchester Studies*, ii, 2 vols (Oxford, 1985), i, pp. 106–36 passim.

[34] For Deerhurst, see P. Rahtz, L. Watts, H. Taylor and L. Butler, *St Mary's Church Deerhurst* (Woodbridge, 1997); for Repton, which has been studied by Dr Taylor and Professor M. Biddle and Dr B. Kjølbye-Biddle, see *Medieval Archaeology*, 20 (1976), pp. 159–60; Taylor, *Repton Studies* i, ii (1977–79).

[35] For Deerhurst, n. 34; for Brixworth, D. Parsons, 'Brixworth, Northamptonshire, All Saints' Church' in *The Blackwell Encyclopedia of Anglo-Saxon England*, ed. M. Lapidge, J. Blair, S. Keynes and D. Scragg (Oxford, 1998), pp. 74–75, with bibliography.

[36] See R. Cramp, 'Excavations at the Saxon Monastic Sites of Wearmouth and Jarrow', *Medieval Archaeology*, 13 (1969), pp. 21–66, and further details in later numbers of the same journal, esp. 16 (1972), 148–52; H. M. and J. Taylor, *Anglo-Saxon Architecture*, i (Cambridge, 1965), pp. 338–49, 432–46.

size or importance, overshadowed by the great Norman abbey of Tewkesbury two miles away along the river Severn, to which eventually it was made a cell. The relative neglect of Deerhurst and Repton after the Conquest indicates the decline in their standing; and there are plenty of positive pieces of evidence from the eleventh and twelfth centuries of the establishment of parish rights in lesser churches; eleventh and twelfth century fonts, for example, are extremely common.[37]

Evidence for the shape and extent of the jurisdiction of these ancient minster churches, and the manner of their decay, is occasionally presented in quite a concrete form in charter or record evidence. The forces which led to the breakdown were evidently the positive demand of landlords and leading tenants for manorial, village, parish churches; and the relatively weak grip of the ecclesiastical authorities in the tenth and eleventh centuries. In Kent ecclesiastical authority remained strong; and there are lists of parishes in the late eleventh-century *Domesday monachorum* of Christ Church Canterbury which show how the parishes were grouped together in their annual demands for chrism, and the payments which (quite contrary to canon law) they made for it.[38] Here we may see a structure still based on the old mother churches, quite different from the rural deaneries which were soon to replace them; but yet the individual parish churches were already for many purposes in full existence. In various parts of the west country, apparently for quite a different reason – the slow development of parochial organisation – the traces survived even longer. As late as 1175–77 a group of eminent papal judges delegate met in the presence of King Henry II to try to sort out the tangled case of the prebends and the churches of the Berkeley Hernesse – the district in Gloucestershire in the lower Severn valley which surrounds the still noble church and castle of Berkeley. This is a fascinating story, whose details have been elicited by Professor Brian Kemp.[39] The old mother church was served by a community of nuns, which fell into decay and disappeared in the mid eleventh century, leaving their rights quite ambiguously distributed among the local landowners and clergy. Some of these clergy were canons of Berkeley, priests, that is, of the old mother church, although they do not seem to have resided there; some of

[37] See F. Bond, *Fonts and Font Covers* (London, 1908; repr. London, 1985).

[38] *The Domesday Monachorum of Christ Church Canterbury*, ed. D. C. Douglas (London, 1944), pp. 77–79, cf. pp. 5–14; Barlow, *The English Church* (n. 1), pp. 179–82, with a map on p. 181; Brett, *The English Church under Henry I* (n. 21), pp. 164–66.

[39] B. Kemp, 'The Churches of Berkeley Hernesse', *Transactions of the Bristol and Gloucestershire Archaeological Society*, 87 (1968), pp. 96–110; cf. A. Sabin, 'St Augustine's Abbey and the Berkeley Churches', ibid., 89 (1970), pp. 90–99; *GFL*, no. 73, pp. 106–7; C. N. L. Brooke, *The Church and the Welsh Border* (Woodbridge, 1986), pp. 67–69.

the local landowners claimed proprietary rights in some of the parish churches of the district. In the disordered period of King Stephen's reign, in the 1140s, they began to distribute these with a liberal hand. Gloucester abbey received gifts from one of the lords of Berkeley,[40] and one of the canons commended himself to them and became their clerk. So Gloucester came to have a stake in the Hernesse. The other lord of Berkeley founded Bristol abbey and gave his new foundation a share of the churches of the Hernesse. Finally, another of the canons, who was an influential chaplain of the Empress Matilda, claimant of the English throne and mother of the future Henry II, commended himself to the empress; and on this basis she claimed all the churches of the Hernesse and gave them to Reading abbey. Thus when King Stephen died and Henry II succeeded, three great abbeys had overlapping claims to the churches of the Hernesse, and the *cause célèbre* smouldered on until 1175–77, when the papal judges delegate finally settled it by compromise. The effect is that we know the shape of this ancient unit of jurisdiction and the churches which were subject to the old minster of Berkeley with some precision; and we can see in the manner of its disintegration the way in which the rights or claims of landlords, and of the clergy of the minster itself and of the parishes, all provided ambiguous but arguable foundations for legal claims.

Reading abbey had been founded by the empress's father, King Henry I: it was indeed the chief of his many foundations, and in the abbey church he was buried.[41] It was the summit of a pyramid of acts of contrition characteristic of this extraordinary man, made up in equal measures of most of the gargantuan sins of the age, yet widely admired as a model of piety and justice too.[42] Reading abbey was an act of kingly contrition in a special sense; for he gathered together the churches and endowments of the three other religious houses (apart from Berkeley) known to have been suppressed under the tolerant eye of his predecessor, King Edward the Confessor, in the mid eleventh century.[43] As with Berkeley, the story behind Reading's endowments is the story of disintegrating minsters and communities; and one of these, Leominster in Herefordshire, has enabled Professor Kemp to reconstruct a substantial area under the jurisdiction of an old minster

[40] 'In the period 1152–4 Roger of Berkeley was finally dispossessed of the manor of Berkeley ... in favour of Robert FitzHarding' (Roger was the heir of Roger of Berkeley I-III who had held it since the Norman Conquest), Brooke, *The Church and the Welsh Border*, p. 68; cf. *The Complete Peerage* by G. E. C., revised edition by V. Gibbs et al. (London, 1910–59), ii, pp. 123ff, esp. p. 125.

[41] Cf. below, pp. 151–4, and references to the work of Professor B. Kemp, p. 151 n. 40.

[42] Cf. esp. the judgment of Orderic, vi, pp. 448–53; cf. the editor's comments, i, pp. 43–4.

[43] See below, pp. 153–4.

church; the place name still records the dominance of the church: for it means the minster by the streams or rivers.[44] When Reading acquired Leominster (like Berkeley, once served by a community of nuns) the parish churches of the district were still being built; and the monks were careful to obtain charters covering the whole jurisdiction of the minster – that is, listing churches in all the villages, whether they had yet been built or not. This is the clearest example known to me of the formation of parishes within the area of jurisdiction of an old minster. It is relatively well documented because the old minster and its dominance over the early area of jurisdiction survived into the early twelfth century, to the age of charters and episcopal confirmations; and especially because it caught the attention of King Henry I in his curious mood of antiquarian penitence.

Most of the recent work on the growth of medieval parishes and the breakdown of the older, larger units, has involved a combination of documentary and topographical research, always with an element of historical geography, sometimes aided by archaeology; and in some cases efforts have been made by experts in field archaeology to trace the history of boundaries and estates back through many centuries. A good example of the combination of historical and topographical evidence is the Cambridge thesis of Dr Patrick Hase:[45] by close study of all the historical evidence he was able to gather, and by inference from the relation of parish boundaries to wider geographical features, he has conjecturally reconstructed the whole pattern of early ecclesiastical geography in Hampshire, and attempted to show how the break up of the larger areas is related to the formation of parochial jurisdictions. There are many detailed studies of parochial history on a local scale; one of the most succinct and valuable is that contained in Dr Owen's *Church and Society in Medieval Lincolnshire*.[46] Let us consider two of her examples. First, Castle Bytham, on the edge of forest country in southern Lincolnshire, a large parish which,

> until 1284 ... preserved something of its pre-Conquest collegiate status, with three canonries, or portions, in the churches of Castle Bytham, Little Bytham, and Holywell. In addition, in two secondary settlements at Counthorpe and Aunby there was at least one parochial chapel and a preaching cross. Finally, within the

---

[44] On Leominster B. R. Kemp, 'The Monastic Dean of Leominster', *EHR*, 83 (1968), pp. 505–15; also Kemp, 'Some Aspects of the *Parochia* of Leominster in the Twelfth Century' in *Minsters and Parish Churches* (n. 21), pp. 83–95; *GFL*, p. 392; for the name, E. Ekwall, *The Concise Oxford Dictionary of English Place-Names* (4th edn, Oxford, 1960), p. 295. Kemp has also published another useful study of an early mother church, 'The Mother Church of Thatcham', *Berkshire Archaeological Journal*, 63 (1967–8), pp. 15–22.

[45] See n. 21.

[46] Lincoln, 1971 (cf. n. 20), esp. ch. 1.

main village and serving the castle, which was at the height of its importance during the twelfth century, was a bewildering array of lesser chapels: St Mary in the Castle, St Thomas in the Barbican, St Mary Magdalen below the Castle, and St John Baptist belonging to the hospital of 'Herberdist'. The parish churches here survive still, but the chapels have almost vanished ...[47]

Here we have in miniature many elements in our story. First of all, it is an echo of the Berkeley Hernesse, in that an early collegiate church survived into the twelfth century – in this case on into the late thirteenth – with its jurisdiction relatively intact. The proliferation of private chapels and oratories, even if many of these were comparatively late, must often have been paralleled in other cases; so too the record we have here of a village cross – which we have every reason to suppose was a common provision in innumerable villages before any parish churches were built there. Equally characteristic is the end product: the minor churches which could naturally grow into parish churches, that is, served reasonably distinct village communities, in the end won parish status and survived; the chapels served their turn and passed away.

This example is relatively clearly dated; the other is timeless.[48] Lincoln cathedral stands on a fine ridge of high ground, and north of it there stretched a Roman road, an ancient traffic artery still very much in use. Along the edges of the high ground, at a respectful distance from the road, are lines of medieval villages; and the parishes run up to the road in long narrow strips from lower ground beyond the village centres, all ending on the road. In this case, at some date unknown – but in a legal, definitive sense, presumably about the year 1000 or a little later – an area of ecclesiastical jurisdiction very likely based in Lincoln itself was broken into these intelligible, rational fractions. But it is also highly likely that they represent much older estates. If one travels a fair distance to the south west of Lincoln, down another Roman road, the Fosse Way, until one comes into the west country, into Gloucestershire, one finds an identical pattern undoubtedly of great antiquity; here the Fosse Way climbs over ridges of the Cotswold hills, and the villages mostly lie about it (as in my other example) again at a respectful distance.[49] One of the villages a little to the west of the Fosse way on this stretch is Chedworth, famous for its Roman

[47] Owen, *Church and Society*, p. 8.
[48] Owen, *Church and Society*, pp. 2–3 and fig. 1.
[49] C. Oman, 'Concerning Some Gloucestershire Boundaries', in *Essays in History Presented to R. L. Poole*, ed. H. W. C. Davis (Oxford, 1927), pp. 86–97, esp. pp. 93–94, and map facing p. 86; a paper which owed much to C. S. Taylor's papers, reprinted in *Gloucestershire Studies*, ed. H. P. R. Finberg (Leicester, 1957), pp. 17–51.

villa and Roman mosaics, found adjacent to the medieval church.[50] But before it climbed onto the Cotswolds the road passed through a belt of very different country. Here the ancient pattern, whatever it was, was broken up by the great ecclesiastical landlords of the neighbourhood – the cathedral priory of Worcester, the abbeys of Evesham and Pershore and others – probably in the late tenth and early eleventh centuries, and so deeply did they score their rights into the landscape that, when the shire boundaries were redrawn in these regions at the turn of the tenth and eleventh centuries, islands of Worcestershire lay scattered about in Warwickshire and Gloucestershire; these islands were not tidied away until the 1930s.[51] There are features of this region which probably still reflect the Roman occupation; the boundaries of the diocese of Worcester until the Reformation preserved the boundaries of the seventh- and eighth-century Hwicce;[52] the shire boundaries reflected the facts of land-holding about the year 1000; the parishes hunted now with this pack of hounds, now with that – some reasserted ancient estate boundaries, others accepted new ones, according to the patterns of land-holding and social and ecclesiastical authority asserting themselves in the tenth and eleventh and twelfth centuries. A little to the west of the Fosse Way, behind Chedworth, lies Withington, a charming Cotswold village subjected to intensive study by the late Professor Finberg.[53] He found traces of Roman survival in the estate history and boundaries of Withington. These are conjectural. What is certain is that one of a group of curious family minsters, or monasteries, was formed here in the late seventh century, under the wing of the bishop of Worcester; that it was hereditary for two or three generations in the family of the Abbess Dunne, and eventually reverted to the bishop, under whose eye it continued for a while a minster church.[54] In the end, at a date unknown, the local villages formed their own parishes, and Withington was left within its ancient boundaries, with a village, estate, manor and parish all within the limits of an ancient estate. In the late 1970s Mr Christopher Taylor and Mrs Frances Brown, archaeologists surveying the whole of Northamptonshire for the Royal Commission on Historical Monuments

[50] On Chedworth see especially I. A. Richmond, 'The Roman Villa at Chedworth', *Transactions of the Bristol and Gloucestershire Archaeological Society*, 78 (1959), pp. 5–23.

[51] Oman, 'Concerning some Gloucestershire Boundaries'; C. S. Taylor, *Gloucestershire Studies*; H. P. R. Finberg, *Early Charters of the West Midlands* (Leicester, 1961), pp. 228–35.

[52] See below, ch. 2, p. 22 and n. 13.

[53] H. P. R. Finberg, *Roman and Saxon Withington* (Leicester, 1955; revised edition in Finberg, *Lucerna*, Leicester, 1964, pp. 21–65).

[54] Finberg, *Roman and Saxon Withington*; Finberg, *Early Charters of the West Midlands*, pp. 32, 35, 38 (nos 5, 21, 32), 84–5, 176, 178.

for England, showed that medieval estate and parish boundaries in that shire may reflect the pattern of settlement of much earlier times.[55]

There is much more work to be done, evidently, in this fruitful field of research; meanwhile it is clear that many parish boundaries mark, in a general way if not in detail, the reassertion of older estate units, forming or reforming themselves within the wider ambience of the old minsters; but that there are many too which reflect new patterns of settlement and new estate boundaries of the tenth, eleventh and twelfth centuries.

Thus we return to the pattern or model with which we began this survey: first, the division of the diocese, often a tribal area, into large units, served by minsters; then the decay of the minster communities and their strength – in the north, and often elsewhere too, much hastened by the Viking raids and settlements of the ninth and tenth centuries;[56] and finally the reassertion of a pattern of parochial units, of parishes, essentially conforming to the pattern of village communities or of local estates – though never ceasing to show a bewildering variety of local differences.

In conclusion, to set the story into perspective, let us look more closely at two examples of large areas influenced by the Viking settlements in the west and north west, the same two which I briefly introduced to show how in these regions the small parish never fully asserted itself in the middle ages. Kirkby Ireleth sits by the estuary of the Duddon; the church is dedicated to St Cuthbert. The dedication is recorded in the fifteenth century; unfortunately fourteenth-century evidence suggests an earlier dedication to St Mary: none the less the dedication to Cuthbert may possibly go back behind the Vikings to the work in this area of missionaries from St Cuthbert's Lindisfarne in the north east.[57] Kirkby sits near the sea,

[55] Frances Brown and C. C. Taylor, 'Settlement and Land Use in Northamptonshire: A Comparison between the Iron Age and the Middle Ages', in *Lowland Iron Age Communities in Europe*, ed. B. Cunliffe, T. Rowley, S. Pryor, British Archaeological Reports International Series (Supplementary), 48 (Oxford, 1978), pp. 77–89. I am indebted to Mr Taylor for knowledge of this paper and for discussion of his work. Taylor has also studied the place of the parish church and other elements in villages of complex plan; see esp. *Medieval Archaeology*, 21 (1977), pp. 189–93.

[56] On this see especially P. Sawyer, *The Age of the Vikings* (2nd edn, London, 1971); cf. the discussion by K. Cameron, *Scandinavian Settlement in the Territory of the Five Boroughs: The Place-Name Evidence* (Nottingham, 1965); Cameron, 'Scandinavian Settlement in the Territory of the Five Boroughs: The Place-Name Evidence: Part II', *Mediaeval Scandinavia*, 3 (1970), pp. 35–49; and elsewhere.

[57] See reference in n. 19. *VCH Lancashire*, vii, p. 387n., cites a fifteenth-century document for the dedication to St Cuthbert, but another of 1336 which refers to the church of St Mary. This may be due to an easy mistake (there was no commoner dedication than to the Blessed Virgin); or to a double dedication, which was not uncommon. But it may also simply be the

betokening the sea-base from which the church came back to these regions; the name means the 'by' or village with the church in Old Norse. The parish stretched for nearly fifteen miles or so, but it was in due course broken up into smaller units; and the earliest and most important of these, at Broughton-in-Furness, also lies near the estuary. Here a subtantial modern church of the nineteenth century replaces what originally was a tiny chapel of the late twelfth century or earlier;[58] and it lies on low ground near the flat marshes whose streams were presumably once navigable. The little town of Broughton has climbed the hillside above it over the centuries, and the church is left on its own, as at St Just in Roseland, a reminder that the clergy came originally from the sea. West Kirby in Wirral is somewhat similarly placed: it is also the 'by' with the church in a large parish, and it also lies near the sea.[59] The village names of its parish are a palimpsest of local history, with British, Anglo-Saxon, Norse and Irish elements. One is called Irby, the 'by' or village of the Irish, a reminder that the Norse who resettled this region in the early tenth century, and in due course became Christian, came immediately from the Norse settlements in Ireland. Hence too the patron saint of West Kirby church, St Bridget: an Irish saint of the sixth century, but doubtless in West Kirby a part of the Irish Norse world of the tenth and eleventh.[60] In these two cases we can see both Christianity and the medieval parishes in the making together; here was no peaceful growth, but a pattern laid by the Viking invader, christened by the missionaries who converted him, and then left essentially unaltered for many hundreds of years.

It is doubtless true that all the rural institutions of Christendom are palimpsests on which many different centuries have scored their marks: in the church of medieval England the dioceses reflect the geography of the seventh and eighth centuries above all, the parishes of the tenth to twelfth.

Note 57 *continued*
fact that the dedication to Cuthbert is no older than *c*. 1400. The list attributed to Prior Wessyngton of Durham, which gives the dedication to Cuthbert, was printed with a critical commentary, and study of dedications to the saint (of which there are three in the Furness peninsula) by A. Hamilton Thompson, 'The MS List of Churches Dedicated to St Cuthbert, Attributed to Prior Wessyngton', *Transactions of the Architectural and Archaeological Society of Durham and Northumberland*, 7 (1936), pp. 151–77; for Kirkby Ireleth see esp. pp. 159–60, 170, 176.

[58] See n. 19, and the plan in Koop, *Broughton in Furness* (n. 19), p. 31, for the first rebuilding in the eighteenth century.

[59] See n. 18.

[60] See Brooke and Keir, *London, 800–1216* (n. 5), pp. 139–40, acknowledging the help of P. Hodges.

2

The Diocese of Hereford, 676–1200

My themes are the see, the bishopric and the bishops of Hereford, 676–1200. Joseph Hillaby has shown grave reason to doubt whether the see of Hereford really dates from 676.[1] I shall say something of how I think that case stands; I shall also say something of the special character of the diocese as a frontier bishopric in the Welsh march – Hereford in Wales as the twelfth-century exchequer clerks habitually called it; and I shall try to reveal it, as it comes into the clear light of day in the twelfth century, in the activities of the two great twelfth-century bishops, Robert de Bethune, the austere canon regular from Llanthony, and Gilbert Foliot, the monk from Cluny and Gloucester. I shall find it as a geographical expression and (I hope) leave it as a diocese.

For a quarter of a century, with many interruptions – from 1942 to 1967 – I was engaged, first with my father, then with Dom Adrian Morey, in studying Gilbert Foliot, bishop of Hereford in the mid twelfth century, and editing his letters and charters; and my first article, in collaboration with my father, was a study of the Hereford cathedral chapter in the twelfth century, published in 1944.[2] Since then, the church in Hereford itself has been studied archaeologically by Mr Shoesmith,[3] and in a Cambridge thesis by my pupil Dr Alison Pearn as one of a group of Mercian towns.[4] The

The F. C. Morgan Lecture for 1992 (see pp. xv–xvi), first published in *The Transactions of the Woolhope Naturalists' Field Club*, 48 (1994), pp. 23–36.

[1] J. Hillaby, 'The Origins of the Diocese of Hereford', *Transactions of the Woolhope Naturalists' Field Club*, 42 (1976–78), pp. 16–52. In preparing this lecture I was particularly indebted to the kind help of Mr Joseph Hillaby and Dr Julia Barrow; and in revising it to Professor Simon Keynes, who kindly showed me his chapter in the forthcoming *History of Hereford Cathedral*.

[2] Z. N. and C. N. L. Brooke, 'Hereford Cathedral Dignitaries in the Twelfth Century', *Cambridge Historical Journal*, 8 (1944), pp. 1–21; supplement in no. 3 (1946), pp. 179–85.

[3] Though A. T. Bannister, *The Cathedral Church of Hereford: Its History and Constitution* (London, 1924) still repays study.

[4] Alison Pearn, 'Origin and Development of Urban Churches and Parishes: A Comparative Study of Hereford, Shrewsbury and Chester' (unpublished Cambridge Ph.D. thesis, 1989); and the studies of R. Shoesmith, e.g. 'St Guthlac's priory, Hereford', *Transactions of the Woolhope Naturalists' Field Club*, 44 (1984), pp. 321–57.

cathedral and the diocese have been investigated by Dr Julia Barrow, whose edition of the bishops' charters – the episcopal *acta* of the diocese – from 1072 to 1234 was published in 1993.[5] Her introduction carries a succinct and penetrating account of the early history of the see, especially illuminating on the twelfth century. In 1990 appeared Patrick Sims-Williams' *Religion and Literature in Western England, 600–800*, which sets the origin of the sees of Hereford and Worcester in a wide religious, cultural, political and social context. The Welsh aspect of the story has been especially illuminated by Professor Wendy Davies, whose early work threw floods of light on the ecclesiastical history of south-eastern Wales, including the ancient kingdom of Erging, now southern Herefordshire.[6] They do not all agree at all points; but my aim will be to draw out the elements on which we can firmly base our story; and for the rest, where they are not at one, attempt to tread as delicately as Agag.

The historian who wishes to understand the conversion of England in the seventh and eighth centuries has to grapple with two fundamental facts not easily reconciled to one another. Anglo-Saxon England was the one part of the Roman empire wholly pagan, and so, ripe for an entirely new pattern of church organisation. But it had been part of Roman Britain which in its later phases was Christian; there were Christian churches in abundance in Wales and Scotland and along the borders of the Saxon conquest – and a considerable no man's land whose status is to us obscure and was always ambiguous.[7] From the eighth century on Offa's Dyke was the frontier between these two worlds. Like all frontiers it gives much too precise an impression: it lay in the heart of a frontier zone. The frontiers of England and Wales were not precisely drawn until 1974, and down to the nineteenth century there were some differences between so-called national and diocesan frontiers here and there.[8] But for our purpose Offa's Dyke would serve well enough if it were not for the notorious fact that it leaves much of Herefordshire out.[9] If we examine the churches and the patron saints of southern Herefordshire – Herefordshire south and west of the River Wye – we find them predominantly Welsh; this was the old

    [5] *English Episcopal Acta, 7, Hereford, 1079–1234* (London, 1992).

    [6] Esp. Wendy Davies, *An Early Welsh Microcosm: Studies in the Llandaff Charters* (London, 1978); *The Llandaff Charters* (1979).

    [7] P. Sims-Williams, *Religion and Literature in Western England, 600–800* (Cambridge, 1990), ch. 3; for general background, Charles Thomas, *Christianity in Roman Britain to AD 500* (London, 1981).

    [8] R. N. Hadcock, *Ordnance Survey Map of Monastic Britain* (2nd edn, 1953); D. M. Smith, *Guide to Bishops' Registers of England and Wales* (London, 1981).

    [9] The classic study is still Sir Cyril Fox, *Offa's Dyke* (London, 1955).

kingdom of Erging. It once stretched much further east, since Ariconium, which lies well to the east of the Wye, seems to have given the kingdom its name.[10] But in the period we are studying, from the seventh to the twelfth centuries, the Wye was its frontier, which underlines the very peculiar fact that the English overlords and bishops who made Hereford the centre of this see placed it on the frontier.

The old Roman sees which survived, after many vicissitudes, in most of Italy and France, and in some places elsewhere too, had been fairly precisely based on the small provinces of the late Roman empire. Their centres lay in Roman cities. This pattern was and is most complete in Italy, where the Roman cities most fully survived, and every city had its bishop. In England the church had to start afresh after the mission of St Augustine sent by Pope Gregory the Great in the 590s.[11] One of the main keys to mission strategy was the loyalty of tribes to their king; and the conversion of the king and the unity of the tribe were central to the policies and hopes of the missionaries. The story is far from simple; but it was broadly speaking true that dioceses and tribal areas had the same boundaries; and in many cases the medieval diocesan frontiers tell us more than county boundaries about early and mid Saxon political geography. Thus the kingdom of Kent had two sees, at Canterbury and Rochester; the South Saxons one, at Selsey (later at Chichester). London was the see of the East Saxons, with the Middle Saxons thrown in for good measure; the East Angles had sometimes one, sometimes two in early days; the West Saxons expanded from one to five, and so forth. The period when the pattern became fully established was the pontificate of Theodore, archbishop of Canterbury from 668–9 to 690, more specifically the 670s. Theodore was a Greek Syrian monk living in Rome and of advanced age when the pope laid hands suddenly upon him in 668 and sent him off to England to be archbishop of Canterbury. Theodore found the church in chaos. In the newly formed kingdom of Mercia, recently converted and a great power in the land, there was no bishop at all. Mercia covered the whole of the midlands and a good deal of the west country, from Leicester to Hereford, and competed with Northumbria for dominance in the island as a whole. One of Theodore's first acts when he arrived in England in 669 was to call the saintly and retiring Bishop Chad out of Lastingham and send him to Wulfhere king of Mercia. Like the later Franciscans, Chad was in the habit of performing his missionary work on foot; but Theodore was an old man in a hurry, and personally

---

[10] Sims-Williams, *Religion and Literature*, p. 45.

[11] See esp. H. Mayr-Harting, *The Coming of Christianity to Anglo-Saxon England* (1972; 3rd edn, 1991); and for what follows, above, ch. 1.

hoisted him onto a horse and sent him riding into Mercia.[12] Chad effectively founded the see of Lichfield; but in Theodore's eyes this was only a makeshift arrangement. He determined to break Mercia up into smaller, more manageable units. He seems to have had some trouble with his fellow bishops, but to have found allies in the kings of Mercia, and, above all, in the pope. Early in the 670s there were seven bishops in England. In 679 the pope decreed that there should be an archbishop and twelve bishops. 'To make up this number', says Patrick Sims-Williams, 'we should have to include the dioceses of the Hwicce and the Magonsaetan [the sees later called Worcester and Hereford], and indeed their bishops, Bosel and Putta, attest an authentic charter already in 680, alongside their spiritual and temporal overlords, Theodore and Æthelred of Mercia' (Wulfhere's successor).[13] To this Mr Hillaby would object that there was no bishop of the Magonsaetan at this date and that Putta by this date had no see at all. We are in deep waters.

The see of Hereford was formed out of the most westerly portion of Mercia. Of this there is no doubt. By about 800 the region it covered was known as the kingdom of the Magonsaetan, the folk of Maund, a sub-kingdom of Mercia.[14] The see was to retain in fossilised form its ancient frontiers even when the counties of Shropshire, Herefordshire and Gloucestershire were formed. For the medieval diocese of Hereford included half Shropshire, all Herefordshire and Gloucestershire west of the Severn.[15] By the same token the see of Worcester occupied the territory of the Hwicce which stretched as far west as the Malvern hills. The name of the Magonsaetan does not appear in seventh- or eighth-century texts – unlike the Hwicce which is undoubtedly an ancient name. By 800 the see was firmly established at Hereford and about the same time the see is first (in surviving documents) called the see of the Magonsaetan; by 800 we are on firm ground. If we ask why its early history is so obscure the answer, I think, is really quite simple: because the Venerable Bede did not know about it.

It might be said with pardonable exaggeration that what Bede tells us about the early history of the English church is secure knowledge; and what he omitted we can never know. There are other sources; and Bede was not infallible. But it is an extraordinary chance that the story of the early English church should have been recorded by the most accurate and historically

---

[12] Bede, *Historia ecclesiastica*, iv, 3, ed. B. Colgrave and R. A. B. Mynors, OMT (Oxford, 1969), pp. 336–37.

[13] Sims-Williams, *Religion and Literature*, pp. 87–88.

[14] Ibid., p. 40.

[15] D. M. Smith, *Guide to Bishops' Registers*, p. 95.

minded scholar of the early middle ages; I have little doubt Bede deserves that title.[16] But he could only pass on, as he carefully points out in his celebrated preface, what he had been able to discover.[17] He knew much of the history of his own Northumbrian church; and he was able to gather good sources from Canterbury and Rome and other sees. He seems to have sent round a kind of circular letter of appeal for information; and it is only too abundantly clear that the bishop of this part of Mercia (whatever he was called) never answered his letter; if he had, we would know more. This is not a unique circumstance. Lindsey (that is, the kingdom of Lincolnshire) is passed over in a silence almost as deep.[18] We cannot expect much light on our story from Bede.

Bede does tell us the story of a man called Putta, who was bishop of Rochester, whose see was devastated in 676 by the king of Mercia; so Putta – a learned man and very musical, so Bede tells us, but not energetic in practical affairs – took himself off (strangely enough) to the bishop of Mercia who gave him a church and a small estate where he lived happily ever after, going round churches improving their music.[19] Now by a curious chance the early bishops' lists give the name of Putta to the first bishop of Hereford.[20] These lists, like Bede, are not infallible – it is odd that another like source, Cuthbert's epitaph, omits Putta; but the lists are based on good tradition and worth serious attention. This coincidence has led to the traditional view that Putta, after leaving Rochester, founded the see of Hereford in or about 676. But no scholar who has read Bede's text carefully – neither Mr Hillaby, nor the late Professor Wallace-Hadrill nor Professor Sims-Williams – has reckoned that Bede can be talking about the first bishop of Hereford.[21] Yet it is a striking coincidence: a Bishop Putta goes into Mercia in 676 and about the same time (if the bishop's list is correct) a Bishop Putta becomes established in western Mercia – and lo, a

[16] See C. N. L. Brooke, 'Bede as Historian', forthcoming. For bibliography see J. M. Wallace-Hadrill, *Bede's Ecclesiastical History of the English People: A Historical Commentary*, OMT (Oxford, 1988).

[17] Bede, *Historia ecclesiastica* (n. 12), praefatio, esp. pp. 6–7.

[18] Although he acknowledges a letter from the bishop of Lindsey (ibid.) – but no such letter from the bishop of Hereford. In understanding Bede's use of sources I am deeply indebted to D. P. Kirby, 'Bede's Native Sources for the *Historia Ecclesiastica*', *Bulletin of the John Rylands Library*, 48 (1965–66), pp. 341–71.

[19] Bede, *Historia ecclesiastica*, iv, 12, pp. 368–69.

[20] Hillaby, 'The Origins' (n. 1), pp. 21–28 and refs.

[21] Hillaby, 'The Origins', pp. 17–19; Wallace Hadrill, *Bede's Ecclesiastical History*, p. 150 (prudently qualified by, 'if Bede's information was right'); Sims-Williams, *Religion and Literature* (n. 7), pp. 97–98.

Bishop Putta witnesses that rare bird, a genuine early Mercian charter, of the year 680.[22] Putta was not a common name: this one or these two men are the only Puttas known to have held bishoprics in Anglo-Saxon England. That may not be quite so remarkable as it seems, for there is reason to think it was not so rare a name in early times as it later became. There are various Puttas only recorded in place-names – such as the Putta whose wharf gave its name to Putney, and the Putta whose meadow gave its name to Putley in Herefordshire, interestingly enough.[23] So it could be chance; but it's an odd chance. Mr Hillaby goes further, and suggests that the bishops' list is wholly in error: that Putta, bishop of Hereford, never existed.[24] This is perfectly possible; but it might be thought a little peremptory. I have another explanation; but I am not at all sure it is correct. If it is not, then Mr Hillaby may well be right – and in any case I think he is right most of the way.

The papal letter of 679 strongly suggests that a bishopric in western Mercia was at least intended; without it one cannot make up the number twelve. Granted the vagaries of St Wilfrid at this time, and other difficulties, it is actually very hard to count the number precisely. But it really does look as if the pope had been told about a new see in western Mercia. That is not to say that it existed. But if Putta was roaming in western Mercia performing episcopal and musical functions, it might well have been reckoned that he was a kind of precursor of the bishops who were firmly settled there soon after. The papal letter of 679 registered an intention; the bishops' list recorded the tradition that Putta was a kind of proto-bishop of Hereford. Or again Bede, who knew so little about western Mercia, may simply have misled us; he is giving us the Rochester not the Hereford end of the story – Putta may really have been bishop of western Mercia after all: this is perhaps the most likely solution. I doubt if we shall ever know: all that seems clear to me is that a see in western Mercia was plotted by Archbishop Theodore in the 670s.

There have been doubts about what title the first bishop used, and about where the see was first founded. The only precise evidence is from a letter of Gilbert Foliot, which I published (not for the first time) in 1967.[25] Gilbert

[22] Sims-Williams, *Religion and Literature*, p. 88, citing P. Sawyer, *Anglo-Saxon Charters: An Annotated List and Bibliography* (London, 1968), no. 1167. On the origins of the diocese, see also J. Barrow, in *English Episcopal Acta*, 7 (1992), pp. xxvii–xxix, and the studies of S. R. Bassett there cited.

[23] E. Ekwall, *Concise Oxford Dictionary of English Place-Names* (4th edn, Oxford, 1960), p. 375, s. n. Putley, Putney.

[24] Hillaby, 'The Origins', esp. p. 28.

[25] *GFL*, p. 300, no. 227.

writes as ex-bishop of Hereford (he had been translated to London in 1163) to his cousin Robert Foliot, bishop-elect in 1173 or 1174, asking him to confirm the rights of the church of Ledbury 'for the sake of the episcopal see which it held long since and out of reverence for the holy bishops whose bodies lie there'. A letter of the 1170s is hardly cogent evidence for the events of the 670s, and there are various possible explanations; it is possible that there was confusion in the tradition since Hereford as well as Ledbury may have lain in the old district of Lydas. If so the see may always have been at Hereford – as has been suggested; and it certainly settled there in quite early days.[26]

The land of the Magonsaetan, western Mercia, the diocese of Hereford, whatever we call it, remained a frontier province. To the exchequer clerks of the twelfth century the centre of it was still 'Hereford in Wales'.[27] Offa's Dyke might indicate with sufficient clarity where Mercia ended and Wales began; but there were to be for many centuries minor fluctuations in the diocesan frontiers, which show that there was frequent activity on the border.[28] Further south, on the bank of the Wye opposite Hereford itself, and to the south west, lay the old Welsh kingdom of Erging, now southern and south-western Herefordshire – between the Wye and Wales; and here we are in territory much more constantly disputed. Its history between the seventh and the eleventh centuries is little known; but it is clear from the survival of Welsh collegiate churches (*clas* churches or minsters), and the frequency of dedications to Welsh saints, that we are in a region predominantly Welsh in the early middle ages. In particular, this is the centre of the cult of St Dyfrig or Dubricius, who was alleged in the twelfth century to have been the first bishop or archbishop of Llandaff.[29]

Hereford was still very much a frontier city in 1055, when it was sacked

[26] The history of Lydas is very obscure and depends essentially on the grant of an estate of thirty hides 'in the district called Lydas' to St Milburga of Wenlock, 675–90, H. P. R. Finberg, *The Early Charters of the West Midlands* (Leicester, 1961), p. 138 (no. 404), pp. 202–5, 209–10; P. H. Sawyer, *Anglo-Saxon Charters*, no. 1798. This has been identified as a district whose name survives in Lyde Brook and Lyde, near Hereford. For a full discussion see B. Copleston-Crow, *Herefordshire Place-Names* (Oxford, 1989), pp. 11–13, 166–67: 'Lyde is a well-evidenced OE stream name *Hlyde* "the loud one".' It is probable that Gilbert Foliot had Ledbury in mind – it is still a great minster church – though Lydbury North has been suggested, Sims-Williams, *Religion and Literature* (n. 7), p. 91.

[27] 'Herefortscir' in Wal', *Pipe Roll 2–4 Henry 11*, ed. J. Hunter (London, 1844, repr. 1930), p. 50, is a typical entry.

[28] C. N. L. Brooke, *The Church and the Welsh Border* (Woodbridge, 1986), pp. 10–12.

[29] On Erging, see Brooke, *The Church and the Welsh Border*, pp. 10–11; Sims-Williams, *Religion and Literature*, pp. 45–46. On Dyfrig, Brooke, *The Church and the Welsh Border*, p. 10 and refs; Wendy Davies, *Early Welsh Microcosm* (London, 1978), pp. 139–54.

by the victorious Welsh prince, Gruffydd ap Llywelyn, who had just acquired supreme power in south as well as north Wales, and was in effect king of the whole of Wales. In 1055 he made an alliance with Ælfgar son of the earl of Mercia, who was in feud with Earl Harold son of Godwin, the leading English potentate of the 1050s and 1060s, the future king of 1066. In October 1055 Gruffydd and his ally sacked Hereford, killing some of the canons. Peace was patched up at a meeting between Gruffydd and Harold at Billingsley in Erging. Soon after, the old bishop of Hereford died, and in March 1056 the warrior Bishop Leofgar, one of Harold's chaplains, was appointed to the see. But in June of the same year he set out at the head of the local levies and fell in battle with Gruffydd ap Llywelyn.[30]

Meanwhile, at Whitsun 1056 (so it seems), a man called Herewald was consecrated bishop for Erging. The only things certain about Herewald are that he bore an English name – as did his son Leofric or Lifris, later master of St Cadoc of Llancarvan and archdeacon of Gwent – and that he was consecrated in England, probably by the archbishop of York, since Canterbury was occupied by the notorious Stigand.[31] By 1104, when Herewald died, he was bishop in Glamorgan, and his successor Urban, another member of his family, it seems, claimed that he had all along been bishop of Llandaff. Now Urban was in effect the founder of the see of Llandaff, whatever had been there before him; and his life was dedicated to the attempt to prove that it had once been an archiepiscopal see – and so in no way subject to the rival archiepiscopal see of St Davids – and that its boundaries included Erging and other territories also claimed by the bishops of Hereford. The Book of Llandaff enshrines these claims in a dazzling collection of forgeries: but though the saints' lives and the charters in the Book of Llandaff contain a great deal of fiction, they are also based on a remarkable quantity of fact; and it is a very delicate matter to elucidate quite what it amounts to.[32] But the essence of the matter so far as it concerns Herewald seems tolerably clear. He started in Erging, presumably as a puppet of the bishop of Hereford, operating in territory devoid of episcopal care and politically dominated by Gruffydd ap Llywelyn. But when Gruffydd's power collapsed, and Gruffydd himself was killed in 1063, the English could

[30] For these events, see J. E. Lloyd, *A History of Wales* (3rd edn, London, 1939), ii, pp. 364–68. For the accession of Leofgar, see W. Stubbs, *Registrum sacrum anglicanum* (2nd edn, London, 1897), p. 36.

[31] J. G. Evans and J. Rhys, *The Text of the Book of Llan Dav* (Oxford, 1893), pp. 265–66, corrected in Brooke, *The Church and the Welsh Border*, p. 92 n. 189; cf. ibid., pp. 92–94; W. Davies, 'The Consecration of Bishops of Llandaff in the Tenth and Eleventh Centuries', *The Bulletin of the Board of Celtic Studies*, 24 (1974–76), pp. 53–73, at pp. 64–66.

[32] Cf. Brooke, *The Church and the Welsh Border*, ch. 2; W. Davies, *An Early Welsh Microcosm*.

redraw the border and the bishops of Hereford lay claim to Erging. The eventual result of this was that Herewald found himself progressively excluded from his original territory, but went on to perform episcopal functions further south and west, until he became effectively bishop of Glamorgan. It is clear that in the process the puppet bishop set up by the English had gone native, and become effectively Welsh; and his son Lifris became the master of one of the most charismatic shrines in south Wales, that of St Cadoc.[33] To Lifris we owe the earliest surviving Life of Cadoc, a strange medley of legend and folklore, portraying a far from attractive picture of its hero, who is more conspicuous for acts of power than of mercy or loving-kindness. We have no reason to suppose the historical St Cadoc was like this: the portrait was aimed at the enemies and rivals of Llancarfan in the late eleventh century. By the time it was completed the English enemy had been replaced by the Norman: the Normans invaded Glamorgan in or about 1093 and St Cadoc faced the most serious threat of all. Llancarfan was handed over by its conqueror, Robert Fitzhamon – founder of Tewkesbury abbey and ancestor of the earls of Gloucester – to Gloucester abbey, which threatened to colonise it and claim its relics.[34] In a dazzling epilogue to the Life of Cadoc, Lifris explained that the relics were not in Llancarfan at all – they were in Benevento in south Italy. At the end of his life Cadoc had been transported miraculously (by air) to Benevento, changed his name to Sophia, and died and been buried in the abbey of St Sophia in Benevento. Now there was undoubtedly such an abbey in the eleventh century, dedicated to Santa Sophia, that is, Holy Wisdom; the rest is pure fiction, doubtless intended to frustrate the abbot of Gloucester should he come demanding the relics. They are not here – they are a thousand miles away.[35]

In the next generation a leading Norman royal clerk, Queen Matilda's chaplain Bernard, was to follow Herewald's example in remodelling the rival see of St Davids. He had been in charge of the see of Hereford for a time in 1101–2, and was called 'priest of the church of Hereford' when he made his profession of obedience to the archbishop of Canterbury on his consecration as bishop of St Davids in 1115.[36] But, like Herewald, he soon

[33] Brooke, *The Church and the Welsh Border*, pp. 73–74, 92–94; and for what follows, ibid., pp. 70–89.

[34] Brooke, *The Church and the Welsh Border*, pp. 64–65; cf. J. E. Lloyd, *A History of Wales* (n. 30), ii, p. 402.

[35] Brooke, *The Church and the Welsh Border*, pp. 87–89.

[36] Brooke, *The Church and the Welsh Border*, pp. 28–29; *Calendar of Documents Preserved in France*, ed. J. H. Round (London, 1899), no. 1138; M. Richter, *Canterbury Professions*, Canterbury and York Society (1973), p. 117, no. 11.

became absorbed in Welsh customs and traditions. He made St Davids a diocese on the Anglo-Norman model with archdeacons and rural deans; but he fought a long and heroic battle to vindicate its independence of the see of Canterbury. He and Urban of Llandaff were rivals, not allies: rivals for large stretches of diocesan territory and for the title archbishop. Neither achieved all his ambitions; but they set a new pattern on the Welsh church for many generations to come. Hereford meanwhile could rejoice that the tide of battle had flowed further west; and though it suffered many anxious moments – especially in the late 1130s when the Welsh rose against the Norman invaders after the death of King Henry I, the shape of the diocese became more secure, with Erging or Archenfield, to give it its Anglicised name, securely part of it.

While these dramas were fought out on the frontier, the see was developing new pastoral patterns, much like other English sees in the late Saxon period, if a little slowly. In its simplest terms, the missionary church in early and mid Saxon times had established centres in major churches or minsters; from these, communities of priests performed pastoral functions over a wide stretch of territory. But in late Saxon times the dominance of the minster in pastoral care had broken down; rivals had appeared in the shape of parishes, much smaller units, sometimes the equivalent of villages. In many parts of England the formation of parishes came well before the conquest, and is lost in the mists of time. In some measure this may well have occurred in the see of Hereford. But some of the minsters retained their pastoral grip into the twelfth century. A notable example of this is Leominster.[37]

There are few words more ambiguous than 'minster'. It is the Old English equivalent of the Latin *monasterium*, and so it starts by meaning a monastery; but the institution and the word passed through so many vicissitudes that by the eleventh and twelfth centuries the word minster in contemporary texts can mean a monastery in the full sense of the word, or a large church served by a community of priests, or any large church, or any church at all:[38] and the antiquaries of the nineteenth century confused the matter further by designating certain particular cathedrals – York, for example, and its pro-cathedrals, Beverley and Ripon – as 'minsters'. We cannot forget the word since it meets us constantly in medieval texts. So we have to give it some definition before we use it.

[37] For this process in general and for the minsters, see above, ch. 1; *Minsters and Parish Churches: The Local Church in Transition, 950–1200*, ed. J. Blair (1988). On Leominster, see J. Hillaby, 'Early Christian and Pre-Conquest Leominster: An Exploration of the Sources', *Transactions of the Woolhope Naturalists' Field Club*, 45 (1987), pp. 557–685.

[38] Above, ch. 1, p. 9.

I use the word in the sense of a large church serving a district which was something between a diocese and a parish. This is not a perfect definition, but it avoids being too precise in a world where almost all our information is imprecise. The minster at Leominster must over several centuries have been served by a group of priests whose parish comprised a wide district fifteen miles or so across. How exactly they did it, we cannot tell: to what extent they carried the sacraments into the villages is totally unknown. But in early days it is not likely that there were many churches apart from the mother church in Leominster: their spread came slowly. As well as the priests there was a religious community of nuns. According to eleventh-century legend it had been founded by Merewalh, son of Penda king of Mercia, the first king of the Magonsaetan; and it may well be that when he was converted he founded or refounded the minster. But the name Leominster contains a Celtic or Welsh element; it may even be a translation of a Welsh name;[39] in later times it claimed some relics of St David, and the legends of St David himself claimed that the saint visited Leominster.[40] It is quite likely that there had been a Welsh monastery here before the Anglo-Saxon invasion. This is speculative; to its later history Mr Hillaby has added considerably by his suggestion – based on some very interesting evidence – that an early eleventh-century prayer book in the Cotton collection in the British Library was written at, or for, the nuns of Leominster.[41] This apart, the only well-recorded event in its history is its dissolution in 1046. The rapacious family of Earl Godwin, Harold's father, found an easy prey in the convents of nuns of the west country. Godwin himself suppressed Berkeley abbey in Gloucestershire; his son Swein carried off the abbess of Leominster and the property of her abbey with her.[42] The story of Leominster was not forgotten. In November 1120 the White Ship was wrecked off the Norman Coast, and Henry I's only legitimate son perished in the disaster. In King Henry's make-up cruelty and piety were strangely mingled. He was one of the most unattractive of a harsh line of kings; yet he won golden opinions from monastic chroniclers for giving his subjects peace and security, and for his lavish generosity to the religious orders. His most elaborate foundation was Reading abbey; and he endowed it with what remained in royal hands of three religious houses which had been suppressed

[39] Sims-Williams, *Religion and Literature*, p. 56.

[40] Hillaby, 'Early Christian and Pre-Conquest Leominster', pp. 600–5.

[41] Ibid., pp. 628–54.

[42] On Berkeley, see B. R. Kemp, 'The Churches of the Berkeley Hernesse', *Transactions of the Bristol and Gloucestershire Archaeological Society*, 87 (1968), pp. 96–100, esp. p. 101; Walter Map, *De nugis curialium*, ed. M. R. James, revised C. N. L. Brooke and R. A. B. Mynors, OMT (Oxford, 1983), p. 416 n. 1. On Leominster, see *Heads*, p. 214; and below, p. 153 and n. 45.

in the reign of Edward the Confessor: it seems to have been a grandiose
act of penance for his royal line, by which he hoped to find forgiveness (as
he may be supposed to have seen it) for the sins which had been so fearfully
punished in the White Ship. The three houses were Reading itself, formerly
a convent of nuns; a male house at Cholsey in Surrey; and Leominster.[43]
And so it was that the monks of Reading came to be lords of Leominster
until the Dissolution. Their magnificent church in Leominster still tells its
story after the refoundation. In the early 1120s, when Reading was founded,
the monks of Reading acquired the church; in 1139 they settled a community
of monks there, whose church is represented by the Norman aisles; a part
of it was doubtless reserved for the parish. In the fourteenth century the
church was extended, new aisles added, and a great part of it at least
made into a parish church on the grandest scale. Meanwhile, in 1123 the
bishop of Hereford, Richard de Capella, listed the churches, or anyway
the villages, which comprised the whole area formerly served by the priests
of Leominster. He listed thirty-nine villages; and even that evidently did
not comprise the whole extent of what had formerly been Leominster's,
but only what could still be retained by the monks of Reading.[44] For the
break up of the old region into smaller parishes was under way. It had
clearly not gone very far, for if it had, it is very unlikely that so much could
have been salvaged. The bishop very likely included some villages, perhaps
many, which as yet had no church: it was a kind of insurance for the monks
– when churches were built there, they would be part of their domain.

One of the most spectacular exhibits in the English Romanesque Exhibition in the Hayward Gallery in London in 1984 was the gorgeous
Romanesque sculptured font from St Michael's church in Castle Frome, a
little to the east of Hereford.[45] This is an outstanding specimen of a group
of noble fonts in this region dating from the early to mid twelfth century;
and in their turn they reflect a school of sculpture with its centre in
Herefordshire. 'The style is a mixture of local and western French elements
but the base suggests knowledge of Italian art', writes Professor Zarnecki,
the eminent art historian, who has always had a particular interest in the
sculpture of Herefordshire, of which Kilpeck provides perhaps the outstanding example.[46] George Zarnecki inspired and planned the Romanesque

[43] See below, p. 153.
[44] B. R. Kemp, 'Some Aspects of the *Parochia* of Leominster in the Twelfth Century', in
Minsters and Parish Churches (n. 37), pp. 83–95. For Bishop Richard's charter see ibid., pp. 83,
92 n. 3.
[45] *English Romanesque Art, 1066–1200* (Exhibition Catalogue, 1984), pp. 65, 178, no. 139.
[46] Ibid., p. 178; cf. G. Zarnecki, *Later English Romanesque Sculpture, 1140–1210* (London, 1953),
pp. 9–15.

Exhibition, and made the font from Castle Frome, magnificently restored and displayed, a central feature. For him, kindly and humane man though he is, the font is an expression of noble craftsmanship. It must be that for all of us; but to me it is equally a symbol of twelfth-century pastoral care, a dramatic assertion by local patrons and a local community that the parish church is theirs, that the children of the village are baptised in their midst. For both George Zarnecki and me it is a cosmopolitan object in which the crafts and concerns of Herefordshire mingle with those of Christendom at large. Fonts survive in very large numbers from the eleventh and twelfth centuries, and represent the development of the parish as the social and religious centre of a community.[47] The village church and the village font had taken the place of the older minsters. The larger *parochiae*, the regions of minsters like Leominster, had been broken into smaller units.

It did not happen so everywhere. In Cheshire and Lancashire, for example, and further north, much larger parishes survived through the twelfth century, when the canon law of parishes became established and parish boundaries fossilised. Bunbury in Cheshire retained a parish of twenty-four small villages; at the end of the Wirral peninsular West Kirby (the *by* or village with the church in the Norse tongue) and Bebington, counted twenty villages between them.[48] Ulpha in Cumbria, by the River Duddon, once formed the centre of a parish running about fifteen miles from its base at Kirkby by the estuary to the top of Wrynose pass. But the Normans, by an absurd judgement of Solomon, made the river divide two parishes, Kirkby and Millom, each enormously long and narrow. The advent of the new canon law in the twelfth century left a palimpsest, showing a variety of stages of development. But over most of the country, the division into small parishes was well advanced – though parishes still vary greatly in size.

There is thus a marked contrast between the parishes of much of this region (for all their variety) and those of Cheshire and the north west. But the contrast between the English parishes and those of Italy is even more marked. There the large font in a small parish church is replaced by a single large baptistery, in which the babies of a whole city and its region – of a whole diocese, that is, were baptised. Such baptisteries had been common in the early church, and survive for example in Poitiers. But in Italy they were revived and rebuilt and continued to flourish in the central middle ages: hence the magnificent baptisteries of Parma and Florence and Pisa. The

[47] F. Bond, *Fonts and Font Covers* (London, 1908; repr. with additional plates in colour, 1985); colour pls 1–2 are of the font at Castle Frome.

[48] Above, p. 18; for what follows, above, pp. 17–18. The pre-Norman history of the Duddon valley is conjectural, but this seems the most probable explanation of the strange boundary formed by the river.

font and the baptistery represent two different models of baptism, and two different models of a parish. In the early church when the baptised were mostly adults, it was common to have a long preparation in Lent and a great baptism of the catechumens at Eastertide. But as it became more and more common to baptise babies – and as the notion developed that if the babies died unbaptised they could not go to heaven – the practice of individual baptism of quite small babies grew common. In Italy the old practices carried on, somewhat modified; in the north individual baptism prevailed; and it came to be the special mark of a parish church – of the church of a worshipping community – that it should have a font and that its priest should baptise the children of the parish. Indeed, if we asked for a definition of a parish church, then one could say that it was the worshipping centre of a community, to which the people paid their tithes, in whose font their babies were baptised and in whose churchyard they were buried.[49]

I end with two most notable of the twelfth-century bishops of Hereford: Robert de Bethune, canon regular and prior of Llanthony, a saintly man and a notable pastor, bishop from 1131 to 1148; and Gilbert Foliot, monk of Cluny and abbot of Gloucester, bishop from 1148 to 1163, then bishop of London till his death in 1187, the man who brought the diocese of Hereford into the main stream of the English church, but whose later life was marred by his bitter strife with Thomas Becket.

The first of the post-conquest bishops who is more than a name to us was Robert of Lorraine, a notable scholar and scientist, who had a hand in bringing to England the abacus – a sort of primitive computer, vital to the development of literate accounting.[50] The twelfth-century bishops included no great warriors, and the early ones were from the commonest stock of English bishops of the mid and late middle ages, that is to say, royal clerks (as we should say, civil servants). Robert de Bethune and Gilbert Foliot represented a new departure: long before, in the tenth and very early eleventh centuries, monks had had a monopoly of the bishoprics. But by 1100 they had become a rarity, save in the see of Canterbury itself and its satellite, Rochester. Robert had made a career for himself on the Continent as a teacher, then settled down to be a canon regular at Llanthony in Gwent.[51]

---

[49] See below, ch. 5; and for parishes without fonts, p. 10, n. 31. E. Cattaneo, 'Il battistero in Italia dopo il Mille', *Miscellanea Gilles Gerard Meersseman = Italia Sacra*, 15–16 (1970), i, pp. 171–95.

[50] On Robert of Lorraine, see J. Barrow in *English Episcopal Acta*, 7 (London, 1992), pp. xxxv–xxxvii.

[51] On Robert de Bethune, see Barrow in *English Episcopal Acta*, 7, pp. xxxix–xlii; J. Hillaby in *The Friends of Hereford Cathedral: 46th Annual Report* (London, 1980), pp. 21–42. The chief source is the Life by William of Wycombe, ed. H. Wharton, *Anglia sacra* (London, 1691), i,

Llanthony sits in a peculiarly remote spot under the Black Mountain in what is still a wild and romantic site. Here a pair of ascetics – one a hermit, the other a chaplain of Queen Matilda who had seen the light – settled down to lead the regular life at the very beginning of the twelfth century. A few years later Henry I and Matilda were on the search for a religious house, fervent in prayer, which they could richly endow and make into a royal mausoleum and (one suspects) a suitable home for one of Henry's favourite nephews, Henry of Blois, future abbot of Glastonbury and prince-bishop of Winchester.[52] The king and queen threatened Llanthony with what G. K. Chesterton once described as crushing endowments, but the founders rejected the offer. Henry himself went on to found Reading abbey and many other houses. Llanthony remained poor and obscure, a remote haven: a house of canons following the rule of St Augustine not the rule of St Benedict, but in every other way closely similar to the Cistercian foundations of the next generation. In 1135 King Henry died, and south and central Wales, much of it recently conquered by the Normans, was aflame with rebellion almost in a moment. Llanthony was in the firing line, and the canons sought refuge in Gloucester. From then on till the early thirteenth century the two houses were run as one: Llanthony-by-Gloucester was the main headquarters; the old house in Gwent the outlying refuge of the ascetics.[53] But meanwhile the second prior, Robert de Bethune, had become bishop of Hereford. He combined patronage of the religious orders with a strong pastoral sense. His first love was Llanthony, which received much favour; but he gave encouragement to the settlement in Shobdon of the Augustinian canons from Saint-Victor in Paris, the great intellectual centre, who later moved to Wigmore; whose second abbot, Andrew of Saint-Victor, was one of the most notable biblical scholars of the twelfth century.[54] He also helped in the foundation of St Guthlac's priory at Hereford. St Guthlac's had once been a collegiate church within the city: from 1143 it became a substantial priory, dependent on Gloucester abbey, outside the walls.[55] The see already had an archdeacon and rural dean, so it seems; and the cathedral chapter had a dean and other dignitaries and fairly

pp. 293–321; and also ed. B. Parkinson, 'The Life of Robert de Bethune by William de Wycombe' (unpubl. Oxford B. Litt. thesis 1951).

[52] On Henry I and Llanthony, see below, ch. 8, p. 151 and n. 39; and ibid. for the similar interest in Montacute priory and its possible link with Henry of Blois: cf. *Heads*, p. 121. For Henry I's spectacular patronage of Henry of Blois, see below, pp. 151–2.

[53] *Heads*, pp. 172–73.

[54] J. C. Dickinson and P. T. Ricketts, 'The Anglo-Norman Chronicle of Wigmore Abbey', *Transactions of the Woolhope Naturalists' Field Club*, 39 (1969), pp. 413–46, at pp. 422–27. On Andrew see refs to the studies of B. Smalley in *Heads*, p. 190, esp. her *Study of the Bible in the Middle Ages* (2nd edn, Oxford, 1952), pp. 112–85.

[55] J. Barrow in *English Episcopal Acta*, 7 (1992), p. xli and no. 21.

numerous canons. Robert seems to have infiltrated a regular element into the chapter; to have divided the see into two archdeaconries and to have made one of his Llanthony canons first archdeacon of Shropshire.[56] The formation of the Herefordshire parishes went on apace.

Robert de Bethune had had to bear the threat of Welsh incursions into his see after the revolt of 1136. He also suffered from the feuds of Stephen's reign, at their height in 1140 when Geoffrey Talbot and Milo of Gloucester (future earl of Hereford) besieged it and made the cathedral into a castle.[57] In later years fighting was sporadic; and it was Gilbert Foliot's business to restore the see after the anarchy of King Stephen's reign. In a measure he had performed this role already as abbot of Gloucester.[58] For Bristol and Gloucester were the chief centres of power of the younger Matilda, the empress, Henry I's daughter and Stephen's cousin and rival; and Gilbert, as abbot of Gloucester, was one of her staunchest supporters. But in the course of the 1140s a new star rose in the person of Theobald, archbishop of Canterbury, whose fame has been somewhat eclipsed by his more celebrated successor Thomas Becket; but who was in his day one of the most remarkable archbishops Canterbury had known. When England was a divided country, Theobald made it his business to hold the church together, to make a unity of the province of Canterbury under the ultimate jurisdiction of the pope – indeed he claimed primacy over all England as his predecessors had done; and Gilbert seems to have been his chief contact in the west country – his spy, one might almost say, save that they seem to have corresponded, and even on occasions met, quite openly. Gilbert, still abbot of Gloucester, set off for the papal council at Reims in 1148, to which the archbishop went in spite of Stephen's attempts to prevent him. There Robert de Bethune died and Theobald arranged for Gilbert to succeed him.[59] It was a very tricky appointment politically. At first Gilbert was very much *persona grata* with the young Prince Henry, Matilda's son, pretender to the throne; but Henry was deeply incensed when Theobald made Gilbert do homage and swear fealty to Stephen. Yet the archbishop managed to smooth these difficulties over, and eventually to bring off his greatest diplomatic coup by making peace between Stephen and Henry in 1153. When Stephen died, Henry II succeeded him. Gilbert soon became one of his

---

[56] *GFL*, pp. 116–17, no. 18; *GF*, p. 268.

[57] *Gesta Stephani*, ed. K. R. Potter and R. H. C. Davis, OMT (2nd edn, Oxford, 1976), pp. 108–11.

[58] For what follows, see *GF* (1965), chs 5–7. On Theobald, see ibid., pp. 88–94; A. Saltman, *Theobald, Archbishop of Canterbury* (London, 1956).

[59] *GF*, pp. 96–97.

closest associates among the bishops, so close that Henry had him translated to London in 1163.

With Gilbert's translation our story must end. Looking back, it seems quite a natural thing for a bishop to be translated from Hereford to London. Three other bishops of Hereford have trodden the same path; and in the fourteenth century, and sometimes later, translation commonly deprived Hereford of its bishops. But in 1163 it was a very strange event. In the early church the removal of a bishop from one see to another was forbidden – it was a kind of divorce; the bishop was married to his see. So it was always the case that translation required papal dispensation; and partly because of the ancient prejudice, partly out of reluctance to involve the pope directly in appointments, translation was a very rare event. From time to time bishops moved up to Canterbury or York. But it was not until the fourteenth century – when all bishops were coming to be appointed (in the pope's view at least) by the pope, that translation became common, and the musical chairs so characteristic of the late medieval and early modern church began. The special circumstance in 1163 was that Thomas Becket had recently become archbishop of Canterbury, to Gilbert's sorrow; and the king, who had promoted Becket, had begun to realise that he and Becket were not going to see eye to eye. Henry wanted Gilbert as near to him as possible, at the centre of affairs, to give him support if the problems got worse; and Thomas himself hoped to find in Gilbert a man who would keep Henry from dangerous courses. So the pope, who at this stage regarded Gilbert as a moderating influence, readily agreed to his translation. In the event Gilbert did help to prevent some of Henry's more extreme courses, but was no peacemaker: he and Becket became embittered enemies; when Thomas was murdered Gilbert was under his ban.[60] It took him a long time to win absolution. In his later years he never (so far as we know) visited Hereford again. But in 1173–74 a cousin called Robert Foliot became bishop of Hereford, and the relations between London and Hereford remained close and cordial for many years to come: Foliots flourished in Hereford until well into the thirteenth century, and Gilbert meanwhile had filled the archdeaconries of the see of London with his nephews.[61] It was to Robert as bishop-elect that Gilbert wrote on behalf of the church of Ledbury, sanctified (as he supposed) by the tombs of the bishops, their predecessors.

I have dedicated many years to studying the life and letters of two notable

[60] For these events see ibid., pp. 98–103, and ch. 9.

[61] On Robert Foliot, see J. Barrow in *English Episcopal Acta*, 7 (1992), pp. xliv–xlv; on Gilbert Foliot's family, *GF*, ch. 3, esp. pp. 44–45, 272–74. For what follows see n. 25.

twelfth-century churchmen, Gilbert Foliot and John of Salisbury. John was a close follower of Becket, and at the height of the controversies between them, in 1166, he wrote a celebrated series of letters in which he denounced Gilbert's role and labelled him Achitophel, after the evil counsellor of King David's court who had led the young Absalom into rebellion.[62] John wrote in anger, and enjoyed the vigour of his own rhetoric; but his words inspired a celebrated apostrophe by Dom David Knowles on the ambiguous character of this notable bishop of Hereford and London.

> And now we come ... to the most enigmatic figure of all, to the man of probity whom even a pope reverenced for his austerity of life, the mirror of religion and glory of the age, the luminary who shed a lustre even on the great name of Cluny; ... the Achitophel who gave counsel ... against his master; the Judas, who made a pact upon the body of Christ, the church of Canterbury.[63]

Gilbert was a strange mixture of good and less good qualities, and certainly not colourless; and Robert de Bethune had some qualities of sanctity. These were bishops of high distinction: Hereford was no distant borderland, hidden away in the Welsh march. Its bishops were as cosmopolitan figures as its sculptors.

---

[62] See esp. John of Salisbury, *Letters,* ii, pp. 152–57, no. 175.
[63] D. Knowles, *The Episcopal Colleagues of Archbishop Thomas Becket* (Cambridge, 1951), pp. 37–38.

3

York Minster from the Ninth to the Early Thirteenth Centuries

The first golden age of Northumbrian Christianity comprised the lifetime, and work, of Bede, down to his death in 735.[1] In the same year Pope Gregory the Great's original intention that York should be the seat of an archbishop was realised; and under its first archbishops the see and the school of York flourished, and became the first home of the great scholar Alcuin later in the century. The early ninth century saw the school and church of York continue, but the Viking onslaught – though its precise impact has been much discussed and disputed – brought the first age of Northumbrian Christian culture to decline. I take up the tale in the late ninth century.

In 855 the Viking army wintered in England for the first time. By 867 the Danes were occupying East Anglia, and in the following year they went north, crossed the Humber and captured York. The Northumbrians suspended their civil wars for long enough to attack them; and, in spite of the death of both their kings, the English seem to have negotiated a truce which left them in possession of the city; but in 869 the Danes were in York again. Simeon of Durham, drawing upon earlier northern annals, records the fact that Archbishop Wulfhere, who had received the pallium in 854, was 'reinstated' in 873 and died in 892 in the thirty-ninth year of his episcopate, after which the see was vacant for eight years.[2] Very little of its ancient reputation seems to have survived at York. Asser tells us that King Alfred 'was wont to say' that 'at that time' (the decade after 871) there were 'no good scholars in all the kingdom of the West Saxons',[3] and he

First printed in *A History of York Minster*, ed. G. E. Aylmer and R. Cant (Oxford, 1977), pp. 12–43.

  [1] This chapter originally comprised the second half of a chapter on the minster from 627 to the early thirteenth century: the first part was written by the late Professor Rosalind Hill with characteristic grace and insight, and this I have summarised in the first paragraph above.

  [2] Simeon of Durham, *Opera omnia*, ed. T. Arnold, RS, 2 vols (London, 1882–85).

  [3] *English Historical Documents*, i, ed. D. Whitelock (2nd edn, London, 1979), p. 292; *Asser's Life of King Alfred* (Oxford, 1904; revised edn 1959), c. 24, p. 21.

brought in learned men from abroad and from western Mercia to fill the gap. Of Northumbria he did not speak at all.

For the first half of the tenth century there is little recorded history of the church of York. The city was occupied in turn by the Danes, the armies of the West Saxon successors of Alfred, and Norse raiders from Ireland. It was not until the reign of Edgar (959–75) that the English were safely in possession of the whole of Northumbria. It does not, however, appear that these years were a time of entire depression, either for the material prosperity of York or for the state of its Christian population. As so often happened, the Vikings, who were prepared to trade as well as to ravage, brought a measure of prosperity; Byrhtferth's *Life of St Oswald* describes York in about 980 as a densely populated city, full of Danish merchants, even if its buildings were somewhat down-at-heel.[4] Some of the Danes were even showing an interest in Christianity, perhaps as an insurance against risks in the future life, perhaps in order to facilitate relations with the English, perhaps from genuine conviction. There were archbishops still in York, though they are little more than names to us, and the minster survived and even remained a centre of Christian worship. As early as 895 a Danish king, Guthfrith, who was converted to Christianity, was buried in it,[5] and in 934 King Athelstan made it a very substantial grant of land.[6] Roger of Wendover, who seems to be using here some earlier source, records that in 946 King Eadred presented it with two large bells.[7]

In 956–58 Oscytel, translated from the see of Dorchester, became archbishop. He was a near relation of the saintly Oda, who since 942 had held the see of Canterbury as a notable reformer, and his undoubtedly Scandinavian name strengthens the probability of the story that Oda's father was a pagan Dane who had come to England in the war-band of Hubba and Ivar the Boneless. Oscytel was a personal friend of St Dunstan, and therefore almost by definition a reformer, although very little is known of his work. He was succeeded, after the very short pontificate of Edwald, by his 'near earthly kin' (probably a nephew) St Oswald, bishop of Worcester.[8] Oswald

---

[4] *Historians of the Church of York*, ed. J. Raine, RS, 3 vols (London, 1879–94), i, p. 454; see n. 11.

[5] Æthelweard, *Chronicle*, ed. A. Campbell, NMT (Edinburgh, 1962), p. 51.

[6] *Early Yorkshire Charters*, i, ed. W. Farrer (Edinburgh, 1914), no. 1, with sceptical comments by W. H. Stevenson; but see *English Historical Documents*, i, no. 104, pp. 548–51, where it is defended by Professor Whitelock; full bibliography in P. H Sawyer, *Anglo-Saxon Charters* (London, 1968), no. 407.

[7] Roger of Wendover, *Flores historiarum*, ed. H. O. Coxe (English Historical Society, London, 1841–42), i, p. 399; *English Historical Documents*, i, p. 283.

[8] *Historians of the Church of York*, i, p. 420.

held the two sees together until his death in 992. This seems to have been a deliberate arrangement, probably made in order to build up the depleted and exhausted church of York by linking it to one of the richest parts of western Mercia. Oswald was one of the three outstanding personalities of the tenth-century reformation in England, the others being St Dunstan and St Æthelwold. Unfortunately for historians, the man who wrote his biography was a person of flowery style and strongly conventional ideas, and he was also much more interested in Oswald's doings as bishop of Worcester and as abbot of Ramsey than in his activities at York. Desiring above all things to emphasise Oswald's saintliness, he gives us very little of the man's individuality. However, a few facts do emerge. Oswald was distinguished from his youth by a strong desire to learn and to teach, and at the monastery of Fleury, to which he had gone to study the principles of the reformed Benedictine rule, he learned the whole office by heart, 'wishing to teach his own countrymen what he had learned from strangers'.[9] He had a notably beautiful voice and, at least at Ramsey,[10] he established a strong musical tradition. Whenever he came to York, he always went first to his church.[11] In spite of the fact that he suffered painfully from rheumatism,[12] he seems to have tried to carry out visitations of his see; it is recorded that he went to Ripon, established monks there in the place of secular clergy, and provided a new shrine for the relics of St Wilfrid and his companions.[13] The one incident recorded in detail about his life in York is the story of a mouse which died suddenly after eating some of the blessed bread which the archbishop was accustomed to distribute to his guests at the beginning of a feast.[14] It is an odd tale, but it serves at least to illustrate the decorous behaviour which the archbishop expected to prevail at his parties. We may believe that at York, as at Worcester, his death was marked by such public lamentation that 'merchants left their bargaining, and women their distaffs and their weaving'.[15]

The union of two substantial sees in the hands of a single saintly bishop is a puzzle; nor is it made easier by the numerous cases of similar pluralism in the two generations between Oswald's death and the Norman Conquest.

[9] Ibid., i, p. 419.

[10] Ibid., i, pp. 417, 464.

[11] Ibid., i, p. 454; on Byrhtferth's *Vita Oswaldi* see Whitelock in *English Historical Documents*, i, pp. 911–12 and refs, e.g. to D. J. V. Fisher, 'The Anti-Monastic Reaction in the Reign of Edward the Martyr', *Cambridge Historical Journal*, 10 (1952), pp. 254–70; and see esp. edn of Byrhtferth, *Vita Oswaldi*, by Michael Lapidge, OMT, forthcoming.

[12] *Historians of the Church of York*, i, p. 467.

[13] Ibid., i, pp. 462–63.

[14] Ibid., i, pp. 454–55.

[15] Ibid., i, p. 472.

Some of the bishops were men of exemplary piety, like Oswald's two successors, Ealdwulf, formerly abbot of Peterborough, who held both Oswald's sees from 995 till his death in 1002, and Wulfstan the homilist, translated from London to the double see in 1002.[16] Some of the pluralists seem to have been practising a mere abuse; and this was recognised in the case of one of the later archbishops, Ealdred, who tried to hold Worcester with York at his translation in 1061, but was ousted by the pope from Worcester a year later. It was notorious in the case of Ealdred's contemporary at Canterbury, Stigand, who was found to be holding the sees both of Canterbury (1052–70) and of Winchester even after he had complaisantly surrendered the see of East Anglia to his brother.[17] Edward the Confessor was particularly tolerant of bishops who accumulated wealth in unusual ways, and some of the English cathedrals benefited permanently from his tolerance, York included. But in the era of the movement for ecclesiastical reform of which popes like Nicholas II, who drummed Ealdred, were the centre, episcopal pluralism, along with clerical marriage and other ancient customs, were fiercely attacked. Evidently St Oswald had grounds of a more acceptable character than Ealdred's for combining the sees.

If such pluralism is strange in a saint, even stranger is the contrast between the two cathedrals to which it draws our attention; and this is of particular interest, for it provides us with the first real insight we have into the nature of the minster's clergy. From the time of St Oswald until the dissolution of the monasteries Worcester was one of the English cathedrals served by a chapter of monks. Oswald at Worcester and Æthelwold at Winchester were the founders of this practice, often said – with some exaggeration – to be unique to Britain.[18] Under Oswald himself and his immediate

[16] For what follows, see F. Barlow, *The English Church, 1000–1066* (2nd edn, London, 1979); D. Whitelock, 'The Dealings of the Kings of England with Northumbria in the Tenth and Eleventh Centuries', in *The Anglo-Saxons: Studies Presented to B. Dickins*, ed. P. Clemoes (London, 1959), pp. 70–88; J. M. Cooper, *The Last Four Anglo-Saxon Archbishops of York*, Borthwick Papers, 38 (York, 1970). On Ealdwulf, see references in *Heads*, p. 59. On Wulfstan see esp. D. Whitelock, 'Archbishop Wulfstan, Homilist and Statesman', in *Transactions of the Royal Historical Society*, 4th series, 24 (1942), pp. 25–45; Whitelock, 'Wulfstan at York', in *Franciplegius: Medieval and Linguistic Studies in Honor of Francis Peabody Magoun, Jr*, ed. J. B. Bessinger, Jr, and R. P. Creed (New York, 1965), pp. 214–31; and Whitelock's edn of *Sermo Lupi ad Anglos* (3rd edn, London, 1963); *Homilies*, ed. D. Bethurum (Oxford, 1957). A number of works written by or connected with Wulfstan are edited, with commentary, by Dorothy Whitelock in *Councils and Synods*, i, 1, pp. 402–506.

[17] Barlow, *The English Church, 1000–1066*, pp. 86–90, 76–81.

[18] On their monasticism, see D. Knowles, *The Monastic Order in England* (2nd edn, Cambridge, 1963), chs 3–4; at one time or another a fair number of chapters on the continent were monastic, and a large number had chapters of canons regular.

successors, and again under the last eminent Old English bishop, Wulfstan II (1062–95), Worcester cathedral was a notable centre of monastic observance. York was never monastic, nor were either of the other minster churches under the archbishops' immediate control – Ripon or Beverley – served by monks in the tenth or any later century; indeed, there were no monastic communities at all in England north of the Trent in the tenth and early eleventh centuries. Northumbria in general, and the vale of York in particular, are full of monastic remains; a few are of the age of St Wilfrid and Bede; the great majority are monuments to the Norman age; none was late Old English. When Thomas, the first Norman archbishop of York, arrived, he is supposed to have found merely the remnant of a group of secular canons in the minster – three of a total never more than seven.[19]

Beside this, let us set another contrast. A document purporting to be of 1092 portrays the aged Bishop Wulfstan presiding over a synod in the crypt of his cathedral which settled many issues, including the status of the parish churches in Worcester itself.[20] We now know that this document is a forgery of the twelfth century; but it establishes the views and aims of the monks of Worcester of that period nonetheless. It claims that by ancient custom there was only one parish, that of the cathedral, and that the various other ancient churches of the city were subordinate to the cathedral. Such a claim might have been regarded as quite normal by an Italian bishop of the age; it was stranger to English ears, for the eleventh and twelfth centuries saw the proliferation of tiny parishes attached to tiny parish churches in many English towns. By the end of the eleventh century York certainly had eleven, and probably far more; by 1200 it had forty. By then Lincoln, Norwich and Winchester had even more numerous parish churches, and London almost one hundred within the walls.[21]

The reasons most commonly alleged for Oswald's pluralism are the poverty of the see of York and the paganism of its inhabitants. The Viking invasions – it has often been thought – had made large areas of eastern and northern England pagan at worst, missionary country at best. Oswald and his successors attempted its reconquest from bases in the south and south west. While they marched out towards York from a base by the Severn, their neighbour the bishop of Dorchester – the vast see which was to be moved to Lincoln after the Norman Conquest – nestled by the

---

[19] Hugh the Chanter, *The History of the Church of York, 1066–1127,* ed. C. Johnson, M. Brett, C. N. L. Brooke and M. Winterbottom, OMT (Oxford, 1990), pp. 18–19.

[20] See below, p. 73.

[21] See below, pp. 75, 82–6.

Thames.[22] The pagan element among the north-eastern Vikings no doubt made York an insecure base for a bishop in the mid and late tenth centuries and for a time reduced the temporalities of the see. There has been much argument as to how thickly the Scandinavian invaders settled in the northern Danelaw, in Lincolnshire and Yorkshire. The most striking evidence of the situation at the time of St Oswald's death is provided by the coins struck by the moneyers of York.[23] They show first of all that it was considered a major centre of economic activity; in the mid eleventh century there were as many moneyers at York as in London itself. By the standards of the day it was a large and prosperous town. Analysis of the names of the moneyers on the coins shows a marked preponderance of names of Viking origin. On the coins of the London mint in the reign of Æthelred the Unready (978–1016) all but a handful of the moneyers have Old English names; in Lincoln and the towns of the east Midlands there is a notable Scandinavian element, rising in Chester to a quarter. In York the Scandinavian names amount to forty, swamping the English (thirteen) and Celtic (five). By this date the Vikings had been in York for a century, and some English parents may have been giving their children Norse names. But when all allowances have been made, it is difficult to escape the conclusion of the expert who has analysed this striking evidence; that York was still 'a primarily Norwegian colony'; and that 'the integration of the settlers with the native population was far less complete in York than in any other part of England in which the Vikings settled'.[24]

Virtually all the English bishops between the reign of Edgar and the accession of Cnut (959–1016) had been monks before their consecration. From Cnut's time there was an increasing element recruited from the secular clergy, specially from the royal chapel; there was also an increasing element of rich men inclined to add see to see and pile up money and estates. Religious life and pastoral care took two chief forms, as far as we can tell:

---

[22] See Barlow, *The English Church, 1000–1066*, pp. 163–64, 215–16; D. Whitelock, 'The Conversion of the Eastern Danelaw', *Saga-Book of the Viking Society*, 12 (1937–45), pp. 159–76. See now, Julia Barrow, 'English Cathedral Communities and Reform in the Late Tenth and Eleventh Centuries', in *Anglo-Norman Durham*, ed. D. Rollason, M. Harvey and M. Prestwich (Woodbridge, 1994), pp. 25–39, at pp. 27–28, and references cited.

[23] See the remarkable study by Veronica J. Smart, 'Moneyers of the Late Anglo-Saxon Coinage, 973–1016', in *Commentationes de nummis saeculorum IX-XI in Suecia repertis*, ii (Stockholm, 1968), pp. 191–276, esp. pp. 227–33 for York. For York in this period, see also H. Lindqvist, 'A Study on Early Medieval York', *Anglia*, 50 (1926), pp. 345–94; J. Radley, 'Economic Aspects of Anglo-Danish York', *Medieval Archaeology*, 15 (1971), pp. 37–57 – now revised and supplemented by numerous fascicules of *The Archaeology of York* and other publications of the York Archaeological Trust.

[24] Smart, 'Moneyers', p. 233.

the monastic communities flourished, as at Worcester, and remained in the eleventh century centres of religious life for the laity as well; elsewhere there was a proliferation of parish churches, reflecting self-help by landowners and merchants, and by parish clergy living close to the people. It is rare for us to have evidence of collaboration between the bishop and the parish priests; the outstanding exception is in *The Law of the Northumbrian Priests*, which seems to show us the great legislator Archbishop Wulfstan I at work among the rank and file of his clergy in York.[25]

Wulfstan was almost certainly a monk by origin, but he has won renown in recent generations by the progressive revelation of his work as legislator and pastoral leader; his works consist of eloquent vernacular sermons and legislation both secular and ecclesiastical. 'With great deserts have we merited the miseries which oppress us', he said in his famous Sermon of the Wolf (a play upon his name) to the English – originally a response to the disasters of the end of Æthelred's reign; 'a great breach will require much repair, and a great fire no little water, if the fire is to be quenched at all; and great is the necessity for everyman that he keep henceforward God's laws eagerly and pay God's dues rightly'.[26]

Wulfstan was indeed much interested both in the church's laws and pastoral care and in its revenues. The first half of the famous cartulary of Worcester cathedral, Cotton MS Tiberius A.xiii,[27] was written under Wulfstan's eye, and carefully corrected and annotated by a hand which may well be Wulfstan's own. For another record, also in the British Library, MS Harley 55, fol. 4v, shows us the same hand labelling and correcting a copy of a record of St Oswald relating to some of the properties of the see of York. It seems clear that Wulfstan's base was at Worcester, and it is probable that we owe the survival of this record to the care of the monks of Worcester for his books. But it also seems clear that he cared for his northern see; and pastorally as well as temporally. *The Law of the Northumbrian Priests* may well be, at least in part, from his hand.[28] It is a puzzling document, but in the main it seems to be a very down-to-earth attempt to deal with

[25] Edited with commentary, by D. Whitelock in *Councils and Synods*, i, 1, pp. 449–68. Cf. J. M. Cooper, *The Last Four Anglo-Saxon Archbishops* (n. 16), pp. 8–10, who believes it to be the work of a subordinate, reworked by Wulfstan; Whitelock argued for Wulfstan's authorship. Some of the code was drawn from earlier codes and adapted to the needs of York.

[26] *English Historical Documents*, i, p. 929.

[27] On which see N. R. Ker, 'Hemming's Cartulary', in *Studies in Medieval History Presented to F. M. Powicke*, ed. R. W. Hunt, W. A. Pantin and R. W. Southern (Oxford, 1948), pp. 49–75; it was ed. by T. Hearne in 1723. On Harleian 55, see Ker, *Catalogue of Manuscripts Containing Anglo-Saxon* (Oxford, 1957), no. 225. See Whitelock, 'Wulfstan at York', esp. p. 216.

[28] See n. 25; *Councils and Synods*, i, 1, pp. 450–51; text and translation, ibid. pp. 452–68.

the clergy of a teeming city, and we need not doubt that it reflects life in York in Wulfstan's later years. The clergy were gathered into a guild or club which attempted to enforce standards of practice and behaviour by levying fines; they were in many ways very secular – they frequented taverns, were quarrelsome, liable to put 'unsuitable things' in their churches, say mass before the church was consecrated, celebrate in wooden chalices, bring weapons into church; they had to be reminded that they can only have one wife (a remarkable concession indeed from a celibate archbishop), that they must 'all love and honour one God ... and entirely cast out every heathen practice' (c. 47). We are shown an active missionary clergy close to their flocks in spirit and manner as well as physically, in the tiny churches in which they are admonished not to celebrate festivals in the wrong order; of the larger presence of the minster there is no hint.

Wulfstan's work evidently continued; for the Flemish monk Folcard, who wrote the life of St John of Beverley in the middle of the century, commends Archbishop Ealdred for his synodal reforms.[29] In celebrating the liturgy, the holy church of York – cathedral and diocese – had shaken off its ancient rusticity, decent order had been enjoined, and the clergy told to take off their secular garments and put on decent clerical dress. In Folcard's stately phrases one catches the echo of cosmopolitan contempt for semi-educated provincial clergy, but also of the lively worker priests and whisky priests – an interesting combination – suggested by the Northumbrian Priests' Law.

On Christmas Day 1066 Ealdred anointed and crowned William the Conqueror king of the English in Westminster Abbey;[30] and in 1069 he died. The appointment of his successor marked a new departure in the promotion of Norman clergy. Hitherto, William's nominees had either been members of the Norman feudal nobility, such as his half-brother, Odo of Bayeux, or Geoffrey de Mowbray of Coutances, or pious reforming monks, like Maurilius of Rouen or Lanfranc, very soon to become archbishop of

[29] 'Vita S. Johannis', *Historians of the Church of York*, i, p. 241. Cf. ibid. ii, pp. 342–54, esp. 353–54: a later chronicle, evidently incorporating early material or traditions, which suggests that Ealdred was active in attempting to sustain or revive some kind of communal life in the minsters of the diocese, especially Beverley; and he is said to have built a refectory at York.

[30] See Guy of Amiens, *Carmen de Hastingae proelio*, ed. C. Morton and H. Muntz, OMT (Oxford, 1972), p. lv; Anglo-Saxon Chronicle, MS D, *sub anno* 1068 for 1069; on Ealdred, see Barlow, *The English Church, 1000–1066*, pp. 86–90. For the effects of the Norman Conquest see J. Le Patourel, 'The Norman Conquest of Yorkshire', *Northern History*, 6 (1971), pp. 1–21. On Ealdred's last years and death, see *Historians of the Church of York*, iii, pp. 349–50; cf. pp. 350–54. There is a very interesting reference to the *consuetudo* of the church of York in the time of Edward the Confessor and Archbishop Ealdred in a charter attributed to Henry I (and perhaps genuine), *Historians of the Church of York*, iii, pp. 34–36.

Canterbury and no doubt already marked out for the office. The English bishops were rarely aristocratic either before or after the Conquest. Already in the Confessor's time the majority had come to be recruited from the royal chapel, and although a trickle of monks continued, the majority of William's appointments were of secular clerks who had grown up both in his chapel and household and in the secular cathedrals of Normandy.[31] Many of the bishops of the next generation had held office or a canonry at Bayeux or Rouen; from Bayeux and the Bessin came three of the most remarkable clerical families of the age.[32] First Thomas, treasurer of Bayeux, archbishop of York (1070–1100), whose brother Samson was bishop of Worcester from 1096; and Samson's son, another Thomas, was ultimately to sit on his uncle's throne at York from 1108 to 1114. Next Ranulf Flambard, William II's notorious minister, bishop of Durham (1099–1128), brother and father of other career clerks.[33] Finally Anger or Anskar, Thomas's colleague at Bayeux, who came to London with his wife Popelina and settled in a canonry at St Paul's; they reared at least two sons, one of whom, Audoen, was successively canon of St Paul's and bishop of Evreux, the other, Thurstan, canon of St Paul's and archbishop of York (1114–40).[34] Thurstan began as a favourite clerk of William Rufus, and colleague of Flambard, and ended, in the odour of sanctity, as founder of Fountains Abbey and monk of Pontefract. In his own career he reconciled or settled several of the conflicts of the age: a scion of the old abuse (as some of his contemporaries saw it) of clerical marriage and hereditary benefices, a worldly royal clerk, who was yet the friend and patron of monks; and in a world in which Cistercian monks could engage in bitter conflict with Cluniacs, he founded a Cistercian abbey and died clothed in the habit of a Cluniac. He also settled the primacy dispute between Canterbury and York – settled after a fashion, for it has flared up again times out of number since his death; but no archbishop of York has since been compelled to admit the formal superiority of the archbishop of Canterbury.

Thurstan must be one of the heroes of this chapter, for he is the central figure of the one really notable chronicle to come out of York minster in the Norman period, that of Hugh the Chanter, or Hugh Sottewaine, which

[31] Below, ch. 6; Barlow, *The English Church, 1000–1066*, pp. 76ff; below, pp. 113, 116.

[32] On these families see Brooke, *Medieval Church and Society* (London, 1971), pp. 69–99, esp. pp. 86ff; also Brooke, 'The Composition of the Chapter of St Paul's, 1086–1163', *Cambridge Historical Journal*, 10 (1951), pp. 111–32, esp. p. 124.

[33] R. W. Southern, *Medieval Humanism and Other Studies* (Oxford, 1970), pp. 183–205; Brooke, 'The Composition of the Chapter of St Paul's', pp. 124, 129ff, corrected by D. E. Greenway, *Fasti*, i, pp. 97–98.

[34] D. Nicholl, *Thurstan, Archbishop of York* (York, 1964); see above, n. 32.

is mainly a lively and entertaining account of Thurstan's struggles.[35] But Thomas and his family were in their way no less interesting. Samson was evidently a man with a subtle and cunning mind;[36] and Thomas was one of the founders of the type of secular cathedral which was characteristic of medieval England, and, in a modified form, still lives in York minster.

If we were in a position to ask an instructed clerk of the eleventh or twelfth centuries what sort of folk peopled cathedrals in his day, he would be able without much difficulty to say 'canons or, in a few places, monks'. But if we asked him what kind of people canons were, we could expect an answer much less clear cut. Traditionally, the word 'canon' was supposed to mean a 'rule', and many canons claimed that they took this name because they lived according to a rule.[37] But notoriously some canons were more regular than others. The distinctions in use in the eleventh century went back to the days of Charlemagne and his successor, Louis the Pious, in the early ninth century. These emperors promulgated edicts and presided over councils which provided, on paper at least, for the reform of the very varied, and often very lax, institutes of their empire, and divided the world into monks and canons in a tolerably clear way. Monks lived according to the Rule of St Benedict and were in a fair measure separated from the world; canons lived also according to a rule and a number of customary regulations codified, probably by Amalarius of Metz, in the Council of Aachen of 816–17. These regulations were deeply influenced by the rule of St Benedict, and, had the canons adhered closely to them, they would have been little different from monks, save that their opportunities to work in the world and serve the communities among which they lived were somewhat greater.

By the twelfth century it was possible for some observers to see two types of canon clearly distinct: canons regular, who lived according to the Rule of St Augustine and so were frequently known as 'Augustinian', and canons secular, who lived in their own houses and enjoyed separate incomes. Even then there were secular canons who liked to quote the old saying 'canon

[35] Hugh the Chanter, *History*; on Hugh, canon and precentor (in Latin *cantor*, hence 'Chanter'), see ibid., pp. xix–xxx and p. xxiii for other members of the family Sottewaine, esp. Arnulf and Thomas, who were also canons.

[36] V. H. Galbraith, 'Notes on the Career of Samson Bishop of Worcester, 1096–1112', *EHR*, 82 (1967), pp. 86–101, suggested that he was the author of the Domesday Survey. P. Chaplais has made a stronger case for William of Saint-Calais, bishop of Durham in 'William of Saint-Calais and the Domesday Survey', in *Domesday Studies*, ed. J. C. Holt (Woodbridge, 1987), pp. 65–77.

[37] Cf. K. Edwards, *The English Secular Cathedrals in the Middle Ages* (2nd edn, Manchester, 1967), pp. 1ff (to which I am much indebted in what follows). See also, on canons regular, J. C. Dickinson, *The Origins of the Austin Canons* (London, 1950); *Mendola*, 3 (Milan, 1962); *Libellus de diversis ordinibus*, ed. and trans. G. Constable and B. Smith, OMT (Oxford, 1972).

equals *regula*', and the distinction was nothing like so firm as most modern scholars would have us believe. In the eleventh century it was even less so; for the rule of St Augustine, though ancient, and in some of its versions and lineaments possibly even connected with the great bishop of Hippo, was hardly known in England before about 1100; and the way of life of the secular canons, in the form in which it is known to us from the custumals of the twelfth century and later, was hardly recognised as legitimate before about 1090.

The canons of English cathedrals in the two generations before the Conquest, in so far as we have any information about them, all seem to have paid some sort of lip service either to the *Institutio canonicorum* of 816–17, or to a version of the eighth-century rule of Bishop Chrodegang of Metz, which is sometimes referred to as the expanded Rule of Chrodegang.[38] This bound them to a measure of common life, not only in attending regularly at mass and the round of daily offices in the cathedral, but also eating communal meals in a refectory by day and sleeping together in a dormitory at night. In some, as at St Paul's, it seems to have been not wholly incompatible with some independent use of money and resources; and at the cathedrals, such as York, where the community was very small, a genuine communal life seems unlikely, and it is quite possible, even probable, that cathedral clerks, like other clergy, lived in the world and married.[39] Folcard's preface, confirmed by later evidence, may indicate that Ealdred embarked on a scheme of reform, but Hugh the Chanter tells us that it was Thomas who in his early years introduced or reintroduced canons living the common life at York; in his later years he converted the chapter to conform with the model to which he had been accustomed in Normandy, a fully secular chapter of canons living in their own houses, enjoying the fruits of separate incomes or 'prebends'.

The history of the secular canons on the Continent has yet to be written, and there is much about it which is totally obscure.[40] But we know that in many parts of northern France (and with local differences, in many other regions too) there had grown up in the preceding centuries a type of

---

[38] See D. Whitelock's R. W. Chambers Memorial Lecture, *Some Anglo-Saxon Bishops of London* (London, 1975); and see now J. Barrow, 'English Cathedral Communities' (n. 22).

[39] See Brooke, 'The Earliest Times to 1485', in *A History of St Paul's Cathedral*, ed. W. R. Matthews and W. M. Atkins (London, 1957), pp. 1–99, 361–65, at pp. 11ff, 361ff; *GF*, pp. 188ff and references cited; see above, n. 37. For what follows, see n. 29; Hugh the Chanter, *History*, pp. 18–19.

[40] See literature cited above, n. 37. A pathfinding comparative study is J. Barrow, 'Cathedrals, Provosts and Prebends: A Comparison of Twelfth-Century German and English Practice', *Journal of Ecclesiastical History*, 37 (1986), pp. 536–64.

cathedral chapter which must have been familiar to many of the Norman invaders. This consisted of a group of between twenty and fifty canons, with individual prebends (literally, a prebend means provisions or provender), who lived in houses in the close, met regularly for mass and offices and served the cathedral and, traditionally, also the churches of the neighbourhood. They were directed by a group of dignitaries, to whom various special functions were delegated: such as the dean or provost, the head of the chapter under the bishop, the precentor who ruled the choir, the chancellor who ruled the seal and the school, the treasurer who guarded relics, reliquaries and other treasures, and so forth. Such chapters existed, or were in process of formation, in various Norman cathedrals in the second half of the eleventh century, but much more mature examples were to be seen not far off, in Chartres and Paris and elsewhere.

There was little in the custom of such chapters to prevent the secular canons from being absentees, and doubtless already at this date many of them were engaged in various other activities, in the service of dukes and kings and other bishops; perhaps also in trade and commerce – though the great proliferation of petty bureaucracies, and the great growth of schools and universities, still lay well in the future when Thomas was consecrated archbishop in 1070. Already these chapters formed large and diverse groups of men with manifold concerns in the affairs of the world and the church. Not surprisingly, they were not well regarded by the more ardent reformers of the day. One of the central planks in the platform of the papal reformers was the campaign for celibacy. In cathedral closes, as in parish churches, as far as the evidence allows us to generalise, it was normal in the mid eleventh century for the clergy to be married. In these circles the programme of the papal reformers spelt social revolution, the downgrading of many ladies of the close from wives to concubines; and in the end, their disappearance. From the parishes (in all probability) they never disappeared during the middle ages. The reformers saw the secular chapters of canons as haunts of vice; for the canons set what they regarded as a bad example to the clergy at large, and passed on their prebends to their sons or near relations. Celibacy had been enjoined on all clergy in the orders of sub-deacon and above from the fifth century – in many respects the law was even older than that – and canons, whether in orders or not, were included in this ban in various pronouncements of the late eleventh century.

The law of the church was perfectly clear. Equally so was custom, and custom hallowed these alliances. We have no reason to suppose that Samson's wife and the lady Popelina, mother of Thurstan, were anything but respected and respectable. The reformers were already attacking them, but it was a long time before the law of celibacy deeply affected the life of the close. The best-documented cathedral of the late eleventh and early twelfth centuries, in this respect, is that of London; and we know that at least a third of the canons of St Paul's of that era were married, and a proportion of these passed on their benefices to their sons.[41] The hereditary canons began to disappear in the second quarter of the twelfth century, and were evidently by then regarded by most responsible churchmen as an abuse. But in the eleventh century opinion must have been very divided, and the family men included both native English and Norman canons. Of York before about 1090 we know little, though doubtless Thomas had some of his Norman associates, and possibly a wife, in his entourage. At the neighbouring cathedral of Durham an elderly, learned, married clerk called Eilaf held the office of treasurer until the Norman Bishop William of Saint-Calais replaced the existing community by monks in 1083. Eilaf and his son lived on for another thirty years as priests of the ancient church of Hexham, until canons regular came to oust him in 1113, sent by Archbishop Thomas II.[42] The younger Eilaf was allowed an honourable pension, but could hardly be expected to welcome this harsh intervention. The next year his small son came to tell him that the archbishop was dead – 'True, my son, he is dead who leads an evil life', said he, not believing at first that the boy could know.[43] The son was to grow up to be abbot of the great Cistercian house of Rievaulx, and St Aelred is a very remarkable link between the world of the hereditary priests and the stern, celibate asceticism of the Order of Cîteaux, which was to be the major spiritual force in Yorkshire in the second quarter of the twelfth century.

It was natural for the papal reformers of the eleventh century, as for the Cistercians in the twelfth, to look askance at secular chapters and secular canons. More positively, the campaign for celibacy was part of a movement to turn all clergy into quasi-monks, to separate them from the entanglements of the world and the flesh, to make communities of canons into quasi-monastic convents. The key moment in the formation of these endeavours was the council in the Lateran basilica in Rome in 1059 at which Pope Nicholas II presided over crucial debates and decisions in the formation of

[41] D. E. Greenway in *Fasti*, i; Brooke, 'The Composition of the Chapter of St Paul's', pp. 124ff; Brooke, *Medieval Church and Society*, pp. 92–94; cf. Brooke, *The Medieval Idea of Marriage* (Oxford, 1989), ch. 3.

[42] J. Raine, *Priory of Hexham* (Surtees Society, 1864), pp. 1ff; F. M. Powicke in Walter Daniel, *Life of Ailred of Rievaulx*, NMT (Edinburgh, 1950), pp. xxxivf.

[43] Ibid., p. 72.

the campaign.[44] One such debate was the discussion of the life of canons, the *vita canonica*, which led to a refreshment of the movement and, in the long run, to the discovery, or invention, of the rule of St Augustine and the growth of the Augustinian canons. Immediately, it inspired fresh efforts to enforce the *Institutio canonicorum* of 816–17 and to strengthen the institutes which had sprung from it.

In spite of this council and the movement it fostered, the secular cathedral chapter enjoyed a modest renaissance in the two generations which followed, and this is an ironical aspect of the history of the church in the wake of the papal reform. In no part of western Europe did the secular cathedral chapter flourish more than in England and Normandy in the late eleventh century. Norman chapters were refounded and greatly enlarged and enriched at Bayeux and Coutances, whose bishops were among the Conqueror's leading military advisers and assistants, and represented old corruption in an episcopate well provided with men of more admirable character.[45] In England the situation was complicated by the presence of monastic chapters already at Worcester, Winchester and Canterbury. These looked strange to Norman eyes, and Lanfranc himself evidently had doubts, or was thought to have doubts, about their suitability. Unlike some of his colleagues, and his more imaginative and sympathetic successor, St Anselm, he cared little for English traditions and cults. But he rapidly discovered the advantage of a community which was both regular and able to absorb a group of his own Norman monastic colleagues. In later years he gave encouragement to the formation of monastic chapters at Rochester (1080) by his disciple Bishop Gundulf, and to the establishment of the see of Wells in Bath abbey (1088–90).[46] It is conceivable that in the 1080s the bishops of Dorchester-Lincoln were contemplating a monastic chapter,[47] and such were formed at Durham in 1083 and at Norwich soon after.

[44] Dickinson, *Origins of the Austin Canons*, pp. 29ff; G. Miccoli, 'Pier Damiani e la vita comune del clero', in *Mendola*, 1 (1959), pp. 186ff.

[45] See below, ch. 6, esp. pp. 107–9 and nn. 1, 3; for the Norman chapters see D. Greenway, 'The Influence of the Norman Cathedrals on the Secular Cathedrals in England in the Anglo-Norman Period, 1066–1204', in *Chapîtres et cathédrales de Normandie, congrès des Sociétés Historiques et Archéologiques de Normandie*, ii, *Annales de Normandie*, 1997, pp. 273–82, and studies by David Spear and others in the same volume.

[46] R. A. L. Smith, 'John of Tours, Bishop of Bath, 1088–1122', in Smith, *Collected Papers* (London, 1947), pp. 74–102; J. Armitage Robinson, *Somerset Historical Essays* (London, 1921), pp. 54ff, for the later history of Wells and its relation to Bath; and on this see now F. M. R. Ramsey in *English Episcopal Acta*, 10 (London, 1995), esp. pp. xxii–xxvi.

[47] This suggestion is dismissed by Dr Dorothy Owen in *A History of Lincoln Minster*, ed. D. Owen (Cambridge, 1994), p. 13. But the very puzzling story of the establishment of a monastic community at Stow in 1091 – and the evidence that the full formation of the chapter

What happened elsewhere has never been made entirely clear, although it is well known that secular chapters on the Norman pattern were formed in about 1090 at Salisbury, Lincoln, London and York. 'When he received the archbishopric', says Hugh the Chanter of Thomas I, 'he found everything laid waste as a result of enemy action. Of the seven canons (there had been no more), he found three in the burnt city and ruined church', which he inherited after the rebellion of 1070 and its savage suppression by the Conqueror.

> The rest were either dead, or driven away by fear and devastation. He reroofed and to the best of his ability rebuilt the church, to which he restored the canons whom he had found there; he recalled the fugitives to the service of God and the church, and added to their number; he rebuilt the refectory and dormitory. He appointed a provost to preside over the others and to manage their affairs; he gave manors, lands, and churches himself, and restored those which others had taken away. He bestowed much of his own property on the canons; he apportioned wise and diligent men to be archdeacons in the diocese ... The canons had long lived in common, but the archbishop, after taking advice, determined to divide some of the lands of St Peter's which were still waste into separate prebends, to leave room for a growing number of canons; in this way each of them might be eager to build on and cultivate his own share for his own sake. This was done. Then he appointed a dean, treasurer, and precentor, endowing each of them as befitted the church's dignity, his own, and theirs. He had already established a master of the schools. He founded and built the present church.

Hugh was writing in the late 1120s and Thomas's church has long since departed, though substantial remains have in recent years been brought to light and can be inspected in the new undercroft of the Minster. He 'adorned and furnished it to the best of his power with clerks, books and ornaments: above all else he desired to have good and reputable clerks'.[48]

at Lincoln took place not long before Remigius's death in 1092 – might suggest that Remigius, himself a monk, had toyed with a plan for a monastic chapter.

[48] Hugh the Chanter, *History*, pp. 18–21. On Thomas's church see D. Phillips, *Excavations at York Minster*, ii, Royal Commission on Historical Monuments (London, 1985); and on his work at York, A. Hamilton Thompson in *VCH Yorkshire*, iii, pp. 375–82. There is a reference to the use of chrism pennies for his restoration of the minster in *Historians of the Church of York*, iii, p. 68, in which Thurstan remits the payment, since by his time payment for chrism had come to be regarded as a kind of simony and was forbidden. The formation of the close is indicated by William II's remarkable writ, *Early Yorkshire Charters*, i, ed. W. Farrer (Edinburgh, 1914), no. 127. If space permitted comment could be made on Archbishop Gerard's letter to St Anselm on the canons and Pope Honorius II's letter about an absentee dean (1125–30), which reveal characteristic problems of such a chapter appearing at an early stage, *Historians of the Church of York*, iii, pp. 23–26, 47–48.

Here is the clearest statement for any English chapter of the curious pause which often separates the appointment of the first Norman bishop from the establishment of an openly secular chapter. Yet such a change of mind seems to have been common. In the last decades of the eleventh century the secular chapter with separate prebends ruled by dean, precentor, treasurer, master of the schools, with archdeacons as dignitaries or at least as canons, makes its début at York and Lincoln; in both cases the bishop was far from being a newcomer. In London the formation of prebends and appointment of dean and archdeacons came about the same time; there and elsewhere the other dignitaries followed later – and in most of the other chapters progress towards the model of Lincoln and York took at least two generations.[49] At York, as at Lincoln and London, and probably at Salisbury, the division of the diocese into territorial archdeaconries seems to have coincided with the formation of the new chapter.

Of St Osmund's work at Salisbury we have an early record in two annals preserved, strangely enough, at Holyrood in Edinburgh, and also in the foundation charter of 1091, but it has been suggested that many of the canons of Salisbury preserved the common life until well into the twelfth century.[50] At Lincoln, we are told – and other evidence confirms it – that Remigius instituted twenty-one canons 'according to the rite of Rouen cathedral'.[51] The rites and customs of Rouen had been described in a book written by John of Avranches, archbishop of Rouen from 1067 to 1079.[52] In a late

---

[49] The full story is emerging with the publication of *Fasti*; see also J. Armitage Robinson, *Somerset Historical Essays*; A. Watkin, *Dean Cosyn and Wells Cathedral Miscellanea*, Somerset Record Society (1941), pp. xxv f, 87–89 (on Wells); *English Episcopal Acta*, 10, *Bath and Wells, 1060–1205* (London, 1995), esp. pp. xxiv–xxxvi; H. Mayr-Harting, *Acta of the Bishops of Chichester, 1091–1207*, Canterbury and York Society (1964), pp. 41–48; K. Edwards in *VCH Wiltshire*, iii, pp. 156ff. For what follows, see *GF*, p. 216 and n., corrected by D. E. Greenway in *Fasti* i, iii, iv – and esp. D. E. Greenway, 'The False *Institutio* of St Osmund', in *Tradition and Change: Essays in Honour of Marjorie Chibnall*, ed. D. Greenway et al. (Cambridge, 1986), pp. 77–101. On archdeacons, see below, ch. 7.

[50] See below, p. 127; *Fasti*, iv (1991), pp. xxii–xxiv.

[51] Giraldus Cambrensis, *Opera*, ed. J. S. Brewer, J. F. Dimock and G. F. Warner, RS, 8 vols (London, 1861–91), vii, p. 19; cf. M. J. Franklin in *English Episcopal Acta*, 17, p. 90.

[52] *De officiis ecclesiasticis*, ed. R. Delamare (Paris, 1923), who prints the edition which circulated, but also notes the MS containing an extract which survives in an English twelfth-century MS in Bodleian Library, MS Bodley 843. It includes a list of orders and dignities which had a background in pseudo-Isidore, but is also reminiscent of the dignitaries of Chartres (cf. E. de Lepinois and L. Merlet, in *Cartulaire de Notre Dame de Chartres* (Paris, 1862–65), esp. ii, p. 96 – cf. i, p. 127). It is, however, doubtful that it had any direct link with John (as I used to suppose): see Greenway, 'The False *Institutio*', pp. 100–1. On John's work and its circulation in England, see E. Bishop, 'Holy Week Rites of Sarum, Hereford and Rouen Compared', *Liturgica historica* (Oxford, 1918), pp. 276–300, esp. pp. 277–78, 299–300.

twelfth-century manuscript an extract from John's work lies near a remarkable analysis of the possible dignitaries of a cathedral, which in its turn was
based on observation among other cathedrals and on a text attributed to
St Isidore; and there is evidence that this influenced Salisbury customs, but
not before the mid twelfth century.[53] The cathedral which is most likely to
have influenced the list of dignitaries, Rouen apart, is Chartres, the most
mature among the great chapters of northern France in this age.

No doubt too the customs of Bayeux, from which Thomas and many
other influential canons of this age sprang, affected its English rivals: in
assessing the details we are hampered by the total absence of evidence as
to the liturgical practices of Salisbury, or York, or Bayeux, which can with
any confidence be traced back to the eleventh century. But it is possible
that the bishop of Lincoln worked out with the archbishop of York, and
in some measure with the bishops of Salisbury and London, the new pattern
they all established in the years leading to 1092.

Thus the formation of some of the secular chapters may have coincided
with the years when the see of Canterbury was vacant and the provincial
chapter of Canterbury, of which the bishop of London is still dean and the
bishop of Winchester subdean, was being formed. At first sight it is strange
that these men should wait till the end of their days was approaching – all
save Maurice of London were elderly, and Thomas and Remigius had both
been bishops for twenty years – before embarking on such ambitious
projects. We may venture the hypothesis that it was no chance that it
happened in the only period of the late eleventh and early twelfth centuries
when Canterbury was not ruled by an eminent monk; to put it another
way, when Lanfranc had been removed from the scene they felt free to
found openly secular chapters. This remains a hypothesis merely.[54] In the
grass at Old Sarum, on the hill at Lincoln and in the undercroft at York
lies the physical evidence of their intentions: the full story of their plans,
and changes of mind, may never be known.[55]

The temporal wealth of archbishop and chapter in the later middle ages

[53] As is established by Diana Greenway, 'The False *Institutio*', pp. 87, 88, 100–1. For the
influence of Bayeux, see Greenway, 'The Influence of the Norman Cathedrals on the Secular
Cathedrals in England in the Anglo-Norman Period, 1066–1204', esp. pp. 276–77 (n. 45).

[54] In the original version of this chapter, as in much of my earlier work, I spoke more
positively: see below, p. 000.

[55] For the architectural and archaeological evidence at York, see D. Phillips, *Excavations at
York Minster*, ii (n. 48); for Lincoln, P. Kidson in *A History of Lincoln Minster*, ch. 2; for Old
Sarum, R. Gem, 'The First Romanesque Cathedral of Old Salisbury', in *Medieval Architecture
and its Intellectual Context: Studies in Honour of Peter Kidson*, ed. E. Fernie and P. Crossley
(London, 1990), pp. 9–18.

was substantial. The landed estates formed a single unit under the archbishop's control and probably remained so down to the eleventh century. William of Malmesbury (c. 1125) tells us that Thomas I's successors grumbled that he had impoverished them by being too generous to the chapter;[56] and it seems that a division took place in his time, first between his own and the chapter's lands and, secondly, between the common fund of the chapter and the individual prebends of the canons. It may well be true that the chapter was relatively well endowed; and it was certainly true in later times that some of the offices and prebends of York were exceptionally rich. No chapter could show inequalities of wealth so great among its canons; and the treasurership and the prebend of Masham, in particular, became famous throughout England and indeed to the gates of Rome and of Avignon, as two of the most desirable plums in Christendom.[57]

The prebend of Masham was established by Roger de Mowbray in the late twelfth century for his kinsman Roger, son of Sampson d'Aubigny.[58] It is rare for the story of a prebend to be so precisely known, and most prebends were endowed by the action of the archbishop, the generosity of the king, or a substantial gift (as in the case of Masham) from a local baron or landowner of substance. Some were well endowed, no doubt, for favoured clerks and relations; some to provide a tempting bait to bring promising young clergy to York. In many cases deserted or partly deserted lands were assigned to prebends and dignities: sometimes they grew and flourished; sometimes they languished. None was so precarious as the prebend of St Paul's which fell into the sea – *Consumpta per mare* – but they were widely scattered from Masham in the north west, thirty-three miles from York, to the Newbalds and South Cave to the south east; or Wetwang, Driffield, Langtoft and Grindale to the east.[59] A nucleus lay among St Peter's manors close to York (Osbaldwick, Dunnington, Strensall and Warthill), but the

---

[56] William of Malmesbury, *Gesta pontificum*, ed. N. E. S. A. Hamilton, RS (London, 1870), p. 257. Domesday shows 'the land of St Peter' comprising about 270 carucates in Yorkshire, mostly in the vale of York and Ryedale; see summary and discussion by A. Hamilton Thompson in *VCH Yorkshire*, iii, p. 11. There have been interesting studies of the holdings of archbishop and chapter in the city by A. G. Dickens, 'The "Shire" and Prison of the Archbishop in the Eleventh Century', *Yorkshire Archaeological Journal*, 38 (1952–55), pp. 131–47, and John Harvey, 'Bishophill and the Church of York', *Yorkshire Archaeological Journal*, 41 (1963–66), pp. 377–93.

[57] For all that follows, C. T. Clay, *York Minster Fasti*, Yorkshire Archaeological Society Record Series, 123–24 (1958–59), esp. i, pp. 122–30 on the treasurers; ii, pp. 51–55 on the prebend of Masham; and *Fasti*, vi, forthcoming, esp. lists 5, 34.

[58] *Charters of the Honour of Mowbray, 1107–91*, ed. D. E. Greenway (London, 1972), nos 191, 197, 325–36, also pp. xliii, lxvi; Clay, *York Minster Fasti*, i, nos 34–37; ii, p. 52; *Fasti*, vi, list 34.

[59] See Clay, *York Minster Fasti*, ii, passim, esp. opening map.

scatter of estates in an area heavily devastated after the Norman Conquest makes it natural that their growth should be very variable, and helps to explain why the distinction between prebends rich and poor became so marked.

A few of these chapter estates lay outside Yorkshire. Of these the most interesting are Axminster in Devon, whose wealthy church had been granted by Edward the Confessor to Ealdred, a favourite clerk of Archbishop Ealdred, in the 1060s, and in which the minster retained a substantial interest; and Oddington in Gloucestershire, a surviving fragment of Archbishop Ealdred's holdings in that county.[60] He had been a man of great wealth: in addition to his two bishoprics he had a grip on the abbey of Gloucester, and Archbishop Thomas struggled hard to retain Ealdred's Gloucestershire manors in a *cause célèbre* not finally settled until 1157.[61] Some of the archbishop's endowments went much further back: for they had once (in the tenth century) been given the whole of Amounderness – a substantial part of Lancashire – and had received other rich gifts over the centuries from King Edward to the Norman Conquest.[62] Much must have depended on the personal wealth of bishops like Ealdred.

Yet when Thomas arrived in 1070 he entered an impoverished see. The Conqueror had faced rebellion in the north in 1069 and always feared York and Yorkshire as a centre of Viking sympathisers: he lived under the shadow of the threat of invasion from Denmark or Norway. His answer to this threat was characteristic: a fearful devastation from which the city and the vale took two or three generations to recover fully.[63] The early history of the prebends is not sufficiently clear for us to date their origin with precision. It seems likely that a proportion of both rich and poor prebends goes back to Thomas's time.[64] Early in the twelfth century, in the brief reign of Archbishop Gerard (1100–8), a substantial endowment came from Henry I and Queen Matilda, from which sprang the prebends of Driffield and

---

[60] Ibid., ii, pp. 35–38, 153–155; *Historia et cartularium monasterii S. Petri Gloucestriae*, ed. W. H. Hart, RS, 3 vols, (London, 1863–7), ii, pp. 105ff.

[61] Ibid.; *GF*, pp. 124ff; *GFL*, nos 128–30.

[62] For Amounderness, see above, n. 6. See also the charters in *Early Yorkshire Charters*, i, and Clay, *York Minster Fasti*.

[63] See esp. T. A. M. Bishop, 'The Norman Settlement of Yorkshire', in *Studies in Medieval History Presented to F. M. Powicke* (Oxford, 1948), pp. 1–12, who points out, however, that the waste lands recorded in 1086 cannot be attributed wholly to the Conqueror's armies.

[64] See Clay, *York Minster Fasti*, ii, p. v, who gathers evidence which makes it probable that the prebends of Holme, Grindale, Warthill, Givendale and Sherburn (later three prebends) go back to Thomas's time.

Laughton; later in his reign Henry added Weighton.[65] The middle and later years of Henry I were to see the rapid spread of the Augustinian canons in the diocese, under his patronage; the later years saw the beginnings of the great Cistercian houses. It looks as if, early in his reign, he considered the minster an important centre of loyalty and influence. The Norman kings rarely visited York; they greatly relied on the archbishop and the bishop of Durham, and on their chapters, for the peace and prosperity of the north east.

In the eleventh and twelfth centuries York was somewhat remote from the main centres of political and intellectual activity in the Anglo-Norman world – or so it must have appeared to the Norman career ecclesiastics who filled the see after the Conquest. It was doubtless an important part of Thomas's aim in forming the dignities and prebends to attract men of a calibre to form the nucleus of a flourishing chapter. The evidence is not sufficient to give more than an impressionistic account of the chapter and its members in the twelfth century. But we know enough to see something of the success and failure, of the aims, ambitions and difficulties of the archbishops, and of the leading members of the chapter. The twelfth-century deans included four men who became bishops;[66] but the two at the end of the century – Hubert Walter and Simon of Apulia – were too involved in royal administration to have much time to spare for York. Perhaps the most characteristic figure in the list is Robert de Gant, whose name seems to place him in a well-known baronial family, who was chancellor to King Stephen from 1140–41 until 1154, and who yet managed to be a fairly frequent visitor to York.[67] This combination of service to the chapter and to kings or bishops, or even to the pope, is characteristic of the twelfth century; thereafter the distinction became increasingly clear-cut between a small community genuinely resident and a large number of canons and dignitaries living elsewhere, drawing the revenues of their offices in York but rarely sitting in their stalls.

[65] Ibid., and pp. 20, 49, 81; *Early Yorkshire Charters*, i, pp. 333ff. Gerard's pontificate also witnessed the important and interesting list of chapter privileges printed in *Visitations and Memorials of Southwell Minster*, ed. A. F. Leach, Camden Society (1891), pp. 190–96.

[66] William of Sainte-Barbe (Durham, 1143–52); Hubert Walter (Salisbury, 1189–93; archbishop of Canterbury, 1193–1205); Henry Marshal (Exeter, 1194–1206); Simon of Apulia (Exeter, 1214–23). See Clay, *York Minster Fasti*, i, pp. 1–2; *Fasti*, vi (forthcoming), list 2.

[67] C. T. Clay, 'Notes on the Chronology of the Early Deans of York', *Yorkshire Archaeological Journal*, 34 (1939), pp. 361–78, at pp. 366–70; cf. Clay, 'Notes on the Early Archdeacons in the Church of York', *Yorkshire Archaeological Journal*, 36 (1944–47), pp. 269–87, 409–34, at p. 281 n. 50. There is little precise evidence of non-residence in this period: cf. the absentee dean of the 1120s, *Historians of the Church of York*, iii, pp. 47–48. It is likely that there were far more absentees than we can have evidence of.

The treasurership attracted such men from an early date. After the promotion of St William from treasurer to archbishop, it went first to his cousin Hugh du Puiset, nephew of King Stephen and of Henry of Blois, bishop of Winchester, who was more active (so it seems) in his role as archdeacon of Winchester.[68] When the pope consecrated Hugh to the see of Durham in 1153, he gave the treasurership to a favourite clerk of the archbishop of Canterbury, John of Canterbury; and when John – an able and amiable man, and a peacemaker in the troubles between Thomas Becket and Henry II – went on to be bishop of Poitiers (1162) and later archbishop of Lyon (1182), a royal clerk, Ralph de Warneville, succeeded who was also treasurer of Rouen, and seems to have lived in Normandy.[69] He was followed, probably in 1182, by another eminent royal clerk, no less than Geoffrey Plantagenet, the king's illegitimate son, who also seems rarely to have visited York until he became archbishop (1189–1212).[70] Not all the treasurers were absentees – two of those of the early thirteenth century frequently appear as witnesses among their fellow canons; but the treasurership remained a prize, to attract the greatest connoisseur among English pluralists, Bogo de Clare, son of the earl of Gloucester, in 1285; and Bogo's successor was a Colonna, a member of one of the most powerful families in the papal curia.[71]

The chapter had a life nonetheless and a feeling of community; and like most such amorphous communities it fell prey from time to time to division and faction. The inner story is mostly hidden from us, but the two great *causes célèbres* of the early and mid twelfth century, Thurstan's fight against the primacy of Canterbury and the case of St William, illustrate both the cohesion and the faction.

Thurstan was a newcomer when he first visited York as archbishop.[72]

---

[68] G. V. Scammell, *Hugh du Puiset, Bishop of Durham* (Cambridge, 1956), esp. pp. 7–8; C. T. Clay, 'The Early Treasurers of York', *Yorkshire Archaeological Journal*, 35 (1943), pp. 7–34, at pp. 10–11.

[69] *GFL*, pp. 137–38; Scammell, *Hugh du Puiset*, pp. 12 ff.; Clay, 'Early Treasurers', pp. 11–24; P. Pouzet, *L'Anglais Jean dit Bellesmains* (Lyon, 1927).

[70] On Geoffrey, see below, pp. 66–68 and references in nn. 100–1, esp. to M. Lovatt, 'The Career and Administration of Archbishop Geoffrey of York (?1151–1212)' (unpublished Ph.D. Thesis, University of Cambridge, 1974–75); Clay, 'The Early Treasurers', pp. 24–25. The name 'Plantagenet' was applied to Geoffrey's grandfather, Geoffrey of Anjou, by Ralph de Diceto, *Opera historica*, ed. W. Stubbs, RS, 2 vols (London, 1876), i, p. 291; but otherwise it seems not to have been current until the fifteenth century.

[71] Clay, *York Minster Fasti*, i, pp. 22–30, esp. pp. 26–28; Clay, 'The Early Treasurers', *Fasti*, vi, list 5.

[72] On Thurstan, see Hugh the Chanter, *History*; D. Nicholl, *Thurstan, Archbishop of York* (York, 1964); and references in n. 32 above.

The firm determination he was able to sustain from first to last is striking testimony to a solid body of feeling in the chapter itself to help and support him; to inspire him indeed to endless struggles in what has appeared to most modern commentators a dreary suit. It did not so appear to contemporaries, and of this a notable witness is Hugh the Chanter, a writer of great skill and verve and self-confidence, who dedicated almost the whole of his lives of the archbishops to a detailed narrative of Thurstan's struggles.[73]

Thurstan won because, in the end, the pope was bound to recognise that his case had the sounder historical foundation; and it is a notable fact that the York chapter succeeded without forgery – it is the only major religious community in England of whose early muniments we have any substantial remnant, to whom no suspicion of forgery attaches.[74] Essentially, this was because the canons and the archbishop of York fought a short, sharp battle against the primacy of Canterbury, winning not a total victory but sufficient to make elaborate invention unnecessary.

The see of Canterbury was older and had been effectively metropolitan much longer than York; and the centres of power and wealth in the kingdom, as well as the centres of monastic observance, made York a northern outpost. Between 900 and 1066 there were no mint towns north of the Trent save York and Chester, and no monasteries north of the Wash save Burton-on-Trent. When Lanfranc, a man of wide and cosmopolitan outlook and somewhat imperial ambitions, came to Canterbury in the 1070s, it was natural for him both to assume that Britain, like Gaul, had a traditional primacy dispute, and to look to the king as an ally in forming a united English – or rather British – church, under the primacy of Canterbury. This suited William, who had ambitions, as yet undefined, over Wales and Scotland, and a deep suspicion of the folk of Yorkshire. Thus Lanfranc was able to extract from Thomas I profession of obedience, though not without a struggle.[75] Meanwhile Thomas prepared for a counter-attack: he asserted

[73] Hugh the Chanter, *History*; and above, n. 35. On his reliability, see R. W. Southern, *St Anselm and his Biographer* (Cambridge, 1963), pp. 143, 303–9; below, n. 75 – and esp. Hugh the Chanter, *History*, pp. xiii–xix.

[74] See *GF*, ch. 8; Brooke, *Medieval Church and Society* (London, 1971), ch. 5. The statement in the text is bold, and doubt has been attached e.g. to Athelstan's grant (but see n. 6); and it may have to be modified when the early professions in York Minster Library, MS M2(2)a, fol. 7r-v, and *British Library Harleian MS 533*, ed. R. Horrox and P. W. Hammond, iii (London, 1982), pp. 84–86, 95–97, have been critically examined. I owe these references to the kindness of Miss Katharine Longley and Dr Martin Brett.

[75] See *Canterbury Professions*, ed. M. Richter (Canterbury and York Society, 1973), pp. lvii ff and n. 34; Professor Richter's account is mainly based on Lanfranc's own narrative and other Canterbury sources, since for the period down to the election of Thurstan Hugh the Chanter's account is confused and at times 'distorted', Richter, *Professions*, p. lviii n. He

YORK MINSTER: NINTH TO EARLY THIRTEENTH CENTURIES 59

the claims of his province to jurisdiction not only over the bishopric of Durham but over Cumbria and Scotland, Lindsey (that is, most of Lincoln-shire) and Worcester; and to round the matter off, for good measure, the diocese of Chester, Coventry and Lichfield. These disputes raged incessantly in the late eleventh and twelfth centuries, and to set beside Canterbury's notable collection of professions York possesses copies of a few – and perhaps some of them are of doubtful authenticity – from bishops of Scotland and the Isles.[76] But in the end, though Canterbury retained after a mighty struggle its lordship over Wales, York lost Scotland and the Isles, and was only compensated with Cumbria, where Henry I and Thurstan set up the new bishopric of Carlisle in 1133, though it was never before 1200 the stable seat of a bishop.[77] Thus York won its measure of independence from Canterbury, but lost its claim to a wider empire.

The kings judged these issues by their political implications; the popes, while never ignoring political expediency, by law and precedent. It is a curious irony that if the archbishops of York had been prepared to submit to Canterbury, they might have had wholehearted support from the English king and the English church for their attempts on the Scottish bishops, and might even have won a little more territory in England. They staked much for their own freedom, their own primacy; and one cannot withhold a feeling of admiration and awe for the power of their cause. The canons of York won fervent support even from a newcomer like Thurstan – and, later, from a Canterbury man like Roger of Pont l'Évêque. It is hard for us to recapture the emotions which inspired some of the best minds in Canterbury to cheat and forge,[78] inspired Thurstan and his colleagues at York to face endless litigation, journeys, possible loss of office, revenue and career – and all those who are more than names to us were career ecclesiastics by no means indifferent to the world and the flesh. King Henry I shared

convincingly argues that Hugh's account of the consecration of St Anselm is misleading, p. lxix n. Hugh's credit greatly improves when he becomes an eyewitness and the York case was in the ascendant. See now Hugh the Chanter, *History*, pp. xxxiii–xxxix.

[76] See above, n. 74.

[77] See D. E. Greenway in *Fasti*, ii, p. 19 and references; Nicholl, *Thurstan*, pp. 140–50; H. S. Offler, 'A Note on the Early History of the Priory of Carlisle', *Transactions of the Cumberland and Westmorland Antiquarian and Archaeological Society*, new series 65 (1965), pp. 176–81; J. C. Dickinson, 'Walter the Priest and St Mary's Carlisle', ibid., 69 (1969), pp. 102–14; M. Brett, *The English Church under Henry I* (Oxford, 1975), pp. 26–28, and in Hugh the Chanter, *History*, pp. xxx–xlv (on primacy), xlv–liv (on York and Scotland); H. Summerson, 'Old and New Bishoprics: Durham and Carlisle', in *Anglo-Norman Durham*, ed. D. Rollason, M. Harvey and M. Prestwich (Woodbridge, 1994), pp. 369–80.

[78] See Southern, *St Anselm and his Biographer*, pp. 308–9, and 'The Canterbury Forgeries', *EHR*, 73, (1958), pp. 193–226; cf. above, n. 74.

his father's suspicions of York and the north east; Thurstan must have seemed at his appointment the very type of the courtier-bishop, and his heroic resistance to archbishop and king an incomprehensible nuisance. In the end he won. No archbishop of York has made profession of obedience to Canterbury since.

The idea of primacy in the eleventh century, though it took more than one form, essentially involved jurisdiction, not just an honorific title, set up between the rank and file of the metropolitans and the pope. It could be used, as the archbishop of Lyon sometimes used it, by a close adherent of the papacy set to lord it over the archbishops of Gaul; it could be used, as Lanfranc tried to use it, to establish a local empire in which the primate's authority counted for more than the pope's. In the long run this was the more likely course, and primacy therefore aroused suspicion from the papacy; this, and the very doubtful historical grounds on which the party of Canterbury based its case, secured papal support for Thurstan and the chapter of York. Hugh the Chanter gives a fascinating and probably in the main sound account of the struggles of Thurstan and the canons of York who helped him, culminating in the famous scene in the papal curia in 1123 when the Canterbury monks produced their privileges 'headed with the names of popes of Rome', but with 'no trace of the style of the Roman chancery ...' And when neither seals nor signatures could be found on any of them 'they made up their minds to come back and say that the bulls had either perished or were lost. When they said this, some smiled, others turned up their noses, and others laughed aloud, making fun of them and saying that it was a miracle that lead should perish or be lost and parchment survive'.[79] Perhaps Hugh claimed more knowledge of the matter than he really possessed, for although he was right to think the bulls should have been leaden, papyrus not parchment was used in the chancery down to the eleventh century. But he was right that the privileges were mostly forged, and Thurstan deserved his moment of triumph after his long toil.

In his later years Thurstan showed a wide interest in the spiritual welfare of his see, and is especially well known for fostering the new religious orders, Augustinian and Cistercian, and for his share in founding the great abbey of Fountains.[80] He died, much respected, at the Cluniac priory of Pontefract. He had held together in a single grasp the world of Ranulf Flambard and the court of William Rufus, and the new world of St Bernard

[79] Hugh the Chanter, *History*, pp. 192–95.

[80] Nicholl, *Thurstan*, chs 5–7; on Fountains also D. Bethell, 'The Foundation of Fountains Abbey and the State of St Mary's York in 1132', *Journal of Ecclesiastical History*, 17 (1986), pp. 11–27; L. G. D. Baker, 'The Foundation of Fountains Abbey', *Northern History*, 4 (1969), pp. 29–43.

and his Yorkshire disciples William, first abbot of Rievaulx, and Henry Murdac, monk of Clairvaux, abbot of Fountains and ultimately archbishop (1147–53). In the chapter at York, zeal for his great cause and the archbishop's personality seem likewise to have held a peaceful balance. But peace was superficial and within the chapter, and between the chapter and the new monastic movements, Thurstan's retirement was the signal for fifteen years of strife.

The central character in this story was the enigmatic William FitzHerbert, later to enjoy a strange celebrity as St William of York.[81] William was son of Herbert, chamberlain to Henry I, and came of a family with estates in Yorkshire; his mother was half-sister to King Stephen. He must have seemed marked out for promotion in the early years of Stephen's reign, since Stephen's brother Henry of Blois, as bishop of Winchester and papal legate, shared with the king the distribution of patronage, and a rash of nephews and protégés spread over the English church. The abbot of Fécamp was one of these, and he was marked out for York;[82] but although the chapter argued and the king and legate cajoled for many months, the attempt failed, and the chapter's attention was diverted to a nephew nearer home. We know little of the background to the quarrel which now broke out: the two leading figures in the chapter after the archbishop, Hugh the dean and Hugh the precentor – the Chanter – had recently departed, the dean to become a monk at Fountains, the precentor (probably) to another world.[83] The new dean, William of Sainte-Barbe, shortly to become bishop of Durham, seems to have tried to be a peacemaker; but he found himself in the midst of a battle of archdeacons. William FitzHerbert himself, treasurer since before 1114 (it seems), was also (as invariably in the twelfth century) archdeacon of the East Riding; his chief opponents were Walter of London, archdeacon of the West Riding, and Osbert of Bayeux, Archbishop Thurstan's nephew, archdeacon of Richmond.[84] In January 1141

[81] See D. Knowles, 'The Case of St William of York', *The Historian and Character and Other Essays* (Cambridge, 1963), pp. 76–97, with bibliography on pp. 94–96; Clay, 'The Early Treasurers', pp. 8–10; J. Burton in *English Episcopal Acta*, 5 (London, 1988), esp. pp. xxx–xxxi; life in *Historians of the Church of York*, ii, pp. 270–91, and in the great north window in the north choir transept of the minster (1422–23).

[82] Knowles, 'The Case of St William', p. 80; cf. *GFL*, pp. 109–10, 116.

[83] Clay, 'Notes on the Early Deans', pp. 363–64; above, n. 35; *Fasti*, vi, lists 2, 3. For the possibility that Hugh the Chanter also retired to Pontefract in 1139 and died later, see Hugh the Chanter, *History*, p. 55 n. 3.

[84] Clay, 'Notes on the Early Archdeacons', pp. 277–79, 283, 286; Clay, *York Minster Fasti*, i, pp. 33, 46; Knowles, 'The Case of St William', p. 97; on Osbert see also A. Morey, 'Canonist Evidence in the Case of St William of York', *Cambridge Historical Journal*, 10 (1952), pp. 352–53; *GFL*, pp. 164–65; John of Salisbury, *Letters*, i, pp. 261–62; *Fasti*, vi, Lists 9, 13.

a majority in the chapter elected William the Treasurer as archbishop; but some of the canons, powerfully supported by leaders of the religious orders in the diocese, refused to accept the election. They carried their protest to the gates of Rome – and also, which was of more consequence, to the gates of Clairvaux, where the prophetic figure of St Bernard was roused for the destruction of the archbishop-elect.

So great was the dust raised by the controversy that it is difficult to discern the flame within, or to tell what really was the tinder to the conflict. They objected to William's mode of life and to the manner of his election; they treated him (not without justice) as the pawn of royal intervention, an intervention no less obnoxious for the fact that his uncle Henry, papal legate and bishop of Winchester – the harlot of Winchester as Bernard politely called him – was evidently playing a more forceful part in the affair than King Stephen. 'O happy Winchester, blessed with the glory of a mighty name – to be called a second Rome! O mighty Winchester, who cancels the orders of mighty fathers ...' wrote Bernard with crushing irony after the long *démarches* of 1141–43 and the archbishop's eventual consecration by his uncle under circumstances of doubtful legality.[85] But his letter was not all irony, for he intended his hearers, pope and cardinals, to shudder and take action. 'See to it, father, that disobedience becomes not a common use and an example, that the dignity of Rome be not torn asunder by savage hands, that the authority of Peter be not laid low ... that the religious life of the See of York grow not cool – or rather, be not dispersed and vanish like smoke.' Rome must take the hammer and break the idol that the seducer of Winchester had set up in Peter's Minster: 'May your Holiness prosper and flourish'.[86] The pope died, however, and his successor Eugenius III was a disciple of St Bernard, who knew the fervour and the mettle of the great Yorkshire Cistercians: of Richard of Fountains, devout and normally peaceful, William of Rievaulx, a zealot but in his own way inspired, Henry Murdac, who rather reflected the harsher side of Bernard, Aelred the future abbot of Rievaulx, the most attractive of all the early Cistercians and a man of peace.[87] The idol was removed and Henry Murdac set in his place. Predictably, the king tried to prevent him from taking up office; less predictably perhaps, the people of York showed implacable hostility. After

[85] St Bernard, *Epistola*, 520, *S. Bernardi opera*, ed. J. Leclercq et al., 8 vols (Rome, 1957–77), viii, pp. 480–82 (my own translation).

[86] Ibid.; cf. Knowles, 'The Case of St William', pp. 86–87.

[87] See Knowles, 'The Case of St William'; also Knowles, *Monastic Order*, chs 13–14; Walter Daniel's *Life of Ailred of Rievaulx*, ed. and trans. F. M. Powicke, NMT (Edinburgh, 1950); A. Squire, *Aelred of Rievaulx* (London, 1969); Aelred, *Opera omnia*, ed. A. Hoste, C. H. Talbot and G. Raciti, 2 vols (Turnhout, 1971–89).

his failure to win papal restoration in 1147–48, William visited Sicily, whose king was his distant relative, and stayed with the royal chancellor, an old friend from Yorkshire, Robert of Selby.[88] On his return he brought gifts to his uncle at Winchester, which perhaps included Byzantine objects to inspire the famous Byzantinate pages in the Winchester Psalter of this epoch; and it is possible, even likely, that he brought back from the south relics to comfort his own old age, perhaps in the charming box of Sicilian Muslim manufacture which still adorns the minster at York.[89]

For to York in the end William returned. In 1153 the pope, St Bernard and Henry Murdac all died. At Rome an arrangement was made: William was restored to York, another nephew of Stephen and Henry of Blois, Hugh du Puiset, William's successor as treasurer of York, was promoted to the see of Durham, and John of Canterbury became treasurer.[90] St William's return was a triumphal progress: the famous story of how the bridge at York broke under the throng which gathered to welcome him, and the injured were miraculously restored by his prayers, does not come from a contemporary source; but it seems clearly to represent a consistent tradition at York that William was loved and revered.[91] Even so, it is extremely unlikely that he would have been canonised but for the dramatic conclusion to his earthly story. On his return to England in 1154 he made peace with Fountains, which his supporters had sacked in 1147, and showed every wish to be on good terms with his former enemies. But immediately after celebrating solemn mass in York Minster, he was taken ill, and on 8 June, 1154 he died. Archdeacon Osbert was accused of poisoning him, and although such tales were common and as commonly disbelieved, Osbert failed to clear himself, was unfrocked and became a minor baron.[92] He represented the less admirable side of his uncle Thurstan's legacy.

Meanwhile no time was lost in providing William with a successor. With a speed which excited comment at the time – and must certainly rouse our suspicions that the wily archbishop of Canterbury, Theobald, had been engaged in intrigue – the archdeacon of Canterbury, Roger of Pont l'Évêque, was elected archbishop of York.

[88] See R. H. Pinder-Wilson and C. N. L. Brooke, 'The Reliquary of St Petroc and the Ivories of Norman Sicily', *Archaeologia*, 104 (1973), pp. 261–305, at p. 299 and n. 1, for this incident and Robert's name.

[89] Ibid., pp. 285–86, 296, 299; on the Winchester Psalter, see G. Zarnecki, *Later English Romanesque Sculpture* (London, 1953), p. 30; and, in general, F. Wormald, *The Winchester Psalter* (London, 1973); K. E. Haney, *The Winchester Psalter: An Iconographic Study* (Leicester, 1986).

[90] See above, nn. 68–69.

[91] *Historians of the Church of York*, ii, pp. 275–76.

[92] Above, n. 84; Knowles, 'The Case of St William', pp. 92–94.

Roger (1154–81) and his successor Geoffrey Plantagenet (1189–1212), Henry II's illegitimate son, each contributed something to the tradition of the Minster: Roger by inaugurating the first age of sumptuous building after Thomas I, Geoffrey by persistently quarrelling with the chapter. The true creators of the minster and the chapter as it was in 1215 were Thomas I and Thurstan, heirs of the old style of secular cathedral chapter who yet had the imagination to make something creative and constructive from it. Thurstan had tried to patronise both secular and regular clergy in the spiritual life of the diocese: Ripon, Beverley, Southwell and the distant outpost of St Oswald's Gloucester had been developed along the lines of the York chapter: Cistercian and Augustinian foundations were aided and fostered.[93] Compared with the pontificates of the two sons of Bayeux, Roger's and Geoffrey's seem but an epilogue. Roger was indeed a great builder, and founder of what became the notable chapel of St Sepulchre; and in Geoffrey's time the chapter was more involved in royal and papal politics than ever before.[94] Each pontificate was in its way a remarkable episode, if only for the light it sheds on what had already taken place in York and the vale. But it seems likely that, here as elsewhere, there came to be a growing divorce between archbishop and chapter, a growing division between resident and non-resident canons.

If Theobald hoped to see in Roger a subservient colleague, he was disappointed; and between Roger and Theobald's successor, Thomas Becket, an implacable feud developed. Roger was seriously suspected of stirring the murderers of Becket to action, and after the eclipse and restoration to which Roger had to submit in the early 1170s, the clerks of Canterbury – led apparently by the eminent humanist John of Salisbury – accused their one-time colleague of nameless crimes.[95] The truth of all these accusations is hard to discern. Roger's role in the Becket affair is unattractive; undoubtedly both he and Becket were urged on to their more extreme actions by the old rivalry of Canterbury and York, whose share in the

[93] Nicholl, *Thurstan*, chs 5–7. St Oswald's became Augustinian under Archbishop Henry Murdac.

[94] See below; and cf. Alexander III's letter to Archbishop Roger (1173, *Historians of the Church of York*, iii, p. 78). On Roger, see now esp. M. Lovatt in *English Episcopal Acta*, 20 (London, 2000). On St Sepulchre's see A. Hamilton Thompson, 'The Chapel of St Mary and the Holy Angels, Otherwise Known as St Sepulchre's Chapel at York', *Yorkshire Archaeological Journal*, 36 (1944–47), pp. 63–77; Roger's charter of ordinance and endowment is ed. M. Lovatt, *English Episcopal Acta*, 20, no. 129; *Historians of the Church of York*, iii, pp. 75–77, dated probably 1177–81 by Clay, 'The Early Precentors and Chancellors', p. 133, and by Dr Lovatt.

[95] John of Salisbury, *Letters*, ii, no. 307. The attribution has been doubted, and the text supposed interpolated, but the early MSS leave little doubt that John preserved it among his own letters, as we now have it: see discussion ibid., p. xliv.

dispute has never been fully unravelled. It is equally clear that the old archbishop, Theobald, had trusted both of them, and the quality of his judgement was usually sound; his disciples were men of exceptional parts. In the diocese of York religion was not growing cool in Roger's time. The rich remnant of his work on the minster reflects the temporal prosperity that the church in York enjoyed in the second half of the twelfth century,[96] and the long list of new foundations, Cistercian, Augustinian, and Premonstratensian in particular, reveals an unprecedented flow of recruits and patronage. By the time of Roger's death in 1181 the splendid churches of all the religious houses, and their flocks and fields, must have helped to make Yorkshire a very different heritage from the charred battlefield which Archbishop Thomas I had entered in 1070. Nor need we suppose that Roger played no part in this.

It seems likely that the ferocity of Roger's onslaught on Becket, and his continuing zeal for the rights of his see,[97] reflect a close relationship between Roger and some at least of his chapter; more than personal animosity against a former colleague and rival seems implicit in his dealings with St Thomas, and there is copious evidence that he became, like Thurstan before him, devoted to the interests of his church. The mantle of his office weighed on him; to say that he was a worthy successor of Thurstan would be to go beyond the evidence. In his early years he was in a measure ruled by his chapter; in later years we may believe that he ruled them – perhaps not without friction, like his friend Gilbert Foliot of London;[98] but in Roger's case we lack evidence, just as we cannot tell how deep a mark his own appointments made upon the chapter. Whereas the nephews of Gilbert Foliot proliferated in the archdeacons' and other stalls at Hereford and London, Roger's known family links in the chapter were modest. Very likely this is due to our ignorance; at least one archdeacon was his nephew, and it has been suggested that the Norman Jeremiah, archdeacon of Cleveland and probably author of the Lay Folks' Mass Book may well have been a relation as well as protégé.[99] But it is clear that there was a continuing and important element at York of men already established before his coming. During most of his reign the dean was Robert Butevilain, already archdeacon

[96] On Roger, see now *English Episcopal Acta*, 20, ed. Marie Lovatt, (London, 2000).

[97] See esp. *Gesta Henrici Secundi*, ed. W. Stubbs, RS, 2 vols (London, 1867), i, pp. 104–5, 112–14 (1176); *Councils and Synods*, i, 1, pp. 998–1000; for his part in the events of 1170, see esp. A. Heslin (Dr Anne Duggan) in *Studies in Church History*, ii (1965), pp. 165–78.

[98] *GF*, pp. 204–11.

[99] Suggested in the first edition of this essay. On Jeremiah (below), see Clay, 'Notes on the Early Archdeacons', pp. 412–15; he suggested a 'close association', not specifically relationship (p. 414). On Roger's family, see M. Lovatt in *EEA*, 20, forthcoming. *Fasti*, vi, list 10.

of York at his arrival, promoted dean in 1157–58. Robert lived until 1186, and after his death continuity came to be symbolised by Hamo, precentor from the early 1170s till the late 1190s, then treasurer (1197–99 to 1217); but of his origin we know nothing. Hamo was evidently a leading figure among the local resident canons; the other treasurers were men of the south who owed their place to papal or royal patronage, already an important influence in the recruitment of the chapter, though not to the degree it later became. We have met John of Canterbury and Ralph de Warneville; the space between Ralph and Hamo was filled by the 'roaring devil i' the old play', Geoffrey Plantagenet, illegitimate son of Henry II, later himself archbishop.

Geoffrey had the misfortune to earn the dislike of two of the colleagues in his father's curia to whom we owe much of our knowledge of him, Walter Map the satirist and Roger of Howden the chronicler; more favourable was the view of his biographer, Gerald of Wales.[100] Some recent historians, while marvelling at his exceptional gift for quarrelling with everyone to hand, have reckoned him the one faithful son of Henry II, and have supposed that he may have mellowed in his last years.[101] Of this we cannot be sure, for from 1207 till 1212 he was an exile in Normandy, out of harm's way; but at least it may be said that he seems conscientiously to have objected to his brother King John's high-handed treatment of the church. For the rest, he arrived in York in 1191, to be enthroned on 1 November, and before two years were out he had quarrelled with the chapter, been reconciled, and quarrelled again. It is hard now to discern precisely what caused the battles, and some episodes in the epic may have been collusive or fictitious. Nor can one avoid the suspicion that some ambitious clerks battened on Geoffrey, knowing full well that patronage slipped rapidly through his fingers. When he came to York he was served by two eminent canonists on the make, Master Simon of Apulia and Master Honorius, author of the *Summa decretalium quaestionum*, one of the most remarkable canon law treatises of its day.[102] In 1193–94 Henry Marshal, dean

[100] Giraldus Cambrensis, *Opera*, iv, RS (London, 1873), pp. 355–431; Walter Map, *De nugis curialium*, ed. and trans. M. R. James, C. N. L. Brooke and R. A. B. Mynors, OMT (Oxford, 1983), pp. 478–89, 494–99; Roger of Howden, *Chronica*, ed. W. Stubbs, RS, 4 vols (London, 1868–71), iii–iv, esp. iv, pp. xxxiv–lxxvii.

[101] Stubbs, introduction to Howden, *Chronica*, iv, pp. xxxiv–lxxvii; Decima L. Douie, *Archbishop Geoffrey Plantagenet and the Chapter of York*, Borthwick Papers, 18 (York, 1960); Clay, 'Notes on the Early Deans', pp. 374ff; Clay, 'The Early Treasurers', pp. 24ff; Clay, 'Notes on the Early Archdeacons', pp. 425–30, and in *Early Yorkshire Charters*, iv, ed. C. T. Clay, Yorkshire Archaeological Society Record Series, extra series, 1 (1935), pp. xxv–xxvi. For a full study of Geoffrey, see M. Lovatt, 'The Career and Administration of Archbishop Geoffrey of York'.

[102] For Honorius, see preceding note, and S. Kuttner and E. Rathbone, 'Anglo-Norman Canonists of the Twelfth Century', *Traditio*, 7 (1949–51), pp. 279–358, at pp. 296, 304–16.

of York, was promoted to the see of Exeter, and Geoffrey, after an abortive attempt to appoint his own half-brother, Peter, tried to set Simon in his place; but he rapidly transferred his support to the royal nominee, Philip of Poitou. The king was then a prisoner in Germany, and to Germany went Simon, presently to be joined by Hamo the precentor and three archdeacons. Richard may have been swayed by the fact that his mercurial half-brother now supported Simon's rival, or he may have accepted the chapter's plea that the deanery was an elective office;[103] from 1194 till 1214 Simon remained dean, then followed Henry Marshal to Exeter, and Hamo ruled in his stead. In 1196 Richard I dropped a penny in the pool; while Geoffrey was absent appealing to the pope he made various appointments, including the presentation of Adam of Thorner – evidently a Yorkshireman – to the arch-deaconry of York, in spite of the fact that Geoffrey had already presented his brother Peter, and (for good measure) Peter of Dinan; Richard's nephew Arthur of Brittany urged compromise on the king, and Peter and Adam were permitted to share the profits of the archdeaconry. Adam performed the functions, and when both visited the minster at the same time, which we may reckon a rare event, they occupied the stall on alternate days.[104]

The archbishop's appetite for disputation was not yet quenched, however, and Adam was not left in peace. Geoffrey's most curious adventure came when he set Master Honorius in the archdeaconry of Richmond in 1198. This vast archdeaconry stretched right across to the Lake District, and its revenues were very substantial. The king wanted it for Roger of St Edmund; the chapter installed him; and the archbishop quarrelled with Honorius. But Honorius won; he took his suit to Rome, and there the great canonist received the favour of the pope, obtained his suit, and returned to enjoy his triumph from the safe distance of the court of Geoffrey's rival, Hubert Walter, ex-dean of York, now archbishop of Canterbury.[105]

Geoffrey's adventures continued. They provide us with a comic interlude, which yet throws a beam of light into the obscure history of the chapter. The endless disputes cannot have made the minster an edifying or a comfort-able place; they remind us that pope, archbishop, king and chapter always competed in the later middle ages for control of chapter patronage, and that many of the richest stalls were held by absentees. They reflect, almost in caricature, the long disputes common to many chapters over appoint-ments, especially of the dean, and the division of the chapter between

[103] On this issue see *Historians of the Church of York*, iii, pp. 92ff; *GF*, pp. 205–6; D. Knowles, *The Episcopal Colleagues of Archbishop Thomas Becket* (Cambridge, 1951), pp. 111–12.

[104] For this, and the later vicissitudes to 1201, when Adam's interest in the archdeaconry finally disappeared, see Clay 'Notes on the Early Archdeacons', pp. 425–27; *Fasti*, vi, list 9.

[105] See above, n. 101, and C. R. Cheney, *Hubert Walter* (London, 1967), pp. 164–65.

resident and absentee. But it is clear that the chapter contained a nucleus of local men who genuinely tried to sustain its services as well as its privileges. In the 1190s these included not only Hamo, evidently a married man or at least a father, reflecting the domesticity of an earlier age; but also Hugh Murdac, nephew of Archbishop Henry Murdac, formerly king's clerk and justice, now an old man in his retirement in the chapter; Adam of Thorner, later to enjoy for a time half the stall of the archdeaconry of York; Reginald Arundel, prebendary of Ulleskelf, and his namesake, presumably a relative, Roger Arundel, son of William Arundel of Foston on the Wolds, a subtantial tenant of the Percy see.[106] The list could be extended: the chapter of York, like many, still contained a number of resident canons; and it was more tenacious than most of its liberties and rites. The use of York was one of the few never submerged by the use of Sarum in the late middle ages. The Minster today bears eloquent witness that it was a powerful centre of loyalty and devotion in the thirteenth and fourteenth centuries.

At the end of Geoffrey's reign the chapter seems, however, notably unhappy and divided. Beyond this we cannot go; for such general judgements do not do justice to the variety of personality and outlook, of attitude and sentiment, of such diverse groups as made a twelfth-century chapter; nor is the scattered, scanty evidence, like the bridge over the Ouse, strong enough to bear them.

---

[106] Clay, 'The Early Treasurers', pp. 28–30; Clay, *York Minster Fasti*, i, esp. pp. 82–83, 86, 91–92; ii, pp. 20–21, 75, 98, 106–11; Clay, 'Notes on the Early Archdeacons', pp. 425–28; Clay in *Early Yorkshire Charters*, xi (1963), p. 197; *Fasti*, vi.

4

The Missionary at Home:
The Church in the Towns, 1000–1250

The wide span of years which I have boldly claimed in my title is intended to enmesh and hold together for our inspection the first great age of the medieval city, the tenth and eleventh centuries, when the medieval church first faced the problem of evangelism in growing mercantile communities, and the age when it deployed in the cities and towns of Europe a new army of missionaries in the persons of the friars. The missionary techniques of the friars are familiar and comparatively well documented; the evangelism of the tenth and eleventh centuries is scarcely documented at all. In recent years the dramatic nature of urban history in this early period has been becoming increasingly apparent; and it was in the conviction that the church's hand in it could not wholly escape detection that I chose the title for this essay. Many aspects of this problem have been traced with the closest care; but I justify the breadth and cloudiness of my theme by a conviction that it has rarely been looked at quite from this point of view.

Broadly speaking, St Dominic believed in evangelism by preaching, St Francis in evangelism by example. To both, in the long run, the whole world was their parish, though both concentrated on the towns of western Christendom as their main field of activity. The similarities and the contrasts are exceedingly instructive; all the more so, I believe, for being deliberate. In the ancient controversy as to whether Dominic was influenced by Francis, I hold the heretical opinion that the influence was powerful and decisive; but I am sure that Dominic took pains to avoid the Franciscan model in some respects while following it in others.[1] Late in 1216, if my reconstruction

First published in *Studies in Church History*, 6, ed. G. J. Cuming (Cambridge, 1970), pp. 59–83.

[1] See Brooke, *Medieval Church and Society* (London, 1971), ch. 11, esp. pp. 229–30. In all that relates to the friars I owe a special debt to my wife, Dr Rosalind Brooke, and to the late Professor Dom David Knowles, though neither is to be held responsible for the statement of my views; and for town parishes, among many who have helped me, I should like particularly to acknowledge my debt to the Reverend Gillian Keir, Miss Susan Reynolds,

is correct, Dominic and Francis met in Rome; and Dominic was so impressed that he suggested that the two orders be merged. Francis was by nature the more original and subtle, and he clearly appreciated that Dominic was a man of powerful mind in some ways quite different from his; in any event, he refused to absorb the Dominicans. At this stage Dominic's Order was a tiny community of canons regular, with a special instruction to preach. On his return to Toulouse, Dominic staged a revolution in his community: suddenly and without warning he dispersed them to the four winds. They turned their backs on the heretics among whom they had been working hitherto, and went out to preach to the church at large; they became, as we understand the term, friars. Thus far, and in certain striking details, Dominic seems to be following Francis; but in looking to Paris and Bologna, the great student centres, for recruits and in devising over the years the most precise and sophisticated organisation of its day, he was doing precisely the opposite of Francis. Dominic conceived an order of instructed clerks – not an order of high scholastics, but of trained men – who could travel and preach; and who, while not actually on the road or in the pulpit, would live an ordered, ascetic life on the Premonstratensian pattern in their convents. Francis's recruits were a cross-section of Italian society; but in early days the majority were simple laymen, townsfolk and peasants, who were commonly illiterate.

> We clerks recited the office like other clerks [declared St Francis in his *Testament*]. The laymen recited the *Pater Noster;* and we dwelt in churches gladly, and were simple folk and subject to all men. And I worked, and wish to work, with my hands; and I firmly will that all other brothers work at a craft which is decent and good. Those who know none, let them learn, not out of greed for labour's reward, but *as an example* and to drive out idleness. And when we are not given the reward of our toil, let us turn back to God's table and seek alms from door to door.[2]

Francis himself preached, to humans as well as to animals; but he never regarded preaching as his own main function or that of his order. Still less was he an organiser; he was there to give an example. Preachers formed a small minority in early days, and it was something of a puzzle to those not in the Franciscan secret, so to speak, what the function of most friars was.

Note 1 *continued*
Professor D. A. Bullough and Professor R. B. Pugh. Since it was written the theme has been brilliantly reconsidered by James Campbell, 'The Church in Anglo-Saxon Towns', *Studies in Church History*, 16 (1979), pp. 119–35, and Richard Morris, *Churches in the Landscape* (London, 1989), ch. 5; see also above, ch. 1, and below, ch. 5.

2 *Die Opuscula des Hl. Franziskus von Assisi*, ed. K. Esser (Grottaferrata, 1976), p. 440.

Dominic refused to recruit illiterate laymen; the hierarchy viewed groups of such folk with suspicion, as men inadequately prepared to resist heresy. The leaders of the northern provinces who started the revolt against Brother Elias in the 1230s, the men who admired learning and committee government and all things Dominican, were equally baffled; and their central figure, Hyamo of Faversham, inspired a decree in general chapter forbidding the recruitment of laymen in this sense.[3] By the time that Salimbene came to write his chronicle, they were virtually an extinct species even in Italy, and he describes those he had met in early days with raised eyebrows and without regret. 'They were useless for hearing confessions ... They did nothing but eat and sleep.'[4]

Francis, on the other hand, repeatedly emphasised that lay brothers, by their prayers and their example, formed the centre of his order. It is clear that he was determined to heal the rift between clergy and laity; that he took seriously the danger inherent in the separation of layman and cleric which had been so conspicuous a feature of the papal reform of the eleventh century and its aftermath. The well-educated clergy moved into a high social stratum in a hierarchical society, and if they preached to the poor their words tended to pass over their audience's heads; the rank and file of the clergy failed to live up to the modes and ideals of the papal reform, and were by that token despised and rejected and demoralised. The function of the Franciscans was to fill this gap; like worker priests to live among ordinary folk on their own terms. In a world in which under-employment, poverty and starvation were always at the door, and which lacked the material resources or techniques for curing any of them, it was worse than useless to preach acceptance and submission: Francis's vision and originality consisted in sending out men who rejoiced in poverty as a positive, exciting, romantic thing; who were happy to be poorer than the poor, humbler than the humble, more ignorant than the ignorant. In high society, the romantic subjection to female tyranny portrayed in many romances was the reverse, the deliberate ironic parody of the high society of fact, in which women were commonly drudges and slaves, slaves of the marriage market, of the marriage bed and of the ludicrous dynastic ambitions of their menfolk. But they gained some relief from the literary cult which portrayed them in a contrary role. To abolish poverty was beyond the range of possible imagination in the thirteenth century; but some reconciliation between the

---

[3] See R. B. Brooke, *Early Franciscan Government* (Cambridge, 1959), pp. 243ff.
[4] Ed. O. Holder-Egger, *Monumenta Germaniae Historica, Scriptores*, xxxii (1905–13), p. 102.

doctrine that the world was God's world and the horror of everyday experience could be effected by making poverty a holy thing.[5]

This presupposed a missionary strategy which was essentially silent and subtle; which worked by example more than by preaching. There is a striking similarity in this respect between Francis's general missionary strategy and his particular treatment of heresy. It has commonly been supposed that Dominic was interested in heretics, and especially in the Cathars, and that Francis was not; for Dominic devoted his best energies to preaching against them, and they hardly figure in Francis's writings or the early lives. But if we ask the simple question, which is likely to have known more of the Cathars, the native of old Castile or the merchant's son of Assisi, we must surely say Francis. The valley of Spoleto boasted, or hid, a Cathar bishop; two or three years before Francis's conversion Assisi apparently had a Cathar *podestà*; Pietro Bernardone traded over the ground where they grew thickest.[6] Francis taught, and above all lived, the Catholic life, saying nothing of the heretics, but quietly turning his back on them; Dominic engaged, in early years, in public disputation with them. I suppose we would normally reckon today that Francis had understood the problem better than Dominic; I am sure that Dominic himself supposed so.

If we seek to trace out their attitude, we can study Francis's writings, Dominic's constitutions, the lives of both men and the comments of their contemporaries.[7] Almost all the evidence by which we may compare the attitude of the men who worked in the rising towns two or three centuries before is indirect. Much of this chapter must therefore consist of an attempt to sketch the framework of churches and parishes in the towns; only with such a basis can one hope to penetrate into a very obscure world of religious activity.

It may be wondered whether there is a subject here at all; whether we can hope to know enough about the work of the church in eleventh-century towns to justify the enterprise. We have, at least, some puzzles on our

[5] Cf. the studies of M. Mollat, especially 'La notion de la pauvreté au moyen âge: position de problèmes', *Revue d'histoire de l'église de France*, 149 (1966), 1–17, and references there cited.

[6] Cf. Brooke, *Medieval Church and Society*, p. 160; K. Esser, 'Franziskus von Assisi und die Katharer seiner Zeit', *Archivum franciscanum historicum*, 51 (1958), pp. 225–64, especially p. 239; A. Borst, *Die Katharer* (Stuttgart, 1953), pp. 231ff; M. Lambert, *The Cathars* (Oxford, 1998), pp. 171–74.

[7] On the Dominican sources, see R. B. Brooke, *The Coming of the Friars* (London, 1975), ch. 6 and pp. 162–200; S. Tugwell, ed., *Early Dominicans: Selected Writings* (Ramsey, New Jersey, 1982); on the Constitutions, Brooke, *The Coming*, pp. 289–90; still useful is G. R. Galbraith, *The Constitution of the Dominican Order, 1216–1360* (Manchester, 1925).

hands, and they may make a promising beginning. Let me sketch two contrasts. When the men who had the invidious task of assessing the English church for papal taxation in 1254 came to the diocese of Ely, they found in Cambridge fifteen parish churches, in Ely one; yet they decided, rightly or wrongly, that the one parish in Ely was worth more than the fifteen in Cambridge put together.[8] This does not mean that Ely was a larger or more prosperous place than Cambridge; no doubt the reverse was true. A mercantile community might have large wealth by the thirteenth century but little tithe.[9] Nonetheless, it points a striking contrast. No doubt we shall rehearse numerous explanations – social, economic and legal – before we claim that the men of Cambridge were of more conspicuous piety than those of Ely; but a church at every street corner is a puzzle in any age.

In the twelfth century the monks of Worcester concocted a remarkable document dated 1092 in which the most ancient persons of the three counties adjacent to Worcester were alleged to have sat for three days in the crypt of Worcester cathedral, and decided in the end that Worcester city contained only one parish, that of the mother church, the cathedral, even though it had other and ancient churches.[10] In this the forgers attempted to represent the most conservative point of view as to the number of parishes in the city, combined with a forward-looking view of the rights of the church, of the status in canon law of bishop and parish priest. To this we shall return; for the moment, let us observe the contrast.

In many parts of Europe a jury of ancients would have given a very similar answer in the late eleventh century. In Italy, for example, it was normal for even a large town to remain a single parish down to the twelfth

[8] *Valuation of Norwich*, ed. W. E. Lunt (Oxford, 1926), pp. 212, 218–19. On the early history of parishes, see above, ch. 1; still helpful are G. W. O. Addleshaw, *Beginnings of the Parochial System*, St Anthony's Hall Publications, 9 (York, 1956), and the excellent bibliography in D. Kurze, *Pfarrerwahlen im Mittelalter: ein Beitrag zur Geschichte der Gemeinde und des Nieder-kirchenwesens* (Cologne-Graz, 1966).

[9] In theory, tithes were paid on all kinds of income, and the extent to which non-agricultural tithe disappeared in the twelfth and thirteenth centuries may have been exaggerated; but it is certainly from the twelfth century that this tendency grew, see G. Constable, *Monastic Tithes from their Origins to the Twelfth Century* (Cambridge, 1964), pp. 16ff, especially 17 n. 1; 267–68, especially 268 n. 1; 287ff). Professor Constable's book is the indispensable guide to the tangled history of tithes, although it only covers part of the field: see ibid., p. 1 n. 1, for general books on the subject of this paper. C. Boyd, *Tithes and Parishes in Medieval Italy* (Ithaca, 1952), is of particular interest.

[10] Ed. R. R. Darlington, *Cartulary of Worcester Cathedral Priory*, (Pipe Roll Society, 1968), pp. 31–32; for its origin, see Julia Barrow, 'How the Twelfth-Century Monks of Worcester Perceived their Past', in *The Perception of the Past in Twelfth-Century Europe*, ed. P. Magdalino (London, 1992), pp. 53–74, esp. pp. 60–69.

century; and some small Italian cathedral cities have only one parish to this day.[11] In the larger cities churches might proliferate: in 924 the Magyars are said to have destroyed forty-four churches in Pavia alone, and it is certain that there were something like this number in the city at that time.[12] In Europe at large this would seem a sensational number for the early tenth century, even if small compared with the 133 described by Opicino in Pavia in the fourteenth century.[13] This illustrates the obvious fact that there may be far more churches than parishes, and that in Italy, unlike parts of northern Europe, there was no tendency in the central middle ages for parishes to split, so that eventually the churches which survived had each its parish. In Italy, indeed, it was no uncommon thing to have more than one cathedral in a city. The extreme case was, of course, Rome: the Lateran basilica may be the Pope's cathedral as bishop of the city, but as Pope he has five; and one could say that, just as the altars of the major basilicas were like the major altars of a single cathedral, so the titular churches, the parish churches of the cardinal priests, operated like the side chapels or chantry chapels of a late medieval cathedral. Their incardination in the papal basilicas made them all members of the chapter of the mother church;[14] and in that sense the Roman scene was as elsewhere in Italy – a single cathedral community dominated all the city churches. But the cardinals were parish priests or arch-priests before they had been incardinated into the basilicas, and in that sense provided the pattern and exemplar for the parochial system in the later medieval pattern. The cathedral clergy of Rome were unique in being nomadic; but transhumance was not uncommon in Italy – in Pavia, for instance, there was a summer and a winter cathedral.[15]

A pilgrim to Rome from north-western Europe in the late eleventh

---

[11] See Boyd, *Tithes and Parishes*, p. 53, n. 12.

[12] See D. A. Bullough, 'Urban Change in Early Medieval Italy: The Example of Pavia' , *Papers of the British School at Rome*, 34 (1966), pp. 82–130, esp. pp. 99, 119ff. I am much indebted to Professor Bullough for discussing some of the problems of this Chapter with me, and for valuable advice and references. His study of early Pavia provides an excellent illustration of what the evidence for a well-documented Italian city can reveal. An interesting parallel to Pavia is Dorstad, which is said to have had fifty-five churches before its destruction in the ninth century. See P. Johansen, 'Die Kaufmannskirche im Ostseegebiet', in *Studien zu den Aufängen des europäischen Städtewesens*, Vorträge und Forschungen, ed. T. Mayer (Lindau-Constance, 1958), pp. 499–525.

[13] *Liber de laudibus civitatis Ticinensis*, ed. R. Maiocchi and F. Quintavalle, *Rerum italicarum scriptores*, xi, i (1903), pp. 4ff, especially p. 17 (133, excluding chapels, 'intra urbem', c. 34 in the suburbs); also ed. F. Gianani (Pavia, 1927), pp. 77ff, 91.

[14] See S. Kuttner, 'Cardinalis: The History of a Canonical Concept', *Traditio*, 3 (1945), 129–214.

[15] Cf. Bullough, 'Urban Change in Early Medieval Italy', p. 100.

century might well have been bewildered by the variety which he found. In the west of England occasionally cities like Worcester and Hereford had already a group of churches; but one parish was normal as yet, and commonly only one church before the twelfth century.[16] In the eastern part of England he would find churches very numerous and commonly already very independent: in Lincoln some thirty-five churches already by 1100, which was to rise to about fifty by the end of the twelfth century: in York fourteen at least by 1100, rising to nearly forty by 1200. In contrast, moving a little further south, the modest city of Winchester had over fifty.[17] London had probably already the largest number of parish churches of any city in Christendom, and they were rising fast; by the late twelfth century it had well over a hundred parish churches strictly so called within the area of the city.[18] In parts of France he would find a situation comparable to Cambridge or Canterbury – with a moderate number of parishes rapidly increasing; thus Poitiers and Bourges (to take two cases which have been systematically investigated) each had twenty or thirty parish churches by the eleventh century.[19] But in the Low Countries, Burgundy, the Rhineland and south-western Germany in general he would rarely have found a multiplicity of town churches, let alone of parishes.[20] In Cologne some sort of parochial division of the area within the ancient walls may go back to the ninth century: if so, it is the earliest documented division of a city into parishes in western Christendom. Even in Cologne there was no approximation to the English record: in 1172 it was reckoned to have thirteen parish churches, covering the much larger area then reckoned in

[16] On Hereford see M. D. Lobel in *Historic Towns*, i (London and Oxford, 1969); and above, ch. 2, esp. studies cited in nn. 4–5.

[17] On Lincoln see Sir J. W. F. Hill, *Medieval Lincoln* (Cambridge, 1948), pp. 147ff; on York, *VCH, York*, pp. 365ff; on Winchester, see D. Keene, *Survey of Medieval Winchester, Winchester Studies*, ii (Oxford, 1985), i, pp. 106–36.

[18] See maps in *The British Atlas of Historic Towns*, iii, ed. M. D. Lobel; C. N. L. Brooke and G. Keir, *London, 800–1216* (London, 1975), ch. 6. There were ninety-nine within the walls, a number more in the city suburbs.

[19] D. Claude, *Topographie und Verfassung der Städte Bourges und Poitiers bis in das 11. Jahrhundert*, Historische Studien, 380 (Lübeck and Hamburg, 1960), especially the maps facing p. 196. For Canterbury see W. Urry, *Canterbury under the Angevin Kings* (London, 1967), pp. 207ff, especially pp. 210–11.

[20] F. L. Ganshof, *Etude sur le développement des villes entre Loire et Rhin au moyen âge* (Paris and Brussels, 1943), pp. 47ff; W. Müller, 'Pfarrei und mittelalterliche Stadt in Bereiche Süd- badens', *Neue Beiträge zur südwestdeutschen Landesgeschichte: Festschrift für Max Miller* (Stuttgart, 1962), pp. 69–80. Of exceptional interest is the history of Paris, on which see A. Friedmann, *Paris: ses rues, ses paroisses du moyen âge à la Révolution* (Paris, 1959).

the city.[21] Most other cities of these regions had a single parish, and a single parish church till the thirteenth century – though it was normal (unlike in Italy) for the parish church to be separate from the cathedral, and there were often monastic churches or communities of secular canons as well. Indeed it is common for the site of the parish church to reveal the history of the village community or communities before the town was formed. Thus Dijon had four (later five) parishes, because the town straddles the frontiers of four earlier, rural parishes. In south-western Germany, of fifty-seven towns studied by Dr Müller in his paper on parish and town in this area, two-thirds had single parish churches outside their walls.[22] This reflected in most cases a parochial system laid down before the town; the church remained in the old village centre, and the town within its old parish. Where a church falls within the walls, it is even so sometimes on the edge of the medieval town; where it is in the centre, it is either because the town grew from an old village nucleus or because the town was planned so, was in fact one of Professor Beresford's new towns.[23] But in this area a parish church was evidently not felt to be an essential part of a new town or a new housing estate, so long as the old church was still within reasonable walking distance. To find more than one parish in a town is rare, and that again, as at Dijon, sometimes reflects a division more ancient than the town; sometimes peculiar local circumstances and factions.

Figures by themselves mean little; and the figures I have cited can hardly be interpreted until we have defined what we mean by a parish and a parish church. But I quote these crude statistics at the outset to establish the extraordinary variety of the scene in western Christendom in the eleventh and twelfth centuries.

There is, however, a fundamental ambiguity in any study of the proliferation of churches and parishes, and that is, obviously enough, that not every church was, or became, a parish church; and that parish boundaries evolved, and parish rights and responsibilities developed and altered.[24] From the

[21] See W. Neuss and F. W. Oediger, *Das Bistum Köln* (*Geschichte des Erzbistums Köln*, i) (Köln, 1964), pp. 282ff, especially pp. 286–87. There are several other good studies of the parishes in Cologne: see especially E. Hegel in *Die Kunstdenkmäler im Landesteil Nordrhein*, supplement 1 (1950) and a brief account in G. Addleshaw, *The Early Parochial System and the Divine Office* (London, 1957).

[22] Ganshof, *Etude sur le développement*, p. 49; Müller, 'Pfarrei und mittelalterliche Stadt'.

[23] Müller, 'Pfarrei und mittelalterliche Stadt', p. 76; for Beresford, see below, p. 80 n. 38.

[24] In general, see (for bibliography) H. Feine, *Kirchliche Rechtsgeschichte: die katholische Kirche*, 4th edn (Cologne-Graz, 1964), pp. 411ff; C. Boyd, *Tithes and Parishes in Medieval Italy* (n. 9); D. Kurze, *Pfarrerwahlen im Mittelalter* (n. 8). In earlier times the limitation was sometimes deliberate: as the late Walter Ullmann pointed out to me, the decree of the council of Tribur of 895, attempting to regulate the growth of parishes, should be stressed in this

twelfth century on, the canon lawyers hammered out a doctrine which has a certain simplicity: to your parish, to your parish church and to your parish priest you owed attendance at mass, you owed tithe; and to him and to it you delivered your children to be baptised, and they delivered you to be buried. Burial rights, baptismal rights and tithe, on what we may with rough justice call a normal definition, though local varieties subsisted, were all essential to the making of a parish church; and that is why strict parochial boundaries of the kind familiar to us today can never have existed before the twelfth century; and much of the controversy that has raged from time to time about parochial origins has turned on these definitions. It was commonly assumed in many parts of Europe before the twelfth century that if you were a strong and healthy baby you went to the cathedral baptistery – or some suitable open space – to be baptized by the bishop on Easter Day or Whitsun; and it was commonly assumed or asserted that tithe should be paid to the mother church, not to the individual local village or town church where one worshipped. From the mother church, indeed, tithe was redistributed by the administrators of the welfare church; and that is why the most ancient parish boundaries in anything like our sense of the term are those not of the parish churches but of the diaconates of Rome.[25] Only when it became accepted that tithe was assessed on land, not on persons or on real or total income, and that it could legitimately be used – contrary to the practice of the early church – for the support of the clergy, indeed mainly for the support of the clergy, could parish boundaries in a strict sense be established. Yet to refuse to employ the word 'parishes' for any institution earlier than 1100 would be absurd. Notoriously, *parochia* in early days more commonly meant a diocese (or any large area) than a parish; but it had been regularly used for a small unit of pastoral care long before the twelfth century, and many parishes had stable boundaries, too, long before this era. I do not believe we shall make any sense of the word if we try to use any more precise definition than that a parish church was the place where the folk of a district worshipped regularly; to whose priest they looked for the sacraments, and whom they were expected, in some fairly direct sense, to support. In this sense the churches which sprang up in their thousands in the eleventh and twelfth

context; see the summary of ninth-century decrees on tithe and of the literature in Constable, *Monastic Tithes* (n. 9), pp. 40ff.

[25] See Boyd, *Tithes and Parishes*, pp. 47ff, 129ff. For the Roman 'Diaconiae', see esp. S. Kuttner, 'Cardinalis: The History of a Canonical Concept', in *Traditio* (1945), pp. 129–214, at pp. 178ff; cf. *Atlas of the Early Christian World*, ed. F. Van den Meer and C. Mohrmann (London, 1959), map 27. For baptism in the cathedral outside Italy, cf. Neuss and Oediger, *Das Bistum Köln*, p. 334 (Cologne); and below, p. 78 (Worcester). For what follows, see Constable, *Monastic Tithes*, ch. 1.

centuries were clearly intended to be parish churches, whereas many of the oratories of the fourth, fifth or sixth centuries were not. One has only to compare the ecclesiastical map of London in the late middle ages with the earlier map of Poitiers as reconstructed by Dr Claude to see the force of this.[26] Poitiers had a continuity of religious life almost unique among the cities of north-western Europe; of this the fourth-century baptistery is still the outward symbol. In late Roman and early medieval times it proliferated churches. But these tended to spread in clusters around the cathedral within and the ancient house of Saint-Hilaire without the old city walls. In London in early days no doubt the churches were clustered, and the way St Gregory and St Augustine clung close to St Paul's in later times may well be a survival from such a time.[27] Nor did the final pattern closely resemble a chessboard or a chequer table. But a pattern there was in the end: the characteristic London parish was irregular in shape but fairly compact, covered about three and a half acres and had at its centre a busy street, often a crossroads. The church has clearly been seen, from its inception, as the centre of a pastoral unit.

In theory churches grouped in this way could either be centres of separate pastoral units, as parish churches in the later sense, or outlying chapels of a minster or mother church, as St Helen's, Worcester, and its dependent chapels were viewed by the monks of Worcester cathedral. Orderic Vitalis was baptised in the little church at Atcham 'by the mighty River Severn': the nave walls which witnessed this ceremony in the 1070s substantially survive, though the font has long since gone;[28] but a glance at Francis Bond's *Fonts and Font Covers* reveals how numerous are the Norman fonts which still bear witness that late eleventh- and twelfth-century churches were baptismal churches;[29] and sufficient pre-Conquest fonts survive to show that this was no novelty, even though in the diocese of Worcester in the mid eleventh century folk thronged to the cathedral with their babies to be received into the church at the hands of St Wulfstan, even before he became bishop.[30]

---

[26] For London see above, n. 18; also the map of the *City of London Showing Parish Boundaries Prior to 1907* printed by the London Topographical Society (1959), which in all essentials reflects the situation in 1200. For Poitiers see D. Claude, *Topographie und Verfassung*, esp. pp. 36ff and maps facing p. 196.

[27] Cf. R. E. M. Wheeler, *London and the Saxons* (London, 1935), esp. p. 100.

[28] Orderic, vi, p. 552 (my translation). On Atcham church, see H. M. and J. Taylor, *Anglo-Saxon Architecture* (Cambridge, 1965), i, pp. 30–32.

[29] F. Bond, *Fonts and Font Covers* (London, 1908).

[30] *The Vita Wulfstani of William of Malmesbury*, ed. R. R. Darlington, Camden Third Series, 40 (1928), pp. 12–13; it is noted that he baptised the poor who could not afford to pay the normal fees. On the cathedral as parish church, see M. Franklin, 'The Cathedral as Parish

At the time of the Norman Conquest substantial traces of the organisation of old minsters and mother churches still survived.[31] In most areas their pastoral office had long been substantially replaced by the local proprietary churches. In most areas the Normans rapidly obliterated the traces of the old organisation by introducing the new pattern of archdeaconries and rural deaneries. Where the old pattern was persistent, as in the *parochia* of the old minster church at Leominster in Herefordshire, a curious conflict between old and new developed: Leominster was granted with all its rights to Reading abbey by King Henry I; and these were deemed, as Professor Brian Kemp has shown, to include rights over a substantial part of the ancient *parochia* of Leominster and its churches;[32] indeed, the earliest charter which confirms this grant lists thirty-nine villages and hamlets of the neighbourhood, and it is not clear how many churches and chapels really existed in them at that date: some part of the list was very likely an insurance against new churches which might be built in the future, to ensure that they did not fall outside Reading's net. Such a confirmation is a statement of pious hope rather than of established right; for in some cases at least Leominster's claim could not be upheld, since rights over churches of other kinds were established by rival landlords.

We see here an example of the fundamental confusion between spiritual and temporal rights, out of which the parish system was born. In the eleventh century a parish church was a piece of property; it could pass from father to son, it could be sold; it seems to have been freer than any other substantial piece of property from the shackles of local or feudal custom.[33] In his famous retort to Anselm, William Rufus likened his own relation to the greater abbeys to Anselm's relation to his manors: they were property from which one drew an income.[34] Churches, therefore, must have owners. Ancient churches were owned by bishops and cathedral chapters; some had long been owned by abbeys; a great number were owned by secular landlords who had built them or laid hands on them; a number more were owned by communities of burgesses. The burgesses of Norwich

Church: The Case of Southern England', in *Church and City, 1000–1500: Essays in Honour of Christopher Brooke*, ed. D. Abulafia, M. Franklin and M. Rubin (Cambridge, 1992), pp. 173–98.

[31] For what follows see F. Barlow, *The English Church, 1000–1066* (2nd edn, London, 1979), esp. pp. 179ff, 183ff; *Minsters and Parish Churches*, ed. J. Blair (Oxford, 1988); above pp. 7–17 and references.

[32] B. Kemp, 'Some Aspects of the *Parochia* of Leominster in the Twelfth Century', in *Minsters and Parish Churches*, ed. J. Blair (Oxford, 1988), pp. 83–95, esp. pp. 83, 90–92.

[33] H. Feine, *Kirchliche Rechstgeschichte*, i, pp. 129–78, esp. pp. 139ff for bibliography; U. Stutz, *Geschichte des Kirchlichen Benefizialwesens*, i (Berlin, 1895, new ed. by H. E. Feine, 1961); for England, Barlow, *The English Church*, pp. 186ff and 186n. for references.

[34] Eadmer, *Historia novorum*, ed. M. Rule, RS (London, 1884), pp. 49–50; see below, p. 139.

had fifteen churches; one eminent burgess alone had 2 1/6.[35] Oddest of all, they could be owned by their priest; indeed, it seems fairly clear that, if the secular owner was lacking or had withdrawn into the background, it could be assumed that the church must be owned by its priest. Thus Canterbury Cathedral Priory in the course of the eleventh century collected a little packet of London city churches, because their owners, the parish priests, had become monks at Canterbury and brought their churches with them.[36]

This curious situation had an economic and pastoral aspect. It is notorious that the confusion of spiritual and temporal property helped the growth of the parish system because it was in the interests of a lay owner to realise his assets by building a church and attracting tithe, of which in many cases he might easily be able to enjoy a considerable share. It represents a legal informality of a kind which must make the student of later parish history gasp. Broadly speaking, it was in the twelfth century that the canon law laid its cold hand on the parishes of Europe and froze the pattern which has in many parts subsisted ever since. It is true that many new parishes have been formed, many amalgamated in the intervening centuries; that, for instance, the division of towns into a number of parishes characteristically took place in the twelfth century and later in Italy, and in the thirteenth century in the Low Countries.[37] But this was an orderly, organised process, not the free-for-all it had been in those cities which had been fragmented before the ice age. It depended on the cooperation of all the powers in the land; especially of bishop, king, lay patrons and any religious house which was interested; and in any parish of much size or value, the pope was commonly invited to help before the process was complete. In 1301 the archbishop of York visited the king's new town, Kingston-upon-Hull, and found a funeral procession winding along the Humber to a distant burial church, between a high tide and a gale; with a great effort he succeeded in arranging burial rights for the chapel of Holy Trinity, Hull; but this church, one of the greatest of medieval parish churches, was only truly made a parish church by act of parliament in 1661.[38] From 1200 to the mid nineteenth century the whole of what is now Birkenhead – which included twelve hamlets – was the parish of Woodchurch, the wooden church which served them all; and eight hamlets in the north-west of the Wirral peninsula lay

---

[35] Barlow, *The English Church, 1000–1066*, p. 192.

[36] 'An Early List of London Properties', ed. B. W. Kissan, *Transactions of the London and Middlesex Archaeological Society*, new series, 8 (1940), pp. 57–69; cf. D. C. Douglas and G. W. Greenaway, *English Historical Documents*, ii (London, 1953), 954–56.

[37] See above, pp. 73–75 and nn.

[38] M. W. Beresford, *New Towns of the Middle Ages* (London, 1967), pp. 169ff.

in the parish of West Kirby, the *by* with the church.[39] This is a pattern characteristic of the north west and of the northern marches of Wales. The most striking contrast is in London. By 1200 or so the parish boundaries were drawn; a few may have died in the later middle ages, but in all essentials the parishes survived – even when most of the churches were destroyed in the Great Fire and a majority disappeared altogether from view, and some parishes were amalgamated – until the act of parliament which redrew the boundaries in 1907.[40]

To a Londoner the period before 1200 seems the age of new parish churches *par excellence*; to a native of Florence or Utrecht the twelfth or thirteenth century; to a sojourner in the Wirral peninsula the nineteenth century would seem to be more truly such. These contrasts cannot be fully explained. The visitor to Florence, and to many other Italian cities, cannot fail to notice the baptistery, outward and visible sign of the centuries when all the children of the city were brought to the duomo to be baptised. If my theme was the dead rather than the living, a profitable time might be spent investigating the shifting sites of burial grounds. Within England, where the contrasts are most sharply defined, it is clear that one major factor which could check the escalation of parish churches was the presence of a large, powerful and effective community of monks or canons in the town. For long periods in the tenth and eleventh centuries the sees of Worcester and York were held in plurality. It might therefore seem surprising that their ecclesiastical history in this period should be so different. A part at least of the explanation is that the bishop commonly resided with his community in Worcester; and that, even after the Norman Conquest, the first Norman archbishop of York had great difficulty at first in scraping together a chapter of canons to serve his minster.[41] The community seems to have mattered more than the cathedral in such cases, and this is readily intelligible.

When the Norman bishops were settled firmly in the saddle, they showed by their actions contempt for the organisation and the image of the old English hierarchy: they introduced archdeacons where few if any had lurked before; they redrew frontiers of lesser jurisdiction and established rural deaneries; they rebuilt all the cathedrals on a vast scale. When the clergy of the diocese of Canterbury led their folk to the cathedral in 1080s in the Pentecostal procession, they entered a large new building whose open vista

[39] G. Ormerod, *History of the County Palatine and City of Chester* (2nd edn, by T. Helsby, London, 1875–82), ii, pp. 485, 520.

[40] See above, pp. 75, 78.

[41] So one may deduce from the telescoped narrative in Hugh the Chanter, *History of the Church of York*, ed. C. Johnson, M. Brett, C. N. L. Brooke and M. Winterbottom, Oxford Medieval Texts (Oxford, 1990), pp. 18–19: see above, p. 51.

was dominated not by shrines or altars but by the formidable figure of Archbishop Lanfranc, enthroned in the apse.[42] Whether this was due to the scorn which Lanfranc and his associates poured on their precursors has been much debated; probably not.[43] But there is no question that the pre-conquest church was in many ways very different from its Norman successor. In particular, the incidence of a powerful religious community and an organising bishop was much more sporadic than it later became.

If we plot the towns where parish churches multiplied, we may start in the north country, in York and Lincoln, cities free from communities of any stature before the very late eleventh century, cities which had lived in a pagan world a century before. At Norwich we are still in the Danelaw, though the southern Danelaw, and in a land where communities flourished. But Norwich itself had been the seat neither of a bishop nor of a religious community of consequence before the Conquest; and yet it was one of the foremost English boroughs of the day. A complete catalogue would be tedious, indeed impossible in the present state of knowledge; but the briefest tour must take note of Canterbury, Winchester and London, for there the conditions were at first sight profoundly different. Canterbury never proliferated churches like York or Lincoln or London; yet Canterbury at the height had twenty-two and Winchester nearly fifty; neither was a town of great size.[44] Neither was in the Danelaw; both had religious communities which one would have supposed powerful; and both had rich bishops overseeing them. London has always been a law to itself. It is probable that the chapter of St Paul's was a small and comparatively insignificant affair before the Conquest;[45] and London had already earned something of that

[42] Cf. Brooke, *Medieval Church and Society*, pp. 173–74, and 'Archbishop Lanfranc, the English Bishops, and the Council of London of 1075', *Collectanea Stephan Kuttner*, ed. G. Forchielli and A. M. Stickler, ii = *Studia Gratiana*, 12 (Bologna, 1967), pp. 39–59, at pp. 42–43.

[43] Most recently by R. W. Pfaff, 'Lanfranc's Supposed Purge of the Anglo-Saxon Calendar', in *Warriors and Churchmen in the High Middle Ages: Essays Presented to Karl Leyser*, ed. T. Reuter (London, 1992), pp. 95–108, who denies Lanfranc's scorn; and T. A. Heslop, 'The Canterbury Calendars and the Norman Conquest', in *Canterbury and the Norman Conquest*, ed. R. Eales and R. Sharpe (London, 1995), pp. 53–85, who shows at least that the Canterbury calendar was purged – though St Ælfheah and St Dunstan survived in it, and Dunstan was much honoured; cf. also M. Gibson, 'Normans and Angevins 1070–1220', in *A History of Canterbury Cathedral*, ed. P. Collinson, N. Ramsay and M. Sparks (Oxford, 1995), pp. 38–68, at pp. 43–44.

[44] See above, p. 75 (Canterbury, York, Lincoln), 75, 78 (London); Derek Keene, *Survey of Medieval Winchester* (n. 17), i, pp. 106–36.

[45] The evidence is noted in C. Brooke, 'The Earliest Times to 1485', in *A History of St Paul's Cathedral*, ed. W. R. Matthews and W. M. Atkins (London, 1957), pp. 1–99, 361–65, at pp. 13ff, 18ff, 361, 363; Brooke, 'The Composition of the Chapter of St Paul's, 1086–1163', *Cambridge Historical Journal*, 10 (1951), pp. 111–32; M. Gibbs, introd. to *Early Charters of the Cathedral Church of St Paul, London*, Camden Third Series, 58 (1939), pp. xviff; Julia Barrow, 'English

reputation for independence and power which was the hallmark of its history in the later middle ages.

To push an investigation of what the varieties of parish organisation signify beyond this point is very difficult; in particular because we are in the dark as to the chronology of much church building. Five churches were dedicated to St Olaf in the city of London. They cannot have been dedicated to him before his death in July 1030; yet even in such a case we cannot be sure that one or more were not older churches rededicated. Nonetheless it would be unduly sceptical to leave nothing but cautions by way of explanation of so striking a phenomenon. It is clear that churches could multiply at any date; thus St Bride's, Fleet Street, and St Alban's, Wood Street, have long been supposed from their dedications to be comparatively early, and the spade has proved them so.[46] But it is also most unlikely that the escalation which produced a church for every three and a half acres came earlier than the eleventh century; and it was probably still in progress in the twelfth. In the case of York, Lincoln and Norwich it is really inconceivable that the medieval pattern of churches is older than the tenth and early eleventh centuries, since this area had to be reconverted in that period. It was reconverted to some purpose, however, and the evidence of surviving buildings and of Domesday Book combines to establish Lincolnshire as one of the parts of England most lavishly provided with parish churches before the Conquest.[47] The hypothesis that all these facts suggest is that in eleventh-century England numerous parish churches sprang up precociously where old institutions had grown weak or disappeared; and that the ecclesiastical

Cathedral Communities and Reform in the Late Tenth and the Eleventh Centuries', in *Anglo-Norman Durham, 1093-1193*, ed. D. Rollason, M. Harvey and M. Prestwich (Woodbridge, 1994), pp. 25-39. There was more continuity at St Paul's than elsewhere; even so the indications clearly are that it took a generation to build up the large Anglo-Norman chapter of the 1090s, revealed by D. E. Greenway in *Fasti*, i.

[46] On the cult of St Olaf, see B. Dickins in *Saga-Book of the Viking Society*, 12 (1940), pp. 53-80. Cf. Brooke and Keir, *London, 800-1216*, pp. 141-42. On the excavations at St Bride's and St Alban's, Wood Street, see W. F. Grimes, *The Excavation of Roman and Mediaeval London* (London, 1968), pp. 182ff, 203ff. No such antiquity has been proved for St Swithun London Stone (ibid., pp. 199ff) which appears to be no older than the twelfth century. For an earlier study of these and similar dedications, see R. E. M. Wheeler, *London and the Saxons* (London, 1935), pp. 100ff; cf. Brooke and Keir, *London*, ch. 6, esp. pp. 137-43.

[47] Cf. W. Page, 'Some Remarks on the Churches of the Domesday Survey', *Archaeologia*, 66 (1915), pp. 61-102, esp. pp. 89, 92, with the indications in H. M. and J. Taylor, *Anglo-Saxon Architecture*, 3 vols (Cambridge, 1965-78). Among the more recent literature on churches in Domesday, see esp. J. Blair, 'The Local Church in Domesday Book and Beyond', in *Domesday Studies*, ed. J. C. Holt (Woodbridge, 1987), pp. 265-78; and J. Blair, 'Secular Minster Churches in Domesday Book', in *Domesday Book: A Reassessment*, ed. P. H. Sawyer (London, 1985), pp. 104-42.

geography and the personalities of the bishops in the eleventh century, and especially in the mid eleventh century (between the death of St Olaf and the death of Harold II), hold part of the key to our enigma. In York and Lincoln and Norwich one is in places where bishops held little sway in the century before the Conquest, where old mother churches had long since disappeared. In York and Lincoln indeed there seems clearly to have been a revival, but at the parochial level mainly – though stirred no doubt by the distant patronage of Oswald and Wulfstan I, and later on by the wealth of Ealdred; or in Lincoln's case by the bishops who sat timorously at Dorchester peeping over the brink of their huge see.[48] In East Anglia the revival was in part monastic; but Bury and St Benet Hulme did not represent the activity of the Bishop of Elmham or Hoxne.[49] The see of East Anglia has this in common with Canterbury and Winchester, that in the mid eleventh century it was in the hands of bishops not noted for their pastoral zeal; first of Stigand, then of his brother Æthelmær, bishops for nearly thirty years, and from 1052 to 1070 Stigand combined Winchester and Canterbury and earned the reputation of serving neither.[50]

The church of St Olaf outside the gates of York was built by Earl Siward, Macbeth's conqueror, in the mid eleventh century;[51] and there are many other cases known in which parish churches were built by lesser and greater lords. It has sometimes been assumed from this, and from the copious evidence that parish churches were later the *Eigenkirchen* of manorial lords, that this was the normal process. That is more than the evidence will tell us, and within the towns it seems to me most unlikely. It is really no more probable that the earl of Leicester or his predecessors had built all the seven or so churches in the city which he claimed to own than that they had been built by the city's legendary founder, King Lear.[52] William Page in his

[48] For a criticism of this argument, see J. Campbell, 'The Church in Anglo-Saxon Towns' (n. 1), pp. 127–28. Cf. Barlow, *The English Church*, pp. 215 ff, 227ff, who gives, however, a somewhat more favourable picture of the diocese of York in particular than that suggested here.

[49] For the early sites of the bishopric of East Anglia see references in Brooke, 'Archbishop Lanfranc, the English Bishops, and the Council of London of 1075', *Studia Gratiana*, 12 (1967), pp. 39–59, at p. 41 n. Their history has now been fundamentally reappraised by J. Campbell, 'The East Anglian Sees before the Conquest', in *Norwich Cathedral*, ed. I. Atherton, E. Fernie, C. Harper-Bill and H. Smith (London, 1996), ch. 1. Bury was first established as an ecclesiastical centre by Bishop Theodred of London in the first half of the tenth century, see D. Whitelock, *Anglo-Saxon Wills* (Cambridge, 1930), pp. 2ff, 99ff; both Bury and Hulme owed their first main endowment as monasteries to King Cnut, see D. Knowles, *Monastic Order in England* (Cambridge, 1940; 2nd edn. 1963), p. 70.

[50] Barlow, *The English Church*, pp. 77ff, gives a very fair judgement on Stigand.

[51] *VCH, York*, p. 397.

[52] On the parish churches of Leicester see *VCH, Leicestershire*, iv, pp. 388–89.

book on London's early history tried to align a number of baronial 'sokes' with later parish boundaries.[53] There is no reason to suppose that any of the sokes within the walls were tidy geographical units, nor do we know the outline of any of them; so that the enterprise is pure conjecture. What we do know is the outline of the parishes in some cases, as Miss Honeybourne has shown, we can be tolerably sure that the outline goes back to the mid eleventh century; though in others it must have shifted much later than that.

I suggested long ago that the churches of London were essentially, or largely, neighbourhood churches, like the churches of Norwich: that their site points not to the lord of a soke as their founder in most cases, but to a group of neighbours expressing a common piety.[54] Dedications to St Olaf and St Clement may suggest that some of these groups consisted of communities from other parts of the world,[55] though this can hardly be proved; but St Olaf at least hints at a link with the missionary world of Scandinavia. Professor R. B. Pugh suggested to me that in some or many cases small town churches grew out of earlier crosses at street corners and crossroads. In at least one case this is remarkably documented; that is the church of St James outside Micklegate at York, which Roger the priest (apparently of the early twelfth century) built where the cross had stood.[56] Their subsequent poverty, and the informality of their ownership, naturally followed if they represented the passing mood of piety of a group of neighbours; though the evidence from Norwich shows that the communities which built such churches could be kept in being for some generations; and in those towns which proliferated churches the proliferation continued into the twelfth and thirteenth centuries, suggesting a continuing interest in the movement. Such an interest on the Continent was in a number of cases enshrined in the practice of electing a parish priest. This practice can clearly be traced in many different parts of Europe in the early middle ages, as has been shown by Professor Kurze in his study of this obscure practice.[57] But he has also shown that evidence of it is rare in the twelfth and thirteenth centuries,

[53] *London: Its Origin and Early Development* (London, 1923), ch. 4, and pp. 159ff. For an attempt to relate parishes and wards, etc. in London, see J. Haslam, 'Parishes, Churches, Wards and Gates in Eastern London', in *Minsters and Parish Churches*, ed. J. Blair, pp. 35–43.

[54] Brooke, *Time the Archsatirist* (London, 1968), pp. 20ff. For continental work on churches built by groups of merchants, see esp. P. Johansen, 'Die Kaufmannskirche im Ostseegebiet' (n. 12); cf. also Kurze, *Pfarrerwahlen im Mittelalter* (n. 8), pp. 308–9.

[55] See below, p. 105 n. 37.

[56] *Regesta regum Anglo-Normannorum*, iii, ed. H. A. Cronne and R. H. C. Davis (Oxford, 1968), no. 987.

[57] D. Kurze, *Pfarrerwahlen im Mittelalter*.

and that most of the documented instances from the late middle ages reflect a new movement towards popular participation in certain selected areas of Christendom. There is no decisive English evidence of parochial elections, but it is reasonable to suppose that it may well have been the practice in Norwich, and in other places where communal interest in neighbourhood churches survived.

All the evidence suggests that between priest and people in these tiny parishes there was an intimacy quite unusual in medieval pastoral relations. The Patarini in eleventh-century Milan attacked the Milanese clergy for secular vices – marriage and simony in particular; but the gravamen of their charges was that these folk were separated by their sins from the people at large.[58] In the long run the papal reform, where it succeeded most, separated clergy and people more than ever before, for it laid emphasis before all else on the view that layman and clerk, especially layman and priest, were clean different things. The renaissance of heresy in Milan two generations later has often been attributed to the failure of the Patarini: it could equally well be attributed to their success. If one judges that the separation of clergy and people was one of the most powerful factors in making some parts of Europe fertile soil for heresy in the twelfth century, then one may reckon the intimacy of clergy and people in English towns part of the explanation for the failure of heresy to take root in England in that period.[59] Part of the explanation: for we have here in view a complex phenomenon singularly ill documented. Nor do I wish to imply that ecclesiastical reform in the eleventh and twelfth centuries was in any simple sense damaging to pastoral success. It would be an absurd paradox to portray the clergy of the *Eigenkirchen* as models, the bishops and clergy of the new world as careless of lay concerns and lay opinion. There is a formidable body of evidence to the contrary, and the thirteenth-century English bishops who instructed their clergy to instruct their people to provide baby-sitters when they went out in the evening were not wholly out of touch with the facts of secular life among married folk.[60]

The strength and weakness of the rank and file of the parish clergy in English towns is strikingly revealed in the document known as the *Law of*

[58] C. Violante, *La Pataria milanese e la riforma ecclesiastica*, i (Rome, 1955); idem, 'I laici nel movimento patarino', *Mendola*, 3, pp. 597–697; H. E. J. Cowdrey, 'The Papacy, the Patarenes and the Church of Milan', *Transactions of the Royal Historical Society*, 5th series, 18 (1968), pp. 25–48.

[59] For the general problem see Brooke, *Medieval Church and Society*, ch. 7; many aperçus on this problem are to be found in *Mendola*, 3.

[60] See the prolific synodal statutes in *Councils and Synods*, ii, ed. F. M. Powicke and C. R. Cheney (Oxford, 1964) esp. pt i, pp. 70, 444 and index, *s. v.* Children: safety measures for.

the Northumbrian Priests.[61] It presupposes that a group of priests of a fair size have been banded together into a sort of guild under the direction of the archbishop, and it has many clauses which emphasise the need for discipline and obedience to the archbishop. It is no coincidence that it survives in a collection linked with the most eminent reforming bishop of the early eleventh century, Wulfstan I of Worcester and York; and it seems probable that it represents an attempt by Wulfstan at the end of his life to instil discipline into the clergy of York. Simony and the sale of churches is forbidden, so is bigamy; though it is presumed that a priest will have one 'woman'.[62] That they are parish clergy with baptismal rights seems presumed, a surprising concession from Wulfstan. The list of offences reflects a lively group of clergy given to secular pleasures, such as brawling, drunkenness, and singing in taverns. No doubt it is a mistake to assume that every sin denounced by a medieval reformer was common practice; but parchment was expensive, Wulfstan in earnest and the list hardly likely to have been drawn up by haphazard.

There is no evidence of much of what constitutes pastoral work today, but what the document portrays is a lively group of clergy mingling with the crowd; with a sense of common purpose among themselves, but not separated from the folk among whom they worked by a different mode of life or excessive education. This intimacy with the flock is emphasised by the design of parish churches in pre-conquest and early Norman times. The characteristic little box with a shallow apse, small in a country church, often tiny in a town church, left no space for the celebrant to be separate from the people.[63] It is no coincidence that in the later twelfth and thirteenth centuries many chancels were rebuilt to allow more space; and in the fourteenth and fifteenth centuries these chancels became almost impenetrable boxes; the priests, men living in another world.[64] The open church of Norman times had as its true successor not the divided parish church of the late middle ages but the friars' churches. The friars devised their own architecture in the second generation of their existence, and its sources were complex.[65] Although the Franciscans have never forgotten that they started

[61] Ed. D. Whitelock in *Councils and Synods*, i, ed. Whitelock et al. (Oxford, 1981), i, 1, pp. 449–68. See above pp. 43–44.

[62] *c.* 35, ed. Whitelock, *Councils and Synods*, i, 1, p. 459 (cf. ibid. n. 3).

[63] See A. W. Clapham, *English Romanesque Architecture after the Conquest* (Oxford, 1934), ch. 6 and fig. 33; H. M. and J. Taylor, *Anglo-Saxon Architecture*, 3 vols (Cambridge, 1965–78); Eric Fernie, *The Architecture of the Anglo-Saxons* (London, 1983).

[64] Cf. Brooke, *Medieval Church and Society*, ch. 8.

[65] Cf. esp. G. Meersseman, 'L'architecture dominicaine en XIIIe siècle, législation et pratique', *Archivum fratrum praedicatorum*, 16 (1946), pp. 136–90; and (for England) A. R. Martin, *Franciscan Architecture in England*, British Society of Franciscan Studies (1937).

in the chapel of the Portiuncula, which is the tiniest of boxes, the characteristic hall-church – the large open space designed to suit the preacher
and his audience rather than the celebration of the sacraments – was
essentially a practical, functional solution to the clear needs of the friars
as their work developed; and especially to their needs in northern countries
whose climate is not always suited to preaching out of doors.

There is clearly a link between the forgotten parish clergy of the eleventh-
and twelfth-century towns and the friars. The parish clergy were secular
men, often no doubt with secular vices; they were worker priests, with the
virtues and vices of their kind. They were readily accepted by their flocks
as men of like passions, like St Francis's lay brothers; but the passions were
so like, the assimilation sometimes so complete, that it might be wondered
who was giving an example to whom. A grave misfortune overtook them
in the papal reform; its insistence on celibacy, on the superiority of the
ascetic, monastic, regular life, made the rank and file parish clergy into
second-class citizens.

It is easy to breed misunderstanding with a topic of this character. I am
not delivering an attack on the papal reform. The abuses the reformers
denounced were in many cases genuine abuses; the assimilation they
abhorred often involved standards reminiscent of the whisky priest in
Graham Greene's *The Power and the Glory*. The reformers thought they
had found another way to convert the people, by setting up communities
among them of ascetic clergy with pastoral responsibility. I do not wish
now to enter discussion of the vexed question how much pastoral work
monks and canons regularly undertook in this period.[66] In some cases clearly
much; and one has only to read the *Life of St Wulfstan* or some of the

---

[66] See M. Chibnall's statement of the literature and the issues in 'Monks and Pastoral Work:
A Problem in Anglo-Norman History', *Journal of Ecclesiastical History*, 18 (1967), pp. 165–72,
in which she charitably and reasonably takes me to task for some sentences in *GF*, p. 85 and
n., which may have given a misleading impression of the state of discussion of the topic.
Among other points, she urges (p. 166) that insufficient attention has been paid in the recent
literature to the distinction between temporal rights over churches and spiritual rights, and
between serving the altar and serving the parish; this is a fair point, but it must be clearly
understood that many folk failed to see the first distinction in the late eleventh and early
twelfth centuries, and that the nature of 'parish work' in this period is exceedingly obscure.
Dr Chibnall's article contains valuable evidence on several of the topics discussed here,
especially on the definition of a parish. That it was widely assumed that monks engaged in
pastoral work in some sense is presupposed in many of the documents discussed in Giles
Constable, *Monastic Tithes* (Cambridge, 1964); but see his own cautious appraisal of the
evidence at pp. 145–47 – and in Constable, 'Monasteries, Rural Churches and the *Cura
Animarum* in the Early Middle Ages', *Settimane di studio del centro italiano di studi sull'alto
medioevo*, 28 (1982 for 1980), pp. 349–95, esp. pp. 384–89.

miracle stories of the period to know that a saintly monk and a monastic community could form a pastoral centre of an effective kind. But there was certainly no 'policy' of monastic participation, and council after council of the early twelfth century denounced the practice; there is a curious tension between tithe regulations which presume that monks engage in pastoral work and conciliar decrees which forbid them to do so.[67] This is one of the ways in which, in practice, pastoral work was frustrated by the activities of twelfth-century reformers. Nonetheless, it would be quite false to suppose that the missionary work of the clergy in the streets of Worcester or Cirencester or Gloucester, dominated by great religious communities, was necessarily less effective than in London or Norwich or Lincoln. But it was different, and these towns had opportunities denied to the others.

The parish church in London was a tiny centre for a small community; a local cult centre. St Paul might preside on his hill in the west end of the city, as Thor and Othen presided in the Scandinavian Olympus; but the centre of the religious world for ordinary folk was the small relic, the small stone, the small cross, and the little church which they had built. Into their religion we can hardly penetrate; but certain things we can state with confidence. To build a hundred churches in a space no larger than 350 acres presupposes a degree of sustained devotion unusual in the history of the church – devotion no doubt to other things as well as to God; for St Olaf may represent the loyalties of an alien community and a parish pump, even a status symbol of a modest kind; and as a missionary, Olaf himself had represented the view that conversion should be by force and fraud, if other methods failed. But the central interest, as I see it, of this escalation of churches is that it shows a popular religious movement in its natural setting – it shows what happened if the folk were left to develop their cultus according to their own devices – and the power in a broad sense of a spontaneous missionary endeavour. In the thirteenth century St Francis tried in a modified way to revive the idea of conversion by infiltration and example, and his original inspiration suffered the same fate as the humble, obscure but undoubtedly effective work of the parish clergy of the eleventh and twelfth centuries.[68]

---

[67] See Constable, *Monastic Tithes*, ch. 2, pp. 136ff (esp. p. 144), 165ff.

[68] By the kindness of Professors J. Kloczowski and E. Wisniowski I am able to add references to a study of parish structure in Poland, which could help students of this subject to spread this kind of parochial investigation more widely in a fruitful way: E. Wisniowski, 'Rozwój organizacji parafialnej w Polsce do czasów Reformacji' (Development of Parochial Structures in Poland to the Reformation), in: *Kosciól w Polsci i (= Eglise en Pologne*, ed. J. Kloczowski) (Kraków, 1968), pp. 237–372, esp. pp. 239ff.

5

The Medieval Town as an Ecclesiastical Centre

My theme is the mingling of literary, archaeological and topographical evidence in the study of the church and churches in medieval urban topography. The chief evidence is the physical witness of churches and other buildings, and the major elements are cathedrals, baptisteries, monastic churches and complexes, including hospitals, and parishes and parish churches. Although by the twelfth century there was considerable legal uniformity, there was considerable variety in other ways. The most obvious contrast is between north and south, with cathedral and baptistery in most Italian cities, few baptisteries but more numerous and complex parishes in the north. I look briefly at a number of examples: St Albans and Battle, monastic towns; Old and New Sarum, cathedral cities in an old hill fort and a new planned town; Zürich and Krakow, fine examples of continental cities, with greater churches and less, and friars' churches, grouped in a manner of special interest. Poitiers, where elements of palaeo-Christian organization survived, marks a transition to the south, where we can view the relation of cathedral and town hall in Todi and Siena; and, especially in Pisa, where we see civic pride and religious sentiment and practice in the group deliberately set in the corner of the city wall with the baptistery, cathedral and campanile as its main elements. Finally, beside Pisa, I set London as the most striking contrast: in Pisa parishes came late and slowly, in London they multiplied as nowhere else. My purpose is to sketch these varieties and consider their historical meaning: here is a large field for comparative study which could be made much larger by further topographical and archaeological research.

In recent years the study of medieval urban topography has taken massive strides; yet it is still in its infancy, and no part of it seems more ready for rapid advance than the place of the church and of churches within it. For the place of the churches in early medieval cities has been in the past relatively neglected, and the main reason for this seems to be that students of urban origins have traditionally been social and economic historians – and that in the past economic historians, archaeologists and ecclesiastical historians tended to work apart and rarely meet. Now all this has changed; and it was high time, for a great part of our written evidence for early towns is ecclesiastical, and the archaeologists have become rapidly and increasingly aware how vital churches are to them, if only because they provide so high a proportion of the solid material still available to the investigator. Significant, too, for the changing attitude among historians, was the passage in the 1974 edition of Cinzio Violante's *La società milanese nell'età precomunale*, in which one of the most eminent of Italian medievalists describes how from the study of secular institutions and structures of the early middle ages he has passed to a deeper interest in the history of the church, which provides the bulk of the evidence.[1]

If we seek to combine literary and archaeological evidence to elucidate urban history and topography, the chief document is the physical witness of church buildings. Let me cite two examples. The theory of Carl Stephenson about English urban origins was challenged in its application to Cambridge in a paper by Helen Cam.[2] After deploying a wide range of evidence, documentary, archaeological and topographical, she triumphantly observed that he had never seen the tower of St Benet's church – a splendid Anglo-Saxon fragment in a part of the town where, according to his theory, no Saxon settlement ought to have been. My second example is the wall and moat which a bishop of Bath and Wells built round his palace at Wells in the mid fourteenth century.[3] It was ostensibly a defensive measure against the militant burghers of his little city. However, neither the thin walls slit

First published in *European Towns: their Archaeology and Early History*, ed. M. W. Barley (Council for British Archaeology, London, 1977), pp. 459–74.

[1] C. Violante, *La società milanese nell'età precomunale* (2nd edn, Rome-Bari, 1974). For the wider setting of this study see above ch. 4 and references, and especially R. Morris, *Churches in the Landscape* (London, 1989), ch. 5.

This essay was written for a CBA Conference on European towns, and was a by-product of my work on medieval London with the Reverend Gillian Keir, issuing in Brooke and Keir, *London, 800–1216: The Shaping of a City* (London, 1975) – see esp. ch. 6. I was much indebted to Gillian Keir, and also to Paul Hodges, who worked extensively on parish church dedications in the 1970s. My work owed much to the inspiration of Martin Biddle and Derek Keene in Winchester and London, and of Donald Bullough, Jerzy Kloczowski, Alexander Murray and Cinzio Violante. Some aspects of the theme have been developed in much greater detail by C. Brühl, *Palatium und Civitas*, 2 vols (Cologne-Vienna, 1973–90); and valuable studies are gathered in *Topografia urbana e vita cittadina sull'alto medioevo in occidente, Settimane di studio del centro italiano di studi sull'alto medioevo*, 21 (Spoleto, 1974). Of the very large literature on individual cities a few are noted below: see especially Derek Keene, *Survey of Medieval Winchester, Winchester Studies*, ii, 2 vols (Oxford, 1985).

[2] Helen M. Cam, 'The Origin of the Borough of Cambridge', in Cam, *Liberties and Communities in Medieval England* (London, 1944), pp. 1–18.

[3] D. Knowles and J. K. S. St Joseph, *Monastic Sites from the Air* (Cambridge, 1952), pp. 272–73.

by arrow-holes shaped like crosses – suited to a bishop's home – nor the shallow, beautiful moat, look truly defensive; both are at their most impressive when they face the canons and the close. Thus symbolically the bishop set himself off from both the other corporations of a city which, of all English cities, tells us its ecclesiastical history most plainly on its face.

I wish to deploy now some elements in a comparative study, which will, I hope, illustrate the rich variety of patterns of urban ecclesiastical geography and the interest of the subject. The major elements in our enquiry are four: the cathedral, the baptistery, the monastic church and complex (and its satellite, the hospital) and the parish. Just to enumerate that list reminds us of one of the fundamental contrasts in Christian Europe in the middle ages, that between north and south. In Italy every city of consequence had a cathedral; and many of the more ambitious had two.[4] Sometimes the two were a so-called summer and winter cathedral. In a number of cases the cathedral had first been built outside the walls of a still largely pagan city, and a new cathedral later built within, when the pagans fled, the city decayed and there was plenty of available, Christian space. This however is a peremptory and superficial statement of a complex story; for in Milan the present enormous duomo of the fourteenth and fifteenth centuries, the best documented of all medieval cathedrals, covers the space formerly occupied by no less than two adjacent cathedrals and two baptisteries, in one of which St Augustine was christened.[5] The baptisteries represent the other contrast between north and south. There are, needless to say, many northern cities which contain cathedrals, but there are as many which have never done so, owing to the much larger extent of northern European sees; in central Europe, especially in Poland and Hungary, cathedral cities are very widely separated.[6] There are even a few northern cities, like Poitiers, with baptisteries; but this common feature of a palaeo-Christian complex is rarely found outside the Mediterranean world in the later middle ages, and we shall presently inspect other reasons why it is very significant that Poitiers

[4] C. Violante and C. D. Fonseca, 'Ubicazione e dedicazione delle cattedrali dalle origini al periodo romanico nelle città dell'Italia centro-settentrionale', in *Il romanico Pistoiense: atti del primo convegno internazionale di studi medioevali di storia e d'arte* (Pistoia, 1964), pp. 303–46; D. A. Bullough, 'Urban Change in Early Medieval Italy: The Example of Pavia', *Papers of the British School at Rome*, 34 (1966), pp. 82–130.

[5] Violante and Fonseca, 'Ubicazione e dedicazione', pp. 327–28; E. Cattaneo, 'Il battistero in Italia dopo il mille', *Miscellanea Gilles Gerard Mersseman = Italia sacra*, 15–16, i (Padua, 1970), pp. 171–95, at p. 175.

[6] J. Kloczowski, 'La province ecclésiastique de Pologne et ses évêques', in *Mendola*, 5, pp. 437–44.

rather than, say, Bourges or Paris should retain its baptistery.[7] In a remarkable study of Italian baptisteries after the year 1000, over forty city
baptisteries are noted in a provisional list of those known to have been
rebuilt or extensively restored in the mid or late middle ages.[8] The possibilities of this subject can only be revealed by studying a number of examples;
and I propose to start with the comparatively simple and progress to the
most complex, so that at the end we may confront an exceptionally complex
city of the north (London) with a clear example of the points of similarity
and difference in the south (Pisa). The subject will not be exhausted: this
I can establish simply by observing that the two most spectacular cities of
early medieval Europe I shall omit altogether, since Rome was *sui generis*
and would demand a volume, or a library, on its own; and Cordova was,
and is, dominated by a mosque.[9]

Let us start with simple examples. So far as is known, no English city of
the middle ages save Old Sarum derived from a prehistoric hill-fort;[10] we
have nothing comparable to the Etruscan and Umbrian cities still so
numerous in central Italy. However we have a few *de facto* built on hill-tops.
Such is St Albans, because it grew up round the abbey, which itself was on
the site (actual or supposed) of Alban's martyrdom; and so the present
town has a situation much less convenient than Roman Verulamium below
it by the riverside.[11] Similarly romantic is the site of Battle, which also grew
up round an abbey, and the abbey was designed – as we are told, and must
believe, for no other explanation will serve for such an awkward site – so
that the high altar lay on the spot where King Harold fell.[12] In both cases
we have the situation, not uncommon in northern Europe, of a town
growing up round a substantial monastic community.[13] Old Sarum was the
exception to prove the rule: the moneyers of Wilton looked for a better
defended site about the year 1000, and so for a time the dry and drafty hill
fort became the centre of a town. In Norman times the twin symbols of

[7] D. Claude, *Topographie und Verfassung der Städte Bourges und Poitiers bis in das 11.
Jahrhundert* (Lübeck-Hamburg, 1960).

[8] Cattaneo, 'Il battistero in Italia'.

[9] E. Lévi-Provençal, *Histoire de l'Espagne musulmane,* iii (Paris, 1967), ch. 13.

[10] P. A. Rahtz and J. W. G. Musty, 'Excavations at Old Sarum, 1957', *Wiltshire Archaeological
and Natural History Magazine,* 57 (1958–60), pp. 353–70; M. Beresford and J. K. S. St Joseph,
Medieval England: An Aerial Survey (2nd edn, Cambridge, 1979), pp. 202–4.

[11] W. Levison, 'St Alban and St Albans', *Antiquity,* 15 (1941), pp. 337–59; S. S. Frere, *Britannia*
(London, 1967), p. 332. We await the full publication of the excavations and studies of Martin
Biddle and Birthe Kjølbye-Biddle.

[12] *The Chronicle of Battle Abbey,* ed. and trans. E. Searle, OMT (Oxford, 1980), pp. 36–37,
42–45.

[13] M. D. Lobel, *The Borough of Bury St Edmunds* (Oxford, 1935).

Norman domination – castle and cathedral; the castle to reveal the force of the Normans, the cathedral God's blessing on that force – rose on the hill top, and the townsfolk lived huddled outside the gates. In the early thirteenth century the cathedral clergy and the bishop laid out the most ecclesiastical of towns by the river side at the hill's foot, with the best space allotted to cathedral and close, and beyond the close they allowed space for a tight and tidy grid of streets, with every necessary amenity, especially a market-place and some defences and churches old and new.

Although the situations are markedly different, there is some analogy between the early history of Sarum and the early history of Krakow, founded at the other end of western Christendom about the same time. The original core is on the small hill of the Wawel, which came to house both the royal palace of the first capital of Poland and the cathedral; it was essentially a fortified castle in which the leaders of church and state lived side by side. In later centuries a narrow corridor came to link the foot of the Wawel with the ample planned city which was laid out beyond the market-place. Thus Krakow became a classic example of the northern European model of a city: *castrum* and *burgus*. To this day the castle or palace dominates the cathedral; but great Dominican and Franciscan preaching churches dominate the old market-place, giving food for thought.

Zürich is another northern city in which religion, politics and commerce have been combined in unexpected ways.[14] The centre of the city lies on the Lindenhof, where in the late middle ages the citizens levelled the Zähringen castle which had replaced a modest Roman fort, and planted the lime trees whose children still remind us that no fortress lords it over the people of Zürich. If we look across the River Limatt, whose exit from the Zürichsee has given Zürich its commercial importance, to the Lindenhof, we see not far away what is evidently enough the central parish church, the church of St Peter, and over to the left the Fraumünster and the Grossmünster across the river. The Grossmünster marks the site of the invention of St Felix and St Regula, mythical Roman martyrs whose relics were discovered on this spot, and round whom grew up the great Carolingian mixed house of secular canons and religious nuns; in the twelfth century, to mark the separation of the sexes and the segregation of women, the nuns were moved across the river into a marsh. The Peterkirche is largely in eighteenth-century dress and the Fraumünster mainly gothic; the Grossmünster still represents the first great age of Zürich's prosperity, the twelfth century, and although

[14] Brooke and Keir, *London, 800–1216* (n. 1), pp. 73–5; K. Dändliker, *Geschichte der Stadt und des Kantons Zürich*, i (Zürich, 1908); A. Largiadèr, *Geschichte von Stadt und Landschaft Zürich*, 2 vols (Zürich, 1945); E. Egloff, *Der Standort des Monasteriums Ludwigs des Deutschen in Zürich* (Zürich, 1949).

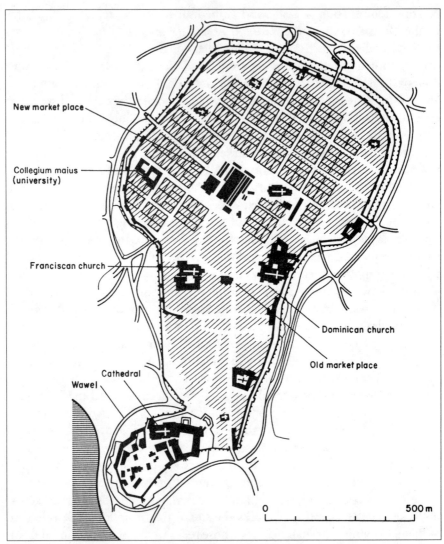

New market place

Collegium maius
(university)

Franciscan church

Dominican church

Old market place

Cathedral
Wawel

0   500 m

1. Plan of Krakow, showing at the base, the hill of Wawel, palace, castle and cathedral;
then the first expansion in the twelfth–thirteenth centuries, with the old market place
and the friars' churches, and finally the new planned town of 1257, with its regular
plots and the new market place carved out of its centre.

the Grossmünster is very much what it became in the sixteenth century,
Zwingli's headquarters, the fine Romanesque sculptures have somehow survived his iconoclasm. But the site of all three reflects earlier passages of history
than their present costume; and, when Zürich became a walled city in the
central middle ages, all three were included within it.

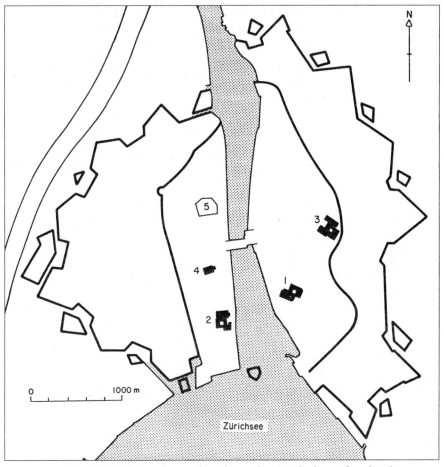

2. Plan of Zürich, based on a plan of 1705, showing the lines of medieval
and post-medieval defences.
1. Grossmünster; 2. Fraumünster; 3. Franciscan convent; 4. St Peter's; 5. Lindenhof.

The final stage in the growth of medieval ecclesiastical Zürich came with the arrival of the friars. The friars seem to have made three contributions to medieval cities: to preaching, to plumbing and to defence. The relation between these is not at first quite obvious, and has never been fully worked out. The friars might have wished to live and preach among the poorest and most neglected section of the community, and Alexander Murray's study of the site of the early Franciscan and Dominican convents in six Italian cities suggests just this – they are usually placed in the new faubourgs, among folk not served by the old cathedral or mother church of the city.[15] However this can hardly have been the only consideration, for the friars were wholly dependent on their patrons and benefactors for their sites and resources. Medieval cities were not segregated into rich suburbs and slums as were those of the nineteenth century; yet there were doubtless fashionable and unfashionable quarters, and the great Florentine churches, for instance, were evidently placed where the Bardi, the Pazzi and their like could pay their respects and their dues to holy poverty. The churches of the friars represent in a striking way the relation between the religious, who had a very clear notion of their own role and function and showed from an early time advanced architectural notions, and the patrons on whom they entirely depended for funds. The friars, in spite of Francis's own emphasis on extreme simplicity and austerity in their buildings, seem to have inherited the Cistercian interest in combining asceticism with good plumbing and decent efficient building. The difference was that the friars built within the walls of towns and the Franciscans in particular were not the owners of their churches; in theory these remained the property of their founders and benefactors, or some local 'friends' or of the Holy See.[16] They came to be in practice, in a quite special sense, municipal buildings. This meant that their builders naturally encouraged and fostered their contribution to water supply and drainage, and even to defence.

In Zürich, as in other cities of what grew to be the Swiss confederation – and very likely elsewhere in northern Europe – it was common practice to site the friars' convents, and especially the Franciscans, immediately inside the city wall.[17] The convent was the property of the municipality (in effect, even if sometimes in theory of the papacy); municipal authorities had ready access in time of need, and obedient, cooperative agents at all times who could be relied on not to build the swarm of tenements or hovels which so easily obscured any medieval urban defensive work. It is to us a strange alliance, but perfectly intelligible.

My last example before we take the experience we have culled to confront the contrasting cities of north and south is Poitiers, where there is an ancient pattern somehow fossilised.[18] The baptistery is a reminder that in Poitiers we are looking at a plan and a structure which has grown up over many hundreds of years and so represents a palimpsest of several epochs. The two fundamental centres are far apart: the cathedral and baptistery in the heart

---

[15] A. Murray, 'Piety and Impiety in Thirteenth-Century Italy', *Studies in Church History*, 8 (1972), pp. 83–106.

[16] M. D. Lambert, *Franciscan Poverty* (London, 1961), esp. chs 2, 3 and 6.

[17] B. E. J. Stüdeli, *Minoritenniederlassungen und Mittelalterliche Stadt*, Franziskanische Forschungen, 21 (Werl/Westfalen, 1969).

[18] Claude, *Topographie und Verfassung* (n. 7).

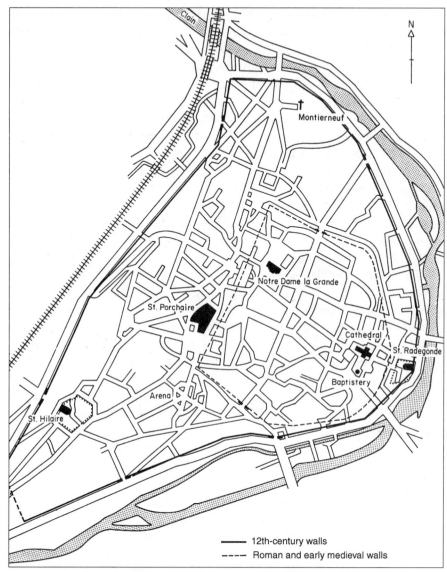

3. Plan of medieval Poitiers, to show the pattern of large churches simplified.
The broken line shows the enceinte of Roman and early-medieval times;
the continuous line shows the new walls of the mid to late twelfth century.

of the old city, the shrine and abbey church of Saint-Hilaire without the
ancient walls. In due course other great churches, collegiate and monastic,
grew up elsewhere in the town, and of these Saint-Porchaire came to be the
most substantial. Every early medieval city had numerous small churches,

oratories and chapels as well as the greater basilicas; in northern Europe in the central middle ages these developed into, or were replaced by, parish churches. Usually there were such vicissitudes in the process that any early pattern was quite destroyed. Thus the parish map of Paris owed more to the centuries of its rapid growth, the twelfth and thirteenth, than to the millennium which preceded them;[19] and the parish boundaries were reorganised by conscious acts of power by Bishop Maurice de Sully, in the late twelfth century, and his successors. The pattern of small churches in Poitiers, in contrast, reflects a much earlier fashion, that for planting oratories round a major centre: Poitiers' churches consist of a series of major stars with satellites about them, and this pattern, though often modified, was never obliterated.

In Rome herself we might see both the characteristics of Poitiers, the great basilicas beset with oratories, and of Paris, a large network of parishes – though here the product of the fourth and not of the twelfth century;[20] but Rome is quite unlike every other Italian city. For although small churches were everywhere built, sometimes in great numbers, they very rarely acquired parochial status. Italy in the central middle ages witnessed the development of two kinds of parishes: the city parish with its centre in the cathedral; and the large country parish or *pieve*.[21] In the late middle ages new parishes were established in the cities, but the idea that the cathedral was the worshipping centre of the whole civic community, and the baptistery attached to it the place where the whole community might be baptised, lasted well into modern times; hence a curious paradox. Italian civic liberty was commonly won, at the latter end, at the expense of the bishop, and the communes were in a sense by definition anticlerical. Yet the cathedral was as much a symbol of civic pride and the baptistery of civic unity as the town hall.[22]

Sometimes this paradox was expressed by permitting cathedral and town hall or halls to smile at one another across the main square of the city; of this Todi is a classic example, for here, in a comparatively modest place, we find the cathedral and three town halls of the late twelfth and thirteenth centuries. Sometimes cathedral and town halls turn their backs on one another, as in Florence and Siena; and at Siena the good citizens of the late

---

[19] A. Friedmann, *Paris, ses rues, ses paroisses du moyen âge à la Revolution* (Paris, 1959).

[20] F. Van der Meer and C. Mohrmann, ed., *Atlas of the Early Christian Church* (London-Amsterdam, 1958), maps 27–29.

[21] C. Boyd, *Tithes and Parishes in Medieval Italy* (Ithaca, 1952).

[22] F. Reggiori, 'Aspetti urbanistici ed architettonici della civiltà comunale', in *I problemi della civiltà comunale*, ed. C. D. Fonseca (Bergamo, 1971), pp. 97–110; Violante and Fonseca, 'Ubicazione e dedicazione' (n. 4).

thirteenth and early fourteenth centuries, while with one hand completing and adorning their lavish duomo at infinite cost – starting indeed a large extension which they never completed – at the same time ensured that the town hall and its tower should dominate what is still one of the most ravishing skylines in Europe.[23] Perhaps it is in Pisa that the Italian civic ideal is most perfectly embalmed;[24] for here the substantial corner of the city, set aside as a religious memorial to the victory over a Muslim fleet in the 1060s which began the great period of Pisan history, is such a memorial still. The new cathedral was laid out and a new baptistery built, and both enshrine elements of design and ornament from every generation down to the age of Nicola and Giovanni Pisano – and some later; and here in the late twelfth century the *torre pendente*, the leaning tower, began to grow and to bend. Later a cloister was added, deliberately commemorative in function; and within the city, on the edge of this divine complex, more practical buildings like hospitals were planted.

In the course of the eleventh and twelfth centuries the pattern of parochial organisation became fixed and its legal status defined. No doubt the roots lay well back in the fourth century; and every epoch since has witnessed changes in the nature and structure of parochial life and organisation. On present evidence the eleventh and twelfth were the most creative. A measure of uniformity was laid on the parishes in the twelfth century by the developing canon law. A parish in its full sense was a worshipping community, whose members gathered in the parish church on Sundays and great festival days, and sometimes more often, who brought their children to be baptised in the church's font and their dead to be buried in its graveyard; to its priest they paid their tithes. The pattern of parish churches and parish boundaries, where it can be traced, has an exceptional interest for the urban historian, since it reveals traces of sentiment and aspiration, settlement and wealth, in a quite unusual way.

No effort was ever made to give any semblance of uniformity to the pattern of city parishes such as the new canon law gave to their legal status. In Italy, where civic pride was far advanced and diocese and city closely identified, the cathedral commonly remained the only or the chief parish centre, at least until the twelfth century. Every variety of number and design can be found in northern Europe; but the contrast is more complete in a group of English cities, where parishes were very numerous. In York there came to be nearly forty by 1200, in Lincoln and Winchester nearly fifty; in

[23] F. Schevill, *Siena: The Story of a Mediaeval Commune* (New York, 1909).

[24] E. Tolaini, *Forma Pisarum* (Pisa, 1967); G. Volpe, *Studi sulle istituzioni comunali a Pisa*, revised edition with introduction by C. Violante (Pisa, 1970).

London nearly one hundred within the walls, that is, roughly a parish to every 3.5 acres.[25]

London is in every way remarkable, above all for the quality of the evidence it provides us. Of the intra-mural churches five were excavated in the mid twentieth century, and Grimes's reports on some of these are of exceptional interest, needless to say; since then the tale has been increased by the City of London Archaeological Unit.[26] We have maps of the parish boundaries which seem for the most part to go back to the twelfth century, some perhaps even further. In most other English towns the number of parishes fluctuated, rising until about 1200, then falling, especially in the fourteenth and fifteenth centuries; the result is that we know little of the earliest boundaries. Between 1200 and 1907 there were only relatively minor changes in the city of London; and although much research will have to be done on late medieval documents before we can be sure precisely how many slight changes of boundary may have occurred, it is sufficiently clear as a general proposition that the boundaries sketched in Ogilby's map of c. 1676 and with greater precision in the Ordnance Survey map of 1878 are those of 1200.[27] This is the more surprising since by the time Ogilby's map was drawn well over a third of the churches had disappeared. The parish churches of London have a special interest because of the unique quality of their witness, which Gillian Keir and I tried years ago to interpret.[28] There is much else that we could say about London's ecclesiastical geography: the history of its religious houses has many striking features, and the refoundation of Westminster Abbey by Edward the Confessor in the mid eleventh century was a vital part of the division of London between the city and Westminster so crucial for the later history of London and the

---

[25] Above, ch. 4, esp. pp. 75, 82–83, 89; Keene, *Survey of Medieval Winchester*, (n. 1), i, pp. 106–36; *Victoria County History, City of York*, pp. 365ff; J. W. F. Hill, *Medieval Lincoln* (Cambridge, 1948), pp. 147ff.

[26] W. F. Grimes, *The Excavation of Roman and Mediaeval London* (London, 1968). For more recent excavations, see J. Schofield and T. Dyson, *Archaeology of the City of London* (London, 1981), esp. p. 39 (St Nicholas Shambles) and Reports of the City of London Department of Urban Archaeology.

[27] Brooke and Keir, *London, 800–1216*, pp. 123ff. This has been modified by the studies of Derek Keene and his colleagues in London; but the history of the parish boundaries cannot be rewritten in detail until the surveys undertaken by Keene's Centre of Metropolitan Studies are much more advanced. For an overview of recent research, see the impressive general account by Derek Keene, 'London in the Early Middle Ages, 600–1300', *London Journal*, 20 (1995), pp. 9–21.

[28] Brooke and Keir, *London*, ch. 6; material supplied by G. Keir for the gazetteer by M. Carlin and V. Belcher in *The British Atlas of Historic Towns*, iii, *The City of London from Prehistoric Times to c. 1520*, ed. M. D. Lobel (Oxford, 1989): see esp. pp. 64, 77, 85–92.

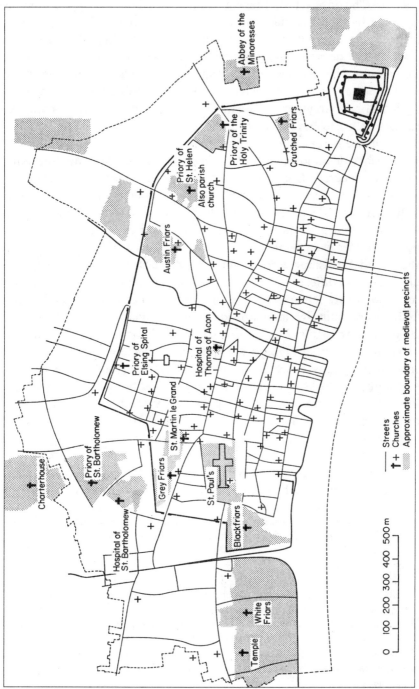

4. Medieval London: plan of the city of London showing the conventual and parish churches; the unnamed churches were parish churches.

Streets
Churches
Approximate boundary of medieval precincts

0   100 200 300 400 500 m

Abbey of the Minoresses

Priory of St. Helen
Also parish church

Priory of the Holy Trinity

Crutched Friars

Austin Friars

Priory of Elsing Spital

St. Martin le Grand

Hospital of Thomas of Acon

Priory of St. Bartholomew

Charterhouse

Hospital of St. Bartholomew

Grey Friars

St. Paul's

Blackfriars

White Friars

Temple

kingdom.[29] The interest of the comparative method in such studies is brought out by the Blackfriars and the Greyfriars, whose splendid precincts and churches lay just within the walls more or less replacing earlier Norman castles – that is on sites strongly reminiscent of Zürich, Bern and Luzern, though no one I believe has hitherto suggested a similar explanation in the case of London to those in the Swiss cities. Perhaps a more subtle explanation is needed, for if Greyfriars in early days was primarily a civic complex, Blackfriars seems to have formed not a civic but a royal enclave.[30]

Above all, the comparative method underlines the peculiarity of the tiny urban parishes of London and other English cities; there is nothing quite like them elsewhere.[31] It is evident enough that these are private churches in origin; and the excavations of St Mary's Tanner Street at Winchester actually revealed a stage in which the church door only opened into a private house.[32] It also showed, more than any of those in London, how many vicissitudes even a modest church with a tiny parish passed through as shape and furnishing were adapted to the tastes and sentiments and religious needs of different generations. But 'private church' is an ambiguous phrase, and we are left mainly to conjecture whether most of the London churches were built by landlords or single magnates, or by groups of neighbours as were the *Kaufmannskirchen* which have been identified in some German towns.[33] Perhaps not quite to conjecture, since once again the map may help us: it seems clearly to indicate that the smaller parishes at least were not blocks of territory in a single hand but groups of holdings, for in every case a substantial thoroughfare provides not – as in a planned town like Salisbury – the frontier of the parish but its core;[34] often a crossroads lies in the midst of a parish.

That the origin of these parishes is obscure is hardly surprising. They represent the popular, lay aspect of piety before and during the age of papal or Gregorian reform. Much of what they stood for – lay property of churches,

[29] A. G. Rosser, *Medieval Westminster, 1200–1540* (Oxford, 1989); Brooke and Keir, *London*, ch. 11; F. Barlow, *Edward the Confessor* (London, 1970), pp. 229ff.

[30] A. R. Martin, *Franciscan Architecture in England*, British Society of Franciscan Studies (1937), pp. 176–204; W. A. Hinnebusch, *The Early English Friars Preachers* (Rome, 1951), pp. 20–55.

[31] See above, ch. 4, esp. p. 75 and n. 20, where somewhat similar conditions are observed in northern and north-central France, especially in Paris.

[32] M. Biddle, 'Excavations at Winchester, 1970: An Interim Report', *Antiquaries Journal*, 52 (1972), pp. 93–131, at pp. 104–5; Keene, *Survey of Medieval Winchester* (n. 1), i, p. 112; ii, pp. 761–3.

[33] P. Johansen, 'Die Kaufmannskirche im Ostseegebiet', in *Studien zu den Anfängen des Europäischen Städtewesens*, Vorträge und Forschungen, ed. T. Mayer (Lindau-Constance, 1958), pp. 499–525.

[34] K. H. Rogers, 'Salisbury', in *Historic Towns*, i, ed. M. D. Lobel (Oxford, 1969).

the proliferation of often very secular priests – was disapproved by the reformers. We have seen the monks of Worcester in the twelfth century claiming that there was but one parish in the city;[35] but even in Worcester there were several traditional centres of lay worship besides the cathedral. This heroic claim serves to underline the difference between Worcester and York, which had been ruled by a common bishop for much of the late tenth and early eleventh centuries. In York there was a multiplicity of tiny churches, and a window is opened into their life by the Northumbrian Priests' Law, which reveals how far even the great reformer Wulfstan I was prepared to go in tolerating the tumultuous clergy of the English towns in the age before the papal reform.[36] He attempted to reduce their wives to one each and their visits to the taverns even further. However, the overall impression is not just of abuse but of a lively clerical community close to the people; it helps us a little to understand why in that age people cared to worship in tiny box churches close to their clergy, rather than, or as well as, enjoying the vast spaces of great romanesque basilicas.

It is in these regions that we must search for the explanation of the numerous tiny parishes. Beyond this, at present, we can only conjecture. For some reason, discipline, and the hold of the bishop and the cathedral, were tighter in the western cities of Worcester and Hereford than in Danelaw cities like York and Lincoln. Perhaps there was Viking influence in London too, for six churches dedicated to St Olaf, one to St Bride and the name of St Clement Danes point to more Viking influence in London than street or moneyers' names, or the usual indicators would suggest.[37] The Vikings will not help us much, for they came to England pagan and what they did here needs some more local explanation. Winchester at least must be pronounced both a very striking example of the phenomenon and almost wholly unviking. We have long speculated on this problem, but it clearly has more to yield still.

The moral of all this is twofold: first that here is an enormous field for comparative study to which we can all contribute with a wandering and observant eye and by meditation on what we see in our wanderings;

---

[35] Above, p. 73 and n. 10.

[36] *Councils and Synods*, i, ed. D. Whitelock et al. (Oxford, 1981), i, pp. 449–68.

[37] On St Olaf and St Bride, see Brooke and Keir, *London*, pp. 137–38, 141–42. St Bride's connection with the Irish Norse was first pointed out to me by Paul Hodges. On the cult of St Clement, see E. Cinthio, 'The Churches of St Clemens in Scandinavia', *Särtryck ur Res Mediaevales Regnur Blomqvist kal. Mai. MCMLXVIII oblatae = Archaeologia Lundensia*, iii (Karlshamn, 1968), pp. 103–16; Cinthio, 'Heiligenpatrone und Kirchenbauten während des frühen Mittelalters', *Acta Visbyensia, 3, Visby-symposiet för historiska vetenskaper 1967* (Visby-Göteborg, 1969), pp. 161–69.

and, secondly, that if only about a tenth out of the century of parish churches in the city of London have been excavated, if our precise knowledge of minute changes of furnishing and structure depends on a tiny scatter of churches in a few parts of Europe only,[38] there is a tremendous archaeological task ahead, especially in cities less liable to destruction than London; in other words that the chief foundation on which this subject can be enlarged is archaeological. Archaeology is not all: there is much to be done with documents, much with dedications, much with maps and more with imagination and insight. It is a subject which starts in crude statistics and ends in all the subtleties of religious sentiment.

[38] A good example is given in M. Biddle, 'Excavations in Winchester, 1970', pp. 106–7.

6

The Bishops of England and Normandy in the Eleventh Century: A Contrast

with Rosalind Brooke

Of the English bishops of the eleventh century, before the Norman invasion in 1066, we commonly know the routes by which they were promoted, very rarely the names of their fathers. The Norman sources answer quite different questions: of the bishops active in the mid and late eleventh century, they more often tell us who their fathers were than any other detail of their early careers.[1] The essential reason for this is that most of the Norman bishops came from families of nobles and successful warriors; most of

First printed in Italian as 'I vescovi di Inghilterra e Normandia nel secolo XI: contrasti', *Mendola*, 6 (1977), pp. 536–45.

[1] The present study is the fruit of work begun as long ago as 1950, when Rosalind Brooke was working in Normandy and Paris on the Norman church in the eleventh and twelfth centuries, with the help of a Pennsylvania State International Fellowship awarded by the International Federation of University Women, and Christopher Brooke was working on the English episcopate in the eleventh and twelfth centuries in Cambridge. Among other materials which we compiled at that time and which have been used by ourselves and other scholars in the intervening years were lists of Norman and English bishops, which we have kept up to date from time to time and form the basis for this communication. Thus our studies are independent of the numerous more recent studies of the Norman church, from which, however, we have greatly profited: see especially Professor David Bates, 'Biography of Odo, Bishop of Bayeux, 1049–97' (unpublished Ph.D. thesis, University of Exeter, 1970) and idem, 'Notes sur l'aristocratie normande: i, Hugues, évêque de Bayeux; ii, Herluin de Conteville et sa famille', *Annales de Normandie*, 23 (1973), pp. 7–38; D. C. Douglas, 'Les évêques de Normandie, 1035–1066', *Annales de Normandie*, 3 (1958), pp. 87–102 = *Cambridge Historical Journal*, 13 (1957), pp. 101–15; M. de Boüard in *L'abbaye bénédictine de Fécamp*, i (Fécamp, 1959), pp. 81–92 (on Mauger of Rouen); and the notes to Orderic, *Ecclesiastical History*, ed. M. Chibnall, esp. iii, OMT (Oxford, 1972), pp. xxvi–xxvii, 84–95; slightly earlier, but very important, is J. Le Patourel, 'Geoffrey de Montbray, Bishop of Coutances, 1049–1093', *EHR*, 59 (1944), pp. 129–61. For later studies, see especially *Les évêques normands du XIe siècle*, ed. P. Bouet and F. Neveux, Colloque de Cerisy-la-Salle, 1993 (Caen, 1995). The dates in *Les évêques normands* should be treated with caution; we await the full critical list in David Spear's forthcoming volume of Norman *fasti*.

the English bishops had been monks, not (so far as we know) of aristocratic family. This is the basic contrast; but thus stated it gives far too simple a picture of what is in fact a singularly interesting contrast, revealing a cross-section of European society in the age of ecclesiastical reform and the root of some fundamental facts in the history of the English church in the middle ages.

Of approximately thirty-eight bishops in Normandy in the eleventh century we have fairly substantial information for only about one half.[2] The majority of these were sons or brothers of substantial figures in the Norman aristocracy, and two were themselves heads of great secular dynasties as well as bishops; two more, Odo of Bayeux and Geoffrey de Montbray or Mowbray of Coutances, strangely combined episcopal office in Normandy, and the refoundation of substantial cathedral chapters, with secular office in England after the Conquest.[3] The only other general feature of the Norman bishops is that they were few and long-lived; the average number per diocese for the century was five, the average length of their episcopate over twenty years. This is a high figure; a fair computation of eleventh-century popes gives them an average of five years each; and if the hazards of the office at that time be considered exceptional, it could be said that a much lower figure was normal in the twelfth century in most areas of western Europe. In the eleventh century the practice of laying hands suddenly on young men of promise was widespread,[4] and long episcopates therefore common; even the English bishoprics produced an average between twelve and fifteen years. In Normandy the high average of twenty years

Note 1 *continued*
    On English bishops, see *Handbook of British Chronology* (3rd edn (London, 1986), ed. E. B. Fryde, D. E. Greenway et al., pp. 209–24 (S. Keynes). Still of use is W. G. Searle, *Anglo-Saxon Bishops, Kings and Nobles* (Cambridge, 1899): our copy has been annotated and brought up to date with the aid of studies noted in *Heads*, pp. 12–16; but the whole subject was laid on a new foundation by F. Barlow, *The English Church, 1000–1066* (2nd edn, London, 1979).

    [2] This is based on our lists (see above). The lists in *Gallia Christiana*, xi (Paris, 1759) are basically sound, since the main sources, Orderic, William of Jumièges, *Acta archiepiscoporum Rotomagensium* (cited from *PL* 147 – after the editions of Mabillon and Martène), and the Coutances *De statu* (*Gallia Christiana*, xi, *Instrumenta*, cols. 217ff) are still the same, and the obituaries and charters were more complete when the materials were collected in the seventeenth and eighteenth centuries.

    [3] See below, and for Odo, D. Bates, 'Biography of Odo'. On Geoffrey de Montbray, see J. Le Patourel, 'Geoffrey de Montbray'; M. Chibnall, 'La carrière de Geoffroi de Montbray' in *Les évêques normands*, pp. 279–93. On the later history of the Mowbray estates and family, D. E. Greenway (ed.), *Charters of the Honour of Mowbray, 1107–1191* (London, 1972).

    [4] The most celebrated case is that of the abbots of Cluny, which reminds us that the appointment of very young men to high office was genuinely thought to be efficacious; it could also be due to family favouritism.

confirms the impression that a large number of the bishops were young members of vigorous, rising, aristocratic families. Odo of Bayeux and Geoffrey of Coutances are good examples; they were the image of the old-fashioned warrior bishop, such as we find in the figure of Archbishop Turpin in the *Chanson de Roland* and the warrior bishop in the war game of chess, who replaced the eastern elephant in the same century.[5] But these two young Normans were both appointed about the time of the accession of Leo IX to the papacy, and Geoffrey was himself present at the dramatic council of Reims in the autumn of 1049, in which Leo inaugurated the era of reform in the presence of the relics of St Rémi.[6] Thereafter there is a change in the nature of the young Duke William's episcopal appointments, a change equally marked in his activities in England after the Conquest.

To observe the nuances in this change, the holders of the best-documented see, the archbishopric of Rouen, will serve as a useful model.[7] The first two were the sons of dukes. The magnificent Archbishop Robert (989–1037) was the first of seven members of the ducal family to grace, or at any rate to occupy, episcopal thrones in Normandy between the early eleventh and the mid twelfth century.[8] He is described to us as a vivid mixture of conflicting elements: as both archbishop of Rouen and count of Evreux, in which capacity he was married and reared a family of children.[9] Robert was the son of Duke Richard I; his successor, Mauger, was the son of Richard II – and so uncle to the reigning duke, the child who was to grow into William the Conqueror – when he was appointed at a tender age in 1037. The Conqueror eventually removed him in 1055, according to contemporary statements for his unworthiness and immoral life; according to some modern historians for political intrigue.[10] Perhaps there is truth in both accounts; for there is no doubt that by the mid 1050s, in spite of a bitter dispute with the reformed papacy over his marriage, Duke William was looking away

[5] H. J. R. Murray, *A History of Chess* (Oxford, 1913); H. M. Garner, 'The Earliest Evidence of Chess in Western Literature: The Einsiedeln Verses', *Speculum*, 29 (1954), pp. 734–50.

[6] C. J. Hefele and H. Leclercq, *Histoire des conciles*, iv, pt 2 (Paris, 1911), pp. 1011–28, especially p. 1018: the bishops of Sées, Lisieux and Bayeux were also there.

[7] See Orderic, iii, pp. xxvi–xxvii, pp. 84ff, and references; and see below.

[8] Brooke, *Medieval Church and Society*, p. 85 n. 36: Robert, Mauger of Rouen; Hugh, bishop of Lisieux, c. 1050–77, grandson of Duke Richard I; Hugh bishop of Bayeux and John of Avranches and Rouen, sons of Rodulf count of Ivry, half-brother of Duke Richard I; Odo of Bayeux, half-brother of William the Conqueror; Richard of Kent, bishop of Bayeux, 1135–42, grandson of King Henry I.

[9] Orderic, iii, pp. 84–85, etc.; cf. William of Jumièges, *Gesta Normannorum ducum*, ed. E. M. C. Van Houts, i, OMT (Oxford, 1992), pp. 128–29, 132–33.

[10] An important study of Mauger and Maurilius is M. de Boüard in *L'abbaye bénédictine de Fécamp* (n. 1), pp. 81–92.

from his family and from old corruption to representatives of the new, cosmopolitan movement of ecclesiastical reform for his clerical advisers. Of these, two were outstanding. First, the German Maurilius was made arch-bishop of Rouen: he was of a family sprung from Mainz, but himself born in Reims, educated at Liège, a teacher at Halberstadt, then monk at Fécamp and abbot in Florence; he had recently returned to Fécamp, still under Abbot John or Jeannelin, one of the main centres of monastic observance in Normandy.[11] Maurilius was archbishop from 1055 until his death in 1067, when the clergy and people of his city looked to have the other major figure of the day, Lanfranc of Pavia and Bec, now abbot of the Conqueror's new abbey in Caen, as his successor.[12] We are told that Lanfranc was elected, but refused;[13] it may well be so – but it seems highly probable that the Conqueror himself already had an even more important post in mind for him, for Lanfranc was soon after appointed to Canterbury.

Maurilius was succeeded by a figure who proves the superficiality of the too simple categories with which we have dealt hitherto. He was John of Avranches, the son of Rodulf count of Ivry, one of the major figures in the Norman aristocracy in the early eleventh century, himself the half-brother of Duke Richard I.[14] John was thus a member both of the ducal dynasty and of a great ecclesiastical dynasty: Archbishops Robert and Mauger were his cousins; Hugh, bishop of Bayeux (c. 1015 – c. 1049) his brother. He had already had a term as bishop of Avranches, and this reminds us how relatively common translation was among the Norman bishops in the early and mid eleventh century. We may, however, assume that John's promotion was different in motivation, say, from the obscure and fascinating episode in 1026 when the bishops of Coutances and Lisieux swapped sees.[15] We may presume that John's advancement to Rouen reflected the credit of his background, life and achievement; for, according to Orderic Vitalis, he was not only nobly born but an ardent reformer.

He ... led a merciless campaign against vice ... For ten years he fulfilled his

---

[11] De Boüard, *L'abbaye bénédictine de Fécamp*; Orderic, iii, pp. 88ff; *Acta archiepiscoporum Rotomagensium*, PL, 147, cols 278–79.

[12] Earlier studies have been replaced by M. Gibson, *Lanfranc of Bec* (Oxford, 1978).

[13] *Acta archiepiscoporum Rotomagensium*, PL, 147, col. 280; Milo Crispin, *Vita Lanfranci*, PL, 150, col. 40.

[14] On John of Avranches, see resumé of paper by C. N. L. Brooke in *Resumés des communications*, Eleventh International Historical Congress at Stockholm (Stockholm, 1960), pp. 120–21; corrected by Diana Greenway, 'The False *Institutio* of St Osmund' in *Tradition and Change*, ed. D. Greenway et al. (Cambridge, 1985), pp. 77–101, at pp. 100–1; and above all Orderic, ii, pp. 200–1, 284–93; iii, pp. 22–23.

[15] *De statu* (n. 2), col. 218.

duties as metropolitan with courage and thoroughness, continuously striving to separate immoral priests from their mistresses: on one occasion when he forbade them to keep concubines he was stoned out of the synod, and fled exclaiming with a loud voice: 'O God, the heathen are come into thine inheritance'.[16]

His successor at Avranches, Michael, was, like Lanfranc, an Italian, and probably a ducal or royal chaplain.[17] If so, he heralds the arrival of the royal chaplains, who became the most successful candidates in Normandy, as they had been somewhat earlier in England, at the end of the eleventh and in the twelfth centuries. With the royal chaplains came the kind of ecclesiastical dynasty which owed little to secular or military prowess, yet was to be so characteristic a feature of the Anglo-Norman scene until the campaign for celibacy brought them down in the late twelfth century. Thus John's successor at Rouen was William Bonne-Ame, son of Radbod, bishop of Sées, and cousin of William, bishop of Evreux.[18] Like John of Avranches, he represented more than one world, for, after a spell as canon and arch-deacon of Rouen, he was monk of Bec and abbot of Caen before returning to Rouen as archbishop. He shows us how the elements in the Norman episcopate – hereditary ecclesiastic and monk, old abuse and new reform – could mingle in a single person. We meet such mixtures several times in the Anglo-Norman episcopate of the early twelfth century, most notably in the brothers Thurstan and Audoen or Ouen, sprung of a married canon of Bayeux and London, married to one wife, according to the fashion of the age, who grew up to be hereditary canons of London and became in due course highly respectable bishops at York and Evreux; Thurstan, as archbishop of York, was to be remembered as the founder of one of the greatest of English Cistercian abbeys, Fountains near Ripon, and to die a Cluniac monk.[19]

By 1140, when Thurstan retired from his diocese, the English and the Norman episcopate had developed a single career structure. It had not been

[16] Orderic, ii, pp. 200–1.

[17] Ibid.; cf. *Regesta regum Anglo-Normannorum*, i, ed. W. H. C. Davis (Oxford, 1913), p. xix and no. 22 – the identification of the chaplain and the bishop is likely, but not certain.

[18] Orderic, ii, pp. 68–70, 254, iii, pp. 22–25; etc.; G. H. Williams, *The Norman Anonymous of 1100 AD* (Cambridge, Massachusetts, 1951), pp. 102ff, gives a useful account of him, though his attempt to identify him as the author of the famous tracts of the 'Anonymous of York' or 'of Rouen' must be reckoned to fail.

[19] C. Brooke in *Cambridge Historical Journal*, 10 (1951), p. 124, and *Medieval Church and Society*, p. 91; D. Nicholl, *Thurstan, Archbishop of York* (York, 1964); *Fasti*, i (London, 1968), pp. 36, 43. On Thurstan, see now introduction to Hugh the Chanter, *History of the Church of York*, ed. and trans. C. Johnson, M. Brett, C. N. L. Brooke and M. Winterbottom, OMT (Oxford, 1990).

so for long. In the late tenth and early eleventh century all the English bishops whose origin is known, save one, had been monks. It is possible that a few more seculars are hidden from our gaze, for we cannot be sure of the origin of about one quarter of the bishops between 990 and 1020.[20] But the monastic dominance is certain and, indeed, well known; it reflects the power of the reforming monastic bishops of the mid tenth century, St Dunstan, St Æthelwold and St Oswald, and the very close relations established between their monastic movement and the royal government in the time of King Edgar (959–75). The monastic bishops lived in a world which regarded monastic involvement in pastoral work as natural and proper. At the same time there is no evidence at all that the English church had a secular higher clergy of any significance in this period; certainly no evidence of a career structure in episcopal service, royal service or the cathedral chapters – all of which were either Benedictine or (in theory at least) living according to a communal, canonical rule.

It is in the reign of the Danish Cnut (1016–35), and specifically in the mid 1020s, that we first meet evidence of royal priests or chaplains who were evidently not monks;[21] and by the end of Cnut's reign they were beginning to infiltrate the episcopate. Under Edward the Confessor the royal chaplains came to dominate the bishoprics, and they were a remarkably cosmopolitan group, including several Germans, mostly Lotharingians, several Frenchmen, and in particular one or two Normans – though the most important of the Normans, Robert of Jumièges, bishop of London and archbishop of Canterbury, had been a monk.[22]

In his interpretation of the English church on the eve of the Conquest, Professor Frank Barlow has emphasised both the English conservatism of the Danish Cnut, and the cosmopolitan links of the English King Edward.[23] In Cnut, however, there is little doubt that we see a man conscious that

---

[20] These figures are based on the lists cited in n. 1, checked by the admirable analyses in Barlow, *The English Church*, especially pp. 62ff, 208ff. See also e.g. J. A. Robinson, *The Saxon Bishops of Wells* (London, 1918); D. P. Kirby, 'The Saxon Bishops of Leicester, Lindsey (Syddensis) and Dorchester', *Transactions of the Leicestershire Archaeological and Historical Society*, 41 (1965–66), pp. 1–8.

[21] Barlow, *The English Church*, appendix B, especially p. 156. The first to enter bishoprics were Ælfwine, bishop of Winchester (1032–47) and Duduc, bishop of Wells (1033–60). See Barlow, *The English Church*, p. 75 and nn. 3, 5; *Ecclesiastical Documents*, ed. J. Hunter, Camden Society (1840), pp. 15–16.

[22] Cf. esp. J. Laporte, 'Les listes abbatiales de Jumièges', in *Jumièges: congrès scientifique du XIIIe centénaire*, i (Rouen, 1955), pp. 435–66, esp. pp. 445, 457.

[23] Barlow, *The English Church*, esp. pp. 65ff, 72, 75, 76ff; idem, *Edward the Confessor* (London, 1970).

English kingship was part of the dynastic and political world of which the German king-emperor, Conrad II, was the centre.

Cnut's Danish realm had a frontier, of course, with Germany, and he and Conrad met in Rome in 1027 in what may be regarded as the central moment of Cnut's reign.[24] In institutions and rituals, indeed, the monarchies of western Europe were never closer together than in the early and mid eleventh century. The royalty of Cnut and Edward is rather obviously symbolised in the characteristic instrument of their governments, the writ – in language and form, and in the shape of seal, thoroughly English; but the image on the seal, even in the time of Edward, from whose reign come the first surviving impressions, was the image of the Emperor Conrad II.[25] It is a reasonable conjecture, impossible of proof, that Cnut began the links with imperial Germany so evident in the recruitment of the Confessor's bishops as well as in the majesty on the great seal; and this could well explain the growth of a secular royal chapel on the German pattern in Cnut's later years.

The monks remained important, however, throughout the century. At Canterbury itself the century opened with two representatives of the tenth century monastic world, Ælfric, who had been the first abbot of the revived abbey of St Albans, and St Ælfheah, recluse and abbot at Bath, then bishop of Winchester, finally archbishop and martyr, slaughtered by the Danes in 1012.[26] All Ælfheah's successors down to the early twelfth century were monks, save for the notorious pluralist Stigand, archbishop from 1052 till 1070; and the Norman conquerors continued the monastic tradition, though with a difference, for Lanfranc of Pavia and Bec, and Anselm of Aosta and Bec, were major figures of the cosmopolitan religious and intellectual world of the mid and late eleventh century.

It is piquant to take our stand in the year 1060, for it represents a point at which the origins of almost the whole of the episcopate are known to us, and it is also the point at which the king's priests, the royal chaplains, were most dominant. There were still monks to be found, Æthelric at Selsey, for example, and Siward at Rochester, one of the most recent appointments; at Lichfield, the chief Mercian see, the bishop was the former abbot of the earl of Mercia's foundation, Coventry abbey; at Hereford and Worcester the bishop, soon to add York to his notable collection, was Ealdred, former abbot of Tavistock, to be remembered (not wholly fairly) as pluralist and

[24] William of Malmesbury, *Gesta regum Anglorum*, ed. R. A. B. Mynors, R. M. Thomson and M. Winterbottom, i, OMT (Oxford, 1998), pp. 324–31.

[25] F. E. Harmer, *Anglo-Saxon Writs* (Manchester, 1952), pp. 94–101; cf. *Facsimiles of English Royal Writs to AD 1100 Presented to Vivian Hunter Galbraith* (Oxford, 1957), pp. xix–xxiv.

[26] Searle, *Anglo-Saxon Bishops* (n. 1), pp. 10–11, 72–73; *Heads*, pp. 27–28, 102; his *Vita*, by Osbern, in *Acta sanctorum bollandiana*, Aprilis, ii (edn of 1866), pp. 628–40, esp. 629–30.

royal favourite more than as monk.[27] But elsewhere the king's priests
are in evidence, led by Stigand, archbishop of Canterbury and bishop of
Winchester, and his brother Æthelmær, to whom Stigand had passed over
the see of East Anglia, since even Stigand found it difficult to hold three
sees.[28] His secular status did not, however, prevent him battening on the
revenues of four or five abbeys; and not all the evidence which has been
found for ecclesiastical reform in this age can disguise the very obvious
fact that Edward in his later years was remarkably complaisant. English
wealth was one of the reasons which brought the Saxon Duduc and the
Lotharingian Giso (1033–60 and 1060–88), successive bishops of Wells, to
seek their fortune in England; also from Lotharingia came Herman, both
king's priest and monk at Saint-Bertin, bishop of the twin sees of Ramsbury
and Sherborne; William of London and Walter, soon to follow Ealdred at
Hereford, were perhaps both Norman; the remaining three were English
king's priests, though Leofric, founder of Exeter cathedral and refounder
of the fortunes of the see of Devon and Cornwall, was educated in
Lotharingia.[29]

Edward's choice of bishops was frankly ambivalent: he allowed Stigand
to hold his sees in spite of grumbles from the Holy See; yet Stigand himself
was second choice to the Norman monk Robert of Jumièges, whom
Edward had had to relinquish after the palace revolution in 1052; his next
appointment after 1060 was the saintly monk Wulfstan to Worcester.[30]

By 1090 Wulfstan was the only survivor of the Old English episcopate.
Royal clerks of Norman or French, or continental origin, had been established in the majority of sees. The Norman monk Remigius from Fécamp
was bishop of Dorchester, now Lincoln, apparently in recompense for
military services, though he died in the odour of sanctity; Norman monks
were also to be found at Durham and Rochester, William of Saint-Calais
and Gundulf, both eminent builders; but Lanfranc himself, the Italian

---

[27] Searle, *Anglo-Saxon Bishops*, pp. 22–23, 60–61; *Anglo-Saxon Chronicle*, MS.E, sub anno
1058; *Heads*, p. 38 (the identification of the bishop of Rochester and the abbot of Chertsey is
not certain).

[28] Barlow, *The English Church*, pp. 77ff, 302ff; for Stigand's abbeys, see *Heads*, pp. 45, 65–66,
esp. p. 65 n. 4.

[29] J. A. Robinson, *Saxon Bishops of Wells; Historiola* (on bishopric of Wells), ed. J. Hunter,
in *Ecclesiastical Documents*, Camden Society (1840); Barlow, *The English Church*, pp. 156, 213ff;
The Exeter Book of Old English Poetry, ed. R. W. Chambers, M. Förster, R. Flower (London,
1933), p. 5. Both the *Historiola* and John of Worcester, *Chronicon*, ii, ed. R. R. Darlington,
P. McGurk and J. Bray, OMT (Oxford, 1995), pp. 476–77, call Duduc *Saxonicus*.

[30] *The Vita Wulfstani of William of Malmesbury*, ed. R. R. Darlington, Camden 3rd Series,
40 (London, 1928). Cf. E. Mason, *St Wulfstan of Worcester, c. 1008–1095* (Oxford, 1990).

turned Norman, had recently died, and so Canterbury was vacant.[31] The men were new and their names revealed the brutal fact of the Norman Conquest; but the pattern was not so different from that of 1060. Yet this disguises greater changes in the making. Some of the Anglo-Norman bishops had responded to the religious fashions of their age by increasing the number of monastic chapters in England. Yet in or about 1090 secular chapters on the Norman model were set up at York and Lincoln and London, and also in St Osmund's Salisbury, soon after the chapters of Bayeux and Coutances had received their finishing touches in the lively old age of Odo and Geoffrey.[32] By the early twelfth century the cathedrals and chapters both sides of the English Channel presented an image very different from that of the year 1000. Yet the balance of monastic and secular bishops continued, so that in Normandy as in England in the early twelfth century a few monastic bishops and a greater number of seculars, with an occasional nobleman among them, presided over churches whose bishops had once been recruited in very different ways.[33] The monastic dominance had long since ceased in England, even though the ethos of the age of

[31] On Remigius, cf. Chibnall in Orderic, ii, p. 144 n. 1; his *Vita* by Giraldus Cambrensis, *Opera*, RS (1861–91), vii, ed. J. F. Dimock, pp. 6, 14ff; D. Bates, *Bishop Remigius of Lincoln, 1067–1092* (Lincoln, 1992). On William of Saint-Calais of Durham, H. S. Offler, 'The Tractate *De iniusta vexacione Willelmi episcopi primi*', *EHR* 66 (1951), pp. 321–41. Cf. esp. M. Philpott, 'The De iniusta uexacione Willelmi episcopi primi and Canon Law in Anglo-Norman Durham', in *Anglo-Norman Durham*, ed. R. Rollason, M. Harvey and M. Prestwich (Woodbridge, 1994), pp. 125–37; and the edition of *De iniusta vexacione* by H. S. Offler, A. J. Piper and A. I. Doyle in *Camden Miscellany*, 34, Camden 5th Series, 10 (1997), pp. 49–104. For William's role in the building of Durham cathedral and formation of its library see *Anglo-Norman Durham*, passim; for the thesis that he was the principal author of Domesday Book, see P. Chaplais, 'William of Saint-Calais and the Domesday Survey', in *Domesday Studies*, ed. J. C. Holt (Woodbridge, 1987), pp. 65–77. On Gundulf of Rochester, R. A. L. Smith, *Collected Papers* (London, 1947), pp. 83–102, and on John of Tours, pp. 74–82. On Gundulf, see also *The Life of Gundulf, Bishop of Rochester*, ed. R. M. Thomson (Toronto, 1977). The secular clerks included John of Tours, bishop of Wells, later Bath, and Robert of Lorraine, bishop of Hereford. Among the obscure cases is Stigand, bishop of Chichester, formerly chaplain to William I, *Fasti*, v, p. 1; *Councils and Synods*, i, 2, 579; John of Worcester, *Chronicle*, iii, ed. P. M. McGurk, OMT (Oxford, 1998), pp. 14–15, and normally supposed a Norman; his name is in origin Old Norse, and might be found both sides of the English Channel.

[32] K. Edwards, *The English Secular Cathedrals in the Middle Ages* (2nd edn, Manchester, 1967), pp. 12–22; and see now above, pp. 51–53, revising my earlier views in the light especially of the work of Professor Diana Greenway.

[33] In Normandy monastic bishops became relatively rare, but Serlo d'Orgères, bishop of Sées (1091–1123) had been abbot of Saint-Evroult, Orderic, iv, p. 252; and Hugh of Amiens of Rouen (1130–64) had been a Cluniac, prior of Lewes and abbot of Reading.

ecclesiastical reform, and the personalities of Lanfranc and Anselm,[34] gave monastic ideals immense power, and monasteries multiplied as never before or since. What is consistent in the English pattern – and a feature of English clerical recruitment throughout the central and late middle ages – is the small number of aristocratic recruits. It cannot be that the sons and brothers of earls and barons lacked means of access to English bishoprics, and in every age a small number may be found on the bench of bishops.[35] But the number is never large, and this can only mean that the Anglo-Norman aristocracy inherited a prejudice which the English seem already to have had: that their sons and brothers should not enter the ranks of the clergy. That this was already so in the late tenth and early eleventh centuries is suggested by the contrast between England and Normandy with which we began.

[34] See n. 12. On monastic growth in England, see D. Knowles and R. N. Hadcock, *Medieval Religious Houses, England and Wales* (2nd edn, London, 1971), esp. appendix 2, pp. 488–95.

[35] It was normal for this proportion to be less than one in six (by any reasonable definition of aristocracy) in late medieval England; see J. R. L. Highfield, 'The English Hierarchy in the Reign of Edward II', *Transactions of the Royal Historical Society*, 5th series, 6 (1956), pp. 115–38, and see p. 115 and n. for other studies. For comparison with France and Germany see B. Guillemain, 'Les origines des évêques en France aux XIe et XIIe siècles', *Mendola*, 5 (1974), pp. 374–407; C. Brühl, 'Die Sozialstruktur des deutschen Episkopats im 11. und 12. Jahrhundert', *Mendola*, 6 (1977), pp. 42–56.

7

The Archdeacon and the Norman Conquest

In a celebrated passage in *The Warden* Anthony Trollope summed up his view of how a diocese was run: either the bishop or the archdeacon did the work; 'either a bishop or his archdeacon have sinecures'; in the see of Barchester at that epoch it was the archdeacon who held the reins.[1] Many years later Trollope was to observe in his *Autobiography* that he doubted if he had ever spoken to a living archdeacon when he first created the character of Theophilus Grantly – one of many such asides from which his reputation has suffered; but in truth the character of the archdeacon is a remarkable mingling of an ancient literary tradition with brilliant human insight. The

From *Tradition and Change: Essays in Honour of Marjorie Chibnall, Presented by her Friends on the Occasion of her Seventieth Birthday*, ed. D. Greenway, C. Holdsworth and J. Sayers (Cambridge, 1985), pp. 1–19.

[1] *The Warden* (1855), ch. 2 (London, 1953, p. 15); cf. *Autobiography* (1883), ch. 5 (London, 1946, p. 96) for what follows. This essay is ultimately based on extensive work on English archdeacons originally undertaken in collaboration with Z. N. Brooke in the 1940s. The notes for this have been used in *GF, GFL, Heads* and elsewhere; and were handed over to the Institute of Historical Research when Professor Greenway began work on *Fasti*. Her studies have carried the investigation much further and deeper, and my debt to her work is to be found in every page and many details of what follows. Details of Norman archdeacons and of the wider context of the Norman Church are partly based on notes prepared by Dr Rosalind Brooke when studying the Norman church in Paris and Normandy in 1950–1; see also n. 23. Since the research for this essay was done general accounts of the subject have appeared by F. Barlow, *The English Church, 1000–1066* (2nd edn, London, 1979), pp. 247–54; *The English Church, 1066–1154* (London, 1979), pp. 48–49, 134–37, 154–56, and M. Brett (*The English Church under Henry I* (Oxford, 1975), esp. pp. 199–211). The admirable discussion by Brett excuses us from more than superficial reference to the archdeacon's functions; and his account has been carried further into the mid and late twelfth century in a series of studies by Brian Kemp: 'Archdeacons and Parish Churches in England in the Twelfth Century', in *Law and Government in Medieval England and Normandy: Essays in Honour of Sir James Holt*, ed. G. Garnett and J. Hudson (Cambridge, 1994), pp. 341–64; 'Informing the Archdeacon on Ecclesiastical Matters in Twelfth-Century England' in *Medieval Ecclesiastical Studies in Honour of Dorothy M. Owen*, ed. M. J. Franklin and C. Harper-Bill (Woodbridge, 1995), pp. 131–49; and his forthcoming edition of *Archidiaconal Acta*, to be published by the Canterbury and York Society.

insight comes out most clearly in Trollope's last farewell to Dr Grantly in *The Last Chronicle of Barset.*

> The archdeacon ... loved the temporalities of the Church as temporalities. The Church was beautiful to him because one man by interest might have a thousand a year, while another man equally good, but without interest, could only have a hundred. And he liked the men who had the interest a great deal better than the men who had it not.[2]

The context explores Dr Grantly's generous efforts to bring the perpetually impoverished Mr Crawley into the bosom of his family, and reveals the archdeacon's better nature; but it also announces a proposition which would have echoed in the mind of many an archdeacon from the twelfth to the early nineteenth century, and helps to explain their reputed devotion to the Church's temporal goods from John of Salisbury, through Chaucer to Trollope himself. 'Purse is the archdeacon's hell', said Chaucer's Summoner, ostensibly quoting a proverb.[3] Two centuries earlier, John had written to an old friend, Nicholas de Sigillo, archdeacon of Huntingdon, a letter of congratulation on his appointment:

> I seem to remember that there was a race of men known in the church of God by the title archdeacons for whom you used to lament, my discerning friend, that every road to salvation was closed. They love gifts, you used to say, and follow after rewards ... The most eminent of them preach the law of God but do it not ... Your friends, and all good men, must thank God and the bishop of Lincoln, who have opened your eyes and revealed to you a path by which this race of men can ... attain salvation ... It is the Lord's doing ...[4]

There was a sharper edge on medieval satire; but the point was the same. Already by the mid twelfth century the archdeacon was a familiar figure, a normal feature of the scene, as open to satire as the pope himself.

A century earlier this would evidently not have been so. There had been a flurry of archdeacons in ninth-century Canterbury; and Canterbury again boasted two or three mythical archdeacons in the early and mid eleventh century.[5] There are a few puzzling references to an archdeacon which suggest that the office existed or at least that the title was familiar; but no single archdeacon can be securely named between 900 and 1066. By the death of Lanfranc in 1089 we have some evidence of an archdeacon in almost every

---

[2] Trollope, *The Last Chronicle* (1867), ch. 83 (Oxford, 1980, p. 878).

[3] *Canterbury Tales, Prologue*, line 658.

[4] John of Salisbury, *Letters*, ii, no. 140, pp. 24–25, with echoes of Isaiah 1:2–3 and Ps. 117 (118):23. Cf. D. E. Greenway in Henry of Huntingdon, *Historia Anglorum*, OMT (Oxford, 1996), p. cxvi.

[5] See below.

diocese; by 1092 the largest of the sees, that of Lincoln, was divided into territorial archdeaconries, and the multiplication of archdeacons spread rapidly in the late eleventh and twelfth centuries. Thus in essence the archdeacon came over with the Conqueror. These facts are well known, though some of them have been doubted or disputed; and there are many aspects of the story still lacking in precision.

To state the matter in its simplest terms, the deacons had been established and appointed in the early church as administrators first of charity and welfare, then of church properties; and the first archdeacons were simply the leading figures among groups of deacons assisting bishops in their sees.[6] This appears to have been the role of the only group of archdeacons known in this country before the Norman Conquest.[7] In 805 the Archdeacon Wulfred was promoted archbishop of Canterbury, and his successors from time to time appointed archdeacons, Ceolnoth even experimenting at the end of his life with a whole posse of them – the names of seven or eight are known, though not all these need have held office simultaneously. Wulfred had instituted the rule of Chrodegang of Metz;[8] and in this rule the senior official and administrator of the chapter is called variously the archdeacon or provost. Thus it was not uncommon in ordinary parlance for a leading deacon or a leading administrator in a bishop's see or cathedral chapter to be called 'archdeacon' in western Europe in the early middle ages, and especially in the ninth and later centuries.

Already by the ninth century an official called an archdeacon had achieved in a number of northern sees – though not in England, so far as we know – a more specific and important administrative role, in essence that which Dr Grantly was to have. Though early evidence is sparse and inconclusive, it seems clear that already by this date it was possible for an archdeacon to control both discipline and temporal administration in a diocese, and

---

[6] Useful brief bibliography in *Oxford Dictionary of the Christian Church* (3rd edn, by F. L. Cross and E. A. Livingstone, Oxford, 1997), p. 97; fuller in A. Amanieu's thorough article 'Archidiacre', in *Dictionnaire de droit canonique*, i (Paris, 1935), cols 948–1004.

[7] For the ninth century see M. Deanesly in *EHR*, 42 (1927), pp. 1–11: N. Brooks, *The Early History of the Church of Canterbury* (Leicester, 1984), pp. 155–57, 160–62. For pre-conquest evidence in general, Barlow, *English Church, 1000–1066* (2nd edn, 1979), pp. 247–54; D. Whitelock in *Councils and Synods*, i, 1, p. 454n.; F. E. Harmer, *Anglo-Saxon Writs* (Manchester, 1952), p. 530.

[8] For Chrodegang in England see esp. *The Old English Version of the Enlarged Rule of Chrodegang*, ed. A. S. Napier, Early English Text Society, 150 (1916); D. Whitelock, *Some Anglo-Saxon Bishops of London* (London, 1975), pp. 27–30. See also n. 20; Brooks, *Canterbury*, pp. 155–57, 160–62.

thus to be the bishop's *alter ego*.[9] It is evident that this was a role which the archdeacons quickly assumed in England after 1066; where they had learned it is not so clear.

In one respect, however, the post-conquest archdeacon retained in the late eleventh and into the late twelfth century a vital feature of his early history: he was, in principle at least, a deacon. The principle was enunciated in English councils of 1102, 1125 and 1127 – following the councils of Poitiers of 1078 and Clermont, 1095 – a repetition which doubtless suggests that it was not universally observed.[10] But in fact all the archdeacons down to the 1190s whose orders we know were deacons. Thus Roger de Clinton, archdeacon of Buckingham, on his promotion to the see of Chester-Coventry in 1129, had to be ordained priest; Robert de Chesney, archdeacon of Leicester, on rising to the bishopric of Lincoln in 1148, likewise had to be ordained priest; the notorious Osbert, archdeacon of Richmond, was ordered to clear himself of the charge of murdering his archbishop by the oath of three archdeacons, 'who were to choose four others, all deacons, to assist them' (adhibitis secum aliis quattuor *diaconis*); Thomas Becket himself as archdeacon of Canterbury was a deacon; John Cumin remained a deacon while he was archdeacon of Bath, to be ordained priest in 1182 after he had handed the archdeaconry over to Peter of Blois – and the tide only began to turn, so far as we know, when Peter's bishop demanded that he take priest's orders.[11] Thus in the eleventh and throughout the twelfth century,

---

[9] See J.-F. Lemarignier in F. Lot and R. Fawtier, *Histoire des institutions françaises au moyen âge*, iii (Paris, 1962), pp. 20–21; for the wider story, A. Hamilton Thompson, 'Diocesan Organisation in the Middle Ages: Archdeacons and Rural Deans', *Proceedings of the British Academy*, 29 (1943), pp. 153–94, is still useful.

[10] *Councils and Synods*, i, 2, pp. 675 and nn. (for 1078, 1095), 739, 747.

[11] In theory, archdeacons who had to be ordained priests before consecration as bishops could have been in yet lower orders; perhaps one or two were; but these documents would probably have recorded such ordinations – and at least the record establishes that they were not priests. For these instances, see *The Chronicle of John of Worcester*, iii, ed. P. McGurk, OMT (Oxford, 1998), pp. 188–89; *Canterbury Professions*, ed. M. Richter (Canterbury and York Society, 67, 1973), p. 45; John of Salisbury, *Letters*, i, no. 16, p. 27; *Materials for the History of Thomas Becket*, ed. J. C. Robertson and J. B. Sheppard, 7 vols., RS (London, 1875–85), iii, p. 188 ('archilevita ecclesiae electus in sacerdotem ordinatur, in crastino … in antistitem consecrandus'), etc.; J. A. Robinson, *Somerset Historical Essays* (London, 1921), pp. 98–99; Peter of Blois, letter 123 in *PL*, 207, cols 358–67, containing an elaborate defence of the proposition that an archdeacon should be a deacon. Other cases are Richard de Belmeis II, ordained deacon when he recovered the archdeaconry of Middlesex in 1138, priest eight days before consecration as bishop, *Radulfi de Diceto Decani Lundoniensis opera historica*, ed. W. Stubbs, RS (London, 1876), i, pp. 251–52; *Canterbury Professions*, p. 48; *Fasti*, i, pp. 2, 15; Paris archdeacon of Rochester was ordained deacon in 1145, *Reg. Roffense*, ed. J. Thorpe (London, 1769), p. 9; Simon Luvel was archdeacon of Worcester, canon of Exeter and a deacon when he died, Exeter Cath. Libr.,

an archdeacon was both an official with fairly distinctive prerogatives, and the chief of the deacons.

Archbishop Ceolnoth experimented with an ambitious hierarchy of portentous officials: a *chorepiscopus* and a team of archdeacons. The experiment died with him, and the *chorepiscopus*, doubtless in his eyes simply an assistant bishop, had always to contend with an ancient prejudice against his existence.[12] He was to reappear briefly in the eleventh century, but no longer in company with an archdeacon; after the Conquest indeed the archdeacon of Canterbury was seen quite precisely as his replacement.[13] For named archdeacons we have very slender evidence between the late ninth century and 1066. John of Worcester entitles Ælfmær, who played a role in the Danish attack on Canterbury in 1011 which culminated in the murder of St Ælfheah, an archdeacon; but he appears to be adding a gloss to the Anglo-Saxon Chronicle.[14] A venerable tradition identifies one Haymo Anglicus as a writer of biblical treatises, as a former monk of Saint-Denis and professor of theology at Paris, who is said to have returned to England and died archdeacon of Canterbury on 2 October 1054. In spite of the apparent precision of the date, the tale appears to be fiction, of a kind very familiar to students of Leland and Bale and Pits. The confusion of Haymo of Auxerre and Haymo of Fulda with an English namesake owes something to Henry of Kirkstede (Boston of Bury) in the fourteenth century; John Bale made him an exile from some Danish invasion and fleshed him out with a career in France; John Pits added to Bale his archdeaconry and the approximate date of his death, *c.* 1054; Thomas Tanner added the

MS 3518, fol. 4. But *c.* 1207 or soon after Henry de Castilion, archdeacon of Canterbury, died a priest, Rouen obituary, M. Bouquet, *Recueil des historiens des Gaules et de la France*, xxiii (Paris, 1894), p. 359.

[12] M. Deanesly, 'The Archdeacons of Canterbury under Archbishop Ceolnoth, 833–870', *EHR*, 42 (1927), pp. 1–11; on the *chorepiscopus*, see W. Levison, *England and the Continent in the Eighth Century* (Oxford, 1946), p. 66 n. 4.

[13] See below, p. 125.

[14] On these early references to archdeacons in general, see W. H. Frere, *Visitation Articles and Injunctions*, i, Alcuin Club Collections, 14 (1910), pp. 41f; p. 45 for Ælfmær; as archdeacon, *The Chronicle of John of Worcester*, ii, ed. R. R. Darlington and P. McGurk, OMT (Oxford, 1995), pp. 468–69. It is just conceivable that he was, or was thought to have been, a monastic archdeacon. According to Leland, *Collectanea*, ed. T. Hearne, iv (2nd edn, London, 1770), p. 7, apparently quoting a twelfth-century source from St Augustine's Canterbury, 'S. Brinstanus, archidiaconus S. Ælphegi' lay in the north porticus of St Augustine's – an intriguing entry. The north porticus contained the early archbishops, but I have not been able to conjecture who this 'Brinstanus' may have been. (For the porticus see H. M. and J. Taylor, *Anglo-Saxon Architecture*, i (Cambridge, 1965), pp. 134–43.)

day.[15] But no contemporary source has been found for any single part of his career. There is more substance in Aluricus archdeacon in Winchester, who is attributed to the time of King Edward (the Confessor) in the Winton Domesday; but even this is a document of c. 1110 and there may be anachronism in it.[16]

St Oswald of Worcester has been credited with an archdeacon, on the much more promising basis of a Worcester document of 1092. This is the famous account of the synod of St Wulfstan, which describes how all the wisest folk of the diocese met in the cathedral crypt and disputed at length on the parochial status of the churches of Worcester, concluding that anciently there had been but one parish in the city of Worcester, that of the cathedral; and that St Oswald had made the prior and his successors deans over all the churches of the city and exempted the churches of the monks from any other deans' or archdeacons' jurisdiction. The document has been shown by Dr Julia Barrow to be a twelfth-century forgery, representing what the monks of Worcester perceived their past to be, probably in the 1140s or 1150s, and it is not good evidence for pre-Conquest history.[17] As Dr Martin Brett has said, 'the phrasing here need not be taken to indicate that the monks thought that such officers were actually at work in Oswald's time';[18] and the whole tenor of the passage is to safeguard the monks' exemption for the future, not give a precise account of the ecclesiastical organization of the past.

For the eleventh century, we are left only with the evidence of the *Northumbrian Priests' Law*, the work of Wulfstan I as archbishop of York between c. 1008 and 1023, which mentions the archdeacon almost in passing, as an official with authority over the priests for which the code is legislating.[19] This, and the references in the Carolingian legislation of Chrodegang familiar in England in the eleventh century, and a stray mention in a glossary of Ælfric, comprise all the unequivocal evidence that the

[15] For Haymo, see Frere, *Visitation Articles*, p. 45; J. Bale, *Illustrium ... scriptorum summarium* (Basel, 1557–9), ii, p. 119; idem, *Index Britanniae scriptorum*, ed. R. L. Poole and M. Bateson (Oxford, 1902), pp. 155–56; J. Pits, *Relationum historicarum tomus primus* (Paris, 1619), p. 186; T. Tanner, *Bibliotheca Britannico-Hibernica* (London, 1748), p. 386. For Kirkstede, see R. H. Rouse in *Speculum*, 41 (1966), pp. 471–99; CUL, Add. MS 3470 p. 72.

[16] F. Barlow et al., in *Winchester Studies*, ed. M. Biddle, i (Oxford, 1976), p. 58; cf. *Councils and Synods*, i, 1, p. 454n.

[17] For text, see *Councils and Synods*, i, 2, pp. 635–69; for evidence that it is spurious, see Julia Barrow, 'How the Twelfth-Century Monks of Worcester Perceived their Past', in *The Perception of the Past in Twelfth-Century Europe*, ed. P. Magdalino (London, 1992), pp. 53–74, at pp. 60–69.

[18] *Councils and Synods*, i, 2, p. 639n.

[19] Ibid., i, 1, p. 454.

word and the office were known in eleventh-century England before the Conquest.[20] The references have been taken to mean that the office was well known, even taken for granted; yet it is very odd that no contemporary source credits anyone with the title. It has been very plausibly suggested that the important York deacon Ealdred, to whom King Edward gave the minster at Axminster in Devon in the early 1060s, held the office described by Wulstan I;[21] and there are deacons in Worcester documents who might well have held similar roles.[22] But there is mighty little evidence that pre-Conquest England had any inkling of the archdeacon as a title or an office.

In Normandy before 1066 the title was certainly known. As often happens, however, with Norman institutions, the title and its function only come out into the clear light of day after 1066, and we have no information from Normandy itself as to the archdeacon's functions – save one clear piece of evidence for archidiaconal jurisdiction in the see of Avranches, not the most forward part of the duchy. What little we know has been set in a clear light by Professors David Bates and David Spear.[23] A scatter of archdeacons appear in the diocese of Rouen in the 1020s, 1030s and 1040s; William Bonne-Ame went from Rouen to be a monk of Bec and abbot of Saint-Etienne at Caen, and eventually returned to Rouen as archbishop.[24] Most

---

[20] *Rule of Chrodegang,* ed. Napier, pp. 16–18; the archdeacon seems not to be named in Amalarius, *Monumenta Germaniae Historica, Concilia,* ii, 1 (ed. A. Werminghoff, 1906), pp. 307–421 (pp. 340f for provosts).

[21] F. E. Harmer, *Anglo-Saxon Writs* (Manchester, 1952), pp. 530–31; cf. ibid., p. 419; *Councils and Synods,* i, 1, pp. 557–59.

[22] For the Worcester *familia* see I. Atkins in *Antiquaries Journal,* 17 (1937), pp. 371–91; 20 (1940), pp. 1–38, 203–29.

[23] D. Bates, *Normandy before 1066* (London, 1982), pp. 215–16, and appendix C, 'A List of Norman Archdeacons to *c.* 1080', pp. 260–62. See now David Spear, 'L'administration épisco-pale normande: archidiacres et dignitaires des chapîtres', in *Les évêques normands du XIe siècle,* ed. P. Bouet and F. Neveux (Caen, 1995), pp. 81–102. A full revised *fasti* for the Norman cathedrals is in progress by Professor Spear: see meanwhile, Spear, 'Les doyens du chapître cathédral de Rouen durant la période ducale', *Annales de Normandie,* 33 (1983), pp. 91–119; 'Les archidiacres de Rouen au cours de la période ducale', 34 (1984), pp. 15–50. Professors Bates and Spear kindly helped me revise this passage, and pointed out the interest of an early settlement between the bishop of Avranches and the abbot of Mont Saint-Michel in indicating a defined archidiaconal jurisdiction in a remote part of Normandy before 1066, cf. J.-F. Lemarignier, *Etudes sur les privilèges d'exemption des abbayes normandes* (Paris, 1937), pp. 159–60.

[24] Bates, *Normandy before 1066,* pp. 260–62; for William Bonne-Ame, see Orderic, ii, pp. 68–69, 254–55, etc.; Spear, 'Les archidiacres', p. 20. Some further details noted in the first edition of this essay will be included in the full deployment of the evidence in David Spear's forthcoming book of Norman *fasti.*

remarkable is the case of Fulk who, according to Orderic, granted a hereditary archdeaconry to Saint-Evroul *in feudo* in the mid eleventh century.[25]
Thus there was evidently a multiplicity of archdeacons in Rouen in the
middle of the century, and at Bayeux in the time of Bishop Odo;[26] one at
least is testified to at Lisieux by *c.* 1050.[27] Most impressive is the evidence
from Sées, which had five archdeacons by 1057, one of them quite specifically
known to be territorial.[28] But there is little other evidence, and even at Sées
the archdeacons were slimmed down later in the eleventh century. What
is certain is that the territorial archdeaconry was known in northern France,
and impinged for a time on at least one Norman see, possibly on several.

After the Norman Conquest the archdeacon was not slow to appear in
the English sees. An early set of conciliar canons, probably of 1070, enjoin
'ut episcopi archidiaconos et ceteros sacri ordinis ministros in ecclesiis suis
ordinent'; the famous writ of William I, formerly dated *c.* 1072, undoubtedly
linked in some way to the council of Winchester of 1076, but not certainly
dated more narrowly than 1072 x 1085, takes the role of the archdeacon in
law and law courts for granted.[29] The first archdeacon to be named, however,
appears to be the monastic archdeacon of Bury, Herman, who wrote the
Miracles of St Edmund, and was probably made archdeacon in or soon after
1071 when the pope defined the area of Bury's exempt jurisdiction.[30] It may
indeed be significant that a monastic archdeacon should appear at this
moment of time, for the rise of the archdeacon and the hardening of
exemption from his (and his bishop's) authority were closely allied – a
point to which we shall recur.

[25] Orderic, ii, pp. 152–53 and n.

[26] For Bayeux, see Bates, *Normandy before 1066*, pp. 261–62. We have to wait until 1092 for
something like a full list of the chapter of Bayeux, which shows four archdeacons; but the
indications are that Bishop Odo (1049/50–97) had established such a complement long before
that date, *Antiquus cartularius ecclesiae Baiocensis*, ed. V. Bourrienne, Société de l'Histoire de
Normandie, 2 vols (1902–3), i, 30. William and Gotzelin occ. 1068 x 1070, *Mélanges*, Société
de l'Histoire de Normandie, 11 (1927), p. 214; Bates, *Normandy before 1066*, p. 261.

[27] Orderic, ii, pp. 18–19; Bates, *Normandy before 1066*, p. 261.

[28] Bates, *Normandy before 1066*, pp. 215, 233 (n. 97), 261–62. Bates notes that the territory
lay outside Normandy and that the documents related to a period when Sées was orientated
'away from Normandy' (p. 215). For evidence of territorial archdeacons elsewhere in northern
France at this time, see Lemarignier, *Etudes sur les privilèges*, pp. 159–60.

[29] *Councils and Synods*, i, 2, pp. 580, 620–24.

[30] See Jane Sayers, 'Monastic Archdeacons', in *Church and Government in the Middle Ages:
Essays Presented to C. R. Cheney on his Seventieth Birthday*, ed. C. N. L. Brooke, D. E. Luscombe,
G. H. Martin and D. Owen (Cambridge, 1976), pp. 177–203, esp. pp. 179–80. Dr A. Gransden
notes however that the title 'archdeacon' is first attached to him in surviving MSS in the
fourteenth century, *Proceedings of the Battle Conference for Anglo-Norman Studies*, 4 (1981),
p. 187 n. 3.

The evidence is scattered and often incidental, but this makes all the more impressive the testimony for the spread of the title and office in the pontificate of Lanfranc (1070–89) and the reign of the Conqueror (1066–87). Thus Lanfranc in his *Monastic Constitutions* explains that a monk in chapter shall be addressed by name and order, not by ancient rank or place of origin – 'Dom Edward the priest' or 'deacon' not 'Dom Edward the archdeacon' or 'of London' – and we only know that this is a specific reference to an archdeacon of London who became a monk at Christ Church Canterbury because he figures in the *Miracles of St Dunstan* by Osbern and Eadmer.[31] Without this evidence we should not know for sure that London had an archdeacon before 1100. They rarely appear in charters in the eleventh century, though the witness-list to the council of London of 1075 supplies Canterbury itself with its first firm reference to Archdeacon Anschetil.[32] A later narrative describes how Lanfranc instituted the first archdeacon to replace the discredited *chorepiscopi*, and it gives the first archdeacon's name as Valerius.[33] Since no one in Lanfranc's household is known to have borne so odd a name it seems likely to be corrupt or invented; but the fact that Lanfranc appointed an archdeacon early in his episcopate need not be doubted. For Salisbury, Orderic provides us with a notice of Gunter of Le Mans, archdeacon of Salisbury, who had retired from the world and become a monk of Battle in time to be abbot of Thorney from 1085.[34] For Exeter, that marvellous record the Exeter martyrology gives three archdeacons before 1100.[35]

Rather more extensive evidence is provided by Domesday Book and its cousins and satellites: these give archdeacons to Wells or Bath, Norwich, Worcester; some of these are mentioned only as tenants, and it is presumption that they plied their archidiaconal trade in the appropriate see; but for most there is little doubt. The evidence is most remarkable of all for Lincoln, where Henry of Huntingdon lists seven territorial archdeacons already in

[31] *The Monastic Constitutions of Lanfranc*, ed. D. Knowles, NMT (Edinburgh, 1951), p. 112, corrected in *Fasti*, i, p. 8 with other references; also Knowles' revised edn in *Corpus consuetudinum monasticarum*, ed. K. Hallinger, iii (Siegburg, 1967), p. 91 and n. – further revised in forthcoming edn for OMT by C. N. L. Brooke.

[32] *Councils and Synods*, i, 2, p. 616; cf. *Fasti*, ii, p. 12. For details in the pages which follow for which references are not given, see Appendix.

[33] H. Wharton, *Anglia sacra* (London, 1691), i, p. 150; for MS evidence (fourteenth century), *Fasti*, ii, p. 12.

[34] See Appendix; and esp. Orderic, vi, pp. 150–53. He may in fact have been archdeacon before the move to Salisbury in the mid and late 1070s, but Orderic would naturally give the see the name familiar when he wrote.

[35] Exeter Cathedral Library, MS 3518; David Blake in *Journal of Medieval History*, 8 (1982), pp. 3–4; and see now *EEA*, xii, p. 306.

office under Bishop Remigius, that is, before 1092; it is a fair presumption
that some at least of these were already in post before Lanfranc died in
1089.[36] Of all the English sees in existence in 1100, only Rochester lacks firm
evidence of an archdeacon by c. 1089,[37] and it is really very improbable that
a see occupied after 1075 by two of Lanfranc's closest disciples, Arnost
(1075–76) and Gundulf (1077–1108), should not have been provided with
every latest improvement. No see in Wales or Scotland or Ireland was
sufficiently under English influence to be drawn into this story, but if the
documents in the Book of Llandaff are to be believed, Llandaff had not
only an archdeacon, but territorial archdeacons in the late eleventh century.[38]

The spread of archdeacons indeed seems to have preceded the reorganisation of the cathedral chapters. By the early twelfth century the archdeacons
were firmly in place as part of the establishment of the new secular chapters
– in the regular cathedral chapters the archdeacon remained until the
Dissolution something of an alien, secular presence. After some preliminary
hesitation, Lanfranc and his colleagues confirmed and extended the monastic
chapters – extended them partly by changing the character of some older
cathedrals, partly by new foundations, partly by the rapacious acquisitions
of some ambitious bishops, absorbing rich and ancient abbeys such as
Coventry and Bath.[39] The anonymous monk who attacked Theobald of
Etampes early in the twelfth century was to include Rouen, Bayeux, York,
London, Salisbury and Lincoln in a catalogue of the notable centres of
communities of clerks, that is, of secular canons.[40] The list is comprehensive,
for Wells (temporarily overshadowed by monastic Bath), Lichfield (whose
bishop had gone to Coventry) and Chichester had to wait till the 1130s and
1140s for effective reorganisation: the new cathedrals, Ely and Carlisle, were
Benedictine and Augustinian respectively; and the rest of the chapters had

[36] For a full study of the Lincoln evidence, see *Fasti*, iii; for Henry of Huntingdon's evidence
as a whole see now the edn by D. E. Greenway, OMT (Oxford, 1996), pp. 590–93.

[37] See also Brett, *English Church under Henry I*, p. 200 and n. 5.

[38] See C. N. L. Brooke, 'St Peter of Gloucester and St Cadog of Llancarfan', in K. Jackson et
al., *Celt and Saxon*, ed. N. K. Chadwick (Cambridge, 1963), pp. 258–322, at pp. 287–88, reprinted
in Brooke, *The Church and the Welsh Border* (Woodbridge, 1986), pp. 50–94, at p. 73 and n.
100. St Davids also had territorial archdeaconries from the time of Bishop Bernard (1115–48):
J. Conway Davies, *Episcopal Acts Relating to Welsh Dioceses, 1066–1272*, i, Historical Society of
the Church in Wales (1946), esp. pp. 241, 270; and see now *St Davids Episcopal Acta*, ed.
J. Barrow, South Wales Record Society, 13 (Cardiff, 1998), pp. 27–30.

[39] Brett, *English Church under Henry I*, pp. 186 f.; see above, p. 50; D. Knowles, *Monastic
Order in England* (2nd edn, Cambridge, 1963), ch. 36.

[40] Ed. R. Foreville and J. Leclercq in *Analecta Monastica* = *Studia Anselmiana*, 41 (Rome,
1957), p. 65.

become Benedictine priories before the end of the eleventh century.[41] For the four chapters of canons on their way to being fully fledged by 1100, there is some evidence to suggest that in three cases a major reorganisation had been undertaken or completed c. 1090–92; and even in London the full establishment of the prebendal system seems to date from c. 1090. But the status of the canons at Salisbury in early days is ambiguous, and they may well have lived a common life for a generation at least.[42] At Lincoln, York and later at Salisbury a pattern of dignities on the continental model was established – with dean, precentor and treasurer at its head – and a schoolmaster, later a chancellor, as well – with the archdeacons usually installed below these dignitaries in chapter and choir. In London the archdeacons came immediately after the dean in precedence and the other dignities only slowly emerged; and we may see here the vestige of a story which could probably be paralleled elsewhere if more evidence had survived. In all these sees, in theory, a semi-regular chapter of canons had existed, or been created or revived, immediately before 1066; and we have seen that in theory at least this was under the surveyance of a superior whose title might have been archdeacon or provost. In the case of York the first Norman archbishop, Thomas of Bayeux, took steps to reestablish this kind of arrangement before establishing the pattern to which he had been accustomed in Normandy; a common life seems also to have been established at Salisbury.[43] It has been conjectured that the late arrival of the fully-fledged secular chapter was due to the resistance of Lanfranc, who not only fostered monastic chapters but may well have wished to see regular canons in the non-monastic cathedrals; and it is noticeable that the flowering of the chapters of canons, including at least three of secular canons – and the first attempt to form the suffragan bishops of the province of Canterbury into a chapter with a dean at its head – seem to approximate to the vacancy after Lanfranc's

[41] Dates in D. Knowles and R. N. Hadcock, *Medieval Religious Houses, England and Wales* (2nd edn, London, 1971), pp. 53–81; for Carlisle, *Fasti*, ii, p. 19.

[42] Above, pp. 51–53. On Salisbury, see now Greenway in *Fasti*, iv, pp. xxii–xxv; T. Webber, *Scribes and Scholars at Salisbury Cathedral* (Oxford, 1992). For correctives on earlier views of Salisbury, see esp. D. E. Greenway in *Tradition and Change* (see n. on p. 117), pp. 77–101. The charter of 1091 for Salisbury, which she has shown to be substantially authentic, evidently enshrines a genuine tradition of a step in the process c. 1089–91, confirmed by the remarkable annal for 1089 in *The Chronicle of Holyrood*, ed. M. O. and A. O. Anderson, Scottish Historical Society, 3rd Series, 30 (Edinburgh, 1938), p. 110. But it is likely that the canons led a common life, possibly following the rule of Amalarius's *Liber officialis*, Diana Greenway in *Fasti*, iv, p. xxiv.

[43] See above, and p. 52. The surviving evidence scarcely *proves* the priority of Bayeux over the English chapters: it is probable and natural to assume that Bishop Odo's work at Bayeux was under way before Thomas departed in 1070.

death, from 1089 to 1093.[44] Be that as it may, it is at least possible that in the time of Lanfranc and in the non-monastic chapters one or more archdeacons held sway until the advent of deans and dignitaries; and in the case of St Paul's this is indeed likely – the most probable explanation for the entrenched position the archdeacons seem to have held already by c. 1090.

This might suggest that the archdeacon of the late eleventh century was as much a power in the cathedral and close as in the diocese. But this is conjectural and, if true, only a temporary phase. For in the same period there began that polarisation of the bishop's and the chapter's jurisdiction which was to make the bishop almost a stranger in his own cathedral in the late middle ages. This process left the archdeacon in an ambiguous state: on the one hand he was the bishop's officer, first and foremost, his right-hand man, his *alter ego*; very probably, if the bishop was Roger of Salisbury or Gilbert Foliot, the bishop's nephew.[45] On the other hand, he was almost invariably a canon, until the fourteenth century, when a price was put on every benefice and prebend and archdeaconries counted as separate items, so that it was possible to be an archdeacon without holding a canonry.[46] In the twelfth century it was still reckoned a virtue that the archdeacon should be a canon, though councils in 1125–27 thundered against other pluralities.[47] We cannot name holders of more than one archdeaconry at any time before the 1180s; but they may have had in mind Hugh the Chanter of York, precentor and archdeacon, or his colleague the treasurer who combined the office with the archdeaconry of the East Riding, and whose successors continued to do so until early in the next century.[48] These

[44] Above, p. 53; cf. *GF*, p. 229. But the new evidence from Salisbury (above, n. 42) compels substantial qualification to the arguments there propounded.

[45] E. J. Kealey, *Roger of Salisbury* (Berkeley, 1972), pp. 272–76; *GF*, pp. 44–9, 204–5, etc.

[46] Cf. C. N. L. Brooke in *A History of St Paul's Cathedral*, ed. W. R. Matthews and W. M. Atkins (London, 1957), pp. 52–53. The exception is Lichfield: only the archdeacon of Chester had a stall there; but between the 1070s and 1220s Lichfield had a status in some ways inferior to Chester and then Coventry.

[47] *Councils and Synods*, i, 2, pp. 740, 748; the second specifically refers to archdeaconries in different sees, a practice which cannot be documented; cf. Brett, *English Church under Henry I*, pp. 210–11.

[48] See C. T. Clay in *Yorkshire Archaeological Journal*, 35 (1940–43), pp. 10–11, 18, 33 etc.; 36 (1944–47), pp. 276–77 – for Hugh the Chanter. On him see also Hugh the Chanter, *History of the Church of York*, ed. C. Johnson, M. Brett et al., OMT (Oxford, 1990), esp. pp. xix–xxiii; and *Fasti*, vi, forthcoming. For a parallel in Lincoln, cf. Richard de Almaria, precentor and archdeacon of Stow, *Fasti*, iii, pp. 12, 45. Godfrey de Lucy almost certainly combined the archdeaconries of Derby and Richmond in the 1180s, *English Episcopal Acta*, 8, ed. M. J. Franklin (London, 1993), p. lii; *English Episcopal Acta*, 16 (1998), p. 116. In the 1190s one man combined the archdeaconries of Carlisle and Durham, *Fasti*, ii, pp. 23, 38.

cases illustrate the intimacy of archdeacons and chapter at York, which reached its peak when Archdeacon Osbert was accused of poisoning the archbishop in 1154.[49]

Yet long before this the archdeacon was clearly associated with the bishop or archbishop in York as well as elsewhere as associates in an alien administration. Few aspects of the ecclesiastical scene are so astonishing or perverse in our eyes as the claims for exemption from bishop and archdeacon made by the cathedral chapters themselves. When the arrangements came out into the full light of day in the thirteenth century, most secular chapters claimed exemption for their estates, and in several, including York, Salisbury and Wells, the dean – or the subdean acting for him – was archdeacon of the cathedral city.[50] These exemptions grew up in various ways at various times, and were subject to frequent attacks by bishops and archbishops. In Lincoln a succession of tough bishops, especially St Hugh and Robert Grosseteste, kept the chapter at bay; but elsewhere a bewildering variety of customs became firmly established. Their origin is obscure; but the most recent study of the York peculiars has made a convincing case, which must apply elsewhere too, that their origin is to be sought in the circumstances of the first generation after the Norman Conquest.[51] They form a dramatic illustration of a phenomenon for which there is widespread evidence: the tightening of ecclesiastical administration by the early Norman bishops after a period of relatively loose control. It is a process desperately hard for us to discern, since it was soon overtaken by the freezing or fossilising effects of the general establishment of the norms of canon law in the twelfth century. But this was widespread in western Christendom; some features of the changes after the Conquest were unique to England. One of these was the development of such local peculiars in the hands of cathedral chapters – which, at least in the present state of knowledge, is not fully paralleled elsewhere. Another is the proliferation of tiny churches and parishes in towns large and small, which gave London one hundred, Winchester fifty and even the modest town of Cambridge about fifteen parishes before 1200.[52] Most of this proliferation evidently took place in the tenth and eleventh centuries, when the hand of authority sat light on these towns; and we see the reaction against it, and the

---

[49] Above, pp. 61, 63.

[50] K. Edwards, *English Secular Chapters* (p. 115 n. 32), pp. 125–34; Sandra Brown, 'Aspects of the History of Peculiar Jurisdictions in the Medieval Church of York' (unpublished D.Phil. thesis, University of York, 1980).

[51] S. Brown, 'Aspects'.

[52] See above, ch. 4; C. N. L. Brooke and G. Keir, *London, 800–1216* (London, 1975), ch. 6; J. Campbell, 'The Church in Anglo-Saxon Towns', *Studies in Church History*, 16 (1979), pp. 119–35, at pp. 126ff.

reaction against Norman authority, most clearly in the synodal decree at Worcester attributed to 1092, forged by the monks of Worcester, probably in the 1140s or 1150s.[53] The synod declared, by heroic simplification, that no proliferation of parishes had taken place in the city – and indeed Worcester was one of the few where this was not wholly untrue; but they also declared the cathedral exempt (since the time of St Oswald) from the sinister pretensions of archdeacons and deans. This was in fact newfangled doctrine, but it confirms the impression from secular cathedrals, that in many quarters an attempt was being made to check the growing pretensions of archdeacons – and this included exempt abbeys, who found it most convenient to parry the bishop's archdeacons by setting up archdeacons of their own.[54] All this may be relatively superficial; but to go deeper and define from the slight traces of evidence precisely what an archdeacon did in the eleventh or early twelfth centuries would carry us too far from our purpose – and the task has been admirably performed, so far as it can be, by Dr Martin Brett and Professor Brian Kemp.[55]

The territorial archdeaconry was firmly established on the Continent by the early eleventh century;[56] and already before 1092 Bishop Remigius of Lincoln had divided his diocese into seven archdeaconries, mostly along the lines (approximately) of shire boundaries. Thus Henry of Huntingdon, who was born late in the eleventh century, claims to have known all of the first seven archdeacons personally. We have unexceptionable evidence that the territorial archdeaconries in the diocese of Lincoln were established this early, and it is natural to assume that when we encounter a multiplying of archdeacons in other sees in the late eleventh or early twelfth centuries, they also represent territorial divisions. This is not easy to prove, and has been doubted;[57] it has been suggested that in some cases there was an

[53] Above, n. 17; and ch. 4.

[54] See Jane Sayers, 'Monastic Archdeacons', in *Church and Government in the Middle Ages: Essays Presented to C. R. Cheney on his Seventieth Birthday*, ed. C. Brooke, D. Luscombe, G. Martin and D. Owen (Cambridge, 1976), pp. 177–203.

[55] See above, end of n. 1.

[56] Lemarignier, in Lot and Fawtier, *Histoire des institutions*, iii, pp. 20–21. For Lincoln and Henry of Huntingdon, see below, p. 135.

[57] See R. R. Darlington, *Cartulary of Worcester Cathedral Priory*, Pipe Roll Society, new series, 38 (1968), p. lxiv; *Acta of the Bishops of Chichester*, ed. H. Mayr-Harting, Canterbury and York Society, 56 (1964), pp. 48–49. The last discussion merely, and correctly, observes the lack of evidence; the other seems to deduce a measure of scepticism from this lack of evidence, and this judgement seems to have been prejudiced by the absence of title in witness lists. Barlow, *English Church, 1066–1154*, p. 49, seems closer to my view. Cf. also J. Scammell, 'The Rural Chapter in England from the Eleventh to the Fourteenth Century', in *EHR*, 86 (1971), pp. 1–21, at p. 7 and n. 3.

intermediate stage, when there was a group of archdeacons here and there without the clear demarcation of function. It may be so; but such indications as exist seem clearly to point the other way.

Scribes of twelfth-century charters seem almost to have deliberately obscured this problem by the way they describe archdeacons. In the eleventh century it had been common for witnesses or 'signatories' to have only their status or order named, not their church or see or shire: Ælfheah the abbot or bishop or archbishop, not abbot of Bath, bishop of Winchester, archbishop of Canterbury; and there are many cases in the two generations following the Norman Conquest in which archdeacons are similarly treated. The normal practice in the twelfth century, however, was to give them the title of the see in which they served. This is well known to all who use twelfth-century charters extensively, but it is worth dwelling on for a moment, since it has obscured the problem we are studying. Armitage Robinson showed long ago that the archdeacons in the diocese of Bath were called, almost indifferently, 'of Bath' and 'of Wells' – with an occasional reference to an archdeacon of 'beyond the Parret'; but he argued very cogently back from thirteenth-century evidence through the known succession of archdeacons in the second half of the twelfth that the distinction into the archdeaconries of Bath and Wells and Taunton (bounded by the Parret) went back to the mid twelfth century and perhaps a good bit earlier.[58] Similarly Sir Charles Clay showed that even the archdeacon of Nottingham or Richmond could be called archdeacon of York, though the former held sway entirely outside the shire and the latter was archdeaon of most of what is now called Cumbria; and the association of the treasurer's office with the archdeaconry of the East Riding creates a presumption that this territorial archdeaconry at least had been formed by the 1090s.[59] There are exceptions. The numerous shires of the diocese of Lincoln and the diversity of the see variously known as Chester and Coventry – and in times more ancient and modern as Lichfield – seem to explain the more frequent early use of archidiaconal titles. There was also some experiment with other versions: 'archdeacon of the bishop', 'archdeacon of the city of London', 'archdeacon of Cambridge' for the archdeacon of Ely; and so forth.[60] Here are a few examples. Armitage Robinson showed in lavish detail that

[58] J. A. Robinson, *Somerset Historical Essays* (London, 1921), ch. 4, esp. pp. 75 (territorial designations), 79–84 (confusion of Bath and Wells).

[59] C. T. Clay, 'Notes on the Early Archdeacons in the Church of York', *Yorkshire Archaeological Journal*, 36 (1944–7), pp. 269–87, 409–34, esp. pp. 270–72. For the East Riding see below p. 137.

[60] *Fasti*, ii, pp. 62, 91 (of the bishops of Norwich and Winchester); *Fasti*, i, p. 8 (London); *Fasti*, ii, p. 50 (Ely, William of Lavington).

Thomas, archdeacon of Wells c. 1195, could be called indifferently of Wells or of Bath, in adjacent charters and adjacent pipe rolls; and that there really had been a Thomas archdeacon of Bath earlier in the 1160s. From London, 1163 x 1178, we have a charter of Bishop Gilbert Foliot 'factum ... apud sanctum Paulum' in the presence of the chapter, witness, 'Radulfo de Dici et Ricardo Foliotth archidiaconis ... canonicis nostris' – whom other documents unambiguously identify as the archdeacons of Middlesex and Colchester.[61]

Anglo-Saxon abbots and bishops normally 'signed' without naming see or abbey, but we could not deduce from this that their local habitation was unfixed or mattered little. By the same token it is abundantly clear that the use of 'archidiaconus' without location was purely a matter of convention, and did not signify that the archdeacon was uncertain of his cure. If we project lists of archdeacons backwards from periods when they are securely placed to periods when we have no territorial designation, we can often deduce with reasonable accuracy where they belong;[62] more important, there are several cases in which as soon, or almost as soon, as we have evidence that archdeacons are multiplying, there is reason to suppose that there were as many archdeacons as a generation or two later when the territorial designations have come out into the open. There are also some subtler indications, such as the order of witnessing.

Students of twelfth-century charters know well that there is some rationality in the order of witnesses, but very few strict rules. Clergy will precede laymen, bishops witness before abbots, and abbots before archdeacons – and so forth; but every rule is broken some time, most were broken frequently. This makes some of the hidden rules the more impressive; and by hidden I mean the cases in which an almost perfect uniformity can be observed in an unexpected place. Thus in charters of the see of London the archdeacon of London himself nearly always witnesses first. This case is particularly striking, since it enables us to deduce that Reinger, who witnesses first in eight cases between 1102 and 1114 x 1115, but is never given a territorial designation, was in fact archdeacon of London.[63] His standing

[61] Robinson, *Somerset Historical Essays*, pp. 81–82, cf. p. 79; *GFL*, no. 429, pp. 468–69.

[62] Cf. *Fasti*, passim; and the discussion in Clay, 'Notes on the Early Archdeacons', *Yorkshire Archaeological Journal*, 36 (1944–47), pp. 285–7.

[63] See *Fasti*, i, pp. 8–9, also citing other evidence. *Charters and Documents Illustrating the History of Salisbury*, ed. W. H. R. Jones and W. D. Macray, RS (London, 1891), pp. 19, 43, 50, might suggest a similar role for the archdeacon of Dorset, but in the earliest charter in which Dorset appears with other archdeacons, he comes third and last, so that no inferences can be made about the early role of his office, E. J. Kealey, *Roger of Salisbury* (Berkeley etc., 1972), p. 254.

may not relate so much to the notion of an *archidiaconus maior* parallel to such continental potentates as the cardinal archdeacons of Autun, Besançon and Toul,[64] but more probably reflects the fact that his was the oldest office in the chapter and its precedence, after the dean's, not seriously challenged until the late twelfth century. But the pattern of archdeacons – four, with London first – which we meet in these early charters, is identical with those of later generations when territorial designations, London, Middlesex, Essex and Colchester, are commonly added; it would seem to be needless scepticism not to think that the territorial division went back before 1102 – indeed, to *c.* 1090.

This much is proved: the territorial archdeaconry was an institution well known to the first generation of Norman bishops and introduced in some sees at least by 1100. For a plurality of archdeacons without separate juris-diction there is no evidence from the eleventh or twelfth centuries. It is a possibility which cannot be wholly discounted. We can be sure what Dr Grantly would have thought of it; we can conjecture what the hereditary archdeacons of Huntingdon or Middlesex would have said to it – and if neither Quintilian nor Cyprian his son ever called themselves archdeacons 'of Colchester' in surviving documents, they had the excuse that they were following convention, and that their Christian names would distinguish them from all other archdeacons living or dead.

[64] See S. Kuttner, 'Cardinalis: The History of a Canonical Concept', *Traditio*, 3 (1945), pp. 129–214, at pp. 159–60 and nn.

Appendix

First References to Archdeacons, Multiplying Archdeacons and Territorial Archdeacons

The advance of *Fasti* and *EEA* since 1985 have made it possible somewhat to abbreviate the original Appendix.

Bath and Wells. Benselin occ. 1086, 1088 x 1106. Three archdeacons occ. 1106. Titles clearly distinguishing Bath, Wells and 'De ultra Parret' occ. 1136 x 1158, F. Ramsey, *EEA*, 10, pp. 216–19 and no. 37.

Canterbury. Valerius said to have been appointed by Lanfranc (above, p. 125). Anschetil occ. December 1074 x August 1075, *Councils and Synods*, i, 2, p. 616; *Fasti*, ii, p. 12.

Carlisle. Carlisle was founded 1133: archdeacons Elias followed by Robert occ. 1133 x 1156, *Fasti*, ii, p. 23.

Chester-Coventry. Two archdeacons probably occ. 1086 x 1087; territorial designations (apart from Chester and Coventry, the names of the see) occ. Derby 1121 x 1126; Shropshire 1127; Stafford 1132, by which date the full complement of five territorial archdeacons were in place. Fasti in *EEA*, 14, pp. 172–79.

Chichester. Lanfranc refers to *uestri archidiaconi* in a letter to the bishop 1070 x 1087, *The Letters of Lanfranc*, ed. H. Clover and M. Gibson, OMT (Oxford, 1979), no. 30, p. 116. Ricoard occurs 1088 x 1118; two archdeacons occur by 1164, but the title of the second archdeaconry, Lewes, is not known before 1204 x 1207, *Acta of the Bishops of Chichester*, ed. H. Mayr-Harting, pp. 48, 212–15, esp. 213.

Durham. The earliest archdeacon occurs before May 1080; two archdeacons occur by *c.* 1127; the territorial title Northumbria (later Northumberland) after 1174. *Fasti*, ii, pp. 37–40; H. S. Offler, 'The Early Archdeacons in the Diocese of Durham', in *Transactions of the Architectural and Archaeological Society of Durham and Northumberland*, 11 (1962), pp. 189–207.

For the earliest date see *Symeonis monachi opera omnia*, ed. T. Arnold, RS, 2 vols (London, 1882–5), i, pp. 114–15; for Northumbria, *Fasti*, ii, pp. 39–40; *Feodarium prioratus Dunelmensis*, ed. W. Greenwell (Surtees Society, 58, 1872), p. 125n. (*c.* 1180 x 1195); G. V. Scammell, *Hugh du Puiset* (Cambridge, 1956), p. 261 (1195).

(*Ely*. Ely was founded in 1109; Nicholas had been archdeacon of Huntingdon, including Cambridgeshire and parts of Hertfordshire, and probably continued to his death *c.* 1110, to be succeeded by William Brito. *Fasti*, ii, p. 50.)

Exeter. The deaths of three archdeacons occ. in the Exeter Martyrology before 1100. The first two died in 1083 and 1084, and it may well be that there were already at least two in the diocese; but this cannot be proved until the 1110s, F. Barlow in *EEA*, 12, pp. 306–10. By 1133 there were already four, the final number, *EEA*, 11, no. 18 gives three; at that date Robert de Warelwast was archdeacon of Exeter: *EEA* xii, p. 306. For full details, ibid., pp. 306–10.

Hereford. Hainfrid or Heinfrid occurs 1085, and from then until 1101/2, V. H. Galbraith in *EHR*, 44 (1929), facing p. 353; Z. N. and C. N. L. Brooke, in *Cambridge Historical Journal*, 8 (1944–46), pp. 14, 183. Two archdeacons of Shropshire (so titled) occur in the time of Bishop Robert de Bethune, 1131–48: *GF*, p. 268.

Lincoln. Seven archdeacons were established in seven territorial archdeaconries by 1092, according to Henry of Huntingdon, ed. Diana Greenway, OMT (Oxford, 1996), pp. 590–91; cf. *Fasti*, iii, pp. 24–41; doubtless some or most of these had held office for some years before 1092. The eighth can be seen emerging from *c.* 1092 down to the first specific reference to an archdeacon of the 'West Riding', *c.* 1145 (of Lindsey) or Stow by the 1150s. *Fasti*, iii, pp. ix, 44–45.

London. For Edward, archdeacon, late monk of Christ Church, see above, p. 125; for the four archdeacons of 1102, see pp. 132–33. Since all appear first in their respective prebendal lists (*Fasti*, i, pp. 45, 51, 63, 71), their appointments presumably occurred *c.* 1090 or earlier. The titles Essex, Colchester occur in 1142 and perhaps earlier; Roger Archdeacon was said by Ralph de Diceto, his ultimate successor as archdeacon from the early 1150s but writing at the end of the century, to be archdeacon of Middlesex before 1127 (*Fasti*, i, pp. 13, 15, 18). In this case a secure succession effectively guarantees that the later territorial distinctions were established by *c.* 1090; we might learn more if we knew when and how the parish of Islington became part of the archdeaconry of London, which was otherwise identical with the City. R. Newcourt, *Repertorium ecclesiasticum parochiale Londinense*, 2 vols (London, 1708–10), i, esp. pp. 676–78; W. E. Lunt, *Valuation of Norwich* (Oxford, 1926), pp. 326–33. Westminster, from St Clement Danes westwards, lay in the archdeaconry of Middlesex, though the abbey and its precincts were exempt.

Norwich. The first known archdeacon, Geoffrey, occurs in *Domesday Book* (London, 1783), ii, fol. 193 (cited *Fasti*, ii, p. 62); two occur probably by 1101 and it seems that there were already at least three in the first decade of the twelfth century (see *Fasti*, ii, p. 62). Professor Greenway notes later evidence that the fourth, Sudbury, was created by the division of Suffolk by Bishop Everard (1121–45), and the territorial title Suffolk first occurs in the 1120s (ibid., pp. 61, 67); it was applied to both archdeacons in the shire. Norfolk and Sudbury do not occur as titles until late in the century (ibid., pp. 65, 70).

Rochester. The first archdeacon occurs 1096 x 1107 (ibid., p. 81; see above, p. 9).

Salisbury. Gunter of le Mans had been archdeacon before becoming monk of Battle and then abbot of Thorney in 1085. There were at least two by 1099 (Everard and Hubald), probably four in the time of Bishop Roger (1102/7– 1139), *Fasti*, iv, pp. 23–24. A clear distinction of the two Wiltshire archdeacons into Salisbury and Wiltshire came much later, and Berkshire is not so named before 1150 x 1151; but Dorset was clearly designated before 1139, and it is reasonable to suppose territorial archdeacons were fully established then – if not earlier (*Fasti*, iv, pp. 23–35).

Winchester. William of Chichester occurs 1078 x 87; two archdeacons occur 1107; 'Surrey' occurs specifically in 1178 (*Fasti*, ii, pp. 91, 94).

Worcester. Ailric occurs 1086 (*Domesday Book*, i, fol. 173r-v); two by 1112; 'Gloucester' from *c.* 1140. *Fasti*, ii, pp. 104, 107; R. R. Darlington, *Cartulary of Worcester Cathedral Priory* (Pipe Roll Society, new series 38, 1968), pp. lxiii– lxiv. Darlington, followed by Professor Greenway, suggested doubt whether there was a territorial division in 1112; but the evidence is of the same character here as in many sees.

York. Hugh the Chanter says that Archbishop Thomas I (1070–1100) apportioned (*divisit*) archdeacons *per diocesim* in a context which suggests a date not late in his pontificate; and he names one in 1093, Hugh the Chanter, *History of the Church of York* (1990), pp. 12–13, 18–19. The obit roll of the abbot of Savigny of 1113 names four archdeacons of York as dead by then: 'Girardo ... Dinando [*for* Durando] ... Rannulfo archidiacono et thesaurario ... Willelmo archidiacono', *Rouleaux des morts du IXe au XVe siècle*, ed. L. V. Delisle (Société de l'Histoire de France (Paris, 1866)), p. 199. Put together with other evidence this suggests at least two, more probably three or four archdeacons in the see already by 1113; and Ranulf's combination of offices seems to show that the union of treasurer and archdeacon of the East Riding had already occurred; the full five archdeacons occur already *c*. 1121 x 1128 (see below). The designation Richmond occurs by 1181, *York Minster Fasti*, i, ed. C. T. Clay, Yorkshire Archaeological Society, record series, 123 (1958), p. 84; Nottingham, East and West Riding by 1135. For all this see studies of C. T. Clay, esp. in *Yorkshire Archaeological Journal*, 36 (1944–47), pp. 269–87; p. 269 for early territorial titles, p. 274 for five archdeacons *c*. 1121 x 1128, pp. 585–87 for other early evidence. See also *EEA*, 5, pp. 123–27; *Fasti*, vi (forthcoming).

8

Princes and Kings as Patrons of Monasteries: Normandy and England, 1066–1135

There is a famous passage in the *Historia novorum* of the English monk, Eadmer, in which he reports a conversation between St Anselm, archbishop of Canterbury, and King William II, on the moral state of England. In the course of it Anselm is reported to have rebuked William for his treatment of the English monasteries, above all for keeping some vacant for years together and enjoying their revenues to the destruction of the monastic life and the disgrace of king and kingdom. 'What is that to do with you?', retorted the king. 'Are not the abbeys mine? Dash it – you do as you like with your manors and shall I not do as I like with my abbeys?' Anselm replied: 'They are yours to defend and guard as their patron (*quasi advocatus*); but not yours to assault or lay waste ...'[1] In another passage Eadmer claims that he was reproducing the exact words of a conversation,[2] and although this was notoriously not the practice of most historians between Thucydides and the eighteenth century when quoting direct speech, Sir Richard Southern has shown in his book on *St Anselm and his Biographer* that it was central to Eadmer's purposes to reproduce discourse, even if not verbatim, at least to give the genuine impression of the spoken word.[3] In this passage we may suppose at least a genuine nucleus, even though there is no reason to suppose that Eadmer reported what he had himself heard; and the succinct, staccato utterance of William Rufus is characteristic of the way in which the king's speech, held up by his pronounced

First printed in *Il monachesimo e la riforma ecclesiastica, 1049–1122*, Mendola, 4 (1968, publ. Milan, 1971), pp. 125–44.

[1] Eadmer, *Historia novorum*, ed. M. Rule, RS (London, 1884), pp. 49–50. Much has been written on the theme of monastic patronage since 1971. For a general view of the patronage of existing houses, see E. Cownie, *Religious Patronage in Anglo-Norman England* (Woodbridge, 1998).

[2] Eadmer, *Historia novorum*, p. 125.

[3] R. W. Southern, *St Anselm and his Biographer* (Cambridge, 1963), p. 333.

stammer, is recorded by Eadmer.[4] But however authentic it may be as conversation, it is also clear that another purpose lies behind Eadmer's presentation: for here is a succinct summary of the whole controversy about the *Eigenkirche*, the proprietary church; here is a brilliant distillation of the great work of Ulrich Stütz and his disciples and followers, presented to us by a contemporary.[5] On the one hand, Rufus drives straight to the heart of the *Eigenkirche*: an abbey to him is simply a piece of property, like a manor. Equally, on the other hand, Anselm states what a Gregorian reformer supposed to be the function of a patron: he is no more and no less than a policeman.

The passage is also a summary of what seems to me to be the interest of my subject: for the Norman kings of England, in their relations to the abbeys of which they were patrons and benefactors, revealed in a remarkable way the range of attitudes and concerns which a patron of our period might show. Not perhaps the whole range, for it is evident that one interest is the comparison and contrast between Anglo-Norman views of the patron's role and those held elsewhere; above all, the well-known difference between the legal standing of the English or French patron and of the German *Vogt*.[6] Something of this will appear as we proceed; but I believe that the practical difference has been somewhat exaggerated by the tendency of historians to concentrate on one or another aspect of a patron's relations with his abbeys; that the real interest of the subject lies more in analysing the nuances of these relations in different situations; and that many recent studies have in one way or another shown this.

I shall also present a picture which is frankly selective, to illustrate a theme rather than to give a comprehensive view of it; partly because I believe that this is more interesting and illuminating in a short essay, and

---

[4] For other passages in Eadmer, see especially pp. 52f, 100ff, 115f; for the king's stammer, William of Malmesbury, *Gesta regum*, ed. R. A. B. Mynors, R. M. Thomson and M. Winterbottom, OMT, i (Oxford, 1998), pp. 566–67.

[5] On the *Eigenkirche*, see the classical studies of U. Stütz, *Geschichte des kirchlichen Benefizialwesens* (2nd edn, by H. E. Feine, Aalen, 1961) and bibliography in H. E. Feine, *Kirchliche Rechtsgeschichte*, i, *Die katholische Kirche* (4th edn, Köln-Graz, 1964), pp. 170–72; for the *Eigenkirche* in England, H. Böhmer in *Texte und Forschungen zur Englischen Kulturgeschichte: Festgabe für Felix Liebermann* (Halle, 1921), pp. 301–53; R. Lennard, *Rural England, 1086–1135* (Oxford, 1959), pp. 288–338; F. Barlow, *The English Church, 1000–1066* (2nd edn, London, 1963), pp. 186ff. For a criticism of Stütz's concept, see S. Reynolds, *Fiefs and Vassals* (Oxford, 1994), pp. 61, 418ff.

[6] On the Vogt, see Feine, *Kirchliche Rechtsgeschichte*, i, pp. 247–48; on the French Avoué see article by R. Laprat in *Dictionnaire d'histoire et de géographie ecclésiastiques*, v, cols 1222–35; on the English patron, see Susan Wood, *The English Monasteries and their Patrons in the Thirteenth Century* (London, 1955).

partly because it seems to be dictated by the nature of our evidence. If we ask, for instance, how much William the Conqueror gave to Saint-Etienne at Caen, or Henry I to Reading or to Cirencester abbey? – we can never hope to give any precise answer. Nor can we tell how much Henry I actually gave to the numerous lesser houses of which he was founder. The documents notoriously hide rather than reveal the nature of many transactions; what purports to be a pious gift will sometimes turn out to be a sale or exchange which caused the donor no temporal loss to balance the spiritual gain he claimed to be achieving. There are many gifts recorded in this period, especially in England, which were generous hopes rather than genuine grants – of churches, for instance. Such were those in the *parochia* of Leominster in Herefordshire, which the donor's successors had little hope of honouring, since other folk had more substantial claims to them; or the churches of the district of Berkeley in Gloucestershire which were given in whole or part to three different monasteries by three different donors, a circumstance which could only be resolved by a series of *causes célèbres*, in which papal judges-delegate and the king cooperated in the second half of the twelfth century.[7] It seems sensible therefore to select certain aspects of the field of this essay on which we can gaze with a clear, unimpeded vision, for particular enquiry.

Of the four Anglo-Norman kings, the first and third, William the Conqueror and Henry I, were men of complex personality who can only be grasped if we see two or three different men under the skin of each; the second and fourth, William II and Stephen, were simpler, though each in his way no less interesting. The trail of devastation still revealed in Domesday Book in 1086 is a monument to the most consistently ruthless king England has had; the close friendship with Archbishop Lanfranc, the fidelity of his married life, and his relations with some of his abbeys, reveal a man with a strong moral sense in some regions of his mind at least, and a genuine piety – perhaps of a largely external kind.[8] William II, William Rufus, was a soldier, a man of the camp, a blasphemer; we may suppose that, like the devils, he believed but he only rarely trembled. When he came near to death's door, he insisted on Anselm's appointment as archbishop, an event

---

[7] Cf. B. Kemp, 'The Churches of the Berkeley Hernesse', *Transactions of the Bristol and Gloucestershire Archaeological Society*, 87 (1968), pp. 96–110. My provisional account, now corrected by Professor Kemp's article, appeared in *Celt and Saxon*, ed. N. K. Chadwick (Cambridge, 1963), pp. 280–82; revised and repr. in Brooke, *The Church and the Welsh Border*, ed. D. N. Dumville and C. N. L. Brooke (Woodbridge, 1986), pp. 67–69.

[8] Two notable studies of the Conqueror are M. De Bouard, *Guillaume le Conquérant* (Paris, 1958; 2nd edn. 1966) and D. C. Douglas, *William the Conqueror* (London, 1964).

which both men subsequently much regretted.[9] Henry I was perhaps the most cruel of his line, and the fact that he acknowledged over twenty illegitimate children is in sharp contrast with his father's record. He was called the lion of justice,[10] partly, I suspect, because a lion is an animal which tears its meat with its teeth and claws. He made a business of government, as Sir Richard Southern has taught us;[11] and yet I find it impossible to believe that business alone explains his gargantuan generosity to his nephews and to one at least of his illegitimate children; his precise insistence on the legitimate inheritance of monarchy; and some aspects of his monastic patronage which seem closely related to these interests. Stephen was an irresponsible soldier, with considerable ability, but without the ruthless consistency of his uncle; and a man with a certain charm and a piety, so far as we can tell, of a wholly conventional kind. Stephen had many weaknesses, but in the end seems the least unattractive of the line.[12]

I propose to take four examples of abbeys which attracted these men's patronage, examples which in the end will involve all four in our gaze, and whose analysis will lead us to broaden our enquiry out to see something like the whole range of our topic.

It is well known that the Conqueror and his wife were related or connected in some way which made their marriage uncanonical; and that in the end the pope only confirmed the bond after many years on condition that each founded an abbey as an act of penance. Caen is now once again a great city; but when I visited it not long after the Second World War its origins were dramatically revealed: for at either end lay the great abbey churches with a city almost swept clear in between. The abbeys were the making of

---

[9] Eadmer, *Historia novorum*, pp. 30ff; cf. Southern, *St Anselm and his Biographer*, pp. 150ff. On William II, see F. Barlow, *William Rufus* (London, 1983).

[10] First recorded by Geoffrey of Monmouth, ed. N. Wright, *The Historia Regum Britanniae of Geoffrey of Monmouth*, i (Cambridge, 1985), p. 75 (of the 1130s); this is in the Prophecies of Merlin, and the point would have been lost unless the phrase could be immediately recognised as a reference to Henry I. The qualities, and perhaps the phrase itself, must have been currently regarded as characteristic of the king: the passage was written *c.* 1135 (for the date, see Wright, *The Historia*, p. xi) shortly before Henry's death, and we may therefore regard it as reflecting his reputation in his later years.

[11] R. W. Southern, 'The Place of Henry I in English History', *Proceedings of the British Academy*, 48 (1962), pp. 127–69, repr. in his *Medieval Humanism and Other Studies* (Oxford, 1970), ch. 11 – a paper to which I am much indebted, although I have tried to develop here aspects of Henry which are in some measure relegated to the background by Sir Richard Southern.

[12] On Stephen, see R. H. C. Davis, *King Stephen* (London, 1967), and the same author's paper in *History* 49 (1964), pp. 1–12; H. A. Cronne, *The Reign of Stephen* (London, 1970); and see now *The Anarchy of Stephen's Reign*, ed. E. King (Oxford, 1994).

Caen; they also ensured that Caen should be a ducal town, a centre of loyalty; and the details of how the Conqueror organised this sleight-of-hand have been skilfully reconstructed by Professor Michel de Bouard.[13] Caen was intended to be a military, commercial and spiritual focus of ducal interest in north-western Normandy, in the Calvados. This was symbolised, and converted into the realm of practical politics, by the placing of the Conqueror's daughter Cecilia first as a nun, then as abbess of the abbey of the Holy Trinity;[14] and of Lanfranc, the great Italian intellectual, who already as prior of Bec had established the foundations of that close intimacy based on mutual respect which was to play so large a part in the Norman settlement of the English church, as abbot of Saint-Etienne.[15] The great abbeys came to form the centre of a close-knit architectural school covering western Normandy – closely linked, needless to say, with the rest of the duchy, and drawing its inspiration from all over France and other parts of western Christendom. In Normandy itself the two abbeys represent a concentration of effort on the eve of the Conquest which prepares one for the staggering achievements of the Normans in England; and the stone vault of the choir of the Holy Trinity was a milestone in the development of Romanesque. It was an achievement comparable to the vaults of Durham cathedral sixty years later, in which were laid the technological foundations necessary for the immensely lofty vaults of the new Gothic cathedrals of the Ile de France in the mid twelfth century. Norman architecture was an aspect of, a phase in, the history of Romanesque architecture throughout Europe; but a striking one, since it represented a concentration of effort, and a scale of effort, not easily paralleled elsewhere.[16]

[13] *Guillaume le Conquérant*, p. 60; cf. M. Fauroux, *Recueil des actes des ducs de Normandie*, in *Mémoires de la société des antiquaires de Normandie* 36 (1961), p. 443; L. Musset, *Les actes de Guillaume le Conquérant et de la reine Mathilde pour les abbayes caennaises*, *Mémoires de la Société des Antiquaires de Normandie*, 37 (Caen, 1967).

[14] She is variously recorded to have joined the community in 1066, *Gallia Christiana*, xi (Paris, 1759), *Instrumenta*, col. 61 or 1075, Orderic, iii, pp. 8–11; iv, pp. 46–47. Probably the earlier date represents simply a declaration of intent; the second its execution. She succeeded the first abbess, Matilda, who died on 6 July 1113, and herself died on 13 July 1126, L. Delisle, *Rouleaux des Morts* (Paris, 1888), pp. 177ff; Orderic, iii, 10–11 and n. 1; iv, pp. 46–47 and n. 2; chronicle of Caen in M. Bouquet, *Recueil des historiens de la France*, xii (Paris, 1781), p. 780. Cf. Douglas, *William the Conqueror*, pp. 394–95.

[15] See esp. *Vita Herluini* in J. Armitage Robinson, *Gilbert Crispin, Abbot of Westminster* (Cambridge, 1911), pp. 95ff; for his relations with William, pp. 97ff; as abbot of Caen, p. 99: in *Works of Gilbert Crispin*, ed. A. S. Abulafia and G. R. Evans (London, 1986), pp. 195ff, 197ff. Cf. M. Gibson, *Lanfranc of Bec* (Oxford, 1978), chs 2, 5, 6, pp. 150–61.

[16] See below, ch. 10. Cf. K. J. Conant, *Carolingian and Romanesque Architecture* (London, 1959), p. 286; A. W. Clapham, *English Romanesque Architecture after the Conquest* (Oxford, 1934).

Lanfranc's former disciple at Bec, St Anselm, expressed firmly in one of his treatises the view no doubt common in his age that only monks had more than a slender chance of salvation.[17] A supreme effort was therefore needed if a secular man with the death of many secular folk on his conscience, like William the Conqueror, was to hope for any degree of mercy on the path to Heaven. But the scale of these buildings also represented in a perfectly clear way two other aims. It is characteristic of the monasticism of this age and of the duchy that they should have been founded to serve a growing town. In the late eleventh century it seemed a natural thing to plant a new abbey close to the heart of a great city, as the first Norman earl of Chester with St Anselm's help planted his abbey in Chester or the peripatetic group who revived monasticism in the north of England settled at last at St Mary's York.[18] These churches came in course of time to have the large naves characteristic of late Romanesque churches. The function of these naves is not profusely documented, but there is much circumstantial evidence to suggest that the motive recorded by Suger for rebuilding the nave at Saint-Denis was a common one — namely to provide space for the milling throngs of lay-folk who came from time to time to worship in the abbey church.[19] At Saint-Denis they came for the festivals of the martyrs whose relics adorned the church; in the Anglo-Norman cathedrals the folk of a whole diocese came for the Pentecostal celebrations. Whatever the occasion, the large nave was partly at least intended to house a large congregation, and this emphasised the close link of monastic community and laity in the late eleventh century, the age when papal reform and popular religion were in harmony, before the new movements and tensions of the twelfth century drew them apart again and so led to the revival of heresy. The large abbeys and cathedrals show us these links on the grand scale; equally characteristic of the age were the foundation of small communities of monks serving a small church, often, it is clear, a parish church, in a town; such, for example, was the community of monks from Gloucester abbey established in the parish church of St Peter in Hereford about 1100.[20]

[17] Cf. Southern, *St Anselm and his Biographer*, p. 101; Brooke, *Medieval Church and Society* (London, 1971), p. 153.

[18] *Cartulary of Chester Abbey*, ed. J. Tait (Manchester, 1920–3), i, pp. xxiiiff; W. Dugdale, *Monasticon anglicanum* (edn of 1817–30), iii, pp. 546, 569; Simeon of Durham, *Opera*, ed. T. Arnold, RS (London, 1882–85), ii, p. 208.

[19] Cf. E. Panofsky, *Abbot Suger on the Abbey Church of St Denis* (Princeton, 1946), esp. pp. 42–43, 88–89, 134–35.

[20] It is suggested in *GFL*, p. 534, that St Peter's was a mere cell before 1143; but the evidence there cited, combined with that in *Historia et cartularium monasterii Gloucestriae*, ed. W. H. Hart, RS (London, 1863–67), i, pp. 86–87, and elsewhere, strongly suggests that it was a small conventual house.

A generation later new winds were blowing. In 1132 a substantial group of the flourishing community of St Mary's York went out into the wilderness to found the great Cistercian abbey of Fountains.[21] In 1143 the bishop of Hereford, who had already seen his city sacked three times in four years in the civil war of King Stephen's reign, joined with the abbot of Gloucester to transplant the monks of Hereford; the community of St Peter and the relics of St Guthlac preserved in a church even more dangerously sited within the castle were collected on an ample and quiet site some distance outside the city walls.[22]

These events serve to underline how characteristic was the foundation of abbeys closely linked with a growing town in the age of William the Conqueror. Equally characteristic was the scale of the churches at Caen, evidently intended not only to house a multitude at great festivals but also to impress. It has often been observed how appropriate was the massive plainness of Saint-Etienne to the crag-like quality of its founder. It was an age acutely sensitive to the physical impression created by a church. In a more sophisticated form, one observes this sensitivity a generation later in the controversy between Abbot Suger and St Bernard and the contrast between Saint-Denis and Clairvaux.[23] The former was designed to attract the multitudes and give them shelter on the great festivals of the saints whose relics the abbey housed: and it was therefore capacious, rich and many coloured; designed to do fitting honour to the saint supposed to be a special devotee of the symbolism of light, and rich in the reflection from jewelled shrines and stained-glass windows. Suger saw in the jewels the reflection of God's glory and thought they brought the mind to God. In the plain, whitewashed barn of a Cistercian church everything, even the proportions, were designed to avoid distraction; the naves were large, but to accommodate lay brothers, not the secular world: Clairvaux was the new Jerusalem, far removed from the gaze of secular men.[24] In a world which was so self-conscious in its attitude to building, and which dedicated such enormous resources to it, we cannot be wrong to see a calculated effect in the great buildings which the Norman conquerors placed

[21] D. Knowles, *The Monastic Order in England* (2nd edn, Cambridge, 1963), pp. 231ff; for discussion of the early documents relating to Fountains, see D. Bethell, 'The Foundation of Fountains Abbey and the State of St Mary's York in 1132', *Journal of Ecclesiastical History*, 17 (1966), pp. 11–27; L. G. D. Baker, 'The Foundation of Fountains Abbey', *Northern History*, 4 (1969), pp. 29–43.

[22] See *GF*, pp. 84n., 85–86.

[23] Cf. Panofsky, *Abbot Suger*; D. Knowles, *Historian and Character and Other Essays* (Cambridge, 1963), pp. 61ff. For what follows, cf. Brooke, *Medieval Church and Society*, p. 172, and references there cited.

[24] St Bernard, letter 64, *Opera*, vii, pp. 157–58; cf. Knowles, *Monastic Order*, p. 22.

on English soil. The Norman cathedrals were (with few exceptions, so far as we know) far larger than their English predecessors. They hoped to fill them on great festivals, especially when the Pentecostal processions brought a flood of pilgrims from every parish in the diocese – and Martin Brett has found evidence to suggest (as one would gather from the buildings themselves) that the Normans deliberately encouraged and developed such gatherings.[25] The enormous churches were also intended to impress the English with the power of the Norman conquerors and the divine favour reflected in the majesty of their churches, represented in the persons of the Norman bishops and abbots. If you entered Saint-Denis in Suger's later years, or if you had entered Canterbury cathedral before the Norman Conquest, the centre of the vista would have been the shrine of the saints, at Saint-Denis raised above the high altar, at Canterbury scattered about, from St Dunstan in the centre to St Wilfrid at the east end.[26] A great relic church is not characteristic of either Normandy or of England immediately after the Conquest. I do not suggest that the Normans were indifferent to relics; but it was not part of their normal assumption in the mid eleventh century that a saint or saints should be visibly the chief inhabitants of a church, although there were, needless to say, important abbeys dedicated to Norman saints such as St Wandrille, St Ouen and St Evroul. In early days after the Norman Conquest, the saints whose relics had been conspicuous in the great churches in England were in some cases actually hidden. This may have been a temporary phase, but there can be no doubt that it was deliberate. In seven years Lanfranc built his new cathedral at Canterbury, and when it was finished neither Dunstan nor Ælfheah – nor Wilfred – were visible; instead, at the centre of the apse, beyond and above the high altar, one was made aware on great festivals of the presence of the archbishop himself.[27] We rarely know how the furniture of the apse of a cathedral or abbey of this period was arranged, but the same was undoubtedly true at Norwich also. In both cases the new church was intended, we may be sure, to impress the crowds who flocked to it with the greatness of the new regime, and the centre of the design and the symbol of the regime was the person of the bishop.

Much of the patronage and benefaction which William the Conqueror offered to Norman and English monasteries was on a very small scale – a

---

[25] M. Brett, *The English Church under Henry I* (Oxford, 1975), pp. 162–64: see p. 186.

[26] Eadmer in Gervase of Canterbury, *Historical Works*, ed. W. Stubbs, RS (London, 1879), i, pp. 7–9; Southern, *St Anselm and his Biographer*, pp. 260ff; cf. Brooke, *Medieval Church and Society*, pp. 173–74.

[27] Ibid.; cf. C. N. L. Brooke. 'Archbishop Lanfranc, the English bishops and the Council of London of 1075', *Studia Gratiana*, 12 (1967) pp. 39–60, at pp. 42ff.

church here, some fields there, petty rights, a slight nod of favour to other men's gifts. Even his larger benefactions could reveal acts of pettiness, and there is a famous story of the knight who claimed that the land on which Saint-Etienne had been founded as the Conqueror was being buried had been taken from his father by force.[28] But there is a clear and precise sense too in which Saint-Etienne and La Sainte Trinité reveal William and Matilda as masters of the grand gesture. When the folk gathered to William's funeral in 1087, they saw in the town and above all in its two great abbeys the outward symbol of William's greatness, and of a faithful marriage; and above all the symbol of the highest feudal bond in the land, the bond between William and his family and God.

The grand gesture appears again, with perhaps a touch of absurdity, in William's most substantial foundation in England. The story of the foundation of Battle abbey comes from the twelfth century chronicle which is partly based on some charters which are notorious forgeries.[29] But there are sound reasons for supposing that it is the form, not the substance of these documents which deceives, and that the story of the abbey's early history is substantially correct. In all Norman monasteries prayers were said for the duke; no doubt when he embarked on his fantastic adventure special prayers were said throughout Normandy. To St Valéry William himself vowed an immediate gift if the saint would help him to a favourable wind. The manor of Tackley in Essex was St Valéry's reward, and every great house in Normandy, especially the two houses at Caen, had its share of the spoils.[30] In 1069 the abbot of Sainte-Trinité-du-Mont at Rouen came with two of his monks to Winchester, and enlisted the support of the great Earl William FitzOsbern. The king, as Dr Matthew has said, 'was in the giving mood and playfully pretended to stab the abbot's hand with a knife as he handed over the manor of Harmondsworth in Middlesex'.[31] In this way small payments were made to all who had helped in the great enterprise.

The story is that, as the Norman army prepared to go into battle on 14 October 1066, the duke vowed to build a monastery on the place where King Harold's standard stood if it was that day successfully captured and

---

[28] Orderic, iv, pp. 106–7; cf. E. A. Freeman, *History of the Norman Conquest*, iv (Oxford, 1871), pp. 718–20, 821–22.

[29] See *The Chronicle of Battle Abbey*, ed. and trans. E. Searle, OMT (Oxford, 1980). On the charters, many of which are forgeries, see T. A. M. Bishop and P. Chaplais, *Facsimiles of English Royal Writs to AD 1100* (Oxford, 1957), pp. xxi ff, E. Searle, 'Battle Abbey and Exemption: The Forged Charters', *EHR*, 83 (1968), pp. 449–80.

[30] D. J. A. Matthew, *The Norman Monasteries and their English Possessions* (Oxford, 1962), pp. 30–31.

[31] Matthew, *The Norman Monasteries*, p. 30.

the English army overthrown.[32] A monk of Marmoutier who was there immediately requested that it be dedicated to St Martin, the soldier turned monk and bishop and one of the chief founders of the French church, whose chief abbey lay at Marmoutier outside Tours. At first sight the story seems a trifle romantic; yet such a story is needed to explain what followed: with a curious mixture of promptitude and reluctance, the Conqueror raised a great abbey with its high altar on the battlefield – and there is no reason to doubt that it stood where Harold's standard had stood and fallen. The abbey was colonised by monks from Marmoutier, to which he had already made some gifts,[33] but dedicated to a saint otherwise not especially connected with William or his line, perched on the top of a small hill where water was hard to find, on a site which was hardly convenient. It became a large and splendid monument to the favour which God and St Martin had showed, against heavy odds, to the Norman invasion. It was another example of the grand gesture, in this case more eccentric than at Caen; for Battle only became a place of any consequence as the result of the abbey's growth; it cannot have been regarded, like the Caen abbeys, as a place immediately under the public eye; as a visible monument it was likely to be less effective. And this may explain why the foundation seems to have been slow to get under way in the Conqueror's early years. He may well have hesitated at the large investment to which he was committed; and accident, such as the drowning of the first abbot, may also have played a part. In the long run the Conqueror arranged for fine buildings, in his favourite Caen stone, for a large community, for extensive endowments, and in all probability for equally extensive privileges; but he died before they had been gathered together in formal documents, and so he left to his son William Rufus the task of completing the foundation.[34]

For the most part William II regarded abbeys, as in the quotation from

---

[32] The tradition is recorded, with circumstantial detail, in the *Chronicle of Battle*, pp. 36–37, 42–46 (of the twelfth century). It is possible that the story grew in the telling, and that the site did not seem so unsuitable in 1066: in the twelfth century monastic communities set increasing store on water supply. Cf. the siting of the Cistercian abbeys in particular.

[33] Fauroux, *Recueil des actes* (n. 13), p. 35, and documents listed there; cf. J. H. Round, *Calendar of Documents Preserved in France*, i (London, 1899), nos 1165ff showing William's interest in Marmoutier before 1066; Fauroux, *Recueil*, no. 228 (= Round, *Calendar*, no. 1173), if genuine, records a confirmation by William's son Robert when his father was about to cross the sea in 1066.

[34] For Rufus' relations with Battle, see *Chronicle*, pp. 96–103 – the vacancy after Abbot Gausbert's death was short by Rufus' standards. The spurious nature of the more important early charters makes it difficult at present to disentangle with precision William II's gifts from William I's, although the fact that the major endowment was completed by the Conqueror is confirmed by Domesday Book.

Eadmer with which I opened, as pieces of property which had unfortunately been alienated by his predecessors to greedy and useless communities of monks; but which could be taxed for their true purpose – to provide William with money for his military adventures – on the happy event of the abbots dying. The longer an abbey was kept vacant, the more benefit the king had from his property, and Anselm's insistence that abbots should be appointed seemed to the king vexatious, if not absurd. Ages of faith always have their crop of blasphemers; but William Rufus was unusual in the frankness of his unconcern, save in an occasional moment of extreme crisis, for the world of the unseen and of the spirit. His values were the values of the camp and the battlefield; and Eadmer, almost in spite of himself, found entertainment in the king's engaging knavery – as he saw it – and even observed something of the strange but intelligible world of values in which Rufus lived. Minor benefaction he may have committed here and there by inadvertence; but so far as we know only two abbeys had any serious grounds to be grateful to him, and it is obviously significant that these were Saint-Etienne at Caen and Battle. He robbed Harold's secular foundation at Waltham to add to the endowments of Saint-Etienne, and he set Battle on its feet by confirming, establishing and probably extending its endowments and privileges.[35] It would be going too far to say that the Battle chronicle speaks well of him, but it is notable for its absence of the invective against Rufus and his exactions which is a monotonous chorus in other monastic histories. William Rufus owed an allegiance to his father which he felt as a strong and religious duty; he owed no such allegiance to God, St Stephen or St Martin: what he did at Caen and Battle was to raise monuments to the great man whose name he carried, and who had designated him his heir and successor to the English throne.

This may be a simplification of a complicated story of which part is hidden from us. It is quite likely that meetings with Anselm brought out a devil in Rufus which made him state his attitude more starkly than was

[35] Cf. Freeman, *Norman Conquest*, v (1876), p. 73 and n.; cf. *Regesta regum Anglo-Norman-norum*, i, ed. H. W. C. Davis (Oxford, 1913), no. 397. He is supposed to have granted the manor of Bermondsey to the monks of that house in 1089; but this may have been a sale, C. N. L. Brooke and G. Keir, *London 800–1216* (London, 1945), pp. 312–14. For Rufus' religion, cf. F. Barlow, *William Rufus* (London, 1983), ch. 3, esp. pp. 115–18 – with details of other monastic benefactions, and a rather different view of his religious outlook. Recent work has added Gloucester abbey to those he favoured: D. Bates, 'The Building of a Great Church: The Abbey of St Peter's Gloucester and its Early Norman Benefactors', *Transactions of the Bristol and Gloucestershire Archaeological Society*, 102 (1984), pp. 129–32; and esp. E. Cownie, 'Gloucester Abbey, 1066–1135: An Illustration of Religious Patronage in Anglo-Norman England', in *England and Normandy in the Middle Ages*, ed. D. Bates and A. Curry (London, 1994), pp. 143–57.

normal. But even so we cannot doubt the sincerity of the outburst quoted at the start: monks and monasteries only seriously interested him when he could view them as property, that is in the simplest and most concrete point in the spectrum of feudal, tenurial and proprietary rights and concerns: the point at which they could be directly exploited to produce money to pay Rufus's mercenaries.

With Henry I we enter a more complex world of ideas. He made a business of government; and that business involved the ruthless and often subtle exploitation of a wide range of financial and judicial resources, and the manipulation of a spider's web of patronage.[36] But he was also, like his father, the master of the grand gesture; and there is a wilful extravagance about his chief acts of patronage, both to the church and to secular men, which makes it plain that Henry had at least two quite different characters under his skin, as we often observe in the personalities of powerful and ambitious men.

Shortly after Henry I's death Peter the Venerable, abbot of Cluny, referred in a famous letter to the former monk of Cluny, Hezelo, who had supervised the building of the great third church at Cluny in St Hugh's time, and said that he 'constructed the material fabric of the new church ..., more than all other mortal men apart from the kings of Spain and England'.[37] It is difficult to discern what precisely lies behind this statement. There is other evidence that Alfonso VI of Leon-Castile and, somewhat later, Alfonso VII were considerable benefactors to Cluny; but the only other precise statement linking Alfonso VI and Henry I is in the De nugis curialium of the English satirist Walter Map, written about 1181.[38] Map tells us that Henry 'completed the monastery of Cluny from its foundations'; and describes how Alfonso had made a start and then withdrawn through meanness, and how Henry then proceeded to build the whole church at his own expense – brushing aside what was left of Alfonso's work – and gave the monks an annual rent of £100 sterling for the upkeep of the fabric. Map had access to good information, but never troubled to relate his stories with historical precision. In this case the close parallel with Peter the Venerable's letter makes it certain that a sound tradition underlies the story; and Henry undoubtedly gave an annual rent to Cluny in 1131 of 100

[36] See Southern, 'The Place of Henry I in English History', Proceedings of the British Academy, 48 (1962), esp. pp. 130ff (= Medieval Humanism, esp. pp. 209ff).

[37] The Letters of Peter the Venerable, ed. G. Constable (Cambridge, Mass., 1967), no. 89, i, p. 229; cf. ii, pp. 157–58.

[38] Walter Map. De nugis curialium, ed. M. R. James, C. N. L. Brooke and R. A. B. Mynors, OMT (Oxford, 1983), pp. 436–39.

marks – not pounds, that is, about two-thirds of the sum named by Map.[39] The most likely reconstruction of events is that Alfonso's benefactions ended with his death in 1109, and that from that point on Henry became the chief benefactor of the third church in its later stages; and this is a remarkable fact, since it must have involved liberating resources on a massive scale for Henry to be remembered as one of the chief builders of this immensely costly church. It is all the more striking because it was only comparatively late in his reign that Henry showed any serious sign of generosity to the monasteries of England or Normandy. His later benefactions were large, eclectic and clearly marked with the king's interest and purpose. The greatest was the foundation of Reading abbey in the early and mid 1120s,[40] an independent house as befitted so royal a foundation – which was to be for Henry what Caen and Battle had been for his parents, and Westminster abbey for Edward the Confessor. It was independent and yet Cluniac, an eccentric combination so late as 1123, when the foundation was formally made; and it is striking testimony to Henry's interest in Cluny that he should wish to have her men and her customs so shortly after the debacle of Abbot Pons – at the point at which modern historians tend to reckon Cluny at a low ebb in its reputation.

It is clear that Henry I's interest in Cluny was connected with the presence there of one of his favourite nephews, his namesake Henry of Blois, son of the count of Blois and of Henry's sister Adela, and brother of the other

---

[39] *Regesta regum Anglo-Normannorum*, ii, ed. C. Johnson and H. A. Cronne (Oxford, 1956), nos 1691, 1713 (1131). Soon after this was first written, Prof. K. J. Conant published his long-awaited *Cluny* (Mâcon, 1968). He cites other evidence (p. 99) to suggest that Henry I's benefactions started early in his reign, and he dates the completion of Cluny III to 1113; it is, however, clear that a part of Map's story belongs to the period after the collapse of the nave in the mid 1120s. He also shows that Alfonso VII (1126–57) was a major benefactor as well as Alfonso VI.

A final estimate of Henry's benefactions before 1120 will have to take into account the evidence relating to Llanthony priory and Montacute priory. To the former Queen Matilda, doubtless with Henry's support, wished to give a large endowment out of the Berkeley estate (see above, p. 33; the evidence is in W. Dugdale, *Monasticon anglicanum*, vi, p. 131) at some period between 1103 and 1118: this was refused by the founders, who wished their priory to remain poor. According to a late source which may well enshrine early tradition, Henry planned to erect the Cluniac priory at Montacute into a great house on another site, but later changed his mind and founded Reading abbey instead. This probably pushes the first adumbration of Reading well before 1120, and it may be that Henry of Blois was destined for first abbot (the evidence is discussed in *Heads*, p. 121 and n. 3).

[40] On the foundation of Reading, see Knowles, *Monastic Order in England*, pp. 281–82. There is a full study in Professor B. R. Kemp's Reading University Ph.D. thesis on Reading abbey; and see Kemp's editions of *Reading Abbey Cartularies*, i, Camden 4th Series 31 (1986), pp. 13–19. For Henry's other foundations, see below.

favourite nephew, Count, later King, Stephen.[41] Sir Richard Southern in his British Academy lecture on Henry I, which has illuminated the reign and a much wider area of English history in brilliant fashion, has emphasised the practical nature of Henry's patronage; and in relation to his nephews the importance to him in his French adventures of strengthening an alliance with the house of Blois and Champagne.[42] But I find it difficult to believe that practical considerations alone can explain the extraordinary contrast between the widely spread, but prudently contrived, enrichment of many of Henry I's servants and barons, and the lavish, not to say crushing, endowment, of his two nephews. Southern has pointed out that Stephen's endowment in the 1110s was matched by an approximately equal endowment for Henry's illegitimate son Robert, earl of Gloucester, in the 1120s, and has suggested that there was an 'obscure palace revolution' which unseated Stephen and replaced him with Robert as the king's favourite relation.[43] This I doubt, for about the time of the supposed palace revolution Stephen's brother Henry was elevated from being a monk of Cluny first to one of England's richest abbeys, Glastonbury, then to its richest bishopric, Winchester; and these two offices he was to hold concurrently until his death in 1171. These three men were provided with royal patronage out of all proportion to what was common or necessary. There is also a marked contrast between Henry's treatment of his close male relations and his treatment of his daughter, the Empress Matilda: on account of a notable scruple for legitimacy he insisted on designating her as his heiress, but he treated her personally as a pawn in the marriage game, sending her off first to one distant marriage then to another. It is plain that Stephen and Henry of Blois and Robert of Gloucester were the king's favourites in a very special sense, and we may be reasonably sure that Henry I's great gifts to Cluny were in part at least intended to provide one of his favourite nephews with a fitting context in which to live.

The endowment of Robert of Gloucester in the 1120s, as is well known, was to fill the sad gap in the royal circle left by the death of Henry's only legitimate son, William, in the disaster of the White Ship in 1120 – to fill the gap, not as heir, since Robert was illegitimate, but as a close relation and favourite. The loss of his heir and the childlessness of his second marriage evidently disturbed Henry's conscience. Throughout his reign, he

---

[41] On Henry of Blois, see p. 259 n. 20 and references cited.

[42] Southern, 'The Place of Henry I', p. 135.

[43] Ibid. Southern's evidence indicates the rivalry of Stephen and Robert for first place among the English nobility in 1127–28, and that Robert was closest to the king in the marriage of his daughter and the count of Anjou. It does not establish any permanent replacement of Stephen by Robert in the king's affections, or any estrangement.

was inclined to make occasional gestures of penance, and to raise monuments to record these gestures. The circular church of the Holy Sepulchre in Northampton was built, it seems, by Henry fairly early in his reign as a friendly gift to the Cluniacs and an acknowledgment of his own failure to go on crusade.[44] Reading was a grand act of penance, and also built to provide himself with a mausoleum as impressive as Saint-Etienne, Caen, and with Cluniac monks to pray for ever for his soul.

There is one other very remarkable and significant element in the endowment of Reading. At its core lay the properties of three ancient abbeys dissolved in the eleventh century: the convents of nuns at Leominster in Herefordshire and at Reading itself, and the house of monks at Cholsey in Surrey.[45]

In the first age of the Viking invasions, in the ninth and early tenth centuries, many monasteries had disappeared; the monastic life indeed was virtually extinct when St Dunstan began to revive it in 940. But between that date and the Norman Conquest, in the days of the monastic revival of the tenth century and later, it was comparatively rare for monasteries to fade away or be dissolved. There may well have been some of which we have no information; but it is likely that we have evidence of as many as were known to Henry I and his advisers, if not of one or two more. He may not have heard of Bedford abbey which flourished very briefly in Edgar's reign and disappeared.[46] He may have known that there had been an abbey at Exeter; if so, he would also have known that it had been converted into the cathedral by Bishop Leofric, and so was irredeemable.[47] Of the four other houses known to us, three were included in what one can regard as the revival in Reading. And after Henry's death there was a curious epilogue which involved the fourth. His widow, Queen Adela, presented

---

[44] *Regesta regum Anglo-Normannorum*, ii, no. 1318 (and p. 344); cf. no. 1317 and note and no. 833, omitting this church; *Monasticon*, v, pp. 191–92. On this and other round churches see M. Gervers, 'Rotundae anglicanae', in *Actes du XXIIe congrès international d'histoire de l'art* (Budapest, 1969; publ. 1972), pp. 359–76.

[45] See Kemp, *Reading Abbey Cartularies*, i, pp. 13–19. Leominster is otherwise known from the abduction of Abbess Eadgifu by Earl Swein in 1046: *Anglo-Saxon Chronicle*, C, *sub anno* 1046; *Chronicle of John of Worcester*, ed. R. R. Darlington and P. McGurk, ii, OMT (Oxford, 1995), pp. 548–49; cf. Freeman, *Norman Conquest*, ii, pp. 89, 545ff. An abbess of Reading occurs c. 1030 in *The Liber Vitae of New Minster and Hyde Abbey, Winchester*, facsimile edn by S. Keynes (Copenhagen, 1996), fol. 26r. For Cholsey, see William of Malmesbury, *Gesta pontificum*, ed. N. E. S. A. Hamilton, RS (London, 1870), p. 193; *Chronicon abbatiae Rameseiensis*, ed. W. D. Macray, RS (London, 1886), pp. 110–11.

[46] Thurcytel abbot of Bedford occurs in 971, but was later expelled, and is almost certainly the same Thurcytel who was later abbot of Crowland, *Heads*, pp. 30, 41.

[47] On Exeter abbey, see *Heads*, pp. 48, 211.

the churches which had formed a major part of the endowment of Berkeley abbey to Reading. The gift was not entirely effective, since her ground for claiming possession of them was tenuous, and other benefactors were busily engaged in presenting part or whole of the complex to other abbeys. These adventures began in the anarchy of Stephen's reign and ended in *causes célèbres* under Henry II.[48] They do not directly concern us: but it is of great interest to see Henry's widow thus attempting, on however doubtful a ground, to complete the work that he had begun.

The foundation of Reading, from one point of view, was therefore restoration to religious uses of a large body of the accessible revenues alienated in the eleventh century. It has often been observed that the preparations were made in the years following the disaster of the White Ship in 1120, in which his only surviving legitimate son perished; and that it represents an act of penitence and prayer. In this context one may say that the grand symbol of penitence for sins which had caused such a disaster to his dynasty, to a man to whom legitimate succession meant so much – as it does to those whom the world thinks to be usurpers – was the restoration of what his predecessors had allowed to be desecrated. Allowed, since in none of these cases had the king been directly responsible for the suppression; in two at least the culprit was Earl Godwin, King Harold's father, for whose acts one might have supposed the Norman kings would have felt little responsibility. But the act of restitution is so striking, and in its way so dramatic, as to leave little doubt that it was deliberate.

If Edward the Confessor was only indirectly responsible for the suppressions which took place in his reign, he bore some blame, since only with royal approval and consent could a great act of endowment or disendowment hope to succeed. This comes out clearly if we make two comparisons: that between Henry's work for Cluny and the Cluniacs with his work for the new communities of canons regular; and that between his acts of patronage and those of his royal nephew and brother-in-law, King Stephen of England and King David of Scotland. If we could count the treasure and assess the capital involved, it seems likely that Cluny and Reading owed more, in a direct, material sense, to Henry I; yet if we look at the whole picture of Augustinian origins in this country, we see that they perhaps owed more to his patronage than to anyone else. The appearance in force – in very large force – of Augustinian canons in England is characteristically the product of Henry's reign, as the spread of the

[48] See above, p. 141 n. 7.

Cistercians is characteristic of the reign of Stephen.[49] From the start the royal family played its part, and Henry's own support must have been essential for the success of his first wife's foundation in 1107 of Holy Trinity Priory in London, the only major religious house to find a home within the city walls. The concentration of effort in which Henry was more closely involved comes later in the reign. In 1123 an Augustianian canon became archbishop of Canterbury; in 1131 another Augustinian, Robert de Bethune, became bishop of Hereford; in the same year Henry launched his other great foundation apart from Reading, the Augustinian abbey of Cirencester, the largest of a group of houses which claimed Henry as founder; in 1133 an Augustinian bishop with an Augustinian chapter were launched in the new see of Carlisle. In his later years Henry had an Augustinian confessor.[50]

The involvement of overlords in monastic foundations is notoriously complex and often almost indefinable. Henry I and Stephen were both in a measure involved in the early years of the famous abbey of Savigny – Henry as duke of Normandy, Stephen as count of Mortain – on whose fiefs most of the abbey's early properties lay. Savigny represented the new urge to austerity and seclusion, and by 1147 its merger into the family of Cîteaux had become a logical step – though not one which commended itself to all of its daughter houses.[51] Stephen as a young man became possessed of the Furness peninsula in north Lancashire, at that date almost at the northern extremity of what was indisputably English territory: its wildness made it suitable for a Savignac colony; its bareness made it a comparatively inexpensive investment; the quality of the observance made its prayers of obvious utility for the future of Stephen's soul. That Stephen had some sense of personal involvement in the new monastic movements may be suggested by the rapid success of the Cistercians in his reign, although much of this was doubtless quite independent of his smile and frown, which were somewhat freely given and even more freely ignored. The conventional, traditional nature of his own piety came to the fore when, as king, he and his wife prepared their mausoleum by founding Faversham abbey in Kent, in precise imitation of Reading: like Reading it

[49] See J. C. Dickinson, *The Origins of the Austin Canons and their Introduction into England* (London, 1950), esp. pp. 125ff; Knowles, *Monastic Order*, pp. 227–66; the foundations are listed in D. Knowles and R. N. Hadcock, *Medieval Religious Houses, England and Wales* (2nd edn, London, 1971).

[50] Dickinson, pp. 126ff; cf. *Cartulary of Cirencester Abbey*, ed. C. D. Ross, 3 vols (London, 1964–77).

[51] Knowles, *Monastic Order*, pp. 250–51.

was Cluniac in observance, yet independent; a burial church, where the souls of king and queen might be remembered till the end of time.[52]

King David I of Scotland is remembered above all for bringing the Scottish lowlands into the Anglo-Norman world, by settling Anglo-Norman barons, by spreading over a wide area monastic communities of various orders, and by other similar activities.[53] Scotland was still a poor country. Monastic houses were never so thick on the ground as in many parts of England. But of those houses which were to have any significance in Scottish history, a majority owed their foundation or revival to David. His French links were evidenced in his patronage of the house of Kelso, daughter of Tiron on the frontier of Normandy and La Perche, a community similar in origin to Savigny. But his benefactions were impartially spread over Benedictine and Augustinian communities, with perhaps a slight partiality shown to the Cistercians. David was a man of piety, and his relations with monasteries show the whole spectrum of an Anglo-Norman monarch's interest: from prayers for himself and his family, through the desire to develop true religious life in his dominions, for missionary enterprise and pastoral work, to the attempt to establish centres of civilising influence and so also, be it said, of royal influence and political stability. His work is a marvellous epilogue and summary of our theme: he reminds us at the end, as we saw at the beginning, that the picture is very complex. I have tried to draw out certain simple guiding principles from this complex world of ideas; but it can only be a valid activity if we remember its complexity. As for the relation of royal patronage to ecclesiastical reform, I hope I have made clear that the relation of these monarchs to that is also not simple; it was part of the world in which they lived; but only a part, commonly a small part, unless they met it reflected in a Lanfranc, an Anselm or a Bernard.

Behind the whole question of a patron's attitude lies the deeper problem of the relation of the patron and the religious influence, the monastic inspiration which forms the community. I began with a quotation which showed this at its most external, in an exchange between William II and St Anselm quoted by Eadmer. I end with the letter in which St Bernard himself announced to Henry I the first steps leading to the first really great Cistercian house in England, that of Rievaulx, in the same year, 1131, that Henry himself was engaged in planting Cirencester Abbey.[54] In this letter the role of Our Lord and the centurion in the gospel are reversed: with a

---

[52] Knowles, *Monastic Order*, pp. 152, 284; *Heads*, p. 49; John of Salisbury, *Historia pontificalis*, ed. M. Chibnall, NMT (Edinburgh, 1956 = OMT, Oxford, 1986), p. 89.

[53] See below, pp. 164–73.

[54] St Bernard, letter 92, in *Opera*, vii, ed. J. Leclercq and J. M. Rochais, p. 241 (my translation); on the foundation of Rievaulx, see Knowles, *Monastic Order*, pp. 230–31.

quiet dignity befitting an approach to an eminent man who was also nearly a stranger,[55] Bernard outlines his scheme, with quiet assurance, in words and similes appropriate to a soldier-king.

> There is a plot of land in your country which is the Lord's – mine and yours – which He would rather die for than lose. I have determined to strive for it; and I am sending recruits from my regiment, who will lay claim to it and – if it please you – revive and settle it with a strong force. And now to this end I have sent scouts ahead whom you see in your presence, who will make prudent enquiry of the state of the case and give me a faithful report. Please help them as messengers of your Lord, and in them do your service to Him. May He lead you – for His own honour, for your salvation, for the safety and peace of your land – happy and illustrious, to a good and peaceful end.

[55] Henry and Bernard met more than once in 1130–31 to discuss the papal schism; one at least of these meetings – but possibly not more than one – must be earlier than the letter; see E. Vacandard, *Vie de S. Bernard*, 4th edn (Paris, 1910), i, pp. 308ff; *Regesta regum Anglo-Normannorum*, ii, no. 1691n.

9

King David I of Scotland as a Connoisseur of the Religious Orders

David I, king of the Scots from 1124 to 1153, was the youngest son of St Margaret, queen of Scotland from *c.* 1069 to 1093, and one of the creative figures in the history of the Scottish kingdom in the mid and late middle ages. He is especially remarkable as the patron of numerous religious houses of a variety of orders; and it is likely that he absorbed his interest in patronage of the religious life from two distinguished women: his mother St Margaret, and his sister Edith or Matilda, wife of Henry I of England.

The authors of 1 Kings (1 Samuel) felt bound to explain, in that incomparable narrative and in the precisest detail, how it was that Samuel came to anoint Jesse's youngest son David as the future king. By the same token we may wonder if Margaret had some prophetic instinct when she gave the name David to her own youngest son. However that may be, he grew up without expectation of the throne, but was able to enjoy the best training that could be had in the richest court in western Christendom, that of Henry I of England where his sister Edith, renamed Matilda, was queen. He grew up a Norman baron, earl of Huntingdon and Northampton, and learned from the unique example of Henry and Matilda what royal patronage to monasteries could be when the founding of new abbeys was at its most fashionable; and he brought to the border country in particular and southern Scotland in general – which he resettled in a vital and definitive way – fellow barons with good Norman names like Bruce; and he set a trail of monastic foundations which are the glory of the border country to this day.[1]

First published in *Mediaevalia Christiana, XIe-XIIIe siècles: hommage à Raymonde Foreville*, ed. C. Viola (Paris, 1989), pp. 320–34.

[1] The fullest recent account is by G. W. S. Barrow, *The Anglo-Norman Era in Scottish History* (Oxford, 1980), which revised E. L. G. Ritchie, *The Normans in Scotland* (Edinburgh, 1954); cf. A. A. M. Duncan, *Scotland: the Making of the Kingdom* (Edinburgh, 1954). For Margaret and David and their work as monastic patrons, see especially Barrow, *The Kingdom of the Scots* (London, 1973); see also the texts in *Regesta regum Scottorum*, i, ed. G. W. S. Barrow (Edinburgh, 1960), pp. 131–62. In this essay I am especially indebted to Barrow, *The Kingdom*

It is recorded of Queen Margaret that on one occasion she harangued a council of Scottish bishops and ordered them to reform their ways – but as she did not speak their language her husband, King Malcolm, acted as interpreter.[2] Now her biographer does not specify the languages of the story; it is clear enough the bishops were Gaelic speaking – and not Latin, for Margaret could have spoken Latin to them. But what was her native language? She had been born and lived as a child in Hungary, where, after the death of St Stephen, the celebrated missionary king, she may have learned to live with a combination of fervent Christianity and wild violence which marked her later milieu in Scotland. I doubt however if she spoke Magyar to her husband and fancy her native language was really English. She was above all a leading representative of the English royal family, an Anglo-Saxon princess, at a time when Edward the Confessor was king and childless. After the debacle of 1066 her brother, Edgar the Atheling, fled with the remnants of his family to the court of Malcolm III of Scotland – best known as the Malcolm who is hailed king of Scotland at the end of *Macbeth*. A contemporary version of the Anglo-Saxon chronicle, very likely written for Malcolm and Margaret's pleasure, describes how he fell in love with her soon after her arrival;[3] at first she resisted him, wishing for a celibate life such as her sister Christina was to enjoy at Wilton and Romsey; but Malcolm pressed his suit with her brother and he gave way, and so did she and they were married. It may well be that it was both a marriage of love and of policy, for it brought the Scottish dynasty into alliance with

of the Scots, pp. 172–87, and the papers by the same author on which this passage was partly based: 'From Queen Margaret to David I, Benedictines and Tironensians', *Innes Review*, 11 (1960), pp. 22–38; and also Geoffrey Barrow's 'Scottish Rulers and the Religious Orders, 1070–1153', *Transactions of the Royal Historical Society*, 5th series, 3 (1953), pp. 77–100. I am also greatly indebted to the rich details contained in I. B. Cowan and D. E. Easson, *Medieval Religious Houses: Scotland* (2nd edn, London, 1976). The essay owes much to Geoffrey Barrow's help and to discussions with Elizabeth Hallam Smith. See Elizabeth Hallam, 'Henry II as a Founder of Monasteries', *Journal of Ecclesiastical History*, 28 (1977), pp. 113–32; 'Aspects of the Monastic Patronage of the English and French Royal Houses, c. 1130–1272', unpublished University of London Ph.D. Thesis (1976).

[2] *Life* of St Margaret of Scotland, probably by Turgot, in *Acta sanctorum bollandiana*, June (1698), ii, pp. 324ff. On St Margaret and her biography, see Derek Baker in *Medieval Women*, ed. Baker (Oxford, 1978), pp. 119–41, esp. pp. 129–32, who warns that some passages of the *Life*, including this, may have been expanded in the course of the twelfth or even the thirteenth century.

[3] *Anglo-Saxon Chronicle* D, BL, Cotton MS Tiberius B.iv, runs to 1079, and is edited in *An Anglo-Saxon Chronicle from British Museum Cotton MS Tiberius B.iv*, ed. E. Classen and F. E. Harmer (Manchester, 1926); cf. translation by D. Whitelock, D. C. Douglas and S. I. Tucker (London, 1961), *sub anno*. The passage is given under 1067, and they are usually reckoned to have been married c. 1069.

the Old English at a time when no one could have been sure that the Norman Conqueror had come to stay in England. Indeed the offspring of that marriage were to legitimise the Anglo-Norman line itself – for when, many years later, King David's one-time steward and friend, the great Cistercian monk St Aelred, provided King Henry II of England with a genealogy fitting for a true English king, he traced his descent not through the Norman line but through Edith-Matilda, Henry I's wife and his grand-mother, and Edith's mother St Margaret, to the Old English line.[4] Whether the marriage of Margaret and Malcolm was thought of as a political alliance or not, it was a highly successful marriage. They came from entirely different backgrounds and had little superficially in common – she was a very devout but also a worldly lady who loved the latest French fashions and was by no means meek or gentle or submissive; he a fairly uncouth warrior. But they were devoted to one another, reared a large family of children – and when Malcolm was killed on one of his raids into England in 1093, Margaret pined for him and was dead within a few days of hearing the news. 'What she had loved, he for love of that love loved too' says her biographer;[5] and the names of the children instantly reveal who was the dominant partner in this remarkable alliance. Edward, Edmund, Edgar, Ethelred, and Edith (the future Matilda, wife of Henry I) all bore English names; not a Scottish name anywhere. Next came Alexander, the most romantic of the names – a reminder perhaps that we are on the verge of the twelfth-century renaiss-ance in whose literary culture Alexander the Great was to be a central figure. It may seem a Scottish name to us, but that is Margaret's doing. By this time Margaret may have felt that her child-bearing days were, or ought to be, drawing to a close – though she may not have been more than in her late thirties – and chose for the boy who proved indeed to be her youngest son the name of David; and carried on with biblical names to give her youngest child the name of Mary.

Her personal piety, her strong character and her cosmopolitan experience and outlook evidently made their mark on many who came into contact with her. A study by Derek Baker in 1978 cast doubt on the picture of her as a traditional saint, constantly engaged in good works and prayer and fasting.[6] But the English chronicle written in her lifetime leaves no doubt that she enjoyed this reputation, that she was a person of quite exceptional devoutness and strength of religious purpose – even if we need also not

---

[4] *Genealogia regum Anglorum*, ed. R. Twysden, *Historiae anglicanae scriptores X* (London, 1652), col. 350; ed. J. P. Migne, *PL*, 195, cols 716–17, following Aelred's very moving account of King David's character and death.

[5] *Acta sanctorum*, June (1698), ii, p. 330.

[6] See n. 2: a study to which I am much indebted. For the English chronicle see n. 3.

doubt that she had her worldly ways too and enjoyed dominating her husband. She may not have had much direct influence on David since he was only about eight when she died, and continental monastic movements made relatively little headway in Scotland before 1100. Yet for all that we may be sure that both Edith-Matilda and David were very much their mother's children.

After Malcolm's death the Scottish kingdom passed through vicissitudes; but from 1097 to 1124 two of Margaret's sons reigned in the northern kingdom, Edgar and Alexander. Meanwhile, soon after 1100, David settled with his sister at the court of Henry I. Henry I was the most extensive monastic patron of the age – or perhaps of any age.[7] He was claimed as founder by literally dozens of religious houses in England and Normandy. He knew how to be generous with economy – and frequently called himself founder of houses other men had paid for – for all sensible patrons of religious houses knew that if Henry favoured them they would survive; if he did not they might founder. But he was also a master of the grand gesture and was capable of wild, romantic extravagance. He spent lavishly towards the rebuilding of the great third church at Cluny in Burgundy, the largest church north of the Alps in its day. He had won the throne by usurpation – however hotly he might have denied it – and had all the earnest desire for legitimacy of the usurper. Furthermore, he had almost innumerable children. The snag was that all but two were illegitimate; and, in the midst of his triumphant career, fate dealt him blow after blow. His wife Matilda died leaving only two children; in the disaster of the White Ship in 1120 the only son was drowned. Henry looked round for salvation both on earth and in heaven. He took another wife but had no more children by her; and he tried to expiate not only his own but all his predecessors' sins by the foundation of Reading abbey – into which he collected with loving care the endowments of religious houses which had been allowed to lapse into dissolution in the previous century; this and Cirencester abbey, his last great foundation, probably cost him in loss of income as much as all the others put together. But they did not impoverish him – nor did they help him to an heir. In every other respect, Henry is the most unattractive of English kings – he was cruel, murderous, harsh,

---

[7] See above, pp. 150–55, on Henry I and p. 156 on David. The chief source is a remarkable reference in *The Letters of Peter the Venerable*, ed. G. Constable (Cambridge, Massachusetts, 1967), no. 89, i, p. 229; cf. ii, pp. 157–58; but see also Walter Map, *De nugis curialium*, ed. M. R. James, revised by C. N. L. Brooke and R. A. B. Mynors, OMT (Oxford, 1983), pp. 436–39, with references at pp. 436–37n. For other aspects of Henry I, see especially Sir Richard Southern, *Medieval Humanism and Other Studies* (Oxford, 1970), pp. 206–33; Judith Green, *The Government of England under Henry I* (Cambridge, 1986).

promiscuous – in all sorts of ways intolerable. But because he was generous to monks and gave peace to England and (even more extraordinary) to Normandy, the gentle chronicler Orderic Vitalis made a hero of him.[8]

Matilda was a remarkable personality in her own right. Like her mother, she was a shrewd mixture of piety and worldliness.[9] One day her brother David found her – so we are told by a very late but good source – washing the feet of lepers in her own chamber.[10] He was struck dumb by the danger and degradation of such a task – but his sister made him kiss their feet. The story was not recorded till well after the days of St Francis, and we may wonder if it was literally true. But two facts we cannot doubt. First, that Matilda really looked after the lepers of London: she founded on the confines of Holborn in London the leper hospital of St Giles in the Fields. The other fact is that David learned from Matilda and her husband how to be a great monastic patron. He learned much else. Henry gave him a great heiress in marriage, Matilda, daughter of Earl Waltheof, and with her he acquired two English earldoms; and until Alexander's death and his own accession to the throne of Scotland in 1124 he was first and foremost an Anglo-Norman feudatory – one of the greatest men in the richest court in Europe. To Henry and his heiress, the younger Matilda, he was steadfastly loyal – even to the point of using his loyalty as an excuse for raiding into England (as his father had done) to attack the usurper King Stephen.[11] It was from the ageing King David that the boy-prince Henry, Matilda's son and the future Henry II, was clothed in the armour of a knight at Carlisle in 1149, when he was sixteen.[12] He settled many parts of southern Scotland with Anglo-Norman barons, like himself, and their followers. In many ways we can discern him imitating Henry I. But we must confine this within reasonable limits: after many years' acquaintance with twelfth-century monarchs I still regard Henry I as one of the most unattractive and David as one of the most appealing of them. Devout, intelligent, loyal David undoubtedly was; but he was not a weak or peace-loving man: no successful twelfth-century monarch could afford to be. In conjunction with his leading bishops he set to work to reorganise the Scottish sees and above all to keep

[8] Orderic Vitalis, i, pp. 43–44; M. Chibnall, *The World of Orderic Vitalis* (Oxford, 1984), pp. 198–99.

[9] R. W. Southern, *St Anselm and his Biographer* (Cambridge, 1963), pp. 188–93.

[10] The fifteenth-century chronicle in the *Cartulary of the Holy Trinity Aldgate*, ed. G. A. J. Hodgett, London Record Society, 7 (1971), pp. 223–24; cf. C. N. L. Brooke and G. Keir, *London, 800–1216: The Shaping of a City* (London, 1975), p. 319.

[11] R. H. C. Davis, *King Stephen* (London, 1967), pp. 38–39, 106–8.

[12] Ibid., pp. 106–7. For what follows, cf. G. W. S. Barrow, *The Anglo-Norman Era in Scottish History* (Oxford, 1980), esp. pp. 97–101.

the archbishop of York, who claimed jurisdiction over Scotland, at bay.[13] He was up against the toughest of Henry I's archbishops, Thurstan of York – a man of similar range of personality to his own; a tough fighter – but also the founder of Fountains abbey. In 1126 they hammered out their first compromise in the court of Henry I. Over territory hotly disputed (we may suppose – for the details are very obscure) between the sees of York and Glasgow, the see of Carlisle was planned; and, after years of further delay and argument, it was actually founded in 1133. All the disputed territory that lay north of the border was handed over to Glasgow, all that lay south to Carlisle. But in 1135 Henry I died and David lost no time in claiming to be lord of Cumbria and settling in Carlisle, from then on his favourite city. The bishop fled and David prepared for more adventures further south. In 1138 he staged his major invasion of north-eastern England; but the redoubtable Archbishop Thurstan, now nearing his end, rallied most of the feudatories of northern England; and the Scottish army – after causing fearful havoc in the north of England – was routed at the Battle of the Standard.[14] We may not pause too long over the havoc David's army caused, for it was hardly different from the suffering the English frequently wreaked when they raided in Scotland – and warfare was endemic and is usually like that. But we cannot doubt the truth of the story, for the best account of the campaign and the battle comes from the pen of St Aelred himself, who was a devoted protégé of David – had been his steward – and reckoned that the king, when not actually engaged in mayhem in Yorkshire, was almost a saint. David's final adventure shows most clearly how his mind worked in the political field. In 1149 the young Henry came to him at Carlisle and was dubbed a knight; and David and his son, another Henry, made a scheme of conquest of the most grandiose. His aim was to set Henry II on the throne of England and redraw the frontier of England and Scotland at the Ribble. It was quite unsuccessful, though Henry became king not long after; and David was lucky to die when he did, for once Henry II was securely on the throne of England, at the end of 1154, he showed no interest at all in the ambitions of the Scottish dynasts to whom he owed so much.

The other general point about David is that his religious foundations reveal the imaginative grasp of a connoisseur. Henry I's great foundation

[13] For what follows see esp. M. Brett, *The English Church under Henry I* (Oxford, 1975), pp. 23–28; D. Nicholl, *Thurstan, Archbishop of York* (York, 1964), ch. 4. On the formation of the see of Carlisle and the archdeaconry of Richmond in the see of York, see Hugh the Chanter, *History of the Church of York*, ed. C. Johnson, M. Brett, C. N. L. Brooke and M. Winterbottom, OMT (Oxford, 1990), pp. liii–liv. On the less amiable side of David, see below at n. 14.

[14] Nicholl, *Thurstan*, pp. 221–28.

had been a traditional Benedictine house with Cluniac affinities; most of his foundations were for Augustinian canons; his wife favoured Augustinians and hospitals particularly, showing a markedly practical bent. But David was at once in the forefront of fashion. He founded – or shared in founding – houses for black monks from Tiron at Kelso, Black or Augustinian canons at Holyrood, Jedburgh and Cambuskenneth, White or Cistercian monks at Melrose, Newbattle, Dundrennan and Kinloss; and he helped his constable to plant White or Premonstratensian canons at Dryburgh.[15] Clearly, like his brother-in-law, he felt the need for the most fervent available prayers and in ample quantity. In all the enterprises of his later life he worked in collaboration with his son, Earl Henry (c. 1114–52), and we cannot tell in detail what Henry contributed to this story. But there is here too a sense of what was most novel and most alive in the religious life of Europe, at a time when the new orders were growing 'like asparagus in May'. If one asks where in western Europe in this period there was a monastic patron who showed the widest and most sophisticated appreciation of the current fashions in the religious life, one answer might be in the south east of Scotland, the heartland of David's foundations. They do not all lie in that region: some are farther afield in Scotland, and he played an important part in the formation of the Cluniac house of St Andrew in Northampton.[16] Nor must we forget that the Benedictine abbey of Dunfermline, which he chose for his burial, owed much to him, whatever kind of foundation Queen Margaret had really made there.[17]

In the eleventh and twelfth centuries men began to look with new and more subtle eyes at the rule of St Benedict, and the old rule of St Augustine was fetched out of oblivion, considerably rewritten, to provide the fundamental model for canons. Modern studies of the religious orders are full of discussions and definitions of the difference between a monk and a canon;[18] but if we were transported back to the twelfth century and asked

[15] See below, pp. 166–71; see also Barrow, *The Kingdom of the Scots*, esp. pp. 173–87. Some doubt attaches to Dundrennan; and the very careful analyses in Barrow 1973 and *Medieval Religious Houses: Scotland* distinguish between contemporary evidence, well-founded tradition and legend which naturally attached David's name to other foundations – for a good example see below, pp. 170–71.

[16] *Royal Commission on Historical Monuments for England, Northamptonshire*, 5 (1984), pp. 52–53; Barrow, *The Kingdom of the Scots*, pp. 174–76 – and scattered references between pp. 173 and 187 on other English houses in which he was interested.

[17] The essential continuity of David's work for Dunfermline with Margaret's foundation is argued in Barrow, *Kingdom of the Scots*, pp. 193–98 and *Medieval Religious Houses, Scotland*, p. 58. For David's burial there see A. H. Dunbar, *Scottish Kings: A Revised Chronicle of Scottish History, 1005–1625* (Edinburgh, 1899), p. 64 (a reference I owe to Elizabeth Hallam Smith).

[18] See below, pp. 213–31, which analyse many recent discussions.

the people of Melrose as they watched the new Melrose abbey rising from the meadows, and the new Jedburgh priory or abbey rising not far away – what is the difference between the monks of Melrose and the canons of Jedburgh? – I am sure that they would have been as confused and baffled as we are. Indeed, it is evident to us that there was often more difference between new and old monastic orders than between monks and canons. Thus the monks of Dunfermline represented traditional Benedictine norms: a relatively large community engaged in public worship in a church to which the faithful from around might come and attend at least in the nave – dividing the rest of their time between spiritual reading and other avocations.[19] In the late eleventh century, and especially in northern France and Burgundy, an intense movement of criticism of this way of life had developed. All monks were sworn to chastity and obedience and personal poverty indeed – but what meant poverty if the community was rich? Monks might have an effect on the world and some of them might spend time in public preaching – but as communities in monasteries they should be cut off, separate from the world. One of the most exciting characters in this movement was Bernard of Tiron, who after being traditional monk, hermit, wandering preacher by turns ended by founding Tiron abbey.[20] There the worship and fervour of traditional monasticism could be mingled with something of these new currents. And the greatest of the daughters of Tiron in the British Isles was Kelso – set up by David before he was king at Selkirk: then moved to Kelso in 1128 on the advice of a French monk who had been David's tutor, and on whom David much relied in his earlier years as king, John, bishop of Glasgow. David is said himself to have visited Tiron before the foundation.[21] The massive westwork of Kelso abbey is one of the finest monuments of Romanesque architecture in Scotland, and of the Norman style beloved of King David, though the surviving buildings are all well after his death. But the west end in its planning and outline is something quite unusual in Britain in this time – a great west work more

---

[19] On Dunfermline see *Medieval Religious Houses, Scotland*, pp. 58–59; Barrow, *Kingdom of the Scots*, pp. 184–85; and for the church and other buildings, D. Knowles and J. K. S. St Joseph, *Monastic Sites from the Air* (Cambridge, 1952), pp. 16–17; *Royal Commission on the Ancient and Historical Monuments of Scotland: Fife, Kinross and Clackmannan* (1933), pp. 106–21.

[20] On Bernard of Tiron see *Vita* by Gaufridus Grossus in *PL*, 172, cols 1367–1446; R. B. Brooke, *The Coming of the Friars* (London, 1975), pp. 50–7; for his context, H. Leyser, *Hermits and the New Monasticism* (London, 1984).

[21] Barrow, *Kingdom of the Scots*, pp. 175–76 (citing *Vita Bernardi*, c. 20, col. 1426), pp. 199–205; *Medieval Religious Houses, Scotland*, pp. 68–70; Knowles and St Joseph, *Monastic Sites*, pp. 60–61; *Royal Commission, Roxburghshire*, i (1956), pp. 240–46; for the influence of Bishop John, see *Regesta regum Scottorum*, i (n. 1), no. 131, p. 192; *Medieval Religious Houses, Scotland*, p. 68.

on the German pattern or model. As one contemplates it in its present setting, there is little to suggest that it was not Benedictine of a traditional pattern.

Monasteries and communities old and new increased with amazing rapidity in the twelfth century; but perhaps the most sensational centre of growth of all was the Cistercian order. In the 1120s some Englishmen came to live with St Bernard at his own abbey of Clairvaux; and in 1131–32 he sent them to Yorkshire to found Rievaulx.[22] Within months the monks of Rievaulx had inspired a group in St Mary's York to secede and set up their own monastery at Fountains, which in the course of 1133 made its submission to St Bernard, and joined the Cistercian order. Only a year or two later one of King David's most brilliant protégés – a young Northumbrian from Hexham called Aelred – happened by chance to visit Rievaulx. He was entranced at once by the beauty of the place and the charm of the life he found there. It was not a charm which would appeal to all of us, or indeed to all at the time. Harsh, cold, monotonous, relentless some of his own recruits were to find it. But Aelred's biographer, Walter Daniel, has left an unforgettable description of Rievaulx as he found it, and its appeal to the young Aelred.[23] So he abandoned King David – anyway for a time – and joined this rapidly growing community; growing so rapidly that in 1136, only four years after its foundation and two years after the entry of Aelred, it was able to send out its first colonies, to Melrose in Scotland and to Warden, far away to the south in Bedfordshire. Not long after, more groups of monks were sent out – to Dundrennan in 1142 and in the next year to Revesby in Lincolnshire.[24] To Revesby went Aelred as first abbot, but he was soon back as abbot of Rievaulx; and the community in his later years comprised 140 choir monks and over 500 lay brothers, so we are told – the largest in the order in its day, we may guess, except Bernard's own

[22] See esp. D. Knowles, *Monastic Order in England, 940–1216* (2nd edn, Cambridge, 1963), pp. 230–45; and for discussion of the origins of Fountains, esp. L. G. D. Baker, 'The Foundation of Fountains Abbey', *Northern History*, 4 (1969), pp. 29–43, at pp. 38ff.

[23] Walter Daniel, *Life of Ailred of Rievaulx*, ed. F. M. Powicke, NMT (Edinburgh, 1950), pp. 10–13; cf. C. Brooke and W. Swaan, *The Monastic World* (London, 1974), pp. 157–61; and on Aelred, Powicke's introduction to Walter Daniel; Knowles, *Monastic Order*, pp. 257–66; A. Squire, *Aelred of Rievaulx* (London, 1969).

[24] *Medieval Religious Houses: Scotland*, pp. 74–76; D. Knowles and R. N. Hadcock, *Medieval Religious Houses: England and Wales* (2nd edn, London, 1971), p. 124; L. Janauschek, *Originum Cisterciensium*, i (Vienna, 1877), pp. 39, 70, 76. *Medieval Religious Houses, Scotland*, p. 75, notes that there is circumstantial, but not 'record evidence' that Rievaulx was mother house of Dundrennan; but it is treated so in the early Cistercian catalogues cited by Janauschek, *Originum Cisterciensium*, p. 70.

Clairvaux.[25] And meanwhile, though Aelred never again lived in Scotland, we do not have to enquire very far where King David could turn for advice on how to found Cistercian abbeys; and if Newbattle and Kinloss, David's last two Cistercian foundations, were both apparently founded from Melrose, all four looked to Rievaulx, and to Abbot Aelred, the Bernard of the north, as their spiritual home and their father, and in Aelred they had a leader as mellifluous as Bernard himself, as inspired – and less abrasive.

In the foundation of Kelso David had already had the help and advice of the bishop of Glasgow, and the same Bishop John was evidently his chief counsellor and colleague in the foundation of Jedburgh in the late 1130s; and at Jedburgh they installed Augustinian canons originally colonised, it seems, from Beauvais.[26] Now Augustinian abbeys in the early twelfth century were basically of two types. When Archbishop Lanfranc had founded St Gregory's priory in Canterbury in the 1070s or 80s at a certain distance from the two Benedictine houses already there, it was clearly meant to serve as a hospital and a practical centre of social and pastoral work in the urban community; and such, we may be sure, was Queen Matilda's purpose in making her own foundation, within the walls of the city of London – likewise Augustinian – and with this kind of Augustinian house David must have been entirely familiar.[27] The other kind is represented by Llanthony on the borders of Wales and England. Here a chaplain of Henry I and a hermit set up house together in one of the most remote, wild and dangerous spots ever chosen for a religious house in Britain. In everything but rule and order Llanthony is like a Cistercian house – in the wilds, in what the Cistercians (harking back to the origins of monasticism) liked to call the desert, utterly remote from the habitations of man. In due course the

---

[25] Walter Daniel, *Life of Ailred*, p. 38. For Aelred's panegyric on David, see *De genealogia* in Twysden, *Historiae anglicanae scriptores* (n. 4), cols 347–50.

It is of great interest that in 1140 (after the foundation of Melrose, but before David's last foundations) David was visited by St Malachy, St Bernard's friend and the creative figure in the reform of the Irish Church, B. T. Hudson, 'Gaelic Princes and Gregorian Reform', in *Crossed Paths: Methodological Approaches to the Celtic Aspect of the European Middle Ages*, ed. B. T. Hudson and V. Ziegler (Lanham, 1991), pp. 61–82, at pp. 62–64. I owe this reference to the kindness of Dr Brendan Smith.

[26] *Medieval Religious Houses, Scotland*, p. 92; Barrow, *The Kingdom of the Scots*, p. 180; Aelred, *Genealogia*, (n. 4), col. 348.

[27] For Canterbury, Knowles and Hadcock, *Medieval Religious Houses: England and Wales* (n. 24), p. 152; *Cartulary of the Priory of St Gregory, Canterbury*, ed. A. M. Woodcock (London, 1956), esp. pp. ix–xi; T. Tatton-Brown, 'The Beginnings of St Gregory's Priory and St John's Hospital in Canterbury', in *Canterbury and the Norman Conquest*, ed. R. Eales and R. Sharpe (London, 1995), pp. 41–52; for London, Holy Trinity Aldgate, Brooke and Keir, *London, 800–1216* (n. 10), pp. 314–25.

canons found it excessively so, and founded a second house in Gloucester which precisely represented the second type of Augustinian house – an urban community very much part of a town.[28] Some of these urban Augustinian communities, like that at Leicester,[29] took over major pastoral responsibilities – so much so that the notion grew up at the time, and has had great vogue in recent times, that Augustinian canons were essentially half way to the world – with a pastoral, outgoing, outward-looking mission. Of many this was true; but of many it was quite untrue – and it is this which makes the difference of monk and canon so confusing to us. David as a young man had been much involved in a plan to make St Andrew's Cathedral an Augustinian house – it did not mature till the 1140s, but it shows his interest already in an urban Augustinian community.[30] The Augustinian house to which David and his brother had looked when recruiting the Augustinian bishop of St Andrew's was Nostell priory in Yorkshire – which was very like Llanthony in conception – founded by Adelold (future bishop of Carlisle) who had been a chaplain of Henry I, and a group of hermits.[31] In Jedburgh, as in Melrose, it seems to me that David himself attempted to follow the idea of setting up houses in remote places. In both cases a new religious house with an old name was established some distance from the old centre: at Melrose about two miles and at Jedburgh about five miles from the former monastery.[32] The towns which we see about these two abbeys came after the abbeys and are a product of them, and at Jedburgh a witness to the transformation of one kind of Augustinian foundation into another. If we ask why David chose to make Jedburgh Augustinian, when many of his foundations were Cistercian, we cannot give a precise answer. But we can make three suggestions. First of all, Jedburgh was above all Bishop John's place – where he chose to be buried; and we may suppose that he had a particular affection for the canons. Secondly, of all the new or relatively new orders of the period, the Augustinian was the most popular, and far and away the majority of Henry I's foundations

[28] For Llanthony see the chronicle in BL Cotton MS Julius D.x, fos 30v–50v, partly printed in W. Dugdale, *Monasticon anglicanum*, ed. J. Caley, H. Ellis and B. Bandinel (London, 1817–30), vi, pt 1, pp. 129–31; see comment below, pp. 227–28. For the sites, see Knowles and St Joseph, *Monastic Sites* (n. 19), pp. 208–11.

[29] A. Hamilton Thompson, *The Abbey of St Mary of the Meadows, Leicester* (Leicester, 1949), esp. ch. 1; cf. below, p. 226.

[30] Barrow 1973, pp. 212–21; *Medieval Religious Houses, Scotland*, p. 96.

[31] *Early Yorkshire Charters*, iii, ed. W. Farrer (Edinburgh, 1916), pp. 133–34; Nicholl, *Thurstan* (n. 13), pp. 130–37; J. C. Dickinson, *The Origins of the Austin Canons and their Introduction into England* (London, 1950), pp. 120–21.

[32] *Medieval Religious Houses, Scotland*, pp. 49, 51, 76, 92.

had been Augustinian – it would be strange indeed if David had not included an Augustinian among his many foundations. And the spread of the orders David patronised strongly suggests that he really was a connoisseur with a sympathy for several and a desire to have the best of what was most fashionable in the religious life in his land. To both Melrose and Jedburgh he gave an ancient name. It almost seems as if he was imitating Henry I, who in Reading revived not one but a trio of lost religious houses, evidently quite aware of what he was doing.[33] Now the tradition about Old Melrose which flourished in his day would certainly have put it under the Rule of St Benedict; and although both monasteries had really been in some kind of lien with Lindisfarne, that is to say houses of monks but not very specifically Benedictine,[34] Old Jedburgh as it was in the late eleventh century may well have seemed to be a decayed house of canons. Later history carried both these great foundations some distance away from David's original conception. Both, and especially Jedburgh, became in effect urban communities. Melrose had a golden age as a centre of Cistercian fervour when St Aelred was the father abbot at Rievaulx and his friend St Waldef or Waltheof, King David's stepson, was abbot at Melrose itself.[35] As for Jedburgh, its fine church was a long time in the building, so that we have something of David still in it, but far more of the late twelfth and thirteenth centuries, culminating in the great west window.[36]

David's patronage can be summarised in a variety of different ways. It can be said that he laid an economic burden on the borders it could never bear – and that it was right and reasonable to transfer them and their lands to the local lairds at the Reformation. Or it can be said that he settled and colonised these territories with advanced farming communities. Or it could be said that he provided the Scottish borders with centres of spiritual life and worship and culture such as they have never enjoyed before or since. However one views it, King David I laid an indelible mark on this part of the country. But there is still Dryburgh to come.

By an irony Dryburgh, the one of these great houses which was not of David's making, best preserved the features which he tried to create – it sits in its rural setting most unspoilt, most beautiful of all the Border

[33] Above, pp. 29–30, 153–54; *Reading Abbey Cartularies*, ed. B. R. Kemp, i, Camden 4th Series (London, 1986), pp. 16–18 and refs.

[34] For Lindisfarne, see brief summary in Knowles and St Joseph, *Monastic Sites* (n. 19), pp. 40–41. On its early history and on the Lindisfarne Gospels, there is an immense literature.

[35] For Aelred see above, n. 23; on Waldef, esp. D. Baker, 'Legend and Reality: the Case of Waldef of Melrose', *Studies in Church History*, 12 (1975), pp. 59–82.

[36] *Medieval Religious Houses, Scotland*, pp. 92–93; Knowles and St Joseph, *Monastic Sites*, pp. 188–89; *Royal Commission on the Ancient and Historical Monuments of Scotland, Roxburgh-shire*, i (1956), pp. 194–209.

abbeys.[37] The canons in a kind of way expressed an appropriate untruth when they later forged a foundation charter attempting to make David their founder. But in fact they were founded by his constable, Hugh de Moreville, in 1150 as David's life was drawing to a close; and though he can hardly have acted without David's consent and support, he started a new fashion in Scotland by choosing the white canons of Alnwick, or Premonstratensians, for his house. It would be nice to know whether he did this to fulfil an ambition of David's to add to his collection of orders – or in defiance of the king's tastes, precisely to give patronage to an order David had ignored. Defiance is not very probable. David certainly knew about white canons: Alnwick, the second house of the order in England, had been founded by Eustace FitzJohn, a great northern baron who had actually fought on David's side at the Battle of the Standard, and who probably regarded David as his potential or actual overlord when he founded the house in 1147–48. It has been alleged that he founded Alnwick – or the Gilbertine Watton soon after – as an act of penance for his involvement in the campaign of the Standard.[38] But it is most improbable that he repented of his friendship with David and his son, and much more likely that we should see his adventures into Premonstratensian and Gilbertine houses as an extension of David's quiver. The Premonstratensians were in most respects extremely like the Cistercians – but they were canons not monks owing to the interest their founder had had in the rule of St Augustine, and in the possibility of setting up an order geared to missionary work and the service of women as well as men – all of which his colleagues and successors frustrated, so that by the 1140s there was little difference to be seen between them and the Cistercians, and so it appeared to the English barons. For between 1132, when Rievaulx was founded, and 1153, when St Bernard and King David died, they spread a mantle of Cistercian houses all over the land; but between 1153 and the end of the century Cistercian foundations were exceedingly rare; in their place Premonstratensian houses were founded in large numbers.[39] In the eyes of their patrons they

[37] Knowles and St Joseph, *Monastic Sites*, pp. 150–51; *Royal Commission on Historical Monuments, Scotland, Berwickshire* (1915), pp. 132–48; for what follows, see esp. *Medieval Religious Houses, Scotland*, p. 101; for the forged charter, *Liber S. Marie de Dryburch*, Bannatyne Club, (Edinburgh, 1847), pp. lxix-lxx; *Early Scottish Charters*, ed. A. C. Lawrie (Glasgow, 1905), p. 436. For the background, H. M. Colvin, *The White Canons in England* (Oxford, 1951).

[38] Knowles and Hadcock, *Medieval Religious Houses: England and Wales*, p. 185; cf. Colvin, *The White Canons*, pp. 53–54.

[39] Below, pp. 216–17; and for what follows, see *Statuta capitulorum generalium ordinis Cisterciensis* i, ed. J.-M. Canivez (Louvain, 1933), p. 45; Janauschek, *Originum Cisterciensium* (n. 24), pp. 131–282.

performed the same function. It is not quite clear why so sharp a caesura was drawn, though it was partly because the Cistercians themselves wished to curtail their own advance and passed a statute forbidding new houses; partly that their reputation suffered an eclipse. So far as the statute is concerned one can only say – it was perfectly obeyed in England, and in central Europe totally ignored. It is a nice puzzle. But this much is clear – that much depended on the relation between fashion among patrons and fashion among recruits. It was no use giving patronage to a community which no one wished to join. It was perhaps a noble act of faith, but of little lasting profit, to join an order to which no one would give support or patronage. Hugh was being forward-looking in choosing the white canons in 1150 – he was just ahead of the rush; and he and they were inspired in their choice of site. But he was not in isolation.

I have said little about women, who certainly had less than their share of patronage in twelfth-century Scotland. Eustace FitzJohn gave support to the order of St Gilbert of Sempringham, who was forming the one successful double order – of women and men – of the day.[40] But it was a very local affair, and Watton was as far north as it successfully penetrated – efforts to plant it in Scotland never matured.[41] So it is pleasant to end by recording the tradition that the house of nuns at Berwick was also founded by King David – though in the history of that house we can be certain of almost nothing.[42] We cannot be certain if David founded it, nor to what order it belonged. I have said that the distinctions between orders were often much less clear-cut than they seem to historians today. The nuns are the best example of all – they hardly seemed to know at times themselves.[43] For this there were two main reasons. First, they depended on chaplains for their services, and often for their administration; and tended to call themselves of the order of whatever chaplains they had for the moment. And, secondly, because the shrewder women discovered advantages in this order or that – they sometimes carried privileges with them; and that is perhaps why the nuns of Berwick sometimes called themselves Cistercian

[40] Colvin, The White Canons, p. 54. For all that relates to St Gilbert and the Gilbertines, see Raymonde Foreville's introduction to The Book of St Gilbert, ed. R. Foreville and G. Keir, OMT (Oxford, 1987); and B. Golding, Gilbert of Sempringham and the Gilbertine Order (Oxford, 1995).

[41] Ibid.; G. W. S. Barrow, 'The Gilbertine House at Dalmilley', Ayrshire Archaeological and Natural History Society Collections, 2nd series, 4 (1955–57), pp. 50–67; Medieval Religious Houses: Scotland, pp. 105–6.

[42] Medieval Religious Houses: Scotland, p. 145.

[43] See especially, Sally Thompson in Medieval Women (n. 2), pp. 242–52; and Medieval Religious Women (Oxford, 1991).

although the Cistercian order knew them not. Whatever St Margaret and her children had done for the religious life of Scotland, they had not made it an inspiring home for women religious. But that is the one qualification to my general theme: that in the work of King David we see as imaginative a patronage of the religious orders as is to be observed anywhere in the Europe of his day.

5. Caen, Saint-Etienne, The West Front. (*Photo, John Crook*)

10

The Normans as Cathedral Builders

In the generation following the Norman Conquest of England in 1066 a start was made in the reconstruction of every cathedral in the land – of almost every major abbey church too, and of innumerable new churches large, medium and small. It is one of the most astonishing building explosions in recorded history. True, it was part of a movement which can be traced all over western Christendom; but nowhere else do we find so marked a concentration of resources in the effort, in so small a land in so short a time. It is a challenge to anyone interested in the history of these buildings – and in the religious sentiment, the art and architecture and the economics of cathedral building – to explain how and why it was done. In it we shall find, in the nature of the case, a mingling of fashion, of function – the uses and needs to which these buildings were put – and religious sentiment.[1]

First, the fashion. It is broadly true to say that the only public buildings in most of western Christendom in the early middle ages were churches, that they performed a great number of functions apart from the obviously religious and liturgical, and that it is therefore perhaps hardly surprising that they were sometimes large. A few enormous churches had survived from the heyday of the Christian Roman empire, especially the largest of

Based on a lecture delivered in King Alfred's College, Winchester on 30 April 1979 under the auspices of the Winchester branch of the Historical Association, and first printed with a reprint of R. Willis, *The Architectural History of Winchester Cathedral*, Friends of Winchester Cathedral (Winchester, 1980), pp. 83–98.

[1] This chapter is a general survey of a vast subject, and I have kept notes to a minimum. In it I have avoided any detailed discussion of matters of style, on which there has been a copious literature, much of it published since 1979. Much recent research is represented by the *British Archaeological Association Conference Transactions*, some of them cited below, and especially by Richard Gem's studies there and elsewhere. It also figures in the many cathedral histories of recent years, most recently of all in chapters by Eric Fernie, 'The Building: An Introduction', and S. Heywood, 'The Romanesque Building', in *Norwich Cathedral: Church, City and Diocese, 1096–1996*, ed. I. Atherton, E. Fernie, C. Harper-Bill and Hassell Smith (London, 1996), pp. 47–58, 73–115 – supplemented by the essential studies of T. Cocke on later restorations, to which we owe the fabric as we know it: 'Change Not Decay: An Account of the Post-Medieval Fabric', ibid., pp. 705–27.

the basilicas in Rome – above all, old St Peter's. There were a few buildings large by any standards scattered about northern Europe too: the abbey of Fulda, where St Boniface was buried, for example, was already substantial in the eighth and ninth centuries. But if we could be transported to the early middle ages with an eye attuned to the great cathedrals and abbeys of the romanesque era, of the eleventh and twelfth centuries, we should find the great buildings of earlier days exceedingly modest. Thus Bede's Wearmouth and Jarrow still in part exist, and they seem now in scale modest parish churches, yet they were the worshipping centres of one of the most flourishing communities of monks in western Europe in the late seventh and eighth centuries.[2]

Between the decline and fall of Northumbrian monasticism in the late eighth and ninth centuries – completed by the Viking raids and conquests – and the revival of monasticism in France, Germany and England in the tenth century, the monastic tradition flourished most obviously in Germany, especially south Germany, in the houses founded by the cosmopolitan group of monks associated with or disciples of St Boniface. Of these one of the most important was Reichenau, the parts of which were in its heyday spread all over the modest island on which it is sited in the Bodensee or Lake of Constance. It flourished as a centre of monastic observance, literature and book illumination in the eighth and ninth centuries, and on into the tenth and eleventh, when a great church was added to the splendour of its *scriptorium*.[3] In the tenth century the main church, the headquarters in the middle of the island, the Mittelzell, was less than a quarter of the building which we see today. In the late tenth and early eleventh centuries it was enlarged to its present size and, allowing for some later work and modern restoration, it is essentially the church of the early eleventh century that survives. We are in the Germany of the Saxon and Salian emperors; and in the world of Ottonian art and architecture; and here more than anywhere else the fashion for large churches began. Greatest of all the surviving German churches of this era is Speyer cathedral, the monument and mausoleum of the Salian emperors; first, the east end and the nucleus of the rest, of Conrad II; next the nave and the whole completed work, of Henry IV, who was buried here in 1106. 'Completed', I say; but Speyer has had a chequered history. In the late seventeenth century Louis XIV gave orders

---

[2] R. Cramp, 'Excavations at the Saxon Monastic Sites of Wearmouth and Jarrow, Co. Durham: An Interim Report', *Medieval Archaeology*, 13 (1969), pp. 21–66, esp. pp. 30–31, 42–45.

[3] The decline of the *scriptorium* in the tenth and eleventh centuries was postulated by a number of scholars, led by C. R. Dodwell and D. H. Turner, *Reichenau Reconsidered* (London, 1965); for a rebuttal of this view, see H. Mayr-Harting, *Ottonian Book Illumination*, 2 vols (London, 1991), i, pp. 203–9.

6. Speyer Cathedral, Nave. (*Photo, John Crook*)

to his armies invading the Rhineland to destroy it, and fearful destruction was wrought; much of what we now see of the nave is nineteenth-century reconstruction. Nonetheless, in scale, conception and design, this is a perfect cathedral of the heyday of early and mid Romanesque; and a remarkable document, since it comes from a part of Europe not reckoned economically advanced in the eleventh century, and from two king-emperors usually reckoned by modern historians not at all seriously interested in spiritual matters. In the end it is a monument to Henry IV, as he lay dying, excommunicate for 25 years, marked as the enemy of Pope Gregory VII, discredited by his aloofness from the First Crusade. The cathedral of course makes clear that in his own eyes, and in the eyes of his immediate supporters, he was by no means cut off from the church and its consolations; and it is a weighty piece of propaganda for the Salian emperors.[4]

By 1066 the fashion for large churches had spread all over northern France and indeed over most of western Europe; the late eleventh and twelfth centuries were to see its zenith. A glance at one or two examples will help us to get a clear view of some of the elements of the world we are studying. First, let us look over the Alps to Milan, to Sant' Ambrogio, the great shrine church built originally by Ambrose himself amid the Roman cemeteries to shelter the holy relics of the obscure Roman martyrs Gervasius and Protasius. Here is a great early Christian basilica to which nearly every century from the fourth to the twentieth has made its contribution. But the nave, the atrium and the canons' tower show that there was a marked concentration of resources precisely in our period, in the late eleventh and early twelfth centuries. The atrium is an ancient feature – the place where the layfolk and the clergy of Milan met before major services, and then processed into the church. But this atrium was rebuilt about 1100. In the meantime there had come to be (by a curious act of archiepiscopal inadvertence) two religious communities serving the same church. In the ninth century the monks were allowed to build the tower on the south, which summoned the faithful to their services; the canons had no such advantage and evidently reckoned they suffered in status and in pocket by having no tower. In the early twelfth century the prosperity of Milan, as of many north Italian cities, was rising to a new peak, and the flow of pilgrims to the shrines in the basilica and of offerings into this and other church coffers was at its height. The canons proceeded to build themselves a tower higher than the monks' but not quite so high as it now appears, since an extra storey was put on

---

[4] On Speyer, see K. J. Conant, *Carolingian and Romanesque Architecture* (2nd edn, Harmondsworth, 1978), pp. 131–35 and pls 87, 91; J. Crook, 'Bishop Walkelin's Cathedral', *Winchester Cathedral*, ed. J. Crook (Chichester, 1993), pp. 21–36, at pp. 30, 32.

top of it in the nineteenth century, but lofty enough; and naturally it brought an angry response from the monks. In 1144 monks and city commune demanded its demolition; but by a stroke of ill luck for the monks, it was one of those rare occasions when the archbishop of Milan, the pope and the emperor were all in accord. They supported the canons, and the tower is there still as a witness both of the generosity of visitors to the church in the early twelfth century and of the political importance of Milan and its churches in the days of the contest of empire and papacy.[5]

A little nearer home, but not too near, is the delectable little pilgrimage town of Conques in the Rouergue in the French *massif central*. Here in the tenth century a small knot of monks brought the relics of Ste Foy, St Faith, a Roman martyr of an obscurity almost equal to that of Gervasius and Protasius in Milan but of great posthumous fame. Her relics performed miracles and, partly for this reason, partly because of its situation on pilgrim routes to the south especially on those heading for Santiago de Compostela in the north of Spain, Faith became an extremely popular saint and her building fund prospered. Prospered, that is, for a time; since the large and splendid church is all of the eleventh century, with a few twelfth-century additions, including the grotesque and fearful last judgement over the west door, which amply illustrated for the sake of pilgrims and other visitors the benefits of good living and good giving and the pains of hell.[6]

Far to the north east of Conques, in the heart of Burgundy, lay the abbey of Vézelay, almost all of it of the early twelfth century; still Romanesque – though the first winds were blowing of the great change in taste and style which was to spread Gothic first over the north of France and then into England, especially to Wells and Lincoln, in the late twelfth century. The first hints of Gothic taste were apparent before the great nave and narthex at Vézelay were quite finished. Still, it represents late Romanesque at its best, and late Romanesque sculpture too, some of the finest that survives. The contrast between the simplicity of Conques and the rich adornment of Vézelay is one to which we shall return. The whole church and monastery is a monument to the period, roughly from 1050 to 1250, when almost everyone believed that St Mary Magdalene lay in Vézelay.[7]

If we survey western Christendom, then, we find plenty of evidence that, and plenty of evidence of reasons why, the late eleventh and early twelfth

---

[5] On Sant'Ambrogio, see C. Brooke and W. Swaan, *The Monastic World* (London, 1974), pp. 219–23, and pls 327–28, 351–57; F. Reggiori, *La basilica di Sant'Ambrogio* (1966).

[6] On Conques and Sainte-Foi, see R. and C. Brooke, *Popular Religion in the Middle Ages* (London, 1984), pp. 26–29, 158–59, and pls 1–2.

[7] On Vézelay, see Brooke, *Popular Religion*, pp. 46–47, 91–94, 163 and pl. 16; Brooke and Swaan, *Monastic World*, pls 112–18.

centuries were a golden age of church building on the grandest scale; and in the display of increasing wealth, in the pursuit of relics and miracles, in the growing love of pilgrim travel – almost the only form of holiday making known to the prosperous or the naturally peripatetic of the age – some of the reasons why money poured into the building funds. We can sharpen the edge of some of these motives. The first two archbishops of Canterbury after the Norman Conquest, the Italians turned Normans Lanfranc and Anselm, were characteristic of the world and monastic milieu in which they lived in believing that most men and women would be damned, and that only monks had a serious chance of heaven. Among the great patrons, Henry I, king of England, famous for his acts of cruelty and violence, of rapacity and cunning, famous too for his horde of bastard children, was equally renowned for his spectacular generosity to the church. His forte was rebuilding, founding, refounding monasteries.[8] Other men put their fortunes large and small into cathedrals.

This kind of large church was a novelty in England at the time of the Norman Conquest. I was one of many who saw the foundations of the pre-Conquest Winchester cathedral when Martin and Birthe Biddle and their colleagues laid them bare nearly thirty years ago.[9] This was indeed a large building – but even so, it seemed dwarfed by the immense, massive base of the Norman west front exposed not far away; and it differed fundamentally from its Norman successor in this respect: the Norman cathedral was one vast room – divided by screens, broken up by the transept, but essentially a single building; the Saxon cathedral was a succession of modest-sized churches tacked on to one another; large in total, but containing no single substantial open hall. It had nothing the least resembling the later Norman nave, whose proportions are still essentially represented in the present immense nave, though when it was rebuilt and adapted in the fourteenth century it was actually somewhat reduced in length.

The old minster at Winchester is indeed the largest pre-Conquest cathedral known; and perhaps it is dangerous to make general statements when so few of its colleagues have been excavated and none survive above ground. They were swept away, and are usually now covered by their successors. It was thus with great anticipation that the excavators working under York minster in the late 1960s and early 1970s searched for the Anglo-Saxon

    [8] See ch. 8, pp. 150–55.
    [9] M. and B. Kjølbye Biddle, *Winchester Studies*, 4 (forthcoming); M. Biddle and D. J. Keene in F. Barlow, M. Biddle, O. von Feilitzen and D. J. Keene, *Winchester in the Early Middle Ages*, *Winchester Studies*, i (Oxford, 1976), pp. 306–13; M. Biddle, *The Old Minster: Excavations near Winchester Cathedral, 1961–9* (Winchester, 1970); J. Crook, 'Walkelin's Cathedral', in *Winchester Cathedral*, ed. J. Crook (n. 4), pp. 21–36.

cathedral; but in that case, very dramatically, they did not find it – they proved that the Roman buildings whose foundations lie all about those of the Norman cathedral were still standing and in use well into the Saxon, Christian period, and that the Saxon cathedral was somewhere else. The best-known surviving foundations of a pre-conquest cathedral are those of the cathedral of East Anglia at North Elmham; the contrast between this modest building about 120 feet long and the cathedral which replaced it at Norwich, well over 400 feet – indeed nearly four times the length, is exceptionally striking and probably exaggerates what was usual.[10] But all the evidence we have suggests that the difference must have been extremely impressive at the time.

The contrast between the early Norman cathedrals and their predecessors took three forms: in size, in situation, and in the cults and devotions which the cathedrals represented. Not only were they large, but a number were moved to quite new cathedral cities. Various explanations of this were given at the time and various have been given since; no doubt there were a variety of factors involved: they were moved to larger and richer towns, to places more readily defensible by bishops representing the conquering Normans in a country uneasily settled. The bishop of Lichfield coveted first Chester for its walls (even though he thought it prudent actually to set his cathedral just outside them) and for the presence of prestigious and generous Norman war lords. But he soon found a better prize in Coventry, a rich monastery which doubled his endowments. The bishop of Dorchester (which lay in Oxfordshire on the edge of a vast diocese) went almost to the other end of his see, and found in Lincoln a rich town and a well-fortified one; but no one who has contemplated Lincoln cathedral standing on its magnificent hilltop site can doubt that Bishop Remigius also had a good eye for a site and a spectacle. In some cases in which the cathedral was already established in its permanent site the Normans so enhanced the situation, or made such spectacular use of it, as to set a wholly new image on the place.

Durham and Winchester are cases in which the Normans took over and adapted, but hardly transformed, existing cults. Durham had been founded as a final home for the much travelled St Cuthbert, whose relics had fled from Lindisfarne when the Vikings came, tried out Chester-le-Street, and finally settled in Durham in the late tenth century. The Normans did not bury or suppress Cuthbert; he ruled over the north east as he always had – though they were in the early twelfth century to give him a new image: for it was only then discovered that gentle, chivalrous Cuthbert had an aversion to women. In Winchester the Normans took over a cathedral

---

[10] See nn. 27, 1.

dedicated to St Peter and with St Swithun's shrine in its centre; the new cathedral was rededicated to Peter, with Swithun given the place of honour behind the high altar.[11] Thus the cults were preserved – though the change was more remarkable than this would suggest, for the tomb of St Swithun, so carefully kept within the bounds of the old Old Minster, was translated in 1093. Elsewhere more violence was done to the cults: at Canterbury Archbishop Lanfranc, with great rapidity, almost completed a new cathedral in the years 1070 to 1077.[12]

The old cathedral had been a diffuse building with several different centres and focal points, including the tombs of St Dunstan and St Ælfheah (or Alphege). The new one was not an enormous building, perhaps not very much bigger than its predecessor; but it had a very substantial nave (as at Winchester, the present nave of Canterbury preserves the proportions of the original; indeed in that case the Norman west tower survived into the nineteenth century), and a modest eastern limb; a single point of concentration, in the high altar dedicated to Christ. But Dunstan and Ælfheah, though revered by Lanfranc,[13] were put underground and out of view. Lanfranc's successor St Anselm presided over the rebuilding of the eastern limb on a much bigger scale, allowing space for splendid new tombs and chapels for his saintly Anglo-Saxon predecessors. The ambiguity in the treatment of Saxon cults reflects something of which we have a great deal of evidence, the striking and curious effort the Normans made to emphasise both change and continuity. At Norwich continuity was preserved by incorporating the ancient synthronon – the bishop's chair from the eastern apse of the earlier cathedral of East Anglia, or one of them. The present arrangement is a modern restoration, but the general purpose is clear. The most curious example is at St Albans – not of course a cathedral in Norman times but a great abbey, one of the two or three richest in the land; and relevant to our theme since there is a good deal of evidence that Lanfranc himself helped his nephew, Abbot Paul, to finance it.[14] No one has ever really studied Lanfranc's buildings as a group; and it may be that we shall end by deciding that his leading protégés, men like Gundulf, monk of Bec

[11] J. Crook, 'St Swithun of Winchester', in *Winchester Cathedral*, ed. Crook, pp. 57–68.

[12] Eadmer, *Historia novorum*, ed. M. Rule, RS (London, 1884), p. 13: 'Ecclesiam ... spatio septem annorum a fundamentis ferme totam perfectam reddidit'. Some architectural historians have doubted the completion of the cathedral in so short a space of time, or glossed the word 'ferme' to mean less than 'very nearly'. But Eadmer was a young monk at the time and knew the facts.

[13] See C. N. L. Brooke's new edition of Lanfranc's *Monastic Constitutions*, ed. D. Knowles (forthcoming); and the literature cited on p. 82 n. 43, above.

[14] Eadmer, *Historia novorum*, p. 15: cf. ibid., p. 37.

and Caen with Lanfranc, then bishop of Rochester – to whose enterprise the building not only of Saint-Etienne at Caen and Rochester cathedral but Rochester castle and the White Tower in the Tower of London have been attributed – had more to do with the designs than he.[15] Nor is there any thread of continuity leading from Saint-Etienne through Lanfranc's Canterbury cathedral, via the crypt of St Mary-le-Bow in the city of London, the archbishop's headquarters in the city at that time, to St Albans cathedral. But perhaps it is not fanciful to see Lanfranc's mind and inspiration behind the adaptation of an image basically Norman-Romanesque to different needs and situations; and also to see his inspiration behind the extreme plainness, the puritan absence of all architectural adornment, which marks them. We have seen that this was in a measure characteristic of the difference between early and late Romanesque – at least it is marked in the contrast between Conques and Vézelay.[16]

But it is exceptionally marked in Anglo-Norman Romanesque, and probably owes something to Lanfranc's personal taste. However that may be, the transepts in Winchester are the most striking surviving example of it; and St Albans presents it with a difference. In the transepts at St Albans there are small columns in the triforium arcade of obviously Anglo-Saxon type; and in the tower Roman tiles to give it yet again a different orientation. The Saxon pillars seem to me most probably intended to express continuity between Saxon and Norman: the ancient abbey and the shrine of the Romano-British martyr Alban survived to give continuity; the great abbey church in its dimensions, scale, idiom, represented change. As for the Roman tiles of the tower, they give the church a uniquely Italian appearance – they remind us of the red brick of Sant' Ambrogio, though indeed one can find this material used over a wide area from Lombardy up into central Germany; and perhaps it is not coincidence that St Albans was built by a nephew of Lanfranc with his uncle's help, that is by two men of Lombard origin.[17] The continuity of cult in the case of most English cathedrals was confined to an incorporeal saint who left no relics for them, or virtually none: to St Peter, who had churches everywhere, especially in Rome; to St Andrew

[15] On Gundulf as builder, see R. A. Brown, H. M. Colvin, A. J. Taylor, *The Middle Ages*, in *The History of the King's Works*, ed. H. M. Colvin, 2 vols (London, 1963), i, pp. 28–31, ii, pp. 806–7.

[16] For the origin of the cushion capital in Germany, and esp. for its appearance in Speyer cathedral, see Crook, 'Bishop Walkelin's Cathedral', in *Winchester Cathedral*, p. 30 and fig. 3.11.

[17] On Abbot Paul, see *Heads*, p. 66; *Gesta abbatum monasterii S. Albani*, ed. H. T. Riley, RS (London, 1867–9), i, pp. 51–61 – for his, and Lanfranc's, building works at St Albans, esp. pp. 53–4.

7. Winchester Cathedral, North Transept. (*Photo, John Crook*)

his brother; or the Blessed Virgin and her son, who ascended into Heaven and left only very slight physical traces, pieces of her veil and of his manger for example, behind. Cuthbert and his pilgrims played their part at Durham; Swithun at Winchester; yet for the most part the Normans built or rebuilt not for pilgrims, nor from the proceeds of relics, but great churches to

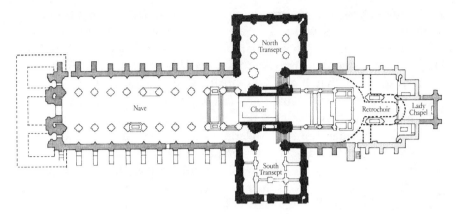

8. Plan of Winchester Cathedral, by John Crook.

universal saints or to God himself. This is a striking feature of the churches of this period: that it seems to have been equally possible, granted the will and a sufficient cause, to build a vast church without the help of relics, *martyrium*, pilgrims or special cult. The Normans were driven by piety – gargantuan churches compensating for gargantuan sins – by the sense of social emulation, by fashion, and because of the novel function they attributed to their cathedrals. This function was of two different kinds: the cathedral was a house, a home, a building whose inhabitants had certain clear cut needs. It was also a symbol, an image, of their power; of God's blessing on their conquest; and we need not doubt that these two motives acted consciously together in inspiring such tremendous buildings.

First, the practical function. We are accustomed to think of the great church as a house for God and the saints to whom it was dedicated; thus in Winchester for God, St Peter, St Paul, St Swithun and all the other saints who had relics, chapels or cults here.[18] Next, for the permanent mortal inhabitants, the bishop and the monks. And finally, for occasional visitors, lay pilgrims and the like. It therefore surprises us to find the east limb, especially God's, St Peter's and St Swithun's, relatively modest; the nave – most of it especially for the layfolk, though the monks no doubt wandered in great processions in it from time to time – the nave simply vast. In a measure this reflected fashion: such a proportion (or as it seems to us disproportion) was not uncommon. But the English cathedrals, led by

---

[18] For the dedications of Winchester cathedral, see A. Binns, *Dedications of Monastic Houses in England and Wales, 1066–1216* (Woodbridge, 1989), p. 90.

Winchester, show it in its extreme form. There seems little doubt that one of the main motives was to provide shelter for very large congregations. When Abbot Suger set about enlarging the ancient abbey church of Saint-Denis on the edge of Paris (as it then was), he tells us candidly that the chief reason was that it was too small for the crush and throng which gathered to celebrate the saint on his festivals and for other great occasions.[19] In Normandy and elsewhere on the Continent there was an ancient custom that on Whitsunday the parish clergy of a diocese led their flocks to the cathedral for a major diocesan celebration; they then gathered the holy oil and chrism blessed by the bishop for use for baptism and unction for the following year, and went on their way rejoicing. So far as we know, there was no such custom in England; indeed Dr Martin Brett has shown that it is extremely probable that it was specifically and self-consciously introduced by the early Norman bishops into English sees.[20] It must have been difficult to acclimatise in this country, for the dioceses were much larger than most of those in France: one has to go to Switzerland and central Europe to find sees as large as Lincoln and York. Candidly, I do not believe that the people of west Cumbria, or Wastdale, Ennerdale or St Bees, who lived throughout the mid and late middle ages in the diocese of York, spent their Whit weekends trekking to York and back; and there are a number of specific cases of compromise arrangements in the larger sees. Even in the smaller sees, one wonders how often the shopkeepers of Southwark came to Winchester on a Pentecostal procession in the middle ages. But one does not indeed have to believe that they came at all – or that every man, woman and child came often even from Kings Worthy or Micheldever, to believe that the establishment of the Pentecostal custom in fact brought

[19] E. Panofsky, *Abbot Suger on the Abbey Church of Saint-Denis* (Princeton, 1946), esp. pp. 86–89.

[20] Brett, *The English Church under Henry I* (Oxford, 1975), pp. 162–4; cf. Brooke, 'English Episcopal *Acta* of the Twelfth and Thirteenth Centuries', in *Medieval Ecclesiastical Studies in Honour of Dorothy M. Owen*, ed. M. J. Franklin and C. Harper-Bill (Woodbridge, 1995), pp. 41–56, at p. 43. But there were undoubtedly links between a cathedral and its diocese earlier than the twelfth century, than the Conquest indeed: cf. ibid. p. 43 n. 7, citing M. M. Gatch, 'Piety and Liturgy in the Old English "Vision of Leofric"', in M. Korhammer, ed., *Words, Texts and Manuscripts: Studies in Anglo-Saxon Culture Presented to Helmut Gneuss on his Sixty-Fifth Birthday* (Cambridge, 1992), pp. 159–79, at pp. 162–67 (a reference I owe to Dr J. Barrow). Michael Franklin, in *English Episcopal Acta*, 8, p. 11, no. 19n., hints at doubts about the authenticity of William Giffard's charter of 1120–29. *English Episcopal Acta*, 8, no. 52 (from an original charter) shows the pentecostal procession as a well-established practice by 1153–71, but allows the parishioners of Bishop's Waltham to go to Bishop's Waltham church instead of the cathedral.

great throngs there; or that the vast nave was often filled for the festivals of St Swithun and other special local occasions.

Furthermore, these great naves were social centres, sometimes too obviously so: a fourteenth-century bishop of London had to protest in the most formal manner against ball games in the cathedral.[21] Again, Winchester was a great royal city, with a palace and a royal castle; doubtless it was expected that royal occasions might take place there and bring throngs of visitors; and in the eleventh and twelfth centuries kings often visited Winchester. If it had been hoped that coronations might take place there, that hope was frustrated by the energy and initiative of the monks of Westminster, led by their devoted prior, Osbert of Clare, who in the mid twelfth century forged a handsome chestful of royal charters and papal bulls to ensure that their abbey had the sole privilege of royal functions and coronations.[22] Martin Biddle and Derek Keene have shown how often the early Norman kings celebrated Easter and other festivals in Winchester, and wore their crowns in the cathedral; and one royal occasion has acquired a particular fame. On 2 August 1100 an arrow struck and killed William Rufus in the New Forest. 'A few of the peasants carried his corpse to the cathedral at Winchester on a horse-drawn wagon, with blood dripping from it the whole way', wrote William of Malmesbury.

> There in the cathedral crossing, under the tower, he was interred, in the presence of many great men, mourned by few. Next year there followed the tower's collapse. I forebear to tell the opinions which were held on this event, lest I seem to believe in trifles – especially since it would have collapsed in any case, even if he had not been buried there, because it was badly built.[23]

In a brilliant passage Martin Biddle and Derek Keene have expounded the relation of the new Norman cathedral to the other buildings round it – to the old minster and the new minster to its north; perhaps to the old monastic buildings to its south; above all to the royal palace to its west, and its obvious relation to the royal importance of the city and other aspects of its life in this period; and they have given us the measurements which reveal just how the original length of the nave stood in the cathedral stakes of western Europe as a whole.[24] It was the longest of all cathedrals; as a

[21] C. N. L. Brooke and G. Keir, *London, 800–1216* (London, 1975), p. 339.

[22] Brooke, *Medieval Church and Society* (London, 1971), pp. 106–10, with references, especially to the works of Dr P. Chaplais.

[23] William of Malmesbury, *Gesta regum*, ed. R. A. B. Mynors, R. M. Thompson and M. Winterbottom, OMT (Oxford, 1998), pp. 574–75: the rather different, earlier version, is also printed ibid. (my own translation).

[24] M. Biddle and D. J. Keene in *Winchester in the Early Middle Ages* (n. 9), pt 4, ch. 3, esp. pp. 289–302, 306–21; for the dimensions see p. 310 n. 3.

church only surpassed by the great third church at Cluny, begun in the 1080s, which was not of course a cathedral but an abbey; Winchester was 533 feet long, and its nearest competitors among the cathedrals were Canterbury (as extended in the early twelfth century) and Norwich, both 454 feet. This placed it far ahead of Sant' Ambrogio (336 feet), even further ahead of the great abbeys in Caen – the Abbaye-aux-Hommes (Saint-Etienne) was a mere 296 feet, the Abbaye-aux-Dames shorter still. Statistics can always mislead, but occasionally instruct; and the last figures remind us of two vital facts in the world in which the Norman cathedrals of England grew. First, that they were part of an Anglo-Norman world, and that we know all too little of the Norman cathedrals in Normandy itself in this period – we have a little of Bayeux, almost nothing of the rest to compare with their English sisters. But we can still see in the remains of Bernai, and the much more substantial if eccentric remains at Mont Saint-Michel, something of what was going up in Normandy through the mid and later eleventh century, before and after 1066; and we can see in these and the great churches at Caen and Jumièges that the Normans in Normandy never aspired to quite the heady grandeur they achieved in England. How shall we put it? In Normandy their rulers were counts or dukes at most, in England kings. But in Normandy they were long established; in England they were newcomers, parvenus. Doubtless this is a superficial statement, but perhaps worth pondering. We cannot weigh motives and causes, but for myself I would lay stress first on the need for space to provide covering for large crowds, joint Norman and Anglo-Saxon crowds; second for an extreme version of the contemporary sentiment that God and his saints liked to be celebrated in churches of immense size. This was not universally held: witness St Bernard, who complained of unnecessary size, and Peter of Bruys, who thought God should be worshipped in the open air; but widely held. And I would place third the status symbol, the desire to impress, to be an outward and visible sign of God's blessing on the Norman conquest and settlement. But these are subjective categories.

The Norman bishops, abbots, monks and canons who became the patrons of the great churches in this country were obviously developing a model and a pattern which they were accustomed to on the Continent; nor were they in the strictest sense innovators. The first great Norman-Romanesque building in this country was Edward the Confessor's Westminster abbey which was conceived and largely built before 1066 – even if we do not have quite literally to believe the famous picture in the Bayeux Tapestry which shows the steeple jack hopping onto the roof with the weathercock to complete the building, just as Edward's body was being carried to his funeral in January 1066. Westminster abbey was a portent; and it was in the next thirty or forty years that the real explosion took place; in the process a new model emerged which was in its turn to influence continental building – a new searching for length and scale; and attempts were made unparalleled in the architectural history of the middle ages to accommodate the whole of Christian society – God, the saints, bishops, monks, canons, layfolk of high and low degree; men and (in spite of St Cuthbert) women – within the frame of a single building. Furthermore, these buildings had a much greater degree of unity than their Old English predecessors or their Gothic successors. We do not know what kind of screens these early Norman churches had. The surviving screens of this period are mostly in Italy, and are not secure analogies. Thus San Clemente in Rome was an early Christian basilica rebuilt to look still like its original in deeply conservative Rome in the early twelfth century; for myself, I think the scale of the sanctuary and choir – the altar approachable from all sides, the screen low enough for vistas to be clearly seen across it – may have been similar in early Norman cathedrals. But the only one for which we have any reliable evidence is Ely, though that was hardly early. The Norman screen of the mid twelfth century survived until the nineteenth and is known from fairly reliable drawings. It was a series of arches supporting a loft or crest which was far too high for anyone to look over it – but it is possible that the arches were open.[25] However we may view the relation of laity to monks in Norman Winchester, we may at least be sure that the line of the roofs and vaults gave a sense of unity which was lacking in the old minster of pre-conquest times, and was to be broken by the immense screens of later centuries, especially by the reredos which firmly and finally separated Christ and St Peter from St Swithun. If we may accept the dates provided by Richard of Devizes' annals, Bishop Walkelin began to build this great church in 1079 or 1080.[26] In 1093 the eastern limb and presumably the crossing, with enough space for the monks, were finished, and in that year the monks moved in in April and in July St Swithun followed them. Precisely how long it took

[25] On the Ely screen see W. St John Hope, 'Quire Screens in English Churches', *Archaeologia*, 68 (1916–17), pp. 43–110, at pp. 86ff and pls ix–x – showing that the screen was a wall 14 feet 6 inches high (perhaps a little lower originally), with three arches, but the arches would not have commanded a view of the high altar, since there was another screen behind it. The study of twelfth-century English screens has been set on new foundation by T. E. Russo, 'The Romanesque Rood Screen of Durham Cathedral: Context and Form', in *Anglo-Norman Durham*, ed. D. Rollason, M. Harvey and M. Prestwich (Woodbridge, 1994), pp. 251–68, esp. pp. 264–65 on Ely – with other evidence from Durham, Tynemouth and Crowland.

[26] Annals of Winchester in *Annales Monastici*, ii, ed. H. R. Luard, RS (London, 1865), p. 32, gives 1079 – p. 37 for 1093 below. But the earlier MS of the annals in Corpus Christi College, Cambridge, MS 339, fo. 22v, gives 1080: see Brooke, 'Bishop Walkelin and his Inheritance', in *Winchester Cathedral*, ed. Crook, pp. 1–12, at p. 11 n. 20.

to complete the nave is not known: Professor Biddle and Dr Keene offer a date in or about 1121 and certainly not much later. Meanwhile, at very much the same time as this church was originally dedicated, came the completion of the Norman cathedral of Lincoln – of which the western limb, preserved in a thirteenth-century Gothic setting like a relic in a shrine – survives; also the first Norman cathedral at Old Salisbury; and the Norman cathedral at York and the first building campaign of Old St Paul's.[27] These four were all secular cathedrals for chapters of canons; but Winchester was not alone among the great monastic churches – there was a throng of abbeys, and at Worcester the one surviving old English bishop, St Wulfstan, lived to see his new cathedral, a thoroughly Norman building.[28] But indeed there is no evident difference in basic idiom or design between the secular and the monastic cathedral; and this is striking. The plan of the cathedrals seems to have depended mainly on fashion and technology. Of this two examples must suffice. Winchester cathedral was originally built with an apse and ambulatory – a passage round the east end, whose replica below ground we can still explore in the crypt. This is a plan obviously suited to churches with major shrines, since it allows for much easier circulation of pilgrims round a shrine behind the high altar (already a common situation) or somewhere in the eastern limb. Thus we find apse and ambulatory plans in most of the great pilgrimage churches of the period – St Martin of Tours (so far as we can reconstruct it), Conques, Santiago de Compostela itself. At Winchester this is obviously appropriate for the shrine of St Swithun, even though in due course it became inadequate, and the large area of the retrochoir was added to give more space in the late twelfth and thirteenth

[27] On Lincoln, see P. Kidson, 'Architectural History', in *A History of Lincoln Minster*, ed. D. Owen (Cambridge, 1994), pp. 14–46, esp. pp. 14–25. On Salisbury see R. D. H. Gem, 'The First Romanesque Cathedral of Old Salisbury', in *Medieval Architecture and its Intellectual Context: Studies in Honour of Peter Kidson*, ed. E. Fernie and P. Crossley (London, 1990), pp. 9–18 (cf. below, p. 192). On York, see Derek Phillips, *Excavations at York Minster*, ii, Royal Commission on Historical Monuments for England (1985), esp. chs 3, 4, 7. On old St Paul's, C. Brooke, 'The Earliest Times to 1485', in *A History of St Paul's Cathedral*, ed. W. R. Matthews and W. M. Atkins (London, 1957), pp. 1–99, 361–65 at pp. 19, 66, 362; the chief sources for our knowledge of old St Paul's are Hollar's engravings in W. Dugdale, *History of St Paul's Cathedral in London* (London, 1658).

[28] *The Vita Wulfstani of William of Malmesbury*, ed. R. R. Darlington, Camden Third Series, 40 (1928), pp. 52–53. On Wulfstan, see Emma Mason, *St Wulfstan of Worcester c. 1008–1095* (Oxford, 1990); on his cathedral, ibid., pp. 117–19 with references to the articles of Richard Gem, esp. 'Bishop Wulfstan II and the Romanesque Cathedral Church of Worcester', in *Medieval Art and Architecture at Worcester Cathedral*, ed. G. Popper, British Archaeological Association Conference Transactions (1978), pp. 15–37.

centuries, in the new Gothic taste.[29] But the same apse and ambulatory plan was also used at Norwich, Chichester and probably at Old St Paul's, none of them pilgrimage churches when designed – even though Norwich was to receive a local boy-martyr in the mid twelfth century and St Paul's was to rediscover St Erkenwald in the same period. This is a striking example of the complex interweaving of function and fashion in determining these designs.

A marked feature of the early Norman work in Winchester, as everywhere, is the thick joints in the masonry; and it is particularly noticeable there on account of the contrast between the thick mortar joints in the transepts and the fine joints of the central tower arches and tower – rebuilt in the early twelfth century after the fall of the first tower. I long ago associated these thick joints with the special circumstances of the Norman Conquest – in which the enormous demands of the Norman patrons for masons must have put an intolerable strain on the supply of skilled craftsmen for a generation or so. But it used to puzzle me that it was possible and safe to build so many buildings of so adventurous a kind with second-rate craftsmen. More recently I came to understand this much better under the instruction of Derek Phillips, the excavator of York minster.[30] His work is of special importance, for two reasons. First of all, he worked for years alongside the engineers who saved York minster from collapse in the late 1960s and early 1970s; and this gave him an experience very rare among archaeologists and architectural historians of how the engineer's mind works, of the engineering involved in a great stone building – rare, but not unique, for Robert Willis, one of the greatest of English architectural historians, was Jacksonian Professor of Engineering ('Applied Experimental Philosophy') at Cambridge. Secondly, Derek Phillips' work gave him an exceptional insight into how the foundations were prepared and laid, and of the basic plan and structure of the Norman York Minster of the late eleventh century. His conclusion is that it was technologically a remarkable achievement, in planning and in the design of footings and foundations; and even more remarkable, it was deliberately designed to be built mainly, not by skilled masons, but by good labourers. I shall not attempt to go into the question of how Norman England could pay for such vast works – a subject on which we know all too little. But we can say this much, securely: in the modern world whether we are building a modest cathedral fast, or a large

[29] It was evidently begun by Bishop Godfrey de Lucy (1189–1204), but there is some evidence which may point to its being started c. 1202: P. Draper and R. K. Morris, 'The Development of the East End of Winchester Cathedral from the Thirteenth to the Fifteenth Century', in *Winchester Cathedral*, ed. J. Crook, pp. 177–92, at pp. 178 and 190 n. 2.

[30] Derek Phillips, *Excavations at York Minster*, ii (n. 27).

cathedral slowly – the case with the two cathedrals I used to see going up in Liverpool when I worked there in the late 1950s and 1960s – the chief cost is labour. In late eleventh century England labour, of a kind, was cheap. In an agricultural society far more hands are needed at harvest time than in the rest of the year: total unemployment is virtually unknown; under-employment, part-time employment, is very common. The extreme of this was ancient Egypt, where the rise and fall of the Nile meant that agricultural labour was hectic for roughly three months of the year, non-existent for the rest; hence a large underemployed labour force which could be hired as a mob for political disturbances – or set to work to build pyramids. The analogy with the Norman cathedrals is obvious: the English labourers were set to good, useful, profitable, religious work by their Norman lords; and ingenious master masons (probably, indeed almost certainly, a mixture of French and English in extraction and training) devised techniques of building suitable for the majority of their labour force. Under the great gothic minster at York we may now explore a good deal of the Norman cathedral in the new undercroft; and see what a remarkable building it was. The east end was probably (not certainly) aisled and of reasonable length; west of the crossing came a huge nave without aisles. In shape and design, as now reconstructed, it closely resembles no other building in the Anglo-Norman world, and its origins, technology apart, are a puzzle. Equally striking is how little it resembles the more conventional Lincoln (so far as we know it), or Herman and St Osmund's Salisbury, which was a modest affair on its windswept hilltop, with a tiny choir and substantial nave, if the excavation reports of 1912–13 are to be trusted.[31]

This emphasises the element of experiment and searching which was an inherent part of the enterprise we have been exploring. It was a great adventure, and it put England in the centre of the Romanesque world for a time. This is most evident in the nave of Durham, where for the first time a wholly satisfactory way of vaulting a vast space in stone was devised – in ribbed vaults with pointed ribs; a hint of Gothic in an otherwise wholly Romanesque setting. And so it was from Durham that the technological base of the even more spectacular adventures of the masons of the Ile de France were derived. Later in the century the taste and the technology of Gothic returned to this country, but with a difference. In Canterbury cathedral choir we may see an early Gothic building almost wholly French

[31] The evidence is very carefully sifted by Richard Gem in 'The First Romanesque Cathedral of Old Salisbury' (n. 27). It is clear that this was begun by Bishop Herman, and it seems likely that it represents his modest concept of a cathedral. When his successor Osmund instituted a chapter of over thirty canons in 1089–91 (see above, p. 52), it seems likely that he anticipated a larger east end – though its erection is currently attributed to Bishop Roger (1102/7–1139).

in style; just as in Henry III's Westminster abbey in the middle of the thirteenth century we see mid thirteenth century Gothic with a strong French element. But elsewhere it was different: the spectacular heights, the love of vertical lines, of the French masons, were deliberately avoided and contradicted by the early English Gothic masons; and so the genius of the Winchester retrochoir, as of Wells cathedral transepts and nave, or St Hugh's choir at Lincoln, lies in the combination of Gothic style with a relatively low building and horizontal lines. But this is an epilogue – intended only to remind us at the end that though later building cannot be compared for concentration of effort and resources to that of the early Norman age – the adventures and experiments, and successes, went on.

11

St Bernard, the Patrons of the Cistercians, and Monastic Planning

If we contemplate the ruins of Rievaulx or Fountains we cannot doubt that their founders had a wonderful eye for a monastic site, even though the beauty of the valleys and of the buildings has been enhanced by the loving art of an eighteenth-century landscape gardener.[1] At Rievaulx we have the contemporary witness of St Aelred's biographer that some of the monks of the twelfth century at least were as charmed by the beauty of the scene as we are.[2] Yet we also know that many blunders were made in choosing sites – numerous shifts and changes are recorded before a number of communities were settled in their final situations: and as for aesthetic appreciation, one of St Bernard's biographers has recorded that the greatest of all the early Cistercians and the chief inspiration of their invasion of England cared not at all for the physical setting or form of the buildings; or so he seems to say.[3] My purpose is to enquire who the founders really were; to see what the documents can tell us about choice of site and building; and in particular to cross-question the *Vita prima* of St Bernard to determine if it has anything at all to tell us about the saint's own tastes and attitudes.

In contemporary parlance a founder or patron was the man who supplied the land and started the endowment of a religious house; and the Cistercians commonly reckoned that such a founder must be responsible for site,

First printed in *Cistercian Art and Architecture in the British Isles*, ed. C. Norton and D. Park (Cambridge, 1986), pp. 11–23.

[1] When this paper was first published, I expressed, and now renew, warm thanks to the editors, to Professor Christopher Holdsworth, Dr Janet Burton and Professor Timothy Reuter for their help and encouragement.

[2] *Walter Daniel's Life of Ailred of Rievaulx*, ed. F. M. Powicke, NMT (Edinburgh, 1950), pp. 12–13; cf. G. Constable, 'Renewal and Reform in Religious Life: Concepts and Realities', in *Renaissance and Renewal in the Twelfth Century*, ed. R. L. Benson and G. Constable (Oxford, 1982), pp. 37–67, at pp. 48–51.

[3] See C. H. Talbot in 'The Cistercian Attitude towards Art: The Literary Evidence', in *Cistercian Art and Architecture*, pp. 56–64, at p. 58.

building fund and endowment – even though that would assuredly mean a measure of collaboration, for Cistercian founders were rarely so rich that they could provide for everything from a single store. But obviously enough there had to be monastic founders too, and especially among the Cistercians – effective cooperation, that is, with the mother house and with the Order. The *Vita prima* and other early narratives tell us a little of how this was accomplished, but rather to tantalise than to inform.

The main period of Cistercian foundation in England fell between 1128 and 1153, and came from three sources. In 1128, by an impulse which has left no record, William Giffard, bishop of Winchester, was moved to settle monks from L'Aumône near Chartres at Waverley.[4] This was to be an important source of Cistercian growth in England; but it has always been overshadowed by the more spectacular foundation of Rievaulx in 1131–32 by the Yorkshire baron Walter Espec under the kindly eye of King Henry I, in unison with St Bernard himself, direct from Clairvaux.[5] From Rievaulx sprang most of the great Yorkshire abbeys and a number more beside. Finally, in 1147, the Norman abbey of Savigny, itself a reformed house similar in inspiration to Cîteaux, agreed to a merger; and in this it carried with it (in some cases at least, so it seems, under protest) the daughter houses of Savigny, including an important group of English houses, most notably Furness and Byland abbeys.[6] By the late 1140s a fair sprinkling of the children of L'Aumône and Waverley – and one, Abbey Dore, from Morimond – had spread about England and the borders of Wales, and an ample growth of the Clairvaux connection, most of them daughters or granddaughters of Rievaulx and Fountains too. The era of growth coincides quite precisely with the last years of Henry I and the reign of Stephen. In 1152 the Cistercian order passed a decree checking further proliferation of new houses,[7] and in the next year St Bernard died. The check in new

---

[4] The Annals of Waverley give 24 November 1128, *Annales Monastici*, ed. H. R. Luard, RS (London, 1864–69), ii, p. 221. It is noticeable that William Giffard died in extreme old age (as one may suppose) *c.* 23 January 1129 (*Fasti*, ii, p. 85), and thus the date proposed by L. Janauschek, *Originum cisterciensium*, i (Vienna, 1877), pp. 17, 286, for the completion of the foundation – 28 October 1129 – would fall well after the founder's death. See Janet Burton, 'The Foundation of British Cistercian Houses', in *Cistercian Art and Architecture*, p. 28.

[5] Knowles and Hadcock, *Medieval Religious Houses: England and Wales* (2nd edn, London, 1971), p. 124; John of Hexham's continuation to the *Historia regum* attributed to Symeon of Durham, ed. T. Arnold, RS (London, 1882–85), ii, p. 285; Janauschek, *Originum cisterciensium*, pp. 22–23.

[6] Janauschek, *Originum cisterciensium*, pp. 95–96; F. M. Powicke in *VCH Lancashire*, ii (1908), p. 115.

[7] Statute of 1152, no. 1, C. Norton, 'Table of Cistercian Legislation on Art and Architecture', in *Cistercian Art and Architecture*, pp. 315–93, at p. 324.

foundations was temporary, especially in central Europe, in Germany and
Poland, where it went on apace into the thirteenth century.[8] In England it
was more definitive. The sort of men who founded houses of white monks
in Stephen's reign founded houses of white canons in the reign of Henry
II: on similar sites with similar buildings and extraordinarily similar aims,
the patrons of the late twelfth century gave their aid to the Premonstratensian
order.

My purpose in this chapter is to ask questions, not to answer them; and
that is fortunate for me, since I do not know the answers to many of them,
nor for some how to set about finding them. Yet they are all quite fundamental to an understanding of how Cistercian sites were chosen, their
foundations made and their buildings built. My first set of questions relates
to the patrons: how did they come to choose the Cistercian order, how did
they communicate with it, what role did they play in choosing the site and
starting the building?[9]

To a monastic founder of the early twelfth century a wonderful variety
of choice was opening, something quite new in the history of monasticism;
and I have long been fascinated by the question of how they chose – to
which there appears to be no contemporary or modern literature to offer
an answer. Men like the historian Orderic Vitalis, or the canon regular of
Liège who wrote the *Libellus de diversis ordinibus*, gave some impression
of the range of order and mode of the religious life; but Orderic was little
read in the twelfth century, and of the *Libellus* only a single manuscript
survives and that incomplete.[10] We can best approach the problem by
looking at a few of the more spectacular patrons and the choices which
they made. Greatest of all the English patrons was Henry I, of whom it has
been said elsewhere that he was, 'like his father, the master of the grand
gesture; and there is a wilful extravagance about his chief acts of patronage,
both to the Church and to secular men, which makes it plain that Henry
had at least two quite different characters under his skin' – a duality which

[8] Janauschek, *Originum cisterciensium*, passim; F. Van der Meer, *Atlas de l'ordre cistercien*
(Amsterdam-Brussels, 1965), corrected in detail by E. Krausen and P. Zakar, 'Kritische Bemerkungen zum *Atlas de l'ordre cistercien* von Frédéric Van der Meer [I]', in *Analecta cisterciensia*,
22 (1966), pp. 279–90; F. Vongrey and F. Hervay, 'Kritische Bemerkungen zum *Atlas de l'ordre
cistercien* von Frédéric Van der Meer [II]', in *Analecta cisterciensia*, 23 (1967), pp. 115–27. For
what follows, see H. M. Colvin, *The White Canons in England* (Oxford, 1951), and R. Mortimer
in *Leiston Abbey Cartulary and Butley Priory Charters*, Suffolk Record Society, 1 (1979), pp. 1–5.
[9] For a more extended treatment, see Janet Burton, 'The Foundation of the British Cistercian Houses', in *Cistercian Art and Architecture*, pp. 24–39.
[10] Orderic, iv, pp. 310–37, and *Libellus de diversis ordinibus*, ed. G. Constable and B. Smith,
OMT (Oxford, 1972).

shows very clearly in his monastic patronage.[11] On the one hand, he was the chief patron of the third church at Cluny; he was the founder of Reading, one of the most lavishly endowed of independent Benedictine houses of the age; the founders of Llanthony actually refused his patronage to avoid being crushed by it. On the other hand, with the maximum economy, he assumed the title of founder to several houses of Augustinian canons and his hand can be seen behind the whole movement which was to spread them over this land almost beyond counting, and brought an Augustinian to the see of Canterbury in 1123 and an Augustinian chapter to the new see of Carlisle at the very end of his reign.[12] It may well be that there is a chain of influence here from his first wife Matilda, who founded one of the most important Augustinian houses in London in 1107–8, and who (if a late but convincing source may be believed) inspired her brother David with an interest in her religious adventures.[13] Later in life, as king of the Scots, David was to emulate his brother-in-law so far as the resources of the northern kingdom permitted. He was indeed himself a connoisseur of the new orders: he planted, or helped to plant, monks of Tiron at Kelso, Augustinian canons at Jedburgh, Holyrood and Cambuskenneth, Cistercians at Melrose, Newbattle, Dundrennan and Kinloss. His constable, Hugh de Moreville, planted Premonstratensian canons at Dryburgh with his approval and support – and that is by no means the end of the story.[14] The foundation of Melrose in about 1136 followed hard upon the entry of David's steward, the English Aelred, as a monk of Rievaulx, about 1134;[15] and this may in part account for the event. But it is in any case clear that David was extremely sensitive to current religious fashions; and though his range was very wide, he was no butterfly: his interest in the Augustinians, for example, in which he followed not only his sister but his brother and predecessor Alexander I, persisted long after the foundation of Melrose. It is possible to discern a wider circle of interests in David's activities: for in the border country, still famous for the beauty of his foundations, he combined an ardent desire

[11] Above, p. 150; cf. pp. 150–55; Walter Map, *De nugis curialium*, ed. M. R. James et al., OMT (Oxford, 1983), pp. 436–9.

[12] J. C. Dickinson, *The Origins of the Austin Canons* (London, 1950), pp. 108–31, esp. pp. 125–26. On the Augustinians, see also D. M. Robinson, *The Geography of Augustinian Settlement in Medieval England and Wales*, 2 vols (Oxford, 1980).

[13] C. Brooke and G. Keir, *London, 800–1216* (London, 1975), pp. 314–25, esp. pp. 318–19; *The Cartulary of Holy Trinity Aldgate*, ed. G. A. Hodgett, London Record Society (1971), pp. 223–24.

[14] For a fuller account, with references, see above, ch. 9.

[15] I. B. Cowan and D. E. Easson, *Medieval Religious Houses: Scotland* (2nd edn, London, 1976), p. 76; Powicke in *Walter Daniel* (n. 2), pp. xxxix–xlvii, 1–16; cf. also A. Squire, 'Aelred and King David', *Collectanea Ordinis Cisterciensium Reformatorum*, 22 (1960), pp. 356–77; Squire, *Aelred of Rievaulx* (London, 1969).

to promote what was best in the religious life of western Europe with the colonisation of what was for him the heart of his kingdom – and its enrichment by the institutions and improvements of the Anglo-Norman kingdom under which he was brought up and the Anglo-Norman baronage of which he was, as to half of him, a member. In this respect he doubtless reckoned his kingdom to include Northumberland and Cumbria, and his sphere of interest much else of England too, down to Rievaulx, where Aelred had become a monk, and Nostell, the Augustinian house with which he remained in closest contact till his closing years,[16] and to his southern earldom of Huntingdon. It is piquant to recall that in his day the southern frontier of Cumbria may have marched with Furness, the northern extremity of the barony of Lancaster, where Stephen, before he was king, had planted monks from the neighbourhood of his Norman caput at Mortain, monks of Savigny, no less, in one of the most notable foundations of the 1120s, the abbey we know as Furness.[17] In religion the circle of Henry I had much in common; in politics they were deeply divided, so that the frontier between Stephen and David became canonised as the frontier of Cumberland and Lancashire north of the sands along the River Duddon.[18]

About 1122 the Yorkshire baron Walter Espec, lord of Warden in Bedford-shire, and recently established by Henry I as a major tenant in chief in Yorkshire, founded, with much help from David and his priory of Nostell, the Augustinian priory of Kirkham, over which he placed in 1123 or so David's stepson, Waltheof, as prior.[19] About 1132 Walter appears as witness to David's charter to his sister's foundation in London; and in the years 1131–32 Walter made the most famous of his foundations, at Rievaulx close to his Yorkshire caput of Helmsley.[20] Here King David's young steward, Aelred, first saw a Cistercian community while on a visit to Walter Espec – and though David and Walter were for a brief space on opposite sides in the Battle of the Standard, it is clear that in many of their interests they

[16] G. W. S. Barrow, *The Kingdom of the Scots* (London, 1973), pp. 168–211, esp. pp. 170–71; W. Rollinson, *A History of Cumberland and Westmorland* (London, 1978), pp. 28–44; A. Armstrong, A. Mawer, F. M. Stenton and B. Dickins, *Place-Names of Cumberland*, English Place-Name Society (1950–2), iii, pp. xxxvi–xxxvii.

[17] F. M. Powicke in *VCH Lancashire*, ii, pp. 114–17.

[18] The final establishment of Cumberland as a shire dates only from Henry II's reign, and the history of the frontier of Lancashire and Cumberland is full of problems.

[19] *Early Yorkshire Charters*, x, ed. C. T. Clay, pp. 143–44; D. Baker, 'Legend and Reality: The Case of Waldef of Melrose', *Studies in Church History*, 12 (1975), pp. 59–82.

[20] *Walter Daniel, Life of Ailred* (n. 2), pp. 10–13; John of Hexham's continuation of the *Historia regum* attributed to Symeon of Durham, ed. T. Arnold, RS (London, 1882–85), ii, p. 285.

were in close touch.[21] Here we see some of the links in a complex chain of great fascination; and we come close to the heart of our problem. For Rievaulx is the classic Cistercian site,

> by a powerful stream called the Rie in a broad valley stretching on either side ... High hills surround the valley, encircling it like a crown. These are clothed by trees of various sorts and maintain in pleasant retreats the privacy of the vale, providing for the monks a kind of second paradise of wooded delight. From the loftiest rocks the waters wind and tumble down to the valley below, and as they make their hasty way through the lesser passages and narrower beds and spread themselves in wider rills, they give out a gentle murmur of soft sound and join together in the sweet notes of a delicious melody.[22]

Thus Walter Daniel, St Aelred's biographer, in his famous rhapsody on the beauty of sight and sound of his monastic home. No one who listens to this, or visits the site, can doubt that it met Cistercian needs to perfection; but Walter Daniel gives no hint, nor does anyone else explain, how the site was chosen. Rievaulx is a good example to put an edge on the question. As the order multiplied it became more difficult to find sites so convenient; they sought a wilderness – and a desert place, observed their enemy Walter Map, 'they do assuredly either find *or make*' – or to put it in the more measured language of Dr Robin Donkin's studies, homesteads and villages were sometimes moved to create the desert they sought.[23]

Two features of Walter Daniel's rhapsody particularly attract my attention: the heartfelt rejoicing in the natural beauty of the site, and the music of the waterways bringing supplies to the abbey. No one who has explored Cistercian sites with any observation can fail to be struck by the solidity and lasting quality of the buildings and the efficiency of the plumbing: drains and conduits are Cistercian hallmarks as surely as commodious valleys and plain austerity. How were these sites chosen?

Walter Espec evidently became enthralled with the order. He set up Rievaulx close to his castle at Helmsley, Warden in Bedfordshire only three or four years later close to his ancestral *caput*; and he even tried, or permitted, a scheme to convert his original foundation of Kirkham from Austin canons to white monks, with what success (or lack of success) might

---

[21] Squire, 'Aelred and King David' (n. 15); Aelred, *Relatio de Standardo* in *Chronicles of the Reigns of Stephen, etc.*, ed. R. Howlett, RS (London, 1884–90), iii, pp. 181–99; *Walter Daniel, Life of Aelred*, pp. xlv – xlvii.

[22] *Walter Daniel, Life of Aelred*, pp. 12–13.

[23] Walter Map, *De nugis* (n. 11), pp. 92–93; R. A. Donkin, 'Settlement and Depopulation on Cistercian Estates during the Twelfth and Thirteenth Centuries, Especially in Yorkshire', *Bulletin of the Institute of Historical Research*, 33 (1960), pp. 141–65.

be anticipated.[24] He is alleged to have died in the Cistercian habit at Rievaulx.[25] How he came to his knowledge of the order is less clear; but he is said to have chosen the site before the monks came to found Rievaulx in 1131–32. When the monks set out St Bernard sent a letter of brilliantly controlled and terse commendation to King Henry I, whom Bernard had met in dramatic circumstances the year before, when he was one of those concerned to see that the English church chose Innocent II in the papal schism.[26] It would be tempting to suppose that Walter Espec was at Henry's court at this time and had himself met Bernard. There is, however, no evidence for this; and it really seems more likely that original contact was made more remotely. Christopher Holdsworth has pointed out to me important evidence of Cistercian links with Yorkshire in the 1120s which may hold the clue.[27] But however it occurred, Walter Espec must have been very well informed on Cistercian needs before he chose the site.

The formal record of early Cistercian foundations, laid out in stately Latin in Janauschek's *Origines cistercienses*, published in 1877, makes dramatic reading enough: the speed with which houses multiplied, especially in the 1130s and 1140s, all over western Europe and beyond, gives one a sense of the thrilling nature of the spiritual adventure involved – and a physical adventure too, with so many groups searching, surveying, choosing sites, negotiating with patrons, sorting out the numerous practical problems, resolving difficulties and disputes. We catch the edge of all this in the sources; we are rarely brought face to face with it. In his account of the Battle of the Standard, Aelred has put into the mouth of the English general, Walter Espec, no less, a fine speech revealing a knowledge of Norman and English history.[28] We do not need to believe in the literal truth of the speech but can accept that he was a man of wide experience and some cultivation.

[24] Dickinson, *The Origins of the Austin Canons* (n. 12), p. 123.

[25] *Cartularium abbathiae de Rievalle*, ed. J. C. Atkinson, Surtees Society, 83 (1889 for 1887), pp. 264–65; cf. *Early Yorkshire Charters*, x, ed. C. T. Clay, p. 144; Powicke in *Walter Daniel, Life of Ailred*, p. xcix.

[26] Letter 92 in *Opera Bernardi*, vii, p. 241; see above, p. 157 and n. 55.

[27] See esp. Bernard's Letter 106 (*Opera*, vii, pp. 265–67) to Henry Murdac, apparently of the 1120s, while Henry was a secular master in York, naming two monks who may already have settled in Clairvaux from Yorkshire in this period; one of whom may have been the first abbot of Rievaulx. Professor Holdsworth has also made important suggestions about choice of site, *Charters of Rufford Abbey*, ed. C. J. Holdsworth, Thoroton Society, i (1972), pp. xxiii–xxvi. For all this see now also P. Fergusson, 'The First Architecture of the Cistercians in England and the Work of Abbot Adam of Meaux', *Journal of the British Archaeological Association*, 136 (1983), pp. 74–86; and Fergusson, *Architecture of Solitude: Cistercian Abbeys in Twelfth-Century England* (Princeton, 1984).

[28] Aelred, *Relatio* (n. 21), pp. 181–99, esp. pp. 183ff.

But neither he nor Aelred has left us any account of the history we should most like to know – the inner story of the foundation of Rievaulx, Warden and the rest.

Nor is it only the patrons whose interests are hidden by our sources. The best account of the spread of the order in the early days comes in the *Vita prima* of St Bernard himself; and there is quite a lot of useful information here about how this or that daughter of Clairvaux came to be established, and even occasionally about the monks who went to form the new houses. But this rarely goes beyond a reference to one of the close associates of St Bernard himself, such as the monk Geoffrey, an expert in the instruction of communities which were converted to the Cistercian way of life *en bloc*, who was sent to receive the community of Fountains in 1133.[29] Now Geoffrey was evidently a choir monk of great experience, a man who could instruct in the customs and liturgy, the way of life and the habit; he and his like can hardly have been experts in food and plumbing too; it is in this region that we are least well informed – and for the interests of this chapter this is the region of greatest significance, for what we most need to know is how the norms and modes of craftsmanship, building and design were planned and disseminated. On this the *Vita prima* tells us very little.

Cistercian planning and architecture are an immensely rich field of enquiry; there is a vast amount which is not known – and more still that I do not know. In asking my questions, therefore, I shall try to presuppose as little as possible of what future research, or the work of those more learned than I, may show. In particular, there are many problems concerning the earliest history of the buildings; the recent discoveries at Fountains have underlined how unsatisfactory our current chronology and architectural history of even the best known sites may be.[30] But no one doubts that the Cistercians established a degree of uniformity and plain simplicity in their buildings which sets them apart even from the other religious orders of the twelfth century, who studied uniformity of plan and function to a degree which is staggering enough and far from understood. The Cistercians established themselves on sites which were remote, preferably in valleys where the river provided excellent drainage, and with streams which brought ample supplies of fresh water to the lavatorium, the kitchen and elsewhere. They built churches large and solid and relatively plain; they built domestic

---

[29] D. Knowles, *Monastic Order in England* (2nd edn, Cambridge, 1963), p. 237; *Vita prima S. Bernardi*, iv, c. 10, in *PL*, 185, col. 327; *Memorials of the Abbey of St Mary of Fountains*, ed. J. R. Walbran and J. T. Fowler, Surtees Society, 3 vols (1863–1918), i, pp. 46–48 and notes; St Bernard, letter 96 (*Opera*, vii, pp. 246–47).

[30] See R. Halsey, 'The Earliest Architecture of the Cistercians in England', in *Cistercian Art and Architecture*, pp. 64–85, at pp. 73–76.

buildings for large communities or small of an equal solidity – made to last; they have the mark of eternity upon them. If we had never heard of St Bernard and knew nothing of their literature, we should deduce that the buildings were for a common way of life; but we should really know more of the striking practical qualities which they reveal than of their spiritual aspirations. And we should assume that these qualities came from within the Order.

In the mid 1130s the elderly Benedictine Orderic Vitalis wrote of them thus:

> They have built monasteries with their own hands in lonely, wooded places and thoughtfully provided them with holy names, such as Maison-Dieu, Clairvaux, Bonmont and L'Aumône and others of like kind, so that the sweet sound of the name alone invites all who hear to hasten and discover for themselves how great the blessedness must be which is described by so rare a name.[31]

'With their own hands' – *proprio labore* – we do not have to interpret this too literally, to assume that every stone in a Cistercian house was laid by Cistercian hands, to perceive that the sites and the buildings themselves presuppose a considerable body of knowledge and expertise in the design of buildings and the necessary crafts associated with them within the order itself. Among the earliest pieces of evidence of the Cistercian attitude to work and practical labour are the famous illuminations from Cîteaux in the books associated with Stephen Harding.[32] These show Cistercian monks engaged in cutting down trees and shaping timber; but they are all caricatures (even if not all intended to be humorous), and the message seems to be – look at us incapable monks, trying to do manual work to which we are not accustomed. If that is the message, it deceives; Cistercian building reeks of professional skill; and if we ask why there is so little trace of it in early Cistercian literature a part of the answer must surely lie in the extraordinary class distinction which was so characteristic of early Cistercian customs, which separated choir monks and lay-brothers – by class I mean not of social origin but of monastic function; though they must often have met, Cistercian monasteries were designed normally to keep them apart.[33] In

[31] Orderic, iv, pp. 326–27.

[32] C. Oursel, *La miniature du XIIe siècle à l'abbaye de Cîteaux* (Dijon, 1926); Oursel, *Les miniatures cisterciennes a l'abbaye de Cîteaux (1109–vers 1134)* (Mâcon, 1960). On the miniatures see now, C. Rudolph, *Violence and Daily Life: Reading, Art and Polemics in the Cîteaux Moralia in Job* (Princeton, 1997); J. France, *The Cistercians in Medieval Art* (Stamford, 1998).

[33] The architectural demarcation, especially in early days, is a marked and curious feature of Cistercian planning. It seems from such evidence as I have seen that the nave was separated from the aisles (which could be used from the first, so far as one can tell, as chapels – cf. the foundations at Rievaulx) and choir by a screen high enough to prevent any view

early days, when the fervour of enthusiasm brought such a multitude of recruits to Cîteaux, it would be surprising indeed if they did not include many skilled craftsmen. Quite a cursory inspection of Cistercian remains surely compels us to believe that there were such; and there are occasional references to lay craftsmen in the order in the literature – but in my observation (which may well be defective) they are very occasional. If we broaden our view and ask how the Cistercians achieved the measure of uniformity which is a mark of their buildings and their sites, then we may see this as a limb or branch of one of the main structures of the Order. They really believed in uniformity, and tried to achieve it by textual work on the rule of St Benedict and on the liturgy.[34] Their efforts at liturgical reform had a limited success – had indeed a ludicrous element, since they tried at first to devise a kind of chant too plain for their many recruits accustomed to traditional Gregorian modes; and they had to set up a committee under St Bernard's direction to devise a compromise formula between new and old.[35] Yet the very attempt is significant. This and other measures depended on the institution of the general chapter which, if not so early a feature as once supposed, may reasonably be assumed to have been in force by the mid 1120s, along with the machinery of statute making and annual visitation. Of the many vexed problems concerning the early statutes I say nothing;[36] but we may be sure that at least in principle every abbot of the order was supposed to be present at the annual general chapter in early days, and that the abbot of a mother house was supposed to visit all his daughters each year. This must often have been in practice delegated. St Bernard himself, to go no lower in the hierarchy, made no attempt to visit all Clairvaux's daughters ever, let alone annually; but we know little

Note 33 *continued*
(see above, p. 189 n. 25, correcting Brooke, *Medieval Church and Society*, p. 166n.). The indications of these screens are clear at Buildwas, and the screen between nave and choir survives intact, if much restored, at Maulbronn. In addition, the lane between the west walk of the cloister and the lay brothers' quarters, which survives in a few cases, notably at Byland, emphasises their exclusion from the paths of the choir monks. This is not to say that they never met, and Professor Holdsworth has pointed out to me, e.g., that one of Aelred's sermons (*PL*, 195, col. 249) seems to presuppose an audience of choir monks and lay brothers combined. This would suggest that lay brothers sometimes joined the choir monks in the chapter house. The evidence, and especially the architectural evidence, needs much more investigation.

[34] C. Waddell, 'The Reform of the Liturgy from a Renaissance Perspective' in *Renaissance and Renewal* (n. 2), pp. 88–109, at pp. 104–9, and references.

[35] Waddell, 'The Reform of the Liturgy', p. 106.

[36] So far as they relate to the themes of this chapter, they were discussed authoritatively by C. Holdsworth, 'The Chronology and Character of Early Cistercian Legislation on Art and Architecture', in *Cistercian Art and Architecture*, pp. 40–55.

of the mechanics of the process, save that he seems to have tried the experiment of making Henry Murdac arch-abbot of Clairvaux's English daughters before he departed to be archbishop of York – with more than one reluctant backward glance – very possibly to the relief of some of his former subjects.[37] What we do know is that the system of visitation caused some disputes as to parenthood, especially in the congregation of Savigny after the merger, but also elsewhere. Thus Kingswood in Gloucestershire was Tintern's daughter, and Tintern was Waverley's sister; both came from L'Aumône near Chartres and L'Aumône from Cîteaux herself – and all of them were involved in a series of disputes in the 1140s and 1150s, the details of which are quite obscure;[38] but they all show that the visitation system was really working with such creaks and groans as we should expect. The Cistercian uniformity reflected a constitution designed in part precisely to that end.

The most elaborate early account of the building of an abbey comes from Bernard's *Vita prima*, and to that document we must now turn.[39] I remember long ago uttering maledictions against Abbot Suger for giving us so many precious details of his work at Saint-Denis, but telling little or nothing of his craftsmen.[40] Partly this may be attributed to his overwhelming egoism; but there also seems to be a kind of snobbery at work, which refuses to give human form to mere mechanicals – though heaven knows these men were not mechanical in the Shakespearean sense. By the same token, perhaps, the authors of the *Vita prima* give no precise details of the names or activities of lay-brothers. But the mischief goes a little deeper, for the book is a notorious example of the curate's egg. It is fundamentally the work of Geoffrey of Auxerre, a modest man, who reckoned himself unworthy to the task, and so summoned a seminar of better authors, as he seems to have supposed, to perform the task; and he set to work in good time while Bernard was still alive. The first book is perhaps the best, since William of Saint-Thierry really knew Bernard intimately, and had that capacity we demand of the best of twelfth-century biographers, of conveying a personal immediacy which stirs the imagination and brings us face to face with its object; and William was provided with copious notes by Geoffrey himself for the parts of the story he knew less well. It is here that we find the

---

[37] D. Knowles, *Monastic Order*, pp. 255–57; Knowles, *Historian and Character and Other Essays* (Cambridge, 1963), pp. 87–91.

[38] *GFL*, pp. 510–13.

[39] *Vita prima S. Bernardi* in *PL*, 185, cols 225–368.

[40] See E. Panofsky, *Abbot Suger on the Abbey Church of Saint-Denis* (2nd edn, by G. Panofsky-Soergel, Princeton, 1979), esp. pp. 20–37. Pages 35–37 draw out his references to his craftsmen, but they remain remarkably anonymous compared with Suger himself.

famous account of how, when Bernard had spent a whole year in the novice chamber at Cîteaux, he still did not know whether the room itself had a vault, 'which we are accustomed to call a ceiling' – *testudo, celatura*:[41] the precise meaning is not plain to me, though the sense is not in doubt. Such was his power of concentration, he was not distracted into observing the ceiling. Similarly, he thought there was only one lancet or light in the east end of the church (it is not quite clear whether the author means nave or choir) whereas there were three. William goes on to say, a little obscurely, that this came naturally to him; that he was not given to sensual curiosity. Geoffrey of Auxerre in the third book tells the famous story of how he journeyed for a whole day by the Lake of Geneva and never saw it, or at least had so little apprehension of it that in the evening he asked his companions where it was.[42] This has been variously interpreted as meaning that Bernard was naturally unobservant, or, to the contrary, that he had so trained his senses that they could avoid all exterior distraction; that it represents in fact a degree of discipline in a man naturally sensitive to nature and art which he had to develop to counter such temptations. I find this excessively paradoxical; yet there is clear evidence that Bernard was sensitive to natural beauty.

We have seen that Walter Daniel revelled in the beauty of Rievaulx, and his description is timed to indicate that this was also part of the attraction of the community for Aelred himself. In the introductory exchange to Aelred's *Speculum caritatis* Aelred playfully tries to excuse himself from literary work on the ground that he is practically illiterate, a man of the kitchens not the schools, who toils in a 'rough and hard retreat, among rocks and hills, where he works with axe and hammer under a rule of silence'.[43] To this Bernard:

I find no terror either in the hard mountain steeps, nor in the rough rocks nor in the hollow places of the valleys, for in these days the mountains distil sweetness and the hills flow with milk and honey, the valleys are covered over with corn, honey is sucked out of the rock and oil out of the flinty stone, and among the cliffs and mountains are the flocks of the sheep of Christ. Wherefore I judge that

[41] *Vita Prima*, i, c. 4 (*PL*, 185, col. 238). See also on this passage the remarks of C. H. Talbot, 'The Cistercian Attitude towards Art: The Literary Evidence', in *Cistercian Art and Architecture*, pp. 56–64, at p. 58.

[42] *Vita prima*, iii, c. 2 (*PL*, 185, col. 306); for a possible medical explanation, see J. F. Benton, 'Consciousness of Self and Perceptions of Individuality' in *Renaissance and Renewal* (n. 2), pp. 263–95, at pp. 268–69.

[43] F. M. Powicke in *Walter Daniel, Life of Ailred* (n. 2), p. lviii, summarising A. Wilmart, 'L'instigateur du *Speculum caritatis* d'Aelred, abbé de Rievaulx', *Revue d'ascétique et de mystique*, 14 (1933), pp. 369–94, at p. 390.

with that hammer of yours you may cut out of those rocks what you would find by your native sagacity in the libraries of the professors, and that not seldom, in the midday heat, you will be aware, under the shade of the trees, of something that you would never have learned in the schools.[44]

This delicious banter no doubt reflects Aelred's tastes more than Bernard's, and, as commonly, Bernard's letter is full of echoes of the Vulgate. But it also echoes Bernard's other famous letter to Henry Murdac: 'You will find among the woods something you never found in books. Stones and trees will teach you a lesson you never learned from masters in the schools.'[45] And both reflect a passage in William of Saint-Thierry's first book of the *Vita prima*, in which he says that Bernard always claimed with a smile to have learned what he knew of the spiritual sense of scripture 'especially from meditating and praying in the woods and the fields ...; and in this he had had no other masters save the oaks and the beeches'.[46] Doubtless we are meant to feel the force of solitude here – the very next chapter has the famous description of the site of Clairvaux *in loco horroris et vastae solitudinis* – echoing Deuteronomy.[47] But there is more to it than that.

William of Saint-Thierry died before Bernard, and the second book, taking the story from the papal schism of 1130, was entrusted to Ernald, abbot of Bonneval, who seems to have been the least intimate with Bernard of the biographers, and the least qualified.[48] The reputation of the *Vita prima* has been a little like the public career of its chief begetter, Geoffrey of Auxerre.[49] After winning his spurs as Bernard's secretary, he eventually became abbot of Igny and then of Clairvaux herself; but owing to some incompetence or

[44] Powicke in *Walter Daniel*, p. lviii; Wilmart, 'L'instigateur du *Speculum caritatis*', pp. 389–94; *Opera S. Aelredi*, ed. A. Hoste and C. H. Talbot, i, Corpus Christianorum continuatio mediaevalis (Turnhout, 1971), pp. 3–6. The passage is full of biblical echoes – Joel 4:18; Deuteronomy, 32: 13, etc.

[45] St Bernard, *Letter* 106 (*Opera*, vii, pp. 265–67); cf. Knowles, *Monastic Order*, p. 221.

[46] *Vita prima*, i, c. 4 (*PL*, 185, col. 240).

[47] *Vita prima*, i, c. 4 (*PL*, 185, col. 241), echoing Deuteronomy 32:10; also part of the service of Lauds on Saturdays, J. Leclercq, *Recueil des études sur Saint Bernard et ses écrits*, ii (Rome, 1966), pp. 173–74, as pointed out to me by Professor Holdsworth.

[48] On Ernald see *Gallia Christiana*, viii, cols 1242–43; Bredero, 'Etudes sur la *vita prima* de Saint Bernard', *Analecta Sacri Ordinis Cisterciensis*, 17 (1961), pp. 1–72, 215–60; 18 (1962), pp. 3–52, at 17 (1961), pp. 253–60; G. Oury, 'Recherches sur Ernaud, abbé de Bonneval, historien de Saint Bernard', *Revue Mabillon*, 59 (1977), pp. 97–127; J. Leclercq, 'Les méditations eucharistiques d'Arnould de Bonneval', *Recherches de théologie ancienne et mediévale*, 13 (1946), pp. 40–56.

[49] *Letters of John of Salisbury*, ii, ed. W. J. Millor and C. N. L. Brooke OMT (Oxford, 1979), p. 558n. and references; N. M. Haring, 'The Writings against Gilbert of Poitiers by Geoffrey of Auxerre', *Analecta Cisterciensia*, 22 (1966), pp. 3–83; A. Bredero, 'Etudes sur la *Vita prima*' (n. 48), *Analecta*, 18 (1962), pp. 3–11.

ill fortune in the complex tangle of the papal schism of the 1160s, he was deposed yet, after a decent interval, became an abbot again at Fossanova and Hautecombe. By the same token the *Vita prima* has recovered a little from the blows struck at it by Professor Bredero and others; but some of the scars remain.[50] Ernald's second book opens with an account of how the French and English kings and the churches of their lands were won over to Innocent II by Bernard's eloquence – an account, as Martin Brett has observed, with judicious understatement, 'to be received with caution'.[51] It is indeed evident that with all the opportunities they had to know the truth, the authors of the *Vita prima* sometimes blundered, from carelessness or partiality or both; in this instance one can only suppose that they read back Bernard's undoubted involvement in the later stages of the schism to its outset. Yet even Ernald rarely goes so far astray as this; and when Geoffrey took up the pen himself for the later books we find solid journeyman's work, at its best vivid and first-hand, at its worst routine and dull hagiography; but always the work of a man who knew Bernard better than we shall ever know him.

Ernald's account of Bernard's mission to Italy in 1134–35, in which he genuinely played an important role,[52] concludes with an account of his return to Clairvaux, where he found his Prior Godfrey and other wise brothers wanting to take counsel with him.[53] 'He and other wise brothers ... sometimes used to force the man of God, whose conversation was in heaven, to come down a little towards the earth, pointing out to him the urgent needs of his house.' In particular they pointed out that the current site of the abbey was too narrow and the church even too small for the number of monks.

> They added that they had pondered on a suitable open space lower down the river, well served by the river itself, with plenty of space for all the monastery's needs, for meadows, farm buildings, plantations and vineyards; and if wood is short in the enclosure, there is a great quantity of stone available to take its place in the building of walls.

At first Bernard was not convinced – the original monastery with its stone

---

[50] Bredero, 'Etudes' (n. 48).

[51] *Councils and Synods*, i, 2, ed. D. Whitelock, M. Brett and C. N. L. Brooke (Oxford, 1981), p. 756 n. 1; see now also T. Reuter, 'Zur Anerkennung Papst Innocenz II: eine neue Quelle', *Deutsches Archiv*, 39 (1983), pp. 395–416; we need not doubt that Bernard was present at some of the meetings in 1130, but the real initiative lay with others. For further light on this, we await C. Holdsworth's forthcoming *Life of St Bernard*.

[52] P. Zerbi, 'I rapporti di S. Bernardo di Chiaravalle con i vescovi e le diocesi d'Italia', *Italia sacra*, 5 (1964), pp. 219–313.

[53] *Vita prima*, ii, c. 5 (*PL*, 185, cols 184–5).

buildings had recently been finished at great expense, and ducts of water had been very expensively fitted out through the offices; if they were to break this up or abandon it, it would be thought frivolous

> or that too much wealth – which assuredly we have not – has made us mad. But indeed it is certain that we do not have a store of money; and I say to you as it is written in the Gospel that he who would build a tower must lay up what he needs to pay for it: otherwise ... it will be said – 'This foolish man began to build, and was not able to finish'.

To which they retorted that as God was sending them recruits he would doubtless send them resources and builders too; and the abbot, delighted by their faith and charity, bent a little to their opinions – but first he prayed ceaselessly to God on the matter, and was vouchsafed several revelations. 'When the news became public, the brothers rejoiced' – and there follows the famous account of the building of Clairvaux II.

> The bishops of the region, noblemen and merchants of the land heard of it, and joyfully offered rich aid in God's work. Supplies were abundant, workmen quickly hired, the brothers themselves joined in the work in every way: some cut timbers, others shaped stones, others built walls, others divided the river, set it in new channels and lifted the leaping waters to the mill-wheels; fullers and bakers and tanners and smiths and other artificers prepared suitable machines for their tasks, that the river might flow fast and do good wherever it was needed in every building, flowing freely in underground conduits; the streams performed suitable tasks in every office and cleansed the abbey and at length returned to the main course and restored to the river what it had lost. The walls which gave the abbey a spacious enclosure were finished with unlooked-for speed. The abbey rose; the new-born church, as if it had a living soul that moveth, quickly developed and grew.[54]

As a vivid account of a great building project – and for its remarkable list of the crafts in which the lay-brothers engaged – we may accept this at face value. We may believe that the brothers took part and that professional craftsmen were needed to help them. But after meditating on it over many years, I am much less clear what we are intended to make of Bernard's own role, still less what was the truth of the matter. The rather artificial conversation piece is characteristic of twelfth-century historical writing and we should not be put off by it, any more than we should doubt Aelred's veracity because he put historical speeches into the mouth of Walter Espec. Ernald seems to be saying: Bernard's conversation was in heaven; when he came down to earth he could be pretty shrewd on practical matters, and

---

[54] *Vita prima*, ii, c. 5 (*PL*, 185, col. 285); C. Brooke, *Europe in the Central Middle Ages* (2nd edn, London, 1987), pp. 76–77.

he understood even about plumbing – which he thought very expensive; when called on to do it he could inspire all manner of local helpers; but essentially his interests lay elsewhere. It might even be argued that Bernard was Mrs Jellyby manquée, wishing to neglect domestic affairs for heavenly discourse and adventures afar off. Whether this was historically true is a question to which I do not see any clear answer. The one thing of which I am entirely convinced is that Bernard cared, at least in a negative sense, very much about the monastic environment – trees and stones, outside the monastic buildings, within 'nothing in the church but bare walls' to quote Ernald again, this time describing what the papal curia encountered when it came in 1131 – and no furnishing to distract the mind.[55] This tunes exactly with the message of the *Apologia*:[56] the attack on echoing space and frivolous ornament is an attack on everything which distracts; the church should be designed to leave the mind and the mind's eye alone.

So much for the written record. What of the evidence of the buildings themselves? Notoriously, a great deal has been deduced about the influence of Bernard's puritanism, and even about his precise prescriptions as to design, from the physical remains. The evidence of the *Apologia*, though not free from ambiguities, makes clear that he held very strong views about the outward appearances of buildings; it is not so clear that they extended to every aspect of artistic creation – just as, in his own performance, he apparently applied a puritanical renunciation of metre and form to his verses, but used every ornament, every variety of rhetoric and mood, to adorn his prose.[57] The problem, however, is whether he gave his mind at all to details of planning. In a celebrated paper in 1953 Dr K. H. Esser laid out a schema of the east end of the churches of the houses descended from Clairvaux.[58] He showed that the basic formula of the square east end was remarkably stable in churches planned in Bernard's lifetime; but after his death, though the formula continued to inspire many abbey churches, there was an outbreak of variety, even of apses, even at Clairvaux herself. The chart is very persuasive. I am not clear how secure is all the evidence on

---

[55] *Vita prima*, ii, c. 1 (*PL*, 185, col. 272); cf. esp. F. Bucher, 'Cistercian Architectural Purism', in *Comparative Studies in Society and History*, 3 (1960–61), pp. 89–105.

[56] *Apologia* in *Opera*, iii, pp. 104–7.

[57] C. Mohrmann in *Opera*, ii, pp. ix ff; cf. Brooke, *Europe in the Central Middle Ages* (2nd edn, London, 1987), pp. 401–4. On the meaning of the *Apologia* see now C. Rudolph, *The 'Things of Greater Importance': Bernard of Clairvaux's Apologia and the Medieval Attitude towards Art* (Philadelphia, 1990), esp. pp. 188–91.

[58] K. H. Esser, 'Über den Kirchenbau des Hl. Bernards von Clairvaux', *Archiv für mittel-rheinische Kirchengeschichte*, 5 (1953), pp. 195–222; cf. C. Brooke and W. Swaan, *The Monastic World* (London, 1974), pp. 152–53, 254 n. 11.

which it is based; those of us who have used Père Dimier's *Recueil des plans* at all extensively know how difficult it is to be sure on what some of the plans were founded.[59] But the basic phenomenon is clear enough. Since Esser's paper, as I understand it, a series of scholars, among them Professor Hahn,[60] have greatly sophisticated our knowledge of Cistercian church architecture; and this has served both to underline the architectural skill and care and knowledge involved in their planning, and also the subtlety of the efforts made – where it was made – to preserve the purity of the formula or formulas. All this seems to speak more of the hidden group of accomplished masons among the lay-brothers of whose existence I conjectured at an earlier stage; it does not at all sound like St Bernard or Brother Geoffrey or their like. Doubtless the craftsmen and the architects listened to Bernard and his colleagues and were inspired by them; the very sharp line that divided choir monks from lay-brothers cannot have prevented serious communication on such themes. But it makes it difficult for us to understand the relationship, since the choir monks who wrote the books were not themselves much involved in it, or did not care to describe it. The length of Ernald's account of the debate, and the elaborate nature of the conversation between Bernard and his colleagues on the rebuilding of Clairvaux, suggest that the author had some special point in mind, perhaps to defend Bernard against the charge of being too much interested in planning and plumbing – who can say? But this is one of many questions which a confrontation of the literary evidence and the buildings leaves ringing in our ears.

[59] M.-A. Dimier, *Recueil des plans des églises cisterciennes* (Grignan-Paris, 1949; supplement, 1967).

[60] H. Hahn, *Die Frühe Kirchenbaukunst des Zisterzienser* (Berlin, 1957). See also the work of P. Fergusson referred to in n. 27.

12

Monk and Canon: Some Patterns in the Religious Life of the Twelfth Century

If you were a religious of the eleventh or twelfth centuries choosing the order in which you were to find your vocation, how did you distinguish order from order, monk from canon? How did you determine gradations of the ascetic life? If you were a founder or benefactor, planning to found a new religious house, how did you determine which order to favour? At a time when asceticism and the religious orders flourished as never before, the choice must have been bewildering. There is a copious contemporary literature arguing the relative merits of this mode and that; and modern scholars have offered a remarkably wide variety of advice.[1] Some have proceeded on the assumption that there must have been a fundamental difference and have pursued it as best they might; others, disappointed in the chase, have doubted if any true difference existed. Some have seen all such differences engulfed in the deeper stream of new impulses and modes which affected every approach to the religious life in this age; others have said that to lose track of such differences is to take a very superficial view

First printed in *Studies in Church History*, 22, ed. W. J. Sheils (Oxford, 1985), pp. 109–29.

[1] From the immense literature I select the following which are particularly helpful: Giles Constable's reprinted studies, *Religious Life and Thought (Eleventh to Twelfth Centuries)* and *Cluniac Studies* (Variorum Reprints, London, 1979–80) and his *Medieval Monasticism: A Select Bibliography* (Toronto, 1976), now supplemented by Constable's fundamental *The Reformation of the Twelfth Century* (Cambridge, 1996); Caroline W. Bynum, *Docere verbo et exemplo: An Aspect of Twelfth-Century Spirituality*, Harvard Theological Studies, 31 (Missoula, 1979) and *Jesus as Mother: Studies in the Spirituality of the High Middle Ages* (Berkeley, 1982); the work of J. C. Dickinson cited at nn. 7 and 41 below; *Mendola*, 3–6 (Milan, 1962–71): *La vita comune del clero nei secoli XI e XII* (3, 2 vols 1962), *L'eremitismo in Occidente nei secoli XI e XII* (4, 1965), *I laici nella 'Societas Christiana' dei secoli XI e XII* (5, 1968), *Il monachesimo e la riforma ecclesiastica (1049–1122)* (6, 1971).

of the meaning of the rules of St Augustine and St Benedict.[2] It is very easy indeed to take an entirely sceptical view; and I propose to start by stating the case for saying there was no difference visible to all in every part of Europe – that no general statement of the difference stands up to close inspection. But to rest the matter there, I am sure, would be superficial and mistaken – and so in the second part of this chapter I embark on the much more hazardous path of determining where the difference lay. I shall try not to add another definition to the scrap heap, but to show by looking at a number of local situations how it might have appeared both externally to a founder and at a deeper level to an educated man with some discernment of different approaches to the ascetic life and religious spirituality. Yet the ultimate abiding impression is of the strangeness of the central fact: at a time when men were seeking their own religious vocation in numbers never before approached in medieval Europe – and patrons lavishing resources on an unparalleled variety of new religious houses – it is especially difficult for us to observe in many cases where the differences lay.

At a superficial level there is an obvious explanation of the paradox. It is often the case that the distinctions most taken for granted are the most difficult for the outsider to discern. In the *Prologue* to the *Canterbury Tales* Chaucer presented a well known conundrum.

> A monk ther was, a fair for the maistrie,
> An outridere, that lovede venerie,
> A manly man, to been an abbot able.
> Ful many a deyntee hors hadde he in stable ...
> The reule of seint Maure or of seint Beneit,
> By cause that it was old and somdel streit
> This ilke monk leet olde thynges pace,
> And heeld after the newe world the space ...
> What sholde he studie and make hymselvene wood [mad],
> Upon a book in cloystre alwey to poure,
> Or swynken with his handes, and laboure,
> As Austyn bit? Howe shal the world be served?
> Lat Austyn have his swynk to hym reserved![3]

---

[2] Cf. for what follows C. Brooke and W. Swaan, *The Monastic World* (London, 1974), ch. 8; the view there expressed of the rule of St Augustine has been severely criticised as too negative. For the rules themselves, see esp. *La règle de S. Benoît*, ed. A. de Vogüé and J. Neufville, *Sources Chrétiennes*, 181–86 (Paris 1971–2); L. Verheijen, *La règle de S. Augustin*, 2 vols (Paris, 1967).

[3] Chaucer, *Canterbury Tales, Prologue*, lines 165–88, ed. F. N. Robinson (Oxford, 1974), pp. 18–19.

There is confusion here, say the commentators; Chaucer has made three rules out of one. The monk must have followed St Benedict's rule if he was really a monk, and there never was a rule of St Maurus; why then this reference to the rival rule of St Austin, St Augustine?

What makes Chaucer's satire so delectable and so lasting is in part at least the marvellous skill with which he creates simultaneously the illusion of an individual and the illusion of a type. The monk is both a general portrayal of a class of men – he might equally well be a black monk or a black canon – and a sharply drawn character, who might be X or Y, people we know well. I call these two marks of his *Prologue* illusions since it seems to me likely that he intended them so. He can hardly have thought all monks and canons were mighty hunters, or all friars rascals, still less all parish priests men of the holy simplicity of his poor parson; indeed he says as much. For some of the individual characters precise originals have been claimed, and J. M. Manly showed indeed that the host carried the name of an actual London innkeeper of the day.[4] But even he admitted that Chaucer seems to have got his wife's name wrong – fortunately, in view of the shrewish character he gives her; and it really makes little difference whether we suppose that Chaucer used traits from known persons of his day or not. I am myself sceptical if there was more drawing from life than was required to catch and entertain his audience; if there had been, the illusion of type would have been difficult to sustain; and I rather suppose that Professor Manly and his successors have been caught in a delicate web of Chaucer's weaving. For the monk, however, Manly contented himself with hinting that he knew who he was or might be, and it was left to Ramona Bressie and after her David Knowles, in what I regard as a rare indiscretion of that great scholar, to trace the lineaments of the monk in William Clown, abbot of Leicester, one of the notable hunting abbots of the fourteenth century.[5] There are indeed links, but for our purpose it is the other limb of Chaucer's satire which counts: his monk was both monk and canon; for they are all one. In most European languages today – and in virtually all before the Reformation – the word monk, *monaco, Mönch, moine, monje*, can equally well mean canon or friar; and it is only in modern English, the one language in Europe devised by folk who knew not monks, that it is a solecism to call Martin Luther, the Austin friar, a monk.

Chaucer's monk was of the late fourteenth century. What happens if we go back into the twelfth century: was it not altogether different then? It is

---

[4] J. M. Manly, *Some New Light on Chaucer* (London, 1926), esp. pp. 78–81; on the monk, p. 262. On Chaucer's portraits, see also below, pp. 300–7.

[5] D. Knowles, *Religious Orders in England*, ii (Cambridge, 1955), pp. 365–66.

hard to give any precise answer to this question. But there is much to suggest that the distinction was often not so apparent as it is to us. We rarely know what passed in a patron's mind, but there are many indications that no fundamental difference was apparent. Among the most notable of twelfth-century patrons was King David I of Scotland, who was evidently a connoisseur: he planted, or had a hand in planting, black monks from Tiron at Kelso, Black Canons at Holyrood, Jedburgh and Cambuskenneth, White Monks at Melrose, Newbattle, Dundrennan and Kinloss, and encouraged his constable to plant white canons at Dryburgh.[6] He doubtless knew a good deal about the different modes of life and customs of these orders and respected it; but there is no evident difference in function, or even in the siting, of the orders. He was only one of a number of patrons who favoured both Augustinians and Cistercians; and although Walter Espec, founder of Kirkham and Rievaulx, did try (it seems) to convert his Austin canons into Cistercian monks – it was a lamentable failure – it is clear that the site and function of a Cistercian house in the 1130s did not appear fundamentally different to him from that of an Augustinian in the 1120s.[7] Most telling is the story of the Premonstratensian canons. In central Europe, so I understand, recent research has attempted to preserve some features of the conventional distinction between Cistercians and Premonstratensians to show that the monks tried to avoid and the canons, in some degree, to foster pastoral work.[8] Both had a role to play in the resettlement of German-speaking people east of the Elbe. Both represent the advance of western ideas and culture. Both were expected to engage in missionary enterprise as well as in the contemplative life. The involvement of the Cistercians in the mission is still under discussion, but it is agreed that the Morimond filiation in central Europe fitted into the landscape more rapidly and readily than their western colleagues, and never attempted isolation and self-sufficiency to the same degree.[9] In England the relation between the orders, in quite a different way, was equally remarkable. Throughout the twelfth century foundations of Austin Canons were popular. The enormous proliferation of tiny houses both of

[6] Some doubt attaches to Dundrennan, and he was not sole founder of them all; see below, ch. 9.

[7] J. C. Dickinson, *The Origins of the Austin Canons and their Introduction into England* (London, 1950), p. 123.

[8] For current research see J. Kloczowski, 'Polonia' in *Dizionario degli istituti di perfezione*, vii (Rome, 1983), cols 45–68, 75–77; and idem, 'Die Zistercienser in Klein-Polen und das Problem ihrer Tätigkeit als Missionare und Seelsorger', in *Die Zistercienser: Ordensleben zwischen Ideal und Wirklichkeit. Ergänzungsband*, ed. K. Elm and P. Joerissen (Cologne, 1983), pp. 71–78.

[9] Ibid. I am much indebted for help in this passage to Jerzy Kloczowski, Urszula Borkowska and Nicholas Coulson.

canons and of monks makes statistics almost meaningless, but it seems to be broadly true that for independent foundations as opposed to cells and minor dependencies canons always led the field. But in the period 1132–52, notoriously, the Cistercians had a marvellous success: almost all the major English and Scottish houses were founded then, and their invasion of Wales and Ireland began.[10] In 1152 the Cistercian general chapter passed its famous decree forbidding new foundations,[11] and in 1153 St Bernard died. Viewed from the perspective of central Europe and the children of Morimond, this decree was nugatory; but, viewed from England and the daughters of Clairvaux in particular, the picture is quite different. There was a virtual stop for a whole generation; and after 1152 Cistercian foundations in England never again became more than a trickle.[12] The Premonstratensians, who only counted a handful of houses before the 1150s, flourished in their stead.[13] The first Premonstratensian house in England was founded at Newsham in Lincolnshire in 1143 and the order spread from there to Alnwick in Northumberland and Easby under the shadow of Richmond castle in Yorkshire in the late 1140s and early 1150s; but the great leap forward began with the foundation of Welbeck in 1153–54, and the kind of patron who had favoured the Cistercians under Stephen was founding Premonstratensian houses, in similar situations, under Henry II. Very characteristic of the great lords of this period was Ranulf of Glanville, Henry II's chief justiciar, who in 1171 founded Butley priory for the Augustinian canons, and in 1183 Leiston for the Premonstratensians.[14]

In exactly the same period the Gilbertine canons enjoyed their heyday.[15] This may have had more to do with the chronology of their founder,

[10] D. Knowles and R. N. Hadcock, *Medieval Religious Houses: England and Wales* (2nd edn, London, 1971), pp. 110–28; I. B. Cowan and D. E. Easson, *Medieval Religious Houses: Scotland* (2nd edn, London, 1976), pp. 72–77; A. Gwynn and R. N. Hadcock, *Medieval Religious Houses: Ireland* (London, 1970), pp. 114–44.

[11] *Statuta capitulorum generalium ordinis Cisterciensis*, i, ed. J.-M. Canivez (Louvain, 1933), p. 45.

[12] Knowles and Hadcock, *Medieval Religious Houses*, pp. 112–28; for the general picture in the order, L. Janauschek, *Originum Cisterciensium, Tomus* i (Vienna, 1877), pp. 131–282.

[13] Knowles and Hadcock, *Medieval Religious Houses*, pp. 183–93; H. M. Colvin, *The White Canons in England* (Oxford, 1951); and see next note.

[14] See R. Mortimer in *Leiston Abbey Cartulary and Butley Priory Charters*, Suffolk Record Society, Suffolk Charters (Ipswich, 1979), esp. pp. 1–5; see also Mortimer in *Bulletin of the Institute of Historical Research*, 54 (1981), 1–16, on Ranulf of Glanville and his family and their foundations.

[15] On the Gilbertines see Rose Graham, *S. Gilbert of Sempringham and the Gilbertines* (London, 1901); *The Book of St Gilbert*, ed. R. Foreville and G. Keir, OMT (Oxford, 1987); B. Golding, *Gilbert of Sempringham and the Gilbertine Order, c. 1130 – c. 1300* (Oxford, 1995).

who died in the same year as Henry II, than with the movements of kings
and patrons; and it is not entirely correct to class the Gilbertines as canons.
They show to perfection, indeed, some of the ambiguities we are investigating. Originally founded to provide a secure institutional framework for
the devout women who gathered round Gilbert at Sempringham, they
rapidly grew into a double order; and in the long run St Gilbert subjected
the nuns to the rule of St Benedict and the men to the rule of St Augustine
– without ever explaining to posterity precisely why he did so.[16] It was
common for nuns in this period to be members of no very definite order
(like the ministering Mr Chadband in *Bleak House*, who was 'attached to
no particular denomination'), but to follow the rule (so far as we can
penetrate into a very obscure region) of their chaplains.[17] This has recently
been made abundantly clear by the work of Dr Sally Thompson. St Gilbert,
like St Norbert, the founder of the white canons, was deeply influenced by
Bernard of Clairvaux; and Gilbert indeed tried to arrange a merger.[18] But
the Cistercians would have nothing to do with women – a stance they
maintained for some considerable time until they awoke one day to find
that there were nuns in their order, a circumstance which bewildered them
as much as it has confused modern historians of the order.[19] As for Norbert,
he was a missionary through and through, and the full Cistercian vocation
was not for him. But orders often have their revenge on their founders;
and to the patrons of the late twelfth century the difference between white
monks and white canons was much less apparent. As for St Gilbert, the
indications are that he thought his menfolk should perform the role of
Martha, his ladies of Mary – and as to why that made Austin's rule
appropriate for the men, Benet's for the women, that is a problem to which
we shall return.

Another very powerful indicator of the common ground between canons
and monks lies in their buildings. Modern scholars have been so much
concerned to discover differences in the planning of the houses of different
orders that they have sometimes lost sight of the fundamental fact that they
liked to live in buildings of an extraordinary uniformity.[20] The characteristic

---

[16] *The Book of St Gilbert*, pp. 48–49.

[17] See Sally Thompson's unpublished University of London Ph.D. thesis on 'English Nun-
neries: A Study of the Post-Conquest Foundations, *c.* 1095 – *c.* 1250' (1984) now publ. as
Women Religious (Oxford, 1991).

[18] *The Book of St. Gilbert*, pp. 40–45.

[19] It has now been admirably clarified by Sally Thompson, 'The Problem of the Cistercian
Nuns in the Twelfth and Early Thirteenth Centuries', *Medieval Women*, ed. D. Baker (Oxford,
1978), pp. 227–52.

[20] See C. N. L. Brooke, 'Reflections on the Monastic Cloister', in *Romanesque and Gothic:
Essays for George Zarnecki*, ed. N. Stratford (Woodbridge, 1987), i, pp. 19–25.

monastic enclosure, with church, cloister, chapter house, dormitory, refectory and parlours grouped in a close-knit unity, was repeated with
remarkably little difference in every part of western Christendom by almost
every order of monks and canons. We cannot trace its origin in the present
state of knowledge, but the structure, and the name of the cloister and
some other parts, is already clear in the famous St Gall plan of the ninth
century.[21] It is fully recorded in surviving buildings and excavated sites from
the eleventh century on, and only began to be seriously modified at the
end of the middle ages. The reason for this modification is clear. The
monastic plan represented the most complex design for a domestic building
or group of buildings known in eleventh- and twelfth-century Europe: even
more complex and articulated than most castles and palaces; it was more
than chance that the English kings used Westminster abbey as the major
element in their greatest palace.[22] But it was always designed for communities
living in common. It had to be severely modified by communities of hermits,
as by the Carthusians; and much change was needed to adapt it to the
living habits of the late middle ages and early modern times, when a greater
diversity of smaller rooms – and ultimately, personal privacy – came to be
accepted in religious houses as in major secular buildings. The monastic
cloister in its heyday was a very remarkable monument both to the living
habits of the central middle ages, and to the communal ritual of monastic
life: the cloister is only the natural centre of a community (at least in the
climate of northern Europe) whose life revolves round ritual processions
conducting the inmates to rooms designed to cater for every phase of their
life and every bodily function. There was sufficient of ritual and meditation
in the life of secular canons for cloisters to be a normal feature of secular
cathedrals in the south and an occasional feature of northern cathedrals –
and it is fascinating to observe how William of Wykeham, who doubtless
enjoyed his own community's cloister on the occasional spring mornings
when he visited Winchester cathedral, implanted a cloister on his academic
communities in Winchester and Oxford.[23] But if we look more generally
at the planning of Oxford and Cambridge colleges in the late middle ages

---

[21] See W. Horn and E. Born, *The Plan of St Gall*, 3 vols (Berkeley, 1979), esp. i, pp. 241–309,
and ii, pp. 315–59 (C. M. Malone and W. Horn on the influence of the plan).

[22] See *The History of the King's Works*, ed. H. M. Colvin, i (London, 1963), ch. 4, pt 4, and
ch. 12.

[23] See G. Jackson Stops, 'The Buildings of New College', in *New College Oxford, 1379–1979*,
ed. J. Buxton and P. Williams (Oxford, 1979), pp. 155–56, 175–77; J. Harvey, 'The Buildings of
Winchester College', in *Winchester College: Sixth Centenary Essays*, ed. R. Custance (Oxford,
1982), ch. 3, esp. p. 81.

– designed within a narrow world for a very precise function, for communities of students all engaged in the same life and the same kind of work – we must be struck by how greatly they differ compared with the monastic enclosures of the whole of Christendom of earlier days.[24]

Within the framework there were differences indeed. The Cistercians achieved a unique degree of uniformity, partly by the centralised organisation of their order, partly by their deliberate efforts in this direction; partly, no doubt, by recruiting expert masons among their early lay brothers. And their monastic complexes normally made much more provision for lay brothers than other orders. Thus lay visitors were forbidden from their churches, and the naves dedicated to the lay brothers; the western range of the claustral buildings provided refectory and dormitory for lay brothers; and in early days at least provision was made for choir monks and lay brothers not normally to meet.[25] In contrast the Premonstratensians, who shared so many of the features of the Cistercians, show the least uniformity, the most irregularity, of all the major orders of the century.[26] In part this may be due to the present state of knowledge; in part to the paucity of evidence for Premonstratensian planning; but it may well be that there was in this region a genuine difference. It cannot, however, be attributed to the fact that one order was of monks, the other of canons, for there are some Augustinian houses which show quite a close imitation of some Cistercian practices, such as the night stair from dormitory to transept.[27]

Most of the literature distinguishing one order from another was controversial, the work of angry men defying their rivals. But there is one work which is wholly eirenical in purpose, the *Libellus de diversis ordinibus*, revived and commented on for us splendidly by Giles Constable and Bernard

[24] See n. 20; R. Willis and J. W. Clark, *The Architectural History of the University of Cambridge and of the Colleges of Cambridge and Eton* (4 vols (Cambridge, 1886; repr. 1988) and the *Royal Commission on Historical Monuments for England*, volumes on *City of Oxford* and *City of Cambridge* (1939, 1959).

[25] See D. Knowles and J. K. S. St Joseph, *Monastic Sites from the Air* (Cambridge, 1952), esp. p. xix; M. Aubert, *L'architecture cistercienne en France*, 2 vols (2nd edn, Paris, 1947), i, p. 317 for lay brothers' choirs; ibid., ii, ch. 4 for lay brothers' quarters; see C. Brooke, *Medieval Church and Society* (London, 1971), p. 166n. – but further consideration of the evidence, e.g. of the choir screen at Maulbronn, Brooke and Swaan, *The Monastic World* (London, 1974), plate 243, makes probable that Aubert was right that lay brothers could not normally see the high altar.

[26] Knowles and St Joseph, *Monastic Sites*, pp. xxii–xxiii, 150–83.

[27] Examples are Cartmel, J. C. Dickinson in *Transactions of the Cumberland and Westmorland Antiquarian and Archaeological Society*, 45 (1946), p. 57; Hexham, plan in W. T. Taylor, *Hexham Priory*, ed. of 1970 at end; Bolton, A. Hamilton Thompson, *History and Architectural Description of the Priory of St Mary, Bolton-in-Wharfedale*, Thoresby Society, 30 (1928), p. 146.

Smith.[28] This is the only surviving work of the twelfth century which sets to work in a systematic way to analyse the differences between monks and canons, and different modes of each, with the specific purpose of showing that they all have a place in God's providence, all are justified in their callings – though not necessarily free from errors and aberrations – and all supported by biblical precedents, if properly understood. Just the thing, we should have said, to appeal to King David and his like. Yet it survives only in one manuscript, and that incomplete; there is no evidence that it strayed from the see of Liège where it was written until it was printed by the Maurists in the eighteenth century and until the manuscript fled to England, probably in the nineteenth.

Even though the author's peaceful intent is unusual in the written literature, it was not unusual in real life. Some of the most zealous of the controversialists were compelled to beat their swords into plough-shares. Even St Bernard, zealous in pursuit of everything corrupt in the traditional monasticism – as he had to be to justify the conversion of many Benedictines and Cluniacs to what he fervently believed to be a better life – was curbed and tamed by Peter the Venerable to speak lovingly and warmly of Cluny itself.[29] Among more ordinary mortals, Gilbert Foliot, the eminent English Cluniac, counted several Cistercians (including Aelred) among his close friends, and delivered one of the frothiest of obituary notices on Bernard himself – a panegyric of his order as much as of the man – immediately after his death.[30] Yet unlike his own former abbot, Peter the Venerable, Gilbert was not always a peaceable man, and he is perhaps most widely known for the violence of his polemics against Thomas Becket. In ordinary intercourse it is likely that good relations between different orders were as common as bad in the heyday of twelfth-century monasticism; doubtless the spirit was abroad so perfectly characterised between the orders of friars in the saying attributed to the Franciscan leader Albert of Pisa – that the Franciscans should dearly love the Dominicans for various good reasons, among others that they sometimes showed them what *not* to do.[31]

The author of the *Libellus* divided the religious of his world into hermits, monks and canons – placing his own order last, as he specifically points

[28] OMT (Oxford, 1972).

[29] This is reflected in Bernard's correspondence with him: *S. Bernardi Opera*, ed. J. Leclercq et al. (Rome, 1957–77), pp. vii–viii, letters 147–49, 228, 265, 267, 364, 387–89, 521 – esp. 228. The polemic – and its opposite – are profoundly studied in G. Constable, *The Reformation of the Twelfth Century*, ch. 4.

[30] *GFL*, no. 108, pp. 146–49; cf. *GF*, p. 77.

[31] Fratris Thomae ... de Eccleston, *Tractatus de adventu Fratrum Minorum in Angliam*, ed. A. G. Little (2nd edn, Manchester, 1951), p. 82.

out to the monkish friend to whom the work was addressed;[32] and the
monks and canons he divides into those who dwell far and those who dwell
near the abodes of men, the more contemplative and the more active as
we should say. He perceives indeed that there are distinctions within monks
and canons more remarkable than those between them – yet this is never
quite distinctly stated, for his purpose is not so much to divide and analyse
as to show the common place all hold in God's purposes. Furthest from
his own way of life (for he was evidently a canon regular living close to
the abodes of men) were the hermits.

> Come then, whoever you are that love the solitary life, and take an example from
> him who was the first to be called just, and receive an increase of good works.
> See also whether our Jesus did anything that could be compared to this kind of
> life. It is written of Him in St John's Gospel: 'Jesus therefore, when He knew
> that they would come to take Him by force and make Him king, fled again into
> the mountain, Himself alone.' Behold my Jesus withdrawing alone into the moun-
> tain, lest the hermit should doubt whether He should live alone in the mountains
> or the wilderness.[33]

Thus 'by withdrawing into the mountain or the desert, as is proper for
hermits, He consecrated their life in Himself'.[34] And the author of the
Libellus goes on to observe from a wide range of biblical precedents that
all recollected folk, not only full-time hermits, may profit from a spell of
solitude. This is very characteristic. He distinguishes carefully the various
modes of the common life – for monks far from human habitation and in
towns and the hubbub of life; for canons likewise in both types of place –
and yet he carefully avoids suggesting that any of these is either perfect or
decadent; he finds a place for all. Even the monks distracted by the affairs
of their tenants and serfs may be reckoned to do it for the sake of their
serfs.[35] The outward looking are justified as well as the inward. It seems a
pity that this gallant ecumenical endeavour commanded so little attention
in its own day.

The perceptions of the Libellus present a formidable obstacle to anyone
who wishes to assert that there was a fundamental and universal difference
between monks and canons in the early twelfth century; and I shall spare
you the details of the many arguments which have been mounted on this
issue. Let me just say that those scholars who have done most to illuminate
and deepen our knowledge of the religious life of the eleventh and twelfth

[32] *Libellus de diversis ordinibus*, pp. 2–3, cf. p. xv.
[33] Ibid., pp. 10–11; cf. John 6:15.
[34] *Libellus*, pp. 12–13.
[35] Ibid., pp. 40–43.

centuries have commonly in the process stressed the variety of experience and aspiration which can be seen within the canonical and the monastic orders. As examples from a larger gathering I cite only Charles Dereine, who especially penetrated into the roots of the more ascetic canonical foundations, Prémontré among them; Jean Leclercq who has specifically argued (perhaps a little too precisely, but from a unique experience of the literature) that though one can discern a 'monastic theology' in this epoch one cannot distinguish a specifically canonical theology from it; and Giles Constable, the tendency of whose many studies is to see all the rich and complex manifestations of the religious life as ultimately part of a seamless robe.[36] A heroic attempt has been made in recent years by Professor Caroline Bynum to find a genuine thread of difference.[37] She sets aside earlier attempts, especially to see clear-cut differences of pastoral role or between the inward- and outward-looking viewpoints of the orders. But she finds a constant theme in the literature of instruction and spiritual direction – that monks emphasise the formation of character, the duty to lead the religious life, to form their own monastic personae, while canons are re-peatedly enjoined to teach by word and example. She admits that it is not wholly watertight – what can one do with a man of such universal charity as Peter of Celle, John of Salisbury's intimate friend, who addresses monks and canons alike with equal concern?[38] I do not doubt that there is a perception in Professor Bynum's work of profound interest, though I share her critics' doubts whether so slender a thread of evidence will bear quite the weight she has perforce to lay on it, and whether one can possibly know from such evidence how the generality of monks and canons viewed themselves.[39]

I wish to take quite a different approach. It has often been observed, to

[36] E.g. Charles Dereine, 'Chanoines', in *Dictionnaire d'histoire et de géographie ecclésiastiques,* xii (1953), cols 353–405; 'Les origines de Prémontré', *Revue d'histoire ecclésiastique,* 41 (1946), pp. 365–406; and 'L'élaboration du statut canonique des chanoines réguliers, spécialement sous Urbain II', 46 (1951), pp. 534–65; cf. Bynum, *Jesus as Mother* (n. 1), pp. 26–27nn.; J. Leclercq, 'La spiritualité des chanoines réguliers', in *Mendola,* 3, i, pp. 117–41; G. Constable, *The Reformation of the Twelfth Century* (Cambridge, 1996). Bynum, *Jesus as Mother,* pp. 25–26, notes scholars who see sharper differences, most notably (and with great subtlety) Sir Richard Southern, *Western Society and the Church in the Middle Ages* (Harmondsworth, 1970), pp. 241–50.

[37] Bynum, *Docere verbo* (n. 1); Bynum, *Jesus as Mother,* ch. 1.

[38] Peter of Celle's *De disciplina claustrali, PL,* 202, cols 1097–1146, is discussed in Bynum, *Docere verbo,* pp. 157–60; Bynum, *Jesus as Mother,* p. 37.

[39] See esp. R. M. Thomson's review in *Speculum* 56 (1981), pp. 598–601, a very perceptive critique, though perhaps not doing full justice to the penetration and subtlety of Caroline Bynum's analyses.

take a profane example, that historically the words Republican and Democrat have meant clean different things in different states and regions of the United States – that the parties are alliances of local groups and factions without any substantial common definition. Yet it would be foolish to deny that the differences have in many times and places been profound, or that the parties have existed. Not to press the analogy too far, it seems natural to suppose that in many local situations a sharper focus may have been discernible than from a global view. Thus a close look at monks and canons in areas such as Bavaria where early houses of Augustinian canons particularly flourished would doubtless be extremely instructive; as too the comparison between Cistercian and Premonstratensian endeavours in what was then eastern Germany at which we have glanced before.[40] But to give a clearer view of the variety and complexity of the local perspective I shall take my examples from Britain, and in doing so traverse ground so clearly and authoritatively covered by the late John Dickinson over forty years ago.[41] I have often had the experience of checking my best ideas on the canons in his book and finding them anticipated there, though I think my purpose and approach is in some ways different from his, and I occasionally differ on the details of the story.

Three of the houses from which the English canons principally sprang point the contrasts and the paradoxes of the story at the outset. St Gregory's at Canterbury was set there by Archbishop Lanfranc as a hospital, that is to say, as a welfare institution in the city – to do work inappropriate to the monks of his cathedral or of St Augustine's abbey – and we may take Eadmer's word for it that he staffed it with regular canons, even though it seems quite clear that its establishment as a full Augustinian house came later.[42] What seems to have happened is that it was converted from a hospital and social service centre (as we should interpret the phrase) into an Augustinian priory in which the hospital was the lesser element; and that is a process often repeated in the twelfth and thirteenth centuries.[43]

---

[40] See esp. P. Classen, 'Gerhoh von Reichersberg und die Regularkanoniker in Bayern und Oesterreich', *Mendola*, 3, i, pp. 304–48 and references; N. Backmund, *Monasticon Praemonstratense*, i, 2 pts (2nd edn, Straubing, 1983); above n. 8.

[41] See Dickinson, *The Origins of the Austin Canons* (n. 7), and many individual studies, e.g. 'The Origins of St Augustine's Bristol', *Essays in Bristol and Gloucestershire History*, ed. P. McGrath and J. Cannon (Bristol, 1976), pp. 109–26.

[42] See *Cartulary of the Priory of St Gregory, Canterbury*, ed. Audrey M. Woodcock, Camden Third Series, 88 (1956), esp. pp. ix–xi. See now T. Tatton-Brown, 'The Beginnings of St Gregory's Priory and St John's Hospital in Canterbury', in *Canterbury and the Norman Conquest*, ed. R. Eales and R. Sharpe (London, 1995), pp. 41–52.

[43] There are examples noted in Knowles and Hadcock, *Medieval Religious Houses*, pp. 155–80 – Cold Norton, Conishead etc.; the most remarkable case is St Bartholomew's London, which

If we examine the grander institutions of the city of London we shall find no such evident contrast between the life and work of a great abbey or cathedral priory and a hospital and social service centre, because there was no great abbey in the city, unless one counts the not too distant Westminster. The chronicle of Holy Trinity Aldgate is in form a much later document, nor is the foundation history of St Bartholomew's contemporary; yet it is clear that both enshrine genuine contemporary traditions of the purposes and activity of their founders, Queen Matilda and Canon Rahere.[44] Matilda, as befitted the daughter of St Margaret and sister of King David I of Scotland, was much interested and involved in religious foundations, and doubtless played a considerable part in inspiring her husband's outbreaks of good works. The story the Aldgate chronicler tells of her brother David's horror in finding her washing the feet of lepers fits the strongly practical pastoral bent of her own foundations – a house of canons in London which was evidently intended to combine pastoral responsibility of some kind with the liturgy and ritual of the religious life;[45] and the leper hospital of St-Giles-in-the-Fields, safely beyond the limit of Holborn – even if the traveller who becomes entangled today in the swirl of streets at the foot of Tottenham Court Road, which mark the site laid out by Matilda, will search in vain for any surviving fields. Even more sharply defined is the purpose of St Bartholomew, founded by a converted courtier in the same court of King Henry I, to improve and care for an insalubrious area just outside the city walls, and allow space both for a large hospital and a community of canons.[46] It is instructive to observe in this case that the interests of the two halves rapidly diverged, so that in the second half of the twelfth century it was thought expedient to separate the house of canons from the hospital, and to put an experienced lay administrator in charge

was founded in 1123 as both priory and hospital, though the hospital may well have been embarked on first; but the hospital was separated from the priory later in the twelfth century, C. Brooke and G. Keir, *London, 800–1216: The Shaping of a City* (London, 1975), pp. 325–28; see N. J. M. Kerling, 'The Foundation of St Bartholomew's Hospital in West Smithfield, London', *Guildhall Miscellany*, 4 (1972), pp. 137–48. See Knowles and Hadcock, *Medieval Religious Houses*, p. 311, for the numerous hospitals served by canons or brothers under the rule of St Augustine without forming regular priories.

[44] Brooke and Keir, *London, 800–1216*, pp. 314–28; chronicle of Holy Trinity, Aldgate in *The Cartulary of Holy Trinity Aldgate*, ed. G. A. J. Hodgett, London Record Society, 7 (1971), pp. 223–33; *The Book of the Foundation of St Bartholomew's Church in London*, ed. N. Moore, Early English Text Society, 163 (1923); also modern English translation by H. H. King and W. Barnard, ed. E. A. Webb (London, 1923).

[45] *Cartulary of Holy Trinity Aldgate*, pp. 223–24; Brooke and Keir, *London, 800–1216*, pp. 318–19.

[46] See n. 43.

of the hospital. Notoriously, it was this separation which saved St Bartholomew's hospital at the Dissolution of the Monasteries; and its survival is
a reminder of Rahere's assumption that canons and welfare went hand in
hand and of his successors' rapid dismantling of his plan.

Examples of Augustinian houses with their origin in hospitals, or with
some evident connexion with pastoral affairs, or at least with city communities, could be multiplied without effort. Let two suffice. At Leicester
successive overlords gathered all the churches of the town by a great act of
power into the hands of communities of canons, first secular, within
the walls, then regular, without.[47] This was the great abbey over which the
mighty hunter, William Clown, later presided. However much or little he
did for the churches of Leicester, it can hardly be doubted that the Norman
lords had taken it for granted that the great church would perform the role
of the ancient minster it replaced, and be a centre of worship and a leader
in the religious life of the town. In this respect the intention seems identical
to that of the founder of St Andrew's priory in the next county town of
Northampton, who was King David's half-brother and predecessor in the
earldom.[48] In this case the original scheme is overlaid by later events, for
new churches were founded and the priory lost much of its patronage; but
so far as one can tell the original conception was the same – save that
St Andrew's was a Cluniac priory, St Mary of the Meadows at Leicester
Augustinian. It is doubtful if Simon de Saint-Liz saw the significance in
this which Matilda or David might have seen; though we may take it that
a Cluniac priory was less well placed in the late twelfth century for defending
its patronage than an Augustinian abbey.[49]

The other example is Cambridge, where we find (so far as we can penetrate
an obscure area of scholarship) the precinct of a house of canons blossoming
into a parish; that is to say that in the late middle ages the immediate environs
of the priory by the river (as a native of Cambridge is likely to say, beside
the gas works) formed the nucleus of a parish which extended over virtually
the whole of the east fields of Cambridge.[50] The origin of this story, which
seems to be (in the present state of knowledge) unique to Cambridge, goes

[47] A. Hamilton Thompson, *The Abbey of St Mary of the Meadows, Leicester* (Leicester, 1949),
ch. 1.

[48] On the churches of Northampton see Michael Franklin, 'Minster and Parishes: Northamptonshire Studies' (unpublished Ph.D. thesis, University of Cambridge, 1982), ch. 2, esp.
pp. 86–98 – cited by kind permission of Dr Franklin; and studies by M. Franklin and others
in *Northamptonshire*, 5, *Royal Commission on Historical Monuments for England* (1984).

[49] See n. 48.

[50] See C. Brooke, 'The Churches of Medieval Cambridge', in *History, Society and the Churches*, ed. D. Beales and G. Best (Cambridge, 1985), pp. 49–76.

something like this. The priory of St Giles was founded by the castle by the Norman sheriff Picot and his pious wife Hugolina about 1092. The late thirteenth-century chronicle which enshrines those facts is cemented by many charters of doubtful authenticity; but on the whole I am inclined to think the story it tells more authentic than its charters – a situation, pace the shade of J. H. Round, only too familiar to students of medieval charters.[51] The site for St Giles was small and water scarce, so early in the twelfth century they were moved to the more salubrious riverside of Barnwell – a description which I am bound to say reads oddly to one who has known from a child the muddy banks of the murky Cam in that region. There they settled round a hermit's cell and ancient chapel of St Andrew.[52] The endowment of the priory of St Giles and St Andrew grew apace, based on the tithes of almost the whole of the west field which became the parish of St Giles, and of the east field, which became (perhaps after the Dissolution) the parish of St Andrew the Less.[53] The parishes of Cambridge were shaped within the city precinct, and the canons' empire among the agrarian tithes was evidently established before the parish boundaries could spread through the fields; and this had the curious consequence that the priory had parochial rights over what was in effect a large parish. The other precinct formed in the eastern fields, that of the nuns of St Radegund, likewise composed a parochial precinct, in that case not so large, but sufficient to preserve in the grounds of its successor, Jesus College, a substantial open space close to the city ditch.[54] In this story, once again, it stands to reason that tithes and pastoral responsibility were intimately linked in early days. In the twelfth century, if one adds the ephemeral community of the canons of the Holy Sepulchre, then canons following Austin's rule came near to monopolising this city of many churches and few inhabitants.[55]

All this supports a familiar pattern – of canons as folk nearer to the city centres, to the ordinary lives of the community, to pastoral care, at least in origin and in principle. But even before Matilda set her hand to Aldgate one of her chaplains, named Ernisius, had gone into partnership with a knight turned hermit to found Llanthony in the bleakest and remotest

---

[51] *Liber memorandorum ecclesie de Bernewelle*, ed. J. W. Clark (Cambridge, 1907), esp. pp. 38–42.

[52] Ibid., pp. 41–42.

[53] Brooke. 'The Churches of Medieval Cambridge', n. 50.

[54] J. G. Sikes and Freda Jones in *VCH Cambridgeshire*, ii, pp. 218–19; A. Gray, *The Priory of St Radegund, Cambridge*, Cambridge Antiquarian Society (1898); *The Atlas of Historic Towns*, ii, ed. M. D. Lobel and W. H. Johns (London, 1975), Cambridge (separately paginated).

[55] Brooke, 'The Churches of Medieval Cambridge', n. 50; M. Gervers, 'Rotundae anglicanae' in *Actes du XXIIe congrès international d'histoire de l'art* (Budapest, 1969; publ. 1972), p. 363.

corner of Gwent under the Black Mountain.[56] John Dickinson has doubted the veracity of the Llanthony chronicle and dismissed it as a thirteenth century compilation with much anachronism in it. This was partly due to the curious way in which it is presented in Dugdale's *Monasticon*. A closer look at the Cotton MS convinced me long ago – and not me alone – that it was mainly written *c.* 1170 and is a more coherent document than had been supposed.[57] It is true that it makes Llanthony in some sense an offshoot of Merton priory which was not founded till 1114, but this very likely means no more than that in due course it received canons from Merton who converted it into the familiar Augustinian pattern. The account of the foundation, and of how Ernisius and William fought off an attempt by the king and queen to make a mighty foundation out of it, seems to me essentially authentic.[58] Yet it would be very puzzling if we had no other examples of Augustinian houses founded on obviously Cistercian sites. Indeed Llanthony outbid the Cistercians before they began; it is doubtful if a site so open to Welsh raids, so remote from other ecclesiastical centres, would really have been acceptable to the Cistercians; and after a generation the canons of Llanthony gratefully accepted an alternative site on the edge of Gloucester. For a while the original home became a cell and Llanthony by Gloucester became an urban Augustinian house notable for its library and school; in the end the two were separated and the old house had a life of its own again.[59] But by then something of the original conception had been forgotten. Yet in 1103, before Cîteaux had been heard of on these shores, we may well believe that for a modest house aiming for obscurity and apostolic poverty, the traditional Benedictine mode seemed too grand, too crushing – like the endowment with which the king and queen threatened it. A number of Augustinian houses were indeed founded in sites similarly remote: such were Nostell, founded by another royal clerk from the same circle, in a similarly remote site; Lanercost, originally as exposed to Scottish raids as Llanthony was to Welsh; and Bolton, due to a move in the early 1150s, from the original home near Skipton, to a site which the early canons must have known was extraordinarily similar

---

[56] W. Dugdale, *Monasticon anglicanum* (edition of London, 1817–30), vi, pp. 129–31. The chronicle in British Library, MS Cotton Julius D. x, fos 30v–50v, and has never been printed in full: for various extracts in print, see *Heads*, p. 172.

[57] Dickinson, *Origins of the Austin Canons* (n. 7), esp. pp. 111–12 and nn.; see refs. in n. 56.

[58] See refs. in n. 56.

[59] *Heads*, pp. 172–73; for its library see N. R. Ker, *Medieval Libraries of Great Britain* (2nd edn, London, 1964), pp. 108–12.

to the Cistercian sites of Rievaulx or Fountains chosen twenty years before.[60] Doubtless the present church at Bolton deceives us as to the original conception, for it is large and spacious and Gothic; the cloister is a reminder of the modesty and simplicity of the first foundation there. The canons of Bolton sought a place for apostolic poverty and simplicity as they interpreted them, remarkable in its contrast to Leicester or Barnwell or to Llanthony by Gloucester. The mantle of Austin was very large and broad; but the example of the first Llanthony, and the long years when both houses were under a single regime, is a reminder that it is not simply that some houses were large and urban, others small and rustic: the conception of early canons' houses could include all these elements together. The many impulses of the religious life of the twelfth century could be combined in a fashion which constantly bewilders us. Yet at Llanthony in 1103 or Leicester in 1143, or in London or Cambridge at any time, the reason why one was surrounded by Austin's men would have seemed tolerably clear. In the local situation it made sense, even if the general condition now defies every effort at definition.

What then of the flow of comment, of Professor Bynum's treatises? Let me say at once that her analysis of the treatises, her revelation of the varieties and richness of attitude they reveal, is of lasting value, even if the conclusions seem relatively slight. For what is established is that there was a tradition in the eleventh and twelfth centuries which emphasised the duty of canons to teach by work and example – *docere verbo et exemplo*. With many qualifications carefully noted she denies that this element appears in their monastic contemporaries.[61] It is an intriguing point, even if we must allow for its limited force. No one doubts that monks sometimes preached or that most of them did so rarely. But it is impossible to believe that the eleventh- and twelfth-century monks were in any doubt or ignorance of the importance of example: it is as if one should say that a schoolmaster – used all his life to emphasise to his friends and colleagues the importance of sound instruction – was totally unaware that his charges also instruct and affect one another. This would be to lay too much weight on a particular literary genre, and in substantial measure Professor Bynum is aware of it. Thus she cites among her monks Abelard and his rule for nuns (reasonably observing that he was 'more pedagogue than monk') and Aelred of

[60] See *VCH Yorkshire*, iii, pp. 195–99 (Bolton), 231–35 (Nostell); *VCH Cumberland*, ii, p. 152 (Lanercost); Dickinson, *Origins of the Austin Canons*, pp. 120–21 (Nostell); Thompson, *Bolton* (n. 27); Sir Charles Clay in *Early Yorkshire Charters*, vii, passim, esp. no. 2 and n. (Bolton).

[61] Bynum, *Docere verbo*, passim.

Rievaulx.[62] Interpretation of Abelard's Rule has been bedevilled by doubts as to the authenticity of the correspondence in which it is embedded. I take it that controversy is dying away; and that we can more clearly see that the rule is a painstaking answer of a not very inspired character to a series of propositions put to him by Heloise, some of them paradoxical. Her letter is manifestly based on the presupposition that example, especially the wrong sort of example, is only too powerful and effective; she quotes Ovid's *Art of Love* to prove the point.[63] And so she demanded, not just a rule – but two documents; the first to be a catalogue of examples of holy women and the part they had played in the life of the church. And if that prolix document is not meant by both Heloise and Abelard to illustrate the positive force of example in the life of nuns, I do not know what it is for; it is certainly not a work of history. Aelred of Rievaulx is a more complex case; and Professor Bynum's analysis of his teaching about example is one of the most subtle and satisfying parts of the book.[64] For she shows that in his treatises he is concerned to set a limit to the value of example; for he is primarily concerned with the monk as learner, and he sees occasions for instance when it is better for a man to be separated from a pattern of life on which he too much depends. The difference here is partly that Aelred proceeds with much greater psychological subtlety than the canons. If one wants Aelred a little more crudely presented, one finds in Walter Daniel's *Life* – an enchanting and often very revealing book, but evidently less sophisticated than Aelred's own writings – the statement that, when Abbot William put the young Aelred in charge of the novices at Rievaulx, his purpose was to make them 'worthy vessels', but also 'examples of perfection to those who truly yearn to excel as patterns of goodness'.[65] We may readily accept that there were many gradations between the most inward-looking or eremitical of religious and the most outward-looking and practical; that in between one will find in the twelfth century men of Aelred's subtlety and ascetic experience who are concerned with the finer problems of advance

---

[62] Bynum, *Docere verbo*, p. 100; cf. pp. 101–4. On changing views of the authenticity of the letters of Abelard and Heloise, see Brooke, *The Medieval Idea of Marriage* (Oxford, 1989; corrected reprint 1994), ch. 4; and refs in J. F. Benton, 'Consciousness of Self and Perceptions of Individuality', in *Renaissance and Renewal in the Twelfth Century*, ed. R. F. Benson and G. Constable, with C. D. Lanham (Cambridge, Massachusetts, and Oxford, 1982–83), pp. 263–95, at p. 266 n. 12.

[63] Letter 5, ed. J. T. Muckle in *Mediaeval Studies*, 17 (1955), pp. 241–53 at p. 242; for what follows letters 6 and 7 (the rule), ed. Muckle ibid., pp. 253–81 and ed. T. P. McLaughlin in *Mediaeval Studies*, 18 (1956), pp. 241–92.

[64] Bynum, *Docere verbo*, pp. 134–37, 188–89.

[65] Walter Daniel, *The Life of Ailred of Rievaulx*, ed. F. M. Powicke, NMT (Edinburgh, 1950), p. 23.

in the religious life, and caring for communities mainly contemplative. This
Professor Bynum has perceived at a deep level. It is not at all the purpose
of this chapter to say that there were no differences. But there were perhaps
no sharp dividing lines: the religious life and religious aspirations resembled
a spectrum, with many subtle shades of colour – many slight differences
adding up in the end to major divisions. And these were often shifting,
and all subject to the many winds which blew. The patron who wished to
found a religious house or the aspirant who sought his vocation might
often be inspired with a dazzling vision; but each must equally often have
been confused and blinded by the profusion of indistinguishable goods laid
out in the shop for his choice.

13

Priest, Deacon and Layman
from St Peter Damian to St Francis

Few incidents in thirteenth-century history have been more often described than the story of the Christmas crib at Greccio.[1] Not long before his death St Francis arranged with a noble layman called John of Greccio to prepare a crib for midnight mass at Christmas, with plenty of hay and real animals, ox and ass, in attendance. Crowds flocked to the place and 'the whole night resounded with jubilation'. Mass was celebrated over the crib. But not by Francis, for he was not a priest but a deacon; and he put on the deacon's vestments, sang the gospel and preached. Strange as it may seem, it is only from this story in the first life by Thomas of Celano, confirmed by some shreds of other evidence, that we know that Francis was in deacon's orders.[2] No explanation is given, no contemporary commentary expounds the fact. Yet it is abundantly clear that his deacon's orders had some profound significance related to his conception of his order and its members, and their relations one to another. It is a curious puzzle to discover what it was.

In the early centuries of the Christian era, as the orders of the Church crystallised, to each a special function was attached.[3] Even the doorkeeper,

First published in *Studies in Church History*, 26 (1989), pp. 65–85.

[1] Thomas of Celano, *Vita prima S. Francisci*, cc. 84–87, *Analecta Franciscana* 10 (Quaracchi, 1926–41), pp. 63–65; trans. R. B. Brooke, *The Coming of the Friars* (London, 1975), pp. 130–31. On all that relates to St Francis, I am indebted to the help of Rosalind Brooke; and, on the lay brothers, to Giles Constable.

[2] Thomas of Celano, *Vita prima*, c. 86 (p. 64); cf. Julian of Speyer, *Vita S. Francisci* (based on Celano), *Analecta Franciscana*, 10, pp. 335, 361, 369; and later sources, e.g. ibid., p. 492. In Celano, *Vita secunda*, c. 219 (ibid., p. 257), St Francis is seen in a vision wearing a purple dalmatic, the deacon's vestment. In *Vita secunda*, c. 193 (p. 241), he prefers a small to a large tonsure: see below, p. 252.

[3] See e.g. articles by A. Michel in *Dictionnaire de théologie catholique*, xi (1931), pp. 1193–405; xiii (1936), pp. 138–61 ('ordre', 'prêtre'); useful references in *Oxford Dictionary of the Christian Church*, ed. E. A. Livingstone (3rd edn, Oxford, 1997), pp. 1189–90, 1325–26.

even the exorcist had his own niche, and it was by no means to be taken for granted that he would rise to be a subdeacon, still less that the deacons, who had the administrative and pastoral duties of the church laid upon them, would ever become priests. In many early monastic communities the monks were not ordained, or anyway not in higher orders; it was the special function of the few priests to celebrate the eucharist for them. The priests had the privilege and duty of celebrating mass; this set them already apart among the clergy, and even the bishop frequently shared in the Latin west the title *sacerdos*. As Melchizedek in the book of Genesis was *rex et sacerdos*, so was Christ in medieval interpretation; and *sacerdos* was a lofty word which would compass a bishop as well as a priest.[4] What was different in the eleventh and twelfth centuries was that the priesthood became in a special sense separated from the rest of society – especially from lay society – on account of its sublime function, and it came to be the normal ambition of innumerable devout clerks to attain the priesthood. The English monk Eadmer, in his *Historia novorum*, quoted the words he heard Pope Urban II utter in Rome in 1099. The pope was laying anathemas on all laymen who claimed the right to grant investiture of churches, and on all clergy who made themselves vassals of laymen. It was a heroic effort to disentangle the spiritual and the secular society of his day – a heroic failure we may think it, since full segregation proved impossible; yet a remarkable success too in the effect it had in creating new social orders. Thus Urban:

> it seemed a horrible thing that hands which had been honoured, even above anything permitted to the angels, with power to create by their agency the God who is the Creator of all things and to offer Him to God the Father for the redemption and salvation of the whole world, that these hands should be degraded by the ignominy of being made subject to hands which were infected by filthy contagions day and night, stained with rapine and accustomed to the shedding of innocent blood.[5]

Pope Urban's statement, as reported by Eadmer, is a brilliant summary of the platform of the reforming papacy, of the Gregorian reform. The priesthood must be separated from the laity, because theirs is the divine

---

[4] Genesis 14:18–20; for his presence in Innocent III's writings, see K. Pennington in *Law, Church and Society: Essays in Honor of Stephan Kuttner*, ed. K. Pennington and R. Somerville (Philadelphia, 1977), pp. 54, 64 n. 32. In the next sentence I speak of the ambition to become a priest as normal. It was never universal: among cathedral clergy, for example, many seem never to have become priests; and though the cathedrals sometimes seem in deliberate reaction against current religious ideals, and many canons perhaps were not especially devout, we have no reason to doubt that many were. For literature, see below, n. 30.

[5] Eadmer, *Historia novorum*, ed. M. Rule (*RS*, London, 1884), p. 114; trans. in R. W. Southern, *Making of the Middle Ages* (London, 1953), p. 132.

function of celebrating the eucharist, of creating – or helping in the work of creation of – the body and blood of Christ on the altar.[6] As so often in the papal reform, we are not contemplating new doctrine so much as an inspired effort to put traditional doctrines, ancient statements of law and practice, into effect. Yet there was development of doctrine too.

The chief theologian, or propagandist, of the papal reform was St Peter Damian: his works were to remain immensely popular for many generations and to be more widely distributed than those of any other writer of his age. He combined an exceptional fervour for the ascetic life of the clergy, be it as monks or canons regular, with a deep learning in the church's law, which added to the authority of his eloquent pen. Here is a characteristic sample.[7]

> Why, O priest, when you should offer yourself sacred, that is as a sacrifice, to God, do you not first refuse to sacrifice yourself as a victim to an evil spirit? For when you fornicate you cut yourself off from Christ's members, and make your body the body of a harlot, as the Apostle bears witness, saying, 'he who is joined to a harlot, is made one body', and again, 'Shall I then take the members of Christ, and make them the members of an harlot?' Far be it. What part therefore have you in the body of Christ, who by luxuriating in seductive flesh have made yourself a member of Antichrist? 'For what fellowship hath light with darkness, or what concord hath Christ with Belial?' Surely you know full well that the Son of God chose the purity of the flesh to that point that He was not born even in pure marriage, but rather from the womb of a virgin? And this too was not sufficient, that she should be a virgin mother only, but the church's faith is that he too who assumed the role of His father was a virgin too. If therefore our Redeemer so loved the wholeness of flowering purity, that He was born not only of a virgin's womb, but was also handled by a virgin foster father, and this while still He rocked in His cradle – by whom, do you think, will He now wish His body to be handled, when in mighty stature He reigns in heaven? If He wished to be touched with pure hands as He lay in his crib, how great a cleanliness will He wish to be touched with now that he is raised on high in His father's glory?

He goes on to emphasise the intimate relation of the priest to his church, of which he is husband and sponsor. Any relationship he may have with one of his spiritual daughters will be incestuous; and he denounced the

---

[6] Cf. *Monumenta Germaniae Historica, Libelli de lite,* i (Hanover, 1891), pp. 223–26 (Humbert, *Adversus Simoniacos*), 348–55 (Manegold of Lautenbach), etc.

[7] Peter Damian, *Opusculum* xvii, c. 3, *PL*, 145, cols 384–85, quoting 1 Corinthians 6:15–16; 2 Corinthians 6:14–15. On Damian and celibacy see C. N. L. Brooke, *The Medieval Idea of Marriage* (Oxford, 1989), ch. 3. On the MSS of his letters and opuscula, see *Die Briefe des Petrus Damiani*, ed. K. Reindel, i, *Monumenta Germaniae Historica, Die Briefe der deutschen Kaiserzeit*, iv, 1 (Munich, 1983), pp. 33–39.

fearful error of the Nicolaite heresy which claimed that the clergy could marry. I do not defend this doctrine: it seems to me far-fetched in the extreme. But we must feel its power if we are to understand the region of human experience we are exploring.

Thus the apotheosis of the priesthood is palpably related to the doctrine of the eucharist. The changes and varieties of the tenth, eleventh and twelfth centuries have recently been set in clear focus by Gary Macy in *The Theologies of the Eucharist in the Early Scholastic Period*,[8] which showed that the development was not so simple or so monolithic as had been supposed. He distinguishes two new tendencies in particular – new since the tradition which laid emphasis on the role of communion in uniting the believer to God in an act leading to salvation also survived. One tradition was to emphasise the relation of the sacrament to the church as a whole: it was a corporate act of God's chosen people: Macy calls this the ecclesiastical tradition. It was very powerful in the twelfth century, and has been powerful in the twentieth; but it was rather overshadowed by a rival tradition in the intervening centuries. This tradition was to emphasise the relation of the eucharist to the body of Christ in its mystical sense, and to make the eucharist a part of the heavenly, symbolic world. The eucharist became ever more sublime, but the act of human communion seemed less essential to it.[9] This was one of the trends which made the private mass of the priest – in which no laymen communicated – so widespread and so popular in these centuries. But we must not be too sweeping: there was a wide variety of attitude and practice, and although by the twelfth century frequent communion for the laity was perhaps becoming rare, and the laity were coming to communicate in bread alone, and to be deprived of the chalice, there were still plenty of voices raised to insist that communion was a vital part of the eucharist and of the life of every Christian.[10] One consequence of the mystical approach was to encourage the tendency in eucharistic theology which concentrated on the sacred nature of the host. In the central scene of the Bayeux Tapestry Harold swears his oath to Duke William: one hand is over a shrine evidently containing relics, the other over a portable

[8] Oxford, 1984.

[9] Macy, *Theologies of the Eucharist*, ch. 3; for the older tradition, see ch. 2. In the early and central middle ages, symbols were often seen as deeply inhering in the things they represented: the modern phrase 'mere symbol' would have baffled theologians of that age. A classic example of eleventh-century priestly eucharistic devotion is John of Fécamp's prayer of preparation, later attributed to St Ambrose: A. Wilmart, 'L'oratio Sancti Ambrosii du Missel Romain', *Auteurs spirituels et textes dévots du moyen âge latin* (Paris, 1932), pp. 101–25.

[10] Cf. St Francis, below, p. 251.

altar covered with little disks, which we may readily interpret as hosts.[11] Of the body of Jesus as He had lived on earth there could be no relics – even though some connoisseurs rejoiced in pieces of His manger and of the loaves with which He fed the five thousand. But the body of Jesus consecrated in the mass was the most powerful relic of all; and the host came to be endowed with all the properties of relics, and to be carried in procession and reserved – not only for the sick, but for special veneration. The full development of this came only in the late middle ages; devotions to the Blessed Sacrament, and all the paraphernalia which came to surround the feast of Corpus Christi – though budding in the thirteenth century – were in full flower and fruit in the fourteenth and even more the fifteenth century. In a similar way the full development of the doctrine of transubstantiation came with Aquinas and Scotus, but the heart of the matter – concentration on the host as an object, and the natural curiosity about its nature, came already in the eleventh century.[12] If the host was a peculiarly sacred object, so were the hands, so was the person, who consecrated it. The eucharist became in a quite special manner the centre of Christian experience, and the priest was sanctified with the bread on his altar.

We might then expect to find in the ordinary terminology of pious writers of the eleventh and twelfth centuries that the priests were set aside from the rest of society as folk with a very special function. The conventional definitions of society, however, made no such distinction.[13] The old threefold categories of those who fight, those who pray and those who work gave the whole clergy a single function, prayer. The more sophisticated lists of the twelfth century distinguished in particular monks, canons and layfolk – or monks, clerks and layfolk. But in all sorts of ways the religious impulses of the age tended to obscure these frontiers and create new ones.

The notion that a monk could, indeed should, normally become a priest, was already well established in the tenth century, the same age which (so far as our records inform us) saw the idea first adumbrated that every priest should normally celebrate mass every day.[14] There was still development

[11] *Bayeux Tapestry*, ed. D. M. Wilson (London, 1986), plates 25–26; for the host as relic, cf. Macy, *Theologies of the Eucharist*, pp. 81–82.

[12] Macy, *Theologies of the Eucharist*, ch. 3, esp. pp. 86–93.

[13] For these definitions, see M. D. Chenu, *Nature, Man and Society in the Twelfth Century*, English trans. by J. Taylor and L. K. Little (Chicago, 1968), esp. ch. 6; and for the older ones, G. Duby, *The Three Orders: Feudal Society Imagined*, English trans. by A. Goldhammer (Chicago, 1980). See now G. Constable, *Three Studies in Medieval Religious and Social Thought* (Cambridge, 1995), ch. 3.

[14] See references in C. Brooke and W. Swaan, *The Monastic World* (London, 1974), p. 253, n. 5 to ch. 6; and for daily mass, esp. S. J. P. Van Dijk and J. H. Walker, *The Origins of the Modern Roman Liturgy* (London, 1960), pp. 51ff.

ahead: it was only in the twelfth and thirteenth centuries that both practices became the norm. But already in the early eleventh century the beautiful little *Liber vitae* of New Minster, Winchester, among the Stowe Manuscripts in the British Library, records the orders and status of the monks; and the community with which the book began in 1031 contained seventeen priests, eleven deacons (of whom one at least was later a priest) and six boys.[15] Bearing in mind that monks were recruited as children, we are shown here a regular *cursus honorum* which could lead all the seniors, if they survived, into the priesthood. Evidence from other houses suggests that this took another century or two fully to accomplish; but it was clearly well on the way. There are occasional intrusions from another social region in these lists: the *conversi*. Some of these are converts and priests – evidently clergy who became monks in middle life. Others are lay converts, who came from secular life; and these, it seems, remained lay – that is, they were not ordained.[16] But the majority of the monks were priests or on the way to the priesthood.

This practice had a devastating effect on the design of great churches. It is notorious that the eleventh century witnessed the building of vast cathedrals and abbey churches on a scale hardly precedented. All manner of reasons can be advanced for this, and fashion clearly played a leading part. But a major element was the provision of altars for very large communities. Thus if every priest in a monastery reckoned to celebrate mass daily – even allowing that there could be two masses, perhaps even sometimes three, at each altar daily – a very large number of altars was needed. The extreme case is recorded at Cluny in the early eleventh century by Rodulfus Glaber where, 'as we ourselves observed, the number of brethren in that house was so great that it was the custom to celebrate mass without interruption from day-break to dinner-time'.[17] The design of large Romanesque churches allowed for a multiplicity of altars spread about the east end and in the transepts; and the pattern of Romanesque triforia suggests that many altars were provided also at first-floor level. If these were not enough, then the nave had to be called into use. The eastern bays of the nave were

---

[15] Brooke and Swaan, *Monastic World*, p. 88 and plates 142–43, reproduce the relevant folios of BL, Stowe MS 944. For a full edition, see *The Liber Vitae of the New Minster and Hyde Abbey, Winchester*, facsimile, ed. S. Keynes (Copenhagen, 1996).

[16] In the mid and late eleventh century the *laicus conversus* or *conversus et laicus* occurs, *Liber vitae*, fos 21v–22r. Thereafter, it is frequently noted by the *conversi* that they were or became priests.

[17] Rodulfus Glaber, *Historiarum libri quinque*, ed. J. France, OMT (Oxford, 1989), pp. 236–37. For the growth of altars in Romanesque churches see the numerous plans in K. J. Conant, *Carolingian and Romanesque Architecture, 800–1200* (Harmondsworth, 1959).

commonly occupied by part of the monks' choir and the screens which separated it from the nave; and the centre of the nave remained (as all indications serve to remind us) the meeting place of the clerical and lay community, even in a monastic church. But altars could be set by the pillars, as is still evident in the nave of St Albans, or in the aisles, as was to be the practice in Cistercian churches from the 1130s on.[18] To us the eucharist in a great community seems of its nature a common festivity, and if we allow that many priests should participate, it seems natural that they do so by concelebration. Deep in the heart of the religious sentiment of the central middle ages lay the notion that priests were set apart to celebrate, and that each represented his vocation by personally celebrating a private mass each day.

Yet it is also clear that there was much diversity of opinion on the role of the priesthood in Christian society. At the end of the twelfth century many of the evangelical aspirations of the day were summed up in the obscure but deeply influential prophecies of the Cistercian (or ex-Cistercian) Abbot Joachim of Fiore.[19] His mind worked inexorably in threes, in three ages and three orders of folk. The first were the married folk, who represented the age of the father, since they were parents too and their special function was to have children. The second was the order of clerks, whose function was not to celebrate the eucharist, which seems to play as little part in his scheme as the hierarchy of the church itself, but rather to pronounce and preach to the people 'the way of the Lord'.[20] The role of preaching is a crucial element in our story, but must be left for another occasion. To Joachim the function of the monks, who formed the third order, was by contemplation to perceive the Love of God; but the more he talked about the monks the more they seemed – to the wishful thinking of thirteenth-century friars – to resemble the Orders of St Francis and St Dominic.[21]

All these words defining the orders of clergy were used in strangely

---

[18] In Brooke and Swaan, *Monastic World*, p. 254, ch. 9, n. 5, it is erroneously suggested that the chapel aisles were a later development: those at Rievaulx and Fountains are evidently twelfth century (see above, p. 203, n. 33). Cf. also the much later chapels added to the nave at Melrose and on the Continent: N. Coldstream, in *Cistercian Art and Architecture in the British Isles*, ed. C. Norton and D. Park (Cambridge, 1986), p. 154.

[19] For what follows, see M. Reeves, *The Influence of Prophecy in the Later Middle Ages* (Oxford, 1969), esp. pp. 135–40.

[20] Reeves, *The Influence of Prophecy*, p. 136.

[21] For the relation of Joachim's prophecies and the mendicants, Reeves, *Influence of Prophecy*, pp. 59–70, 161–273; cf. R. B. Brooke, *Early Franciscan Government* (Cambridge, 1959), pp. 268–72.

ambiguous ways. To us the word priest is wholly clear, for it represents an order which was precisely defined. But the vernaculars played tricks with it, and in Old English a *preost* can be a clerk – in any order or none: a priest in our sense was a mass-priest.[22] Granted this, it is not surprising that 'clerk' had many shades of meaning. This is the most general term for a man who was not a layman – and at times, for a clergyman who was not a monk. A simple tonsure, an elementary hair-cut, set the clerk off from the layman.[23] Like the canon, he was expected to be involved in clerical duties in the world; and the clerical order could comprise all the clergy whatever their function. As we read accounts of it we begin to wonder what limits can be set to the clerical order; and when we read about their claims to lead the apostolic life we wonder if monks are not clerks after all.[24] The apostolic life was the supreme goal in twelfth- and thirteenth-century religious aspiration, and it is hardly surprising that many different orders claimed to lead it. To the monks it was palpable that the common life and common property of the first Christian communities described in Acts 4 foreshadowed the monastic order; theirs was the mode of living of the primitive church. Clerks and canons could counter by pointing out the pastoral, active, preaching work of the apostles, and St Francis took one version of Jesus' charge to his disciples and set it in the centre of his Rule. Nothing could be more apostolic than the direct imitation of the gospel. At first sight these divergent views of the apostolic life seem to justify great diversity of inspiration and practice. But there was a contrary tendency, very well known to all who have studied the religious movements of the twelfth century, towards assimilation between the different modes. A striking example lies in the buildings they lived in. There is an extraordinary uniformity about the monastic complexes which monks and canons of different orders built for themselves in the central middle ages: church and cloister form the centre of groups of buildings following the same fundamental pattern to a quite remarkable degree.[25] The silent witness of the

[22] T. Northcote Toller and A. Campbell, *Supplement* to J. Bosworth, *Anglo-Saxon Dictionary* (Oxford, 1921), p. 681; cf. the king's priests studied by F. Barlow, *The English Church, 1000–1066* (2nd edn, London, 1979), pp. 156–58. For 'maessepreost' see J. Bosworth, *Anglo-Saxon Dictionary* (Oxford, 1898), p. 662; *Supplement*, pp. 628–29; and esp. *Councils and Synods*, i, 1 (Oxford, 1981), pp. 204–5.

[23] On the significance of tonsure in the central middle ages, see G. Constable in *Apologiae duae*, ed. R. B. C. Huygens, *Corpus Christianorum, Continuatio mediaevalis*, 62 (Turnhout, 1985), esp. pp. 72–75. For Francis and tonsure see below, p. 252.

[24] See e.g. M. D. Chenu, *Nature, Man and Society in the Twelfth Century*, trans. J. Taylor and L. K. Little (Chicago, 1968), chs 6 and 7.

[25] Cf. C. Brooke, 'Reflections on the Monastic Cloister', in *Romanesque and Gothic: Essays for George Zarnecki* (Woodbridge, 1987), i, pp. 19–25.

buildings contradicts the noisy pamphlet wars – or rather, it shows, as we can see time and again in the religious impulses of this age, that though the currents flowed in different channels, yet they often scored a common pattern in different parts of the same landscape.

Into this world something of older traditional views had survived, now beleaguered by the ideals of twelfth-century religion. Little treatises were still copied on the functions of the various orders, and some of them were perhaps read.[26] The seven deacons of the city of Rome had survived into this world, but in the late eleventh century they were claiming to be called cardinal, like the old parish priests of Rome, and to be princes of the church; and the day was not far distant when they might even cease to be deacons.[27] In Rome the ancient world and the immediate present always lived side by side – only in Rome could perfect early basilicas like San Clemente and Santa Maria in Trastevere be built in the twelfth century;[28] and it was the confident mingling of fashions of very different ages which helped Rome to be conservative and revolutionary at once. More surprising perhaps is the way in which the notion lingered in northern Europe that an archdeacon should be a deacon.[29] This was an ancient office in new dress; in the tenth and eleventh centuries the archdeacon found a new vocation as a diocesan administrator, and in this guise he was imported into England after the Norman Conquest, as the bishop's alter ego in administering his diocese. In the late eleventh and early twelfth centuries church councils were reiterating the rule that archdeacons should be deacons; and there is a good deal of evidence that, for example, English archdeacons in the twelfth century commonly were. Men like Thomas Becket, archdeacon of Canterbury, retained their deacon's orders till they became bishops, when they were hastily ordained to the priesthood before their consecration. Here was a motive for devout clerks to avoid entering the priesthood, in the hope that they might become archdeacons. True, arch-deacons were not commonly reckoned devout; but it is noticeable that many

[26] Later examples of this ancient mode are the late tenth-century pastoral letter of Ælfric, which includes an account of orders (*Councils and Synods*, i, 1, pp. 202–5); and the twelfth-century tract by Hugh of St Victor, 'De ecclesiasticis ordinibus' incorporated in his *De sacramentis, PL* 176, cols 421–31.

[27] Cf. S. Kuttner, 'Cardinalis: The History of a Canonical Concept', *Traditio*, 3 (1945), pp. 129–214, at pp. 189–98.

[28] See E. Kitzinger, 'The Arts as Aspects of a Renaissance: Rome and Italy', in *Renaissance and Renewal in the Twelfth Century*, ed. R. L. Benson and G. Constable (Cambridge, Massachusetts, and Oxford, 1982), pp. 637–70, at pp. 641–48; and W. Horn, 'Survival, Revival, Transformation: The Dialectic of Development in Architecture and Other Arts', ibid., pp. 711–27, at pp. 719–20.

[29] For what follows, see above, p. 120.

canons remained deacons or less.[30] Canons may well have followed a different
pattern from the priesthood at large; but it would be absurd to question that
some or many of them were devout. Late in the century Peter of Blois,
archdeacon of Bath, fervently defended the proposition that an archdeacon
should be a deacon – but this was because his bishop took a different view.
The archdeacon was second to the bishop in running a diocese, head of all
the clergy of his archdeaconry, and he must lead them in other ways too, or
so the bishop reckoned. He must be a priest: the tide had turned; and from
then on it no longer seemed appropriate that he should be a deacon – and
although the reputation of the medieval archdeacon for rapacity and worldliness hardly supported his role as leading priest of a diocese, the decline in
the practice of keeping archdeacons in deacons' orders is a piquant illustration
of the enhanced role of priesthood among the orders of the church.

Another ancient practice of a rather different kind which died hard in
this epoch was the marriage of the clergy.[31] Among the rank and file of the
parish clergy indeed it is likely that the clerical concubine and the clerical
family survived over much of England (perhaps over much of Europe) to
the Reformation. In England in the early twelfth century there is abundant
evidence that many respectable clergy thought they owned their benefices,
in this sense at least that they could pass them on to their sons. The
hereditary church may well have been encouraged by the increased emphasis
on lineage in secular society in the twelfth century: if a lay fee was hereditary,
by how much the more – some may have thought – the proprietary church.
In St Paul's cathedral we have the edifying picture of hereditary canonries
and even hereditary archdeaconries: when about 1115 Cyprian, archdeacon
of Colchester, succeeded his father Quintilian, the names suggest an inheritance of learning and scholarly interests as well as of the office.[32] Reformers
and bishops and other patrons who wanted the canonries and offices for
their own protégés rapidly brought this condition of affairs to an end. In
well to do parishes the practice lasted much longer; and in the late twelfth

[30] See above, p. 120 and n. 11. Calendars and obituaries of cathedrals give some information
on the orders of canons, though it is never systematic: see e.g. the St Paul's obituaries listed
by D. E. Greenway in *Fasti*, i, p. xiv; the Hereford obituary in R. Rawlinson, *The History and
Antiquities of ... Hereford* (London, 1717), pp. (3)-(31), and the Chartres obituaries in *Obituaires
de la province de Sens*, ed. A. Molinier and A. Longnon (Paris, 1902-), ii. I have modified the
text in the light of discussion with Dr Julia Barrow, to whose advice I am much indebted.

For what follows see Peter of Blois, letter 123, *PL*, 207, cols 358–67.

[31] See C. Brooke, *Medieval Church and Society* (London, 1971), ch. 4; Brooke, *Marriage*, ch.
3, and refs.

[32] Brooke, *Marriage*, p. 87; cf. D. E. Greenway, *Fasti*, i, p. 18. Canons could be priests or
deacons or less (see n. 30); there was legislation against their marrying in this era, whatever
their orders, see C. N. L. Brooke, *Medieval Church and Society*, pp. 74–75n.

century we see something like a scramble to make religious houses rectors of churches since they at least could not be nests of married clergy and hereditary abuse. But these gifts of rectories of local churches were sometimes made in the face of local juries or the like who clearly thought it the custom that the rector's son and heir should succeed.[33] We can imagine Peter Damian giving witness in such a case. The practice was wrong in law, wrong in theology, blasphemous, he might have said, and insulting to the Holy Family; but it was perfectly respectable custom, reflecting a view very far from Damian's – that priests were not so different from other folk, and could acquire property and found dynasties like other men. Their property was spiritual, like the papal monarchy. But it was property nonetheless for that.[34] We can understand why the reforming popes were so urgent in their attempts to separate spiritual from temporal possessions, and deny laity and lay courts any say in spiritual property. But we see again the variety of religious sentiment and practice.

In the long run the reformers succeeded in abolishing hereditary benefices and making most of the higher clergy celibate in practice as well as theory. This had one very remarkable effect on European society whose interest had not been fully assimilated by the social historians. We have been taught that lineage, pride in family, and strategies to ensure the enhancement of family estates and family standing, prospered as never before in twelfth-century Europe.[35] For a knight or a secular landowner it mattered who his father was – who his ancestors were. This was not wholly new: family pride has always been possible, and earlier generations had rejoiced in reciting their genealogies real or feigned. But a more orderly structure of lineage was undoubtedly characteristic of the twelfth century, in secular families and estates. An abbot or bishop was a magnate fully as much as his secular counterpart: in the central event of a secular monarchy, the election or acknowledgement of a new king, spiritual and temporal lords mingled on equal terms: in the eleventh and twelfth centuries at least, it was the archbishop of Canterbury or the archbishop of Mainz who had the first and most crucial voice.[36] The lords spiritual were lords as much as the lords

---

[33] A good example is the church of St Peter, now Little St Mary's, Cambridge, *VCH, Cambridgeshire*, iii, p. 131. In general, see B. W. Kemp, 'Monastic Possession of Parish Churches in England in the Twelfth Century', *Journal of Ecclesiastical History*, 31 (1980), pp. 133–60.

[34] For examples of this highly proprietary attitude to churches, see C. N. L. Brooke and G. Keir, *London, 800–1216* (London, 1975), pp. 131–36, esp. 135–6.

[35] A classic statement of these views is in G. Duby, *The Knight, the Lady and the Priest*, English trans. by B. Bray (New York and Harmondsworth, 1983–84).

[36] Cf. C. Brooke, *The Saxon and Norman Kings* (London, 1963), ch. 2; Brooke, *Europe in the Central Middle Ages* (2nd edn, London, 1987), pp. 208–9.

temporal, but their authority depended not at all on their lineage. It was not that the church was democratic in the modern sense: it has always been exceedingly rare for a peasant to become pope. In some parts of Europe it was common for leading bishops to be brothers or sons of great men, and there was here and there a religious community, especially in Germany, which was the monopoly of a group of noble families.[37] But I deliberately turn to the English evidence since the English was (in the present state of knowledge) the least aristocratic of the regional churches of medieval Europe.[38] Occasionally a royal patron set his heart on promoting a close relation. One of Henry I's favourite nephews, Henry of Blois, enjoyed the see of Winchester with the abbey of Glastonbury *in commendam*, in the jargon of a later age; Henry II's illegitimate son Geoffrey became archbishop of York.[39] But these were exceptional cases, and even the sons of barons were relatively few. None of the archbishops of Canterbury between 1066 and 1200 owed his promotion to his father; none of them was the son of a baron of the first rank.[40] When class distinctions were growing in the secular world, one distinction alone meant more than lineage; the clerical tonsure, the spiritual office, which might justify the order of priest or bishop.

In other words, the greatest social barrier in this society was between clergy and laymen. It even had something of the character of modern distinctions of race and nationality. When they cut the archbishop to pieces in his own cathedral, Becket's murderers were expressing in brutal form a deeply felt prejudice of caste. Many folk naturally felt quite differently: layman and cleric mingled in the same families, and worked together in the service of king or noble or bishop. The links were as intimate as the frontiers. Nonetheless, the division between cleric and lay was fundamental.

So we turn with a special interest to the ambivalent world of the lay monk. We have encountered lay converts, *conversi*, in Winchester in the

---

[37] A. Schulte, *Der Adel und die deutsche Kirche im Mittelalter* (Stuttgart, 1910); but cf. C. Brühl, 'Die Sozialstruktur des deutschen Episkopats im 11. und 12. Jahrhundert', in *Mendola*, 8 (1977), pp. 42–56.

[38] Cf. Brühl, 'Die Sozialstruktur', with R. and C. Brooke, above, p. 116 and n. 35 on the English evidence; cf. also B. Guillemain on the French evidence, 'Les origines des évêques en France aux XIe et XIIe siècles', in *Mendola*, 7 (1974), pp. 374–402.

[39] On Henry of Blois see esp. D. Knowles, *Monastic Order in England* (2nd edn, Cambridge, 1963), pp. 286–93; Knowles, *The Episcopal Colleagues of Archbishop Thomas Becket* (Cambridge, 1950), pp. 34–37, 109–11; G. Zarnecki, 'Henry of Blois as a Patron of Sculpture', in *Art and Patronage in the English Romanesque*, ed. S. Macready and F. H. Thompson (London, 1986), pp. 159–77; and the forthcoming biography by M. J. Franklin.

[40] *Fasti*, ii, pp. 1–5; cf. esp. C. R. Cheney, *Hubert Walter* (London, 1967), pp. 16–17. Hubert Walter's father was a prosperous baron of the second rank, but in any case Hubert owed his promotion to service to the king.

mid eleventh century; and this traditional kind of layman turned monk was common in many parts of Europe at this time. But in the late eleventh century reformed monasteries in various parts of Europe began to acquire a different kind of lay monk, lay brothers who took monastic vows of a kind, but were never expected to enter orders. They first appear in large numbers in the congregation of Hirsau in south Germany in the late eleventh century, and they proliferated in many of the new orders of the twelfth, among the Carthusians, Cistercians, Grandimontines, Premonstratensians and Gilbertines. Sometimes they were noblemen turned religious, like the eccentric count of Nevers who rebuked Louis VII for playing chess when he might have been making up for his failings as a king.[41] More characteristically, they saved monastic leaders from employing lay servants, who could provide too direct a link between enclosed monks and the wider world. They also provided a vocation for throngs of peasants who could not expect access to traditional monastic communities. They look at first sight democratic in tendency; but the irony is that the institution of lay brothers actually sharpened some of the class distinctions of the secular world.

St Gilbert's biographer gives an admirable impression of the philosophy which led the founder of the Gilbertine Order at Sempringham in Lincoln-shire to have not one or two, but four groups within his order.[42] It was founded for women, but from an early date Gilbert formed double com-munities of women and men – the women dedicated to the Rule of St Benedict; the men, whose original function was to assist the women and act as their chaplains, following the Rule of St Augustine.[43] They were canons, not monks. Gilbert was early advised that his nuns should not have secular women to wait on them. 'He was anxious that [their servants] should not report or perform any worldly deed which might offend the nuns' minds.' So he established a group of lay sisters in his order:

> he preached to them contempt for the world and the abandonment of all property; restraint upon the will and the mortification of the flesh; continual work and

---

[41] *Magna vita S. Hugonis*, ed. and trans. D. L. Douie and D. H. Farmer, NMT (Edinburgh, 1961–62); corr. repr. OMT (Oxford, 1985), ii, pp. 55–58; cf. Walter Map, *De nugis curialium*, ed. and trans. M. R. James et al., OMT (Oxford, 1983), pp. 80–81 and n. 2. On the lay brothers see esp. *Mendola*, 5 (Milan, 1968), esp. chs. by J. Leclercq, 'Comment vivaient les frères convers?', pp. 152–76; J. Dubois, 'L'institution des convers au XIIe siècle: forme de vie mon-astique propre aux laics', pp. 183–261; C. D. Fonseca, 'I conversi nelle comunità canonicali', pp. 262–305. In what follows I am much indebted to Constable in *Apologiae duae*, pp. 124–30.

[42] *The Book of St Gilbert*, eds. R. Foreville and G. Keir, OMT (Oxford, 1987), pp. 30–39, 44–49.

[43] Ibid., pp. 48–49, 52–53.

infrequent rest; many vigils and little sleep; extended fasting and bad food; rough clothing with no adornment; confinement within the cloister to ensure that they did no evil and periods of silence lest they speak it; constant prayer and meditation to prevent them from thinking what was forbidden.[44]

A pretty tough assignment, it would seem to us, only tolerable on the assumption that they felt fully a part of the order, sharers in its merits and rewards. After a short interval Gilbert added his fourth estate.

Now because women's efforts achieve little without help from men [I am quoting his male biographer], he took on men, and put those he kept as servants about his house and on his land in charge of the nuns' external and more arduous tasks; some of them he had raised from childhood at his own expense, others were fugitives from their masters freed in the name of religion, and others again were destitute beggars.

In other words, says our author, he went out into the highways and the hedges and compelled them to come in; and he gave them a way of life identical to that of the lay sisters.[45]

In the new orders at large, and especially among the Cistercians, the new type of lay brothers commonly wore beards to distinguish them from the monks, who were clean-shaven, and so they were called *conversi barbati* or *barbati*, the bearded brethren.[46] Some time about the early 1160s, the Cistercian Abbot Burchard of Bellevaux wrote a ponderous little treatise on the significance of beards and of shaving, based on many biblical texts morally and allegorically interpreted, and much misplaced learning, the *Apologia de barbis*. A new edition of this curious work was published in the Corpus Christianorum in 1985 by Professor Huygens, with a learned and entertaining introduction by Giles Constable, making clear many dark places in the history of beards and their significance in the religious life.[47] What emerges first and foremost from Burchard and his commentators is that the beard was preserved as a class distinction. The Cistercian lay brother was clothed like a monk, but his superiors (as the choir monks reckoned themselves) wished to know at a glance with whom they were dealing. In principle indeed, the choir monks and lay brothers were strictly segregated, though not always perhaps quite so much in practice.[48] This is

[44] Ibid., pp. 34–37.
[45] Ibid., pp. 36–39.
[46] See esp. Constable, in *Apologiae duae*, pp. 124–28.
[47] *Apologiae duae*.
[48] Constable, in *Apologiae duae* , p. 129 and n. 416; Leclercq, 'Comment vivaient les frères convers', and Dubois, 'L'institution des convers', in *I laici* (n. 41), pp. 158–60, 234–35, 245–47. For some evidence qualifying the completeness of the segregation, see above, pp. 203–4, n. 33.

one of the oddest features of the Cistercian way of life, and the texts give us no adequate explanation. The Cistercian church was designed so that the centre of the nave formed a choir for the lay brothers; but they were apparently surrounded by screens sufficiently high to prevent them seeing the choir monks to the east or the little chapels and altars in the aisles all about them.[49] Their domestic quarters lay to the west of the cloister, but in early days they were commonly – perhaps normally – forbidden the use of the cloister itself and provided with a separate lane which enabled them to gain access to and from their own quarters without encountering choir monks.[50] Some mingling could not be avoided, but it was kept to a minimum. It was the same with their way of life: they lived under a rule similar to that of the choir monks, but they were forbidden to cross the frontier; they could not learn letters or be ordained – as had some at least of the lay *conversi* of the old type.[51] So clearly were lay brothers of inferior social standing that the Cistercian general chapter actually passed a decree in 1188 forbidding noblemen to become lay brothers.[52]

It has been much disputed whether the Cistercian lay brothers were monks or laymen. Here Constable's learning guides us through a minefield in the most helpful way.[53] Clearly they were subject to religious vows; they had a simple tonsure; they were celibate; they were not in the full sense laymen. Occasional texts refer to lay brothers in this or that order as monks, just as we encounter bearded choir monks from time to time among the

---

[49] D. Knowles and J. K. S. St Joseph, *Monastic Sites from the Air* (Cambridge, 1952), pp. xix–xx and passim; C. N. L. Brooke and W. Swaan, *The Monastic World* (London, 1974), pp. 139–50, and figs 11–12; plates 238, 243; above, pp. 203–4 and n. 33.

[50] For the lane, see esp. Dubois, 'L'institution des convers', in *I laici* (n. 41), p. 234; Knowles and St Joseph, pp. 89 (Byland), 106–7 (Buildwas).

[51] Cf. Leclercq, 'Comment vivaient les frères convers', and Dubois, 'L'institution des convers', in *I laici* (n. 41), pp. 160, 255; cf. *Usus conversorum*, ed. P. Guignard, *Les monuments primitifs de la règle cistercienne* (Dijon, 1878), pp. 276–87, at p. 281, no. 5, p. 283, no. 9, p. 285, no. 13; but see esp. the edition of early versions by J. A. Lefèvre in *Collectanea ordinis Cisterciensium reformatorum*, 17 (1955), pp. 11–39, 'Les traditions manuscrites des *usus conversorum* de Cîteaux'; pp. 65–97: 'L'évolution des *usus conversorum* de Cîteaux', at pp. 92, 94. The prohibition of learning is in both versions, that against a lay brother becoming a monk only in the later version; but it is clearly of quite early date, since it is in the *statuta* which some have attributed to 1119 and is certainly before 1152 (ibid., p. 69); see also *Les plus anciens textes de Cîteaux*, ed. J. de la Croix Bouton and J. P. Van Damme (Achel, 1974), p. 124, no. xxii; and for discussion of date, C. Holdsworth, 'The Chronology and Character of Early Cistercian Legislation on Art and Architecture', in *Cistercian Art and Architecture*, ed. C. Norton and D. Park (n. 18), pp. 44–52.

[52] J. M. Canivez, ed., *Statuta capitulorum generalium ordinis Cisterciensis*, i (Louvain, 1933), p. 108; cf. Dubois, 'L'institution des convers' (n. 41), in *I laici*, p. 261.

[53] Constable, in *Apologiae*, pp. 128–30, esp. p. 128 n. 408; cf. Dubois in *I laici*, pp. 248–60.

shaven. But it is not normal to call the lay brothers monks, and there is abundant evidence that in the twelfth century they were not normally thought of as monks. Some assimilation took place here and there in the thirteenth century, and in the fourteenth lay brothers almost disappeared. But in their heyday in the twelfth century only a few idealists thought them equal to the choir monks.[54] It is not always easy to see the relationship from the lay brothers' viewpoint, since our commentators were choir monks, and Abbot Burchard's jocular, patronising tone is only an exaggerated form of the common snobbery which informs the surviving literature. But it is clear that some lay brothers in several orders achieved positions of trust and responsibility and resented their inferior status. So far as we can penetrate the lay brothers' case in these disputes, they are strikingly reminiscent of the arguments between the administrative and academic viewploint which used to trouble Cambridge colleges thirty years ago. St Gilbert's lay brothers evidently thought he was starry-eyed and unpractical, and were stung by the celebrated scandal of the nun of Watton to accuse him of not keeping nuns and canons sufficiently apart. They were the practical men who knew what was what – and very likely they were often right. But they found little sympathy at the papal curia or among the English bishops for the view that laymen should rule clerics and, after a very long-drawn out dispute, they lost their case.[55] The most dramatic of all the many conflicts in the twelfth century between clerics and lay brothers was in the order of Grandmont. It seems that the founder, in the late eleventh century, had deliberately sought to make the clerks and laymen in his order equal, as part of the extraordinary lessons in humility which mark every aspect of his vocation.[56] I say 'it seems' because the founder, St Stephen, pronounced that 'there is no other rule except the gospel of Christ' and was reluctant to commit his own rule to writing: he renounced his learning in the most literal manner; his disciples had to reconstruct it from the memory of his teaching after his death.[57] In many ways he anticipated Francis; but even

[54] Especially among the Grandimontines: Constable, in *Apologiae*, p. 127 and n. 402; and see below.

[55] *The Book of St Gilbert*, pp. lv-lxii, lxxxiv-xc, 134–67, 343–44.

[56] See J. Becquet, ed., *Scriptores ordinis Grandimontensis, Corpus Christianorum Continuatio Mediaevalis*, 8 (Turnhout, 1968): the early documents give no account of any differences. This was certainly the view of Prior Gerard Iterius (1188–98): see Constable, in *Apologiae duae*, p. 127 and n. 402, citing Becquet, *Scriptores ordinis Grandimontensis*, pp. 397, 431, 473. On Grandmont, the essay of Rose Graham in *English Ecclesiastical Studies* (London, 1929), ch. 9, is still valuable; and see now C. Hutchison, *The Hermit Monks of Grandmont* (Kalamazoo, Michigan, 1989).

[57] Becquet, *Scriptores ordinis Grandimontensis*, p. 5, and for the *Regula*, ibid., pp. 63–99, esp. p. 65. The *Regula*, c. 24, p. 82, rejects the use of written evidence in lawsuits (cf. c. 31, p. 84).

Francis insisted that his rule was written, though as it came to him by divine inspiration its literary form was never sacrosanct till the pope had embalmed it in a bull.[58] No doubt the early constitutions of the Grandimontines are genuine enough, but we can never be sure exactly how and when they were put on parchment, and some of their writings are of the most doubtful authenticity.[59] Still, we may dimly perceive a world in which layman and clerk were equal, and the arrangements of the houses were adapted to fit the needs of the lay brothers as much as of the clerks. After a while the lay brothers naturally took to bossing the clerks; we are told that if the clerks started their services before the lay brothers were ready 'the lay brothers beat them well'.[60] So in this order it was the clerks, the choir monks, who complained; and in the end the popes of the early thirteenth century laid it down very firmly that the clerical priors had authority; the lay brothers were put in their place. Mary had complained of Martha – in contrast to the gospel story;[61] and the priors had to do many things forbidden in the rule to exercise their new authority. For all the many nuances in this story, its tendency is clear: in the religious orders in the twelfth and early thirteenth centuries laymen held a vital role and commanded much respect; but their position was indelibly inferior.

Against this St Francis set his face. Among the first brothers whom Francis gathered in 1209 and 1210 laymen greatly outnumbered clerks.[62] When Pope Innocent III gave verbal approval to the rule in 1210, he caused all, including Francis, to receive a simple tonsure, and once firmly inside a religious order laymen ceased to be lay in some very obvious senses. But we have seen that in most other orders a class distinction as large as that between lay and cleric in the outer world persisted; and it was this that Francis wished to avoid. The distinction between lay and clerical may have been less fundamental in Italy than north of the Alps – there was a tradition of lay education, of a true mingling of laymen and clergy not nearly so evident

[58] In the *Testament* he talks as if every recension of the rule was the same; cf. *Die Opuscula des Hl. Franziskus von Assisi*, ed. K. Esser (Grottaferrata, 1976), pp. 439, 422–24; for the surviving texts of the rule, ibid., pp. 363–404.

[59] See especially the long tirade attributed to the ex-prior against Henry II after the murder of Thomas Becket, *Materials for the History of Thomas Becket*, ed. J. C. Robertson and J. B. Sheppard, RS (London, 1875–85), vii, pp. 450–60, no. 746.

[60] Graham, *Ecclesiastical Studies*, p. 223, citing the poet Guiot de Provins, *Oeuvres*, ed. J. Orr (Manchester, 1915), pp. 56–59, esp. p. 58, lines 1551–60.

[61] What the clerks unctuously observed was that 'they read nowhere that Mary complained of Martha', Graham, *Ecclesiastical Studies*, p. 223, citing Jacques de Vitry, *Historia occidentalis*, c. 19: see now *Historia*, ed. J. F. Hinnebusch (Fribourg, 1972), p. 126.

[62] Only one of the first eleven, Sylvester, was a priest; and the *Regula bullata* of 1223 (c. 7) still envisages that ministers may not be priests.

in France, for example, or England. It is significant that it was an Englishman educated in Paris, Haymo of Faversham, who destroyed Francis's intention in this region sixteen years or so after his death by introducing a constitution effectively forbidding the recruitment of lay brothers in the order.[63] To Haymo it must be a clerical organisation just like any other order – he was following closely in the footsteps of the reformers of the Grandimontines, even more closely the arrangements of St Dominic. Dominic, it seems, greatly admired Francis, but was not inspired by his methods of organisation.[64] Dominic and his successor placed a general chapter at the head of their order, which was in effect a representative committee. Francis also collected a general chapter as the supreme organ of his order, but it was a large, tumultuous, charismatic gathering, a prayer meeting not a parliament.[65] By the same token he was very emphatic that the prayers of his humble lay brothers were as efficacious as those of the most learned doctors,[66] and he clearly envisaged the main function of the rank and file of the brothers as to live a life which would be an example to their neighbours, not to teach or preach or perform sacraments. His mission was to the humble and the poor, and he reckoned his followers needed to be on their level – simple, ordinary folk like them, if they were really to teach them. It is useless to seek out the rights and wrongs of the difficulties and disputes which followed from this.[67] There is little doubt that he feared that his humble lay brothers would be put in a corner by the clerics, and no doubt at all that this is what happened. The gossip chronicler Salimbene joined the order in the late 1230s when there were still copious lay brothers; and when he came to write his chronicle fifty years later he looked back with puzzled amusement at the extinct species which he had observed in early days. What good were they? What could they have been for? They were useless for hearing confessions and performing the other pastoral tasks of the friars of his day. They wore long beards, like Armenians and Greeks. At a provincial chapter at Siena, three hundred brothers were present,

[63] R. B. Brooke, *Early Franciscan Government* (Cambridge, 1959), pp. 243–45, cf. pp. 197–98; for Dominican influence on Haymo's legislation, see ibid., pp. 239–41.

[64] On the relations between Francis and Dominic, see C. Brooke, *Medieval Church and Society* (London, 1971), pp. 222–26; R. B. Brooke, *The Coming of the Friars* (London, 1975), pp. 95–97.

[65] On the Franciscan general chapter, see R. B. Brooke, *Early Franciscan Government*, e.g. pp. 35–38, 42–43, 130–32, 163–66.

[66] *Scripta Leonis*, ed. and trans. R. B. Brooke, OMT (Oxford, 1970; corrected reprint, 1990), no. 71, pp. 210–13 ('lay' not specified in the context but clearly intended to be included); Thomas of Celano, *Vita secunda S. Francisci*, cc. 164, 193, and cf. c. 191, in *Analecta Franciscana*, 10, pp. 225, 241, cf. pp. 239–40; R. B. Brooke, *Early Franciscan Government*, pp. 160–61.

[67] See esp. R. B. Brooke, *Early Franciscan Government*, pp. 51–52, 160–61, 243–45.

including an enormous throng of lay brothers. 'They did nothing but eat and sleep.'[68]

Still, there was much talk of the role of the laity in the church; and in the twelfth and thirteenth centuries much work for lay brothers to perform. In the early thirteenth century it was both natural and extremely difficult to give a lay element in a new religious order a fair share of initiative and authority – while paying due respect to the role of the clergy. The clergy and the sacrament they performed were central to Francis' thinking. 'For St Francis had such reverence and devotion for the body of Christ', wrote his companions,

> that he wished it to be written in the rule that friars, in the provinces where they were staying, should concern themselves lovingly in this matter and should admonish and preach to the clerks and priests to house Christ's body suitably and in a good place. If they did not do so, he wanted the friars to see to it. At one time he wanted to send some friars through all the province with some pyxes, so that wherever they might find Christ's body unlawfully bestowed they might house it honourably in these.[69]

And his reverence was not confined to the sacred elements. In his open letter to all the rulers of the world – to all podestà, consuls, judges, rectors and what have you – after admonishing them to remember that death approaches, he went on: 'I firmly advise you my lords, to set aside every care and business, and gladly receive the most holy body and the most holy blood of our Lord Jesus Christ in His holy commemoration.'[70] And in his *Testament*, in some respects a very individual document, claiming personal and direct inspiration from God – yet also emphasising his submission to the pope and to all the clergy of the world:

> The Lord gave me and gives me such faith in priests, who live according to the model of the holy Roman church, on account of their order [*ordinem*: I think he means orders], that even if they should persecute me I wish to run back to them. And if I had as much wisdom as Solomon, and found poor and humble secular priests in the parishes in which they lived, I would not wish to preach against their will. I wish to fear, love and honour them and all others as my masters; and I do not wish to consider sin in them, because I discern in them the son of God and to me they are masters. I do this because in this world I see nothing of the Son of God most high in a tangible sense, except His most holy

---

[68] Salimbene, *Cronica*, ed. O. Holder-Egger, *Monumenta Germaniae Historica, Scriptores*, xxxii (1905–13), pp. 99–103, esp. p. 102.

[69] *Scripta Leonis*, no. 80, pp. 226–29.

[70] *Opuscula S. Francisci*, ed. K. Esser, pp. 274–75 (in defence of its authenticity, see pp. 270–74); trans. R. B. Brooke, *The Coming of the Friars*, p. 127.

body and blood, which priests receive and priests alone administer to others. This most holy mystery I wish to honour and venerate above all others and to house in precious pyxes.[71]

It was thus not disrespect for priests which led Francis to people his order with laymen – or rather to accept with gladness the very numerous laymen who approached him. The union of priests and laity was fundamental to his conception of the order. But the role of the lay brothers was by no means clearly defined – far less so than in the older orders which were struggling with lay brothers' rebellions over the generation in which he was born and grew up. It was of the essence that Francis should hold the two elements in his order together, and this was presumably the reason why he chose to accept deacon's orders but not be a priest. Maybe it was also an act of humility; but if that was the major point, why a deacon? Like the laymen, he could not celebrate mass; but, like the clergy, he was in higher orders. Yet he did not want to be given a large tonsure when he was shaved; the simple brothers, who had the small tonsure, should have a share in his head.[72] It was a grand symbolic gesture, we may think, linking him to the two wings of his order – and in the long run it was entirely fruitless. But like everything he did, it greatly enriched the world he lived in. Clearly he saw the danger of conflict between clergy and laity, and that one of his main duties was to allay it. We may well suppose indeed that he looked beyond his order to the world about him; to the flourishing, tumultuous, factious Italian city republics at the height of their independent or semi–independent activity. There is a famous story of how he made peace between the bishop and the podestà of Assisi which has the familiar ring of Don Camillo about it.[73] The pattern of government in the Italian cities over the century or more since Pisa deposed its archbishop from secular rule and established its consuls in the early 1080s had been steadily and firmly secular and anticlerical – however much some of the cities had to acknowledge the pope and his legates as their overlords. But Pisa had also shown the way in another activity equally characteristic of the Italian city republics: it had set aside a share of its wealth, and in the long run an immense investment, in beautifying the city with lovely churches.[74] The relation of church and state, of clergy and laity, was exceedingly ambivalent, never more so than in the days of Francis; and he made his order a microcosm of the world

[71] *Opuscula*, ed. Esser, pp. 438–39; trans. Brooke, *The Coming*, p. 117.

[72] Celano, *Vita secunda*, c. 193, *Analecta Franciscana*, 10, p. 241.

[73] *Scripta Leonis*, c. 44, pp. 166–71.

[74] C. Brooke, *Europe in the Central Middle Ages* (2nd edn, London, 1987), pp. 133–35, 142–44 and refs.

he lived in, and a pattern for the reconciliation of clergy and laity. In that sense the lay element in the order was fully lay, however it might be modified in the eyes of the church and in the law of the church by the tonsure and the vows and the rule.

14

John of Salisbury and his World

John of Salisbury was born at Old Sarum, somewhere on that windswept hill, about 1115–20.[1] He died on 25 October 1180, in Chartres, and was buried in a finely carved tomb in the abbey church of Notre-Dame-de-Josaphat.[2] He was by turns student and scholar, an ecclesiastical administrator and advocate in the church courts, and eventually a bishop. He enjoyed a fine career associated with noble places – Salisbury, Paris, Canterbury, Rome, Chartres; but outward circumstances at first sight hardly justify his fame. He was also an author of remarkable books and letters: the *Policraticus* has achieved a modest immortality in two continents at least among the set books for university courses in the history of

Reprinted from *The World of John of Salisbury*, ed. M. Wilks, *Studies in Church History*, *subsidia*, 3 (Oxford, 1984), pp. 1–20.

[1] For the biographical literature on John of Salisbury to 1980, see D. E. Luscombe's paper 'John of Salisbury in Recent Scholarship', in *The World of John of Salisbury*, pp. 21–37, and 'A Bibliography, 1953–82', ibid, pp. 445–57. Still useful are C. Schaarschmidt, *Johannes Saresberiensis* (Leipzig, 1862); C. C. J. Webb, *John of Salisbury* (London, 1932). See also C. N. L. Brooke in *The Letters of John of Salisbury*, i, ed. W. J. Millor, H. E. Butler and C. N. L. Brooke, NMT (Edinburgh, 1955; corr. repr. OMT, Oxford, 1986), pp. xii–xxiv, and in *Letters*, ii, OMT (Oxford, 1979) introduction; Klaus Guth, *Johannes von Salisbury*, Münchener Theologische Studien, Historische Abteilung, 20 (St Ottilien, 1978). It is generally accepted that he was born in Salisbury on the basis of his name (persistently used by contemporaries), and of his own references to the folk of Salisbury and Wiltshire as *gens nostra* in the *Policraticus*, viii, c. 19; ed. C. C. J. Webb (Oxford, 1909), ii, p. 371; cf. vi. 18 (ii, pp. 47–48); Webb, *John of Salisbury*, ed. C. C. J. Webb (Oxford, 1932), pp. 1–2; and to Salisbury cathedral as *mater mea* in *Letters*, ii, no. 137 (p. 16). It would be excessively sceptical to suppose that the surname was only a family name in this case – though it is not wholly impossible – especially as there is some evidence that his family name was *Parvus*, Webb, *John of Salisbury*, p. 1; *Letters*, ii, no. 212, pp. 342–43.

[2] Schaarschmidt, *Johannes Saresberiensis*, p. 59; and full references in *Letters*, ii, p. xlvii n.; esp. to *Cartulaire de Notre-Dame de Chartres*, ed E. de Lépinois and L. Merlet, 3 vols (Chartres, 1862–5) i, p. 20. There is a full account of his tomb, with illustrations, by R. Joly and J. Villette in *Notre-Dame de Chartres*, ii, no. 44 (Sept. 1980), pp. 10–17.

political thought.[3] But no serious student of the history of thought has ever, I believe, set John among the immortals: he lived in the century at whose opening Anselm was already old and Abelard learning his elements; as an original thinker, he was not in that class. John's fame is as a mirror of his age: his career reflects so much which was characteristic of the twelfth century, and his writings show a quite exceptional gift for portraying his contemporaries and showing us his world from the inside. As we read his writings we are alternately enthralled by his vignettes of men and events and shocked by the opportunities he missed. Again and again he lifts the curtain, and we turn to ask for a better view; but like the ghost of Hamlet's father he is no longer with us. Today let us be thankful for his gifts and talents, and enjoy them as we can: if he had given us all we might ask for we could hardly contemplate him and his world in the compass of a single chapter.

His value as a mirror of his world is greatly enhanced by two vital elements in his temperament. In his writings he loved to play with complex irony on the two sides of an issue or a person.[4] Some modern readers have described this as taking an objective view: mercifully it was not quite that, or his comments would be much less interesting and amusing than they often are. It is rather that he enjoyed having the best of both worlds, cutting everybody down to size, while preserving a reasonable respect and sympathy for almost all the men he describes – for he was a man of innumerable friends, with a select, small band of irreconcilable enemies.[5] The other characteristic was his love of travel: like all compulsive travellers, he complains of the rigours and difficulties; and it was normal in the twelfth century to have a watertight excuse for travelling. When he crossed and recrossed the Alps, in the late 1140s and 1150s, we may be sure that he always went as the accredited representative of Theobald, archbishop of Canterbury, to the papal curia.[6] When in his exile in the 1160s he went

---

[3] The *Policraticus* has been made widely known by the translations of bks iv–vi and parts of vii–viii by J. Dickinson (New York, 1927), and of bks i–iii and parts of vii–viii by J. B. Pike (Minneapolis, Minnesota, 1938); see esp. Luscombe, 'John of Salisbury in Recent Scholarship', in *The World of John of Salisbury*, pp. 29ff. It is being reedited by K. S. B. Keats-Rowan in Corpus Christianorum continuatio mediaevalis, vol. i so far (Turnhout, 1993).

[4] See esp. his treatment of St Bernard and Gilbert de la Porrée in the *Historia pontificalis*, cited here from the edition and translation by M. Chibnall, NMT (Edinburgh, 1956); OMT (Oxford, 1986), pp. 15f; or his treatment of Louis VII and his brother the archbishop of Reims – under whose protection John lived in exile, but of whom he wrote with studied ambiguity – in the later *Letters*, for example, nos 136, 144, 176 (pp. 176–9), 223 etc.

[5] Especially Arnulf, bishop of Lisieux: see *Letters*, i, nos 1, 17, 18, 30; *Historia pontificalis*, pp. 54–56 etc.

[6] See *Letters*, i, pp. xii–xxiv; A. Saltman, *Theobald* (London, 1956), especially pp. 169–75.

from Reims also to the mouth of the Rhône and collected the gossip of numerous travellers in those regions, he was officially on a pilgrimage to Saint-Gilles.[7] But if one contemplates his career at large the impression is inescapable: he accepted commissions which took him over much of western Europe because he enjoyed it, enjoyed above all making friends wherever he went. So let us contemplate first of all his work through the places which he knew.

It all began in Salisbury: but of his life and origins there he tells us, alas, almost nothing. He was born under Bishop Roger, the great royal servant, the worldly royal chancellor, a type of old corruption as the ardent ascetic and reformer viewed him, who lived in immense splendour in his castles about Wiltshire, with his amazonian concubine Matilda of Ramsbury (if such was her name), and his tribe of sons and nephews, head of one of the great ecclesiastical dynasties of the age.[8] As we contemplate the tomb of Bishop Roger in the cathedral nave, brought down here from Old Sarum when the cathedral and city were moved in the thirteenth century, we cannot but regret John's silence about him.[9] Yet perhaps we can catch the echo of what his comment might have been. If I had to guess who John's father was, I would conjecture that he was a married canon of Old Salisbury under Roger's patronage.[10] The centre of John's family circle moved in the 1140s or 1150s from Salisbury to Exeter, where he and his full brother Richard held canonries, and at least one half-brother too; and Robert son of Egidia, the half-brother, appears to have been a married canon of Exeter.[11] Perhaps he was married first and a canon later; but there is little in John's letters to him to suggest anything strange in a priest and canon having a

---

[7] *Letters*, ii, pp. xix–xx, xxxviii, 552–53, 576–77 (nos 272, 274).

[8] See esp. E. J. Kealey, *Roger of Salisbury* (Berkeley, 1972). For the doubt as to Matilda's name, see Orderic, vi, pp. 532–33 n. 2. For different aspects of Salisbury cathedral, see D. E. Greenway, *Fasti*, iv, introduction, and T. Webber, *Scribes and Scholars at Salisbury Cathedral, c. 1075 – c. 1125* (Oxford, 1992).

[9] For the identification of the tombs and effigies moved from Old Sarum, see H. de S. Shortt, 'The Three Bishops' Tombs Moved to Salisbury Cathedral from Old Sarum' (Salisbury, 1971) repr. from *Wiltshire Archaeological and Natural History Magazine*, 57 (1958–60), pp. 217–19.

[10] It should be emphasised that this is pure conjecture, though it gains a little colour from the fact that his half-brother was the son of 'Egidia', which may suggest a mother not formally married.

[11] See *Letters* ii, pp. xxv–xxvi and references, especially to D. W. Blake, 'The Church of Exeter in the Norman Period' (unpublished M.A. thesis, University of Exeter, 1970). *Letters*, ii, no. 147 refers to a nephew, apparently Robert's son, and no. 148 to a lady possibly Robert's concubine. See now F. Barlow, 'John of Salisbury and his brothers', *Journal of Ecclesiastical History*, 46 (1995), pp. 95–109; and F. Barlow, ed., *English Episcopal Acta*, 11–12, especially 12, pp. 301–21 – fasti of Exeter Cathedral, 1046–1257.

small son;[12] nor anywhere else, in a large body of writings in which inumerable abuses are condemned, to suggest a special rejection of clerical marriage, save evidently for himself. Ecclesiastical historians have too easily picked up the language of eleventh and twelfth century rhetoric, and divided the clergy into good and bad: the good the ascetics, the celibate, the denouncers of women; the bad the worldly, rich, pluralists with their canonries and bishoprics and women. In practice they lived together often, I would judge, in a harmony difficult for the more ardent modern commentator to grasp.[13] John certainly accepted the other main pillar of Bishop Roger's world: he had in his bones the idea of the career open to talent which would end in canonries and a bishopric: he was a canon of at least two cathedrals in his later years, Exeter and Salisbury:[14] at Exeter he resided intermittently; at Salisbury, for all we know, hardly at all. As for women, he rarely mentions them; and this I presume to be the tact of the celibate who does not wish to press his condemnation of the accepted way of life of his friends. There is a modest bow in one letter to a lady whom I take to be his sister-in-law.[15] When he was an exile for his support to Thomas Becket in the 1160s he sent a message to his mother, then living with the family in Exeter;[16] when he returned from exile on 16 November 1170, after an urgent visit to Canterbury and Westminster,

> I speedily made a visit to my mother, who has been ill these two years, and can joyfully await the day of the Lord now that she has seen me; and I earnestly pray she may have a place in the prayers of yourself and the saints who dwell with you [John is writing to his close friend and host in exile, Peter of Celle, abbot of Saint-Rémi at Reims]. She had received an assurance from the Spirit that she would not see death till she had seen myself and my brother return from exile.[17]

By 2 December we may be sure, and probably some days before, he was

[12] *Letters*, ii, nos 147–48. There are sharp references to incontinent archdeacons in *Letters*, i, nos 14–15, 79; but two of these were written in Theobald's name, and all refer to public scandals – furthermore the archdeacon denounced in nos 14–15 was addressed in ii, no. 253 a few years later in a much more friendly fashion.

[13] Cf. C. Brooke, *Medieval Church and Society* (London, 1971), ch. 4. The celibate element in the Salisbury chapter is brought to life most effectively in Teresa Webber, *Scribes and Scholars*.

[14] *Letters*, ii, p. xlvi n. for Exeter; ibid. no. 152, pp. 52–53, shows that he had revenues in the diocese of Salisbury; and he is specifically called canon of Salisbury in *Materials for the History of Thomas Becket*, ed. J. C. Robertson and J. B. Sheppard, RS 7 vols (London, 1875–85), iii, p. 46.

[15] *Letters*, ii, no. 148 (cf. n. 11 above).

[16] *Letters*, ii, no. 172, pp. 132–33.

[17] *Letters*, ii, no. 304, pp. 716–17.

back in Canterbury:[18] it is easier to fit in this speedy visit to his mother if she had returned to Salisbury to die; but we cannot be certain – it is really more probable that he found her among his family in Exeter.

If we know nothing precise of his relations with Bishop Roger, we are better informed of his modest, but firm friendship with his contemporary, Jocelin de Bohun, the other twelfth-century bishop whose effigy lies now in the midst of Salisbury cathedral.[19] Jocelin came from another great bishop's household, that of Henry of Blois, King Henry I's favourite nephew, King Stephen's brother, bishop of Winchester.[20] Roger and Henry owed everything to Henry I, and were men of ostentation, splendid patrons, politically ambitious. There the resemblance ended. Henry was that comparative rarity in the English church, a high aristocrat bishop; he was also a monk and celibate. John's attitude to him was deliciously ambivalent. In the 1140s he had been a bitter rival to John's master Archbishop Theobald for authority in the English church; and he had been denounced by John's most prestigious early patron, St Bernard of Clairvaux, for undue and unsuitable influence in the disputed election to the archbishopric of York. Bernard, in a heated moment, had referred to Henry in a letter to the pope, as the 'harlot of Winchester'.[21] John's satirical account of Henry's antics in Rome, and his buying up old statues (he was a notable patron of art), are famous.[22] But in the late 1160s Henry became one of the few bishops openly to resist Henry II in his machinations against Becket and won golden opinions from John.[23] Jocelin de Bohun was a minor aristocrat who had won patronage and an archdeaconry from Henry. He had gone to Bologna (or anyway to Lombardy) to study law, had had an affair (so it seems) with an Italian girl; and his son, Reginald FitzJocelin, also a friend of John's, archdeacon in the Salisbury diocese, later bishop of Bath, nearly archbishop of Canterbury – and immortalised in the exquisite Gothic of Wells cathedral of which he was the first major patron – was known as 'the Lombard' on account of his origin.[24] In the 1160s Jocelin fell under

---

[18] Ibid. 2 December was the day of Thomas Becket's arrival in Canterbury: ibid. pp. 720–21.

[19] On the tomb, see Shortt, 'The Three Bishops' Tombs' (n. 9) on Jocelin, D. Knowles, *The Episcopal Colleagues of Archbishop Thomas Becket* (Cambridge, 1951), pp. 17–22, 157 and passim; *GFL*, p. 538 and refs; and now *English Episcopal Acta*, 18, ed. B. Kemp.

[20] On him, see esp. Knowles, *Episcopal Colleagues*, pp. 34f; Knowles, *Monastic Order in England* (2nd edn, Cambridge, 1963), pp. 287–93; L. Voss, *Heinrich von Blois* (Berlin, 1932). Also *English Episcopal Acta*, 8, ed. M. J. Franklin (London, 1993), and Franklin's forthcoming biography.

[21] St Bernard of Clairvaux, letter 520, in *Opera*, viii, ed. J. Leclercq and H. Rochais (Rome, 1977), pp. 480–82.

[22] *Historia pontificalis*, pp. 78–80.

[23] *Letters*, ii, no. 296, pp. 682–85.

[24] *Materials for the History of Thomas Becket*, iii, pp. 524–25; cf. Knowles, *Episcopal Colleagues*, p. 19; *GF*, p. 56 and n.

Becket's displeasure, and John doggedly faced both ways: Jocelin was one of his bishops, Becket his immediate master. His letters show him supporting the archbishop's public thunders while struggling to patch up old friendships behind the scenes.[25]

But we are anticipating. If John's early schooling lay in this neighbour-hood, he will always be remembered as one of the brilliant students of the French schools in the late 1130s and 1140s. Every history of Paris and its schools, and of twelfth-century learning, has in its core a quotation or a summary or an echo of the famous passage in John's *Metalogicon* in which he lists the masters at whose feet he sat. He went abroad in 1136 and 'passed about twelve years in varied studies'.[26] The roll-call is impressive: he came at a crucial time, early enough to hear Abelard's last lectures, late enough to hear a wide variety of other men, Robert Pullen, Robert de Melun, William of Conches, Thierry of Chartres, Gilbert de la Porrée and many others.[27] Once again, we are entranced by what he can reveal in quite a few words, infuriated by the gaps. He does not plainly state whether his whole career as a student passed in Paris, or if he wandered, as many did, among the cities of France. This silence has enabled the Abbé Clerval and others to reconstruct a whole school of teachers in Chartres, and to make John a student in a ghost school in the city by which his body undoubtedly lay.[28] It also gave Sir Richard Southern the occasion for a famous exercise in demolition, in which the school of Chartres was shown to have almost no basis in historical evidence, though its teachers were real men of weight and moment and originality, some of whom may well have taught in Paris.[29]

[25] *Letters*, ii, esp. nos 216–18.

[26] *Metalogicon*, ii, c. 10, ed. C. C. J. Webb (Oxford, 1929) p. 82; ed. J. B. Hall and K. S. B. Keats-Rohan, Corpus Christianorum continuatio mediaevalis (Turnhout, 1991), p. 72; cf. *Letters*, i, pp. xiv–xv.

[27] *Metalogicon* ii, c. 10, pp. 77–83; ed. Hall and Keats-Rohan, pp. 70–73. See O. Weijers in *The World of John of Salisbury*, pp. 109–16; K. S. B. Keats-Rohan, 'John of Salisbury and Twelfth-Century Education in Paris', *History of Universities*, 6 (1986), pp. 1–45.

[28] J. A. Clerval, *Les écoles de Chartres au moyen âge* (Paris, 1895).

[29] R. W. Southern, 'Humanism and the School of Chartres', in Southern, *Medieval Human-ism and Other Studies* (Oxford, 1970), pp. 61–85. For the 'barrage of well-informed but hostile criticism' see Luscombe, 'John of Salisbury in Recent Scholarship' (n. 1), p. 25 and nn.; P. Dronke, 'New Approaches to the School of Chartres', *Anuario de estudios medievales*, 6 (1971), pp. 117–40. In 'The Schools of Paris and the School of Chartres' in *Renaissance and Renewal in the Twelfth Century*, ed. R. L. Benson and G. Constable (Oxford, 1982), pp. 113–37, Sir Richard Southern replied to his critics; see also Southern, *Scholastic Humanism and the Unification of Europe*, i (Oxford, 1995), ch. 2. Cf. *Letters*, ii, p. x, and Luscombe, 'John of Salisbury in Recent Scholarship', pp. 24–5.

I am one of those who found Sir Richard's argument in itself extremely convincing, but still wonder a little if it did not demolish too much. At the very least, can it really be true that so inveterate a traveller as John of Salisbury stayed twelve years in France without studying anywhere but in Paris? It is hard to imagine. However that may be, he sat at the feet of a galaxy of masters; he learned much of philosophy and the whole gamut of the trivium and quadrivium; he studied theology over many years. He laid the foundations of a lifelong enjoyment of rhetoric; his mind was marked by a particular interest in ancient authorities, in philosophic ambiguities, with a love for finding truth, and falsehood, in both sides of a question, which we have seen was to be the mark of his best ironical prose.[30]

One branch of learning was curiously absent from his early schooling, and that was law.[31] Curiously, since if John had had to fill in a form between 1147 and 1176 describing his profession, one perfectly good answer might have been that he was a professional lawyer, for he seems to have been on and off through most of the period chief adviser to the archbishop of Canterbury on appeals to the papal curia, and in the early 1170s adviser on such cases to his close friend, Bishop Bartholomew of Exeter, who was a considerable canonist in his own right, and others.[32] This is only part of the story; but so far as it goes it seems a well-attested fact. The first collection of his letters, mainly covering the years 1156–1161, is one of the most important sources for the history of appeals to Rome from anywhere in Europe in the mid twelfth century; and one may add that this is not only significant but dramatic, since the mid twelfth century saw the transformation of the very nature of papal monarchy by the growth of the appeals system.[33] Yet John has never been very favourably viewed by the professional students of canon law, since his works do not reveal him as a jurist of deep learning, nor has any single gloss on Roman or canon law been successfully attributed to him. We do not even know how he learned his law; though it is possible that it came after his arrival in Canterbury in 1147, and that he learned it from the Bolognese jurist Master Vacarius whom Theobald imported to ensure that the latest Bolognese fashions were understood in

---

[30] See n. 4 above.

[31] See *Letters*, i, pp. xix–xxiii; ii, pp. xii, xlvi and n.

[32] A. Morey, *Bartholomew of Exeter* (Cambridge, 1937); S. Kuttner and E. Rathbone, 'Anglo-Norman Canonists of the Twelfth Century', *Traditio*, 7 (1949–51), pp. 279–358, at p. 295. See now F. Barlow in *English Episcopal Acta* xi, especially pp. xxxix–xli; D. N. Bell, ed., *Bartholomaei Exoniensis contra fatalitatis errorem*, Corpus Christianorum continuatio mediaevalis (Turnhout, 1996).

[33] Cf. *Letters*, i, pp. xxx–xxxvi.

England.[34] Here is an intriguing puzzle. We should certainly recall that later archbishops were content to use a man of even less legal learning, Master Peter of Blois, as their chief advocate in important cases;[35] and that it has often happened that the greatest advocates have been men of more eloquence than learning. John was undoubtedly eloquent, a master of rhetoric; an adept diplomat except on the relatively few occasions when his zeal completely overran his discretion;[36] a man who made friends everywhere and kept them; an avid traveller. For whatever reason, Theobald sent him again and again to the curia, almost from the first. When he wrote the *Metalogicon* in the late 1150s he could say,

> I have been distracted by other tasks, not different merely but inimical to study, so that I could scarcely snatch an hour here and there, and then furtively, to play philosopher. Ten times I have crossed the chain of the Alps since I left England first; twice have I travelled through Apulia; I have done business often in the Roman court on behalf of my superiors and friends; and on a variety of counts I have traversed England, and France too, many times.[37]

In the course of his years as a student John had won patronage from two leading figures of the monastic world, Peter, abbot of Moutier-la-Celle, later of Saint-Rémi, a man who vies with Peter the Venerable of Cluny in the charm and urbanity of his letters to a wide circle of which John always remained the centre; and St Bernard himself.[38] It seems a reasonable guess that John had attracted Bernard's notice as a promising pupil of Bernard's favourite Parisian professor, the English Robert Pullen – like many strong-minded men Bernard divided the world, and especially the academic world,

[34] *Letters*, i, pp. xxii–xxiii; on Vacarius see R. W. Southern, 'Master Vacarius and the Beginning of an English Academic Tradition', *Medieval Learning and Literature: Essays Presented to R. W. Hunt* (Oxford, 1976), pp. 257–86; P. Stein, 'Vacarius and the Civil Law', in *Church and Government in the Middle Ages: Essays Presented to C. R. Cheney* (Cambridge, 1976), pp. 119–37.

[35] Southern, *Medieval Humanism* (n. 29), pp. 107–8; cf. Kuttner and Rathbone, 'Anglo-Norman Canonists', pp. 285–86.

[36] As in the case of his negotiations with the pope on the claims of Henry II to Ireland (*Letters*, i, p. 257 and references) and perhaps *Letters*, ii, nos 174–75, which may be reckoned to have exacerbated feeling between Becket and the English bishops in the summer of 1166.

[37] *Metalogicon* iii, *prologus* (ed. Webb, p. 117; ed. Hall and Keats-Rohan, p. 101); cf. *Letters*, i, pp. xxiv, 256: we cannot be certain if the figure ten is precisely correct, but any reasonable reconstruction of the nature of John's career in the late 1140s and 1150s makes it very plausible.

[38] On Peter see J. Leclercq, *La spiritualité de Pierre de Celle* (Paris, 1946), and the forthcoming edition of his *Letters* in OMT by J. Haseldine; also Haseldine, 'Understanding the Language of *Amicitia*: The Friendship Circle of Peter of Celle (*c.* 1115–1183)', *Journal of Medieval History*, 20 (1994), pp. 237–60; 'The Creation of a Literary Memorial: The Letter Collection of Peter of Celle', *Sacris erudiri*, 37 (1997), pp. 333–79; *Letters*, i, pp. ix–x and passim. Most of his works are in *PL*, 202.

into good men and bad; he was as ruthless in promoting the careers of the good as he was in persecuting the bad. He drove Abelard into the arms of Peter the Venerable, but helped Robert Pullen to the dignity of a cardinal;[39] and he seems to have given John a testimonial which he carried to Canterbury. This was in 1147, and was the first fulcrum upon which John's career rose and fell.[40] An obscure crisis in the late 1150s gave him a period of sabbatical leave to complete his major works, the *Metalogicon* and the *Policraticus*,[41] the even longer period of exile in the 1160s gave him evidently the chance and impetus to embark on the *Historia pontificalis*, an unfinished, semi-satirical, semi-serious essay in history as viewed from the papal curia.[42] For the rest, he was a man of affairs, and his other major writings, the letters, are mainly concerned with the two preoccupations of the 1150s and 1160s: with the administration of Theobald's court and appeals cases, and with the struggle between Thomas Becket and Henry II.[43]

Enough has already been said to reveal the basic theme of this essay. We recall the memory of a man who in a quite extraordinary degree united a local base in England and Salisbury with a cosmopolitan experience characteristic of western Christendom in the twelfth century. Even in exile – perhaps particularly in exile – he revealed himself an Englishman who longed to live in England, anyway for half each year, with a strong sense of loyalty to the people and places from which he sprang; and at the same

[39] F. Courtney, *Cardinal Robert Pullen* (Rome, 1954), ch. 1.

[40] St Bernard, letter 361 (*Opera*, viii, pp. 307–8): it is true that Bernard calls him simply John, but the letter is addressed to Theobald; the circumstances fit John of Salisbury and are not known to fit those of any other of Theobald's clerks; and there is some manuscript authority for the address to John *of Salisbury* in the heading of the letter; see Leclercq and Rochais's apparatus, p. 307, notes to lines 7–8: they cite one surviving manuscript, their MS Rp – cf. p. 235; presumably Mabillon had seen at least one more.

[41] See G. Constable, 'The Alleged Disgrace of John of Salisbury in 1159', *EHR*, 69 (1954), pp. 67–76; *Letters*, i, pp. 257–58.

[42] See *Historia pontificalis*, and M. Chibnall, 'John of Salisbury as Historian', *The World of John of Salisbury*, pp. 169–77; C. N. L. Brooke, 'Aspects of John of Salisbury's *Historia Pontificalis*', in *Intellectual Life in the Middle Ages: Essays Presented to Margaret Gibson*, ed. L. Smith and B. Ward (London, 1992), pp. 185–95. The work is anonymous in the only surviving manuscript, and there has been no detailed discussion of its authorship, since its extraordinary congruence with the manner, career and experience of John were first noted – and the authorship attributed to him – by W. Giesebrecht in his *Arnold von Brescia* (Munich, 1973), pp. 6–7. There are numerous circumstantial points which come readily to hand in favour of his authorship; and the whole case has been laid out by J. McLoughlin, 'John of Salisbury (c. 1120–1180): The Career and Attitudes of a Schoolman in Church Politics' (unpublished Ph.D. thesis, Trinity College, Dublin, 1988), i, pp. 129–47.

[43] *Letters*, i, pp. xxv–xxxviii, ii, pp. xix–xliv; Saltman, *Theobald*, passim.

time a Frenchman, a man of Europe, at home wherever he went.[44] It is particularly striking how important a source he is, in ways large and small, for the history of the papacy and Italy. Let us look at a few of his throwaway lines. In the late 1150s Peter of Celle dedicated his treatise on bread – full of biblical learning, largely on the symbolic and tropological significance of bread in scripture – to John; John's letter of thanks runs on the theme: you have filled me with bread, now I want a drink, for I am an Englishman and therefore (notoriously) a toper; and, in an extraordinary mixture of joyful conviviality and learned allusion, he compared English beer and French wine, rising to the red wine of the Passion and the white which reflects 'the holiness and cleanliness of chastity' and then switching back to his earlier mood with equal suddenness, placing at the bottom of his list of wines those of the Mediterranean. 'I should prefer any to the wine of Falerno or Palermo or Greece which the chancellor of the king of Sicily used to give me to the peril of my life and my salvation.'[45] John is an interesting witness on the obscure but important figure of Robert of Selby, chancellor to Roger the Great of Sicily. For Robert's surname, or place of origin, we rely entirely on another English witness, the chronicler John of Hexham.[46] At one time I supposed that he might have been a fellow citizen of John of Salisbury, for the scribe of the chief manuscript of John of Hexham seems originally to have written an abbreviation mark which would have converted *Salebia* (Selby) into *Saleberia* (Salisbury).[47] But he, or a well-informed colleague, erased the mark and left us guessing, until Martin Brett drew my attention to the reading in the independent manuscript in Paris, which is unambiguously in favour of Yorkshire. Nonetheless, John and Robert link in their different ways the two Norman kingdoms of Sicily and England, and John links them to much in between. Papal affairs apart, John was a witness of a dramatic period in the growth of the Italian cities. Himself a native of a modest northern town – the only ancient hill-fort to be a town in twelfth-century England – he must have felt a certain affinity (such as no Englishman can feel today) in the numerous enchanting hill

[44] The early letters of his exile reveal a strong and continuing desire to return to England; yet many of his letters from Reims also take for granted that he is at home there – for the phrase 'nos Francos' see *Letters*, ii, no. 270, pp. 546–47.

[45] *Letters*, i, no. 33 especially pp. 57–58.

[46] John of Hexham in Symeon of Durham, *Opera omnia*, ed. T. Arnold, RS, 2 vols (London, 1882–85), ii, pp. 318–20.

[47] For the manuscripts see R. H. Pinder-Wilson and C. Brooke, 'The Reliquary of St Petroc and the Ivories of Norman Sicily', *Archaeologia*, 104 (London, 1973), pp. 261–305, at p. 299 n. 1.

towns of central Italy.[48] Two rival legends dominate the historiography of
Siena, one of the greatest of all hill towns: that of its Roman origin, familiar
to visitors to Siena from its adoption in the badge of the wolf of Romulus
and Remus, and that of its Gallic origin associated with Brennus duke of
the Senones as John calls him; and to the Gallic view John is the earliest
surviving witness by several generations.[49] Of the Roman revolution of
Arnold of Brescia, heretic and revolutionary, John is a major source;[50] but
perhaps more remarkable is his place among the contemporary witnesses
for the stirring of the Lombard league against Frederick Barbarossa in the
1160s.[51] In the summer of 1167 the Emperor Frederick Barbarossa sat with
a seemingly invincible army at the gates of Rome. The Italian cities, furnished
with imperial podestà, lay quiet behind him; Pope Alexander III seemed to
have been caught in a trap. His very survival, and with him the chances of
peace of any kind for Thomas Becket and his supporters, seemed doubtful.
But a force more powerful than Frederick intervened; and like Sennacherib
from the walls of Jerusalem the emperor was presently in flight, leaving a
great part of his army, and several of his chief advisers, dead of the plague.
Through the winter of 1167 and 1168 he was a fugitive in north Italy and
in the Alps; and the Lombard cities rose and founded their first league. In
December 1167 the league was formed; in the following spring Frederick
fled to Germany; early in 1168 the fortress city of Alessandria was founded,
witness to this day of the survival of its eponymous hero, Pope Alexander.[52]
When I was concerned to annotate the letters referring to this period, I
was stupefied to find that of many of these events, especially the details of
the emperor's adventures, John is our earliest and even our only witness;
and when the citizens of Alessandria and the Lombard league celebrated
their centenaries in the late 1960s, in key *relazioni* Raoul Manselli noted
the fact that John's letter of June 1168 was the earliest record of the event.[53]

[48] So far as is at present known: there is, for example no evidence that Shaftesbury was ever
a hill-fort or hill-town in prehistoric times. The ancient hill-towns were mostly abandoned
during the Roman occupation of Britain.

[49] *Letters*, ii, no. 240, pp. 456–59 and n. On John and Italy, see R. Manselli in *Popolo e stato
in Italia nell'età di Federico Barbarossa, Alessandria e la Lega Lombarda* (Turin, 1970).

[50] *Historia Pontificalis*, pp. 63–65.

[51] See T. Reuter, 'John of Salisbury and the Germans', in *The World of John of Salisbury*,
pp. 415–25; *Letters*, ii, pp. xxxviii–xxxix. For John and the Lombard League see *Popolo e stato*
(Turin, 1970), especially the paper by R. Manselli; see also Manselli in *I problemi della civiltà
comunale*, Atti del congresso, Bergamo, 1967, ed. C. D. Fonseca (Bergamo, 1971), p. 18 and n.
50; bibliography in F. Cognasso, *Il Piemonte nell'età sveva* (Turin, 1968), p. 843.

[52] *Letters*, ii, nos 272–76, especially (for Barbarossa in the winter of 1167–68), no. 272, and
(for the foundation of Alessandria) no. 276, pp. 588–89.

[53] See n. 51.

'The Lombards to the emperor's shame [wrote John] are building a city in the fortified town called *Roboretum*, near Pavia, which they are calling Alessandria in honour of Pope Alexander and to the destruction of the Pavesi' (Frederick's chief remaining allies). This is still, in Manselli's words, 'L'indicazione più sintetica e precisa dei vari motivi della fondazione di Alessandria' – 'the most precise and concise statement and interpretation of the various motives for the foundation' of the city.[54] Of other aspects of the history of the league, especially Henry II's intrigues with it, which have been too often ignored by English historians, John is our only witness.[55]

This illustrates his cosmopolitan flavour as well as his importance for the understanding of his world. It is equally important, however, to observe that his witness is neither impeccable nor objective. No historian would go to John for a balanced view of Frederick Barbarossa.[56] John had first contemplated the Germans across the French frontier; and as he never visited Germany, so far as we know, he had no German friends nor occasion to modify the kind of part-humorous, part-rhetorical distaste for German political ambitions and German culture which is the most marked blemish in his cosmopolitan make-up. This antipathy was enlarged by three circumstances. He was close, even intimate for a time, with the English Pope Adrian IV; and an ambiguous phrase in one of the letters may well mean that Adrian had hinted an intention to make John a cardinal, prevented by Adrian's early death.[57] Frederick and Adrian, to state the matter coolly, had not found it easy to meet one another half or any part of the way. Then in 1159, when Adrian died, came the double election to the papacy, and Frederick's support for Victor IV, whom everyone of weight in the English church came rapidly to assume was the anti-pope.[58] Finally, when Becket fled from the wrath of Henry II, it was as evident to contemporaries as it is to us that Alexander III's difficulties with Barbarossa (who refused to recognise him as pope) prevented him from wholehearted condemnation of his own most powerful lay supporter, the English king.[59] Hence the sharpness of John's anger against the 'Ex-Augustus' as he liked to call him

[54] *Letters*, ii, pp. 588–89; R. Manselli in *I problemi*, p. 18.

[55] *Letters*, ii, no. 290, pp. 660–61.

[56] See T. Reuter, 'John of Salisbury and the Germans', in *The World of John of Salisbury*, pp. 415–25; *Letters*, i, no. 124; ii, p. 841 (index *s. v.* Frederick).

[57] *Letters*, ii, no. 235, pp. 434–35; cf. *Letters*, i, p. 256.

[58] See Mary G. Cheney, 'The Recognition of Pope Alexander III: Some Neglected Evidence', in *EHR*, 84 (1969), pp. 474–97.

[59] For all this see T. A. Reuter, 'The Papal Schism, the Empire and the West, 1159–1169' (unpublished D.Phil. thesis, University of Oxford, 1975), and Reuter in *The World of John of Salisbury*, pp. 417f. See esp. *Letters*, ii, nos 177, 290, pp. 182–85, 658–61.

(with not quite adequate justification), which inspired him to imagine a formal papal deposition of the emperor, an imaginary event which in its turn inspired later historians to enter into the innocuous Lateran synod of 1167 a fictitious account of the deposition which he was supposed to have witnessed.[60] John is an important witness to quite distant events in his world; but he is not an objective or always accurate witness. Janet Martin has taught us to look with deep suspicion at some of John's references to ancient authorities – he enjoyed teasing us (to give a generous interpretation) with imaginary sources or faked quotations.[61] Similarly, there are many points in his letters in which incidents appear to have been invented or distorted; although this is more commonly to be attributed to distortion by rumour, which he may be reporting in all innocence, than to prejudice. Thus he describes a battle in Germany which cannot have taken place (anyway as he describes it), and attributes a sister to the king of Scots – and an improbable plan to marry her in north Italy – who appears to be unknown to the historical record and perhaps never existed.[62] But his love of ambiguity, and the genuine ambiguity of many of his sentiments, often make him a vivid, authentic contemporary witness so long as we always remember that he was never truly detached from the events he describes.[63] Even the greatest of his enemies, King Henry II, is shown under a dazzling variety of colours: John often refers to him as tyrant, in phrases open or veiled; but equally there are passages of astonishing respect, even reverence; he never doubted that his own future lay in reconciliation to the king, and he tried to have it arranged long before Becket was reconciled.[64] There are some moments of delicious invective. In the summer of 1166 Gilbert Foliot, bishop of London, Becket's strongest opponent among the bishops of the province of Canterbury, managed to get many of the bishops to put their seals to a letter to Pope Alexander in which he defended the king, portraying him as a modest, mild man, astonished by the venom of his old servant the archbishop, just waiting till peace was made before

[60] For Frederick as 'ex-Augustus' and the Lateran synod see *Letters*, ii, no. 242, especially p. 474 and n. 4. But Reuter, 'John of Salisbury and the Germans', pp. 416–19, shows that there was some foundation for John's overstated view of the matter.

[61] Janet Martin, 'John of Salisbury as Classical Scholar', pp. 179–201; also Janet Martin, 'John of Salisbury and the Classics' (unpublished Ph.D. thesis, Harvard University, 1968).

[62] *Letters*, ii, no. 276, pp. 588–89; no. 272, pp. 554–55.

[63] See n. 4. *Letters*, ii, no. 168 (the account of Becket's thunders at Vézelay in June 1166) and no. 304, with its terrifying account of the events of late November and early December 1170, are remarkable examples of the vividness with which he can portray contemporary reactions to dramatic events.

[64] See esp. *Letters*, ii, pp. xxiv–xxv and references.

setting off on crusade, in spite of his devotion to wife and children.[65] Later historians, recalling Henry's violent quarrels with his queen and his sons, and his consistent failure to mount his imaginary crusades in the next decade, have found this very hard to swallow. Doubtless we have the wisdom of hindsight; John is our witness that contemporaries, even in the 1160s, found it sufficiently disingenuous. David Knowles, in a brilliant literary flight, has made it impossible for us to take Gilbert seriously.[66]

> Heaven help us [he is summarising John's rejoinder] what a nerve the man has! 'We do not say [John quotes Foliot] that the king has never been at fault, but we do say that he considers it the sweetest of all tasks to listen to those who tell him he is wrong.' Does he think that anyone in Europe will swallow this?

And John quotes the resounding climax of Horace's epistle, where the poet tells of the man who, once deceived in the streets by a bogus cripple, refuses to hear even the best authenticated tale of woe; the whole street begs the unfortunate to try his story elsewhere: 'Quaere peregrinum! vicinia rauca reclamat' (Go seek a stranger, the whole neighbourhood howls till it's hoarse).[67]

Perhaps the most curious feature of this letter is that it was addressed – and taking it all for all, I am convinced that it was sent – from the security of Reims into England, to the bishop of Exeter, in whose hands, as a loyal subject of King Henry who had (however reluctantly) set his seal to the bishop's letter, John's epistle must have seemed about as safe a possession as a letter bomb.[68] One of the many indications, however, that all this invective should not be taken too literally or too seriously is that it passed, to all appearance, quite freely in and out of Henry's dominions.

So John is not an objective witness to his world; yet he is a vivid, unusual, important witness. And I wish to conclude by sketching the circumstances and contents of two of his most important letters. In doing so I renounce many other possibilities. I could talk of that great treatise of political ideas and all manner of other things, that remarkable and unwieldy fragment of a moral encyclopedia, the *Policraticus*; I could (if I had the learning) discuss

[65] *GFL*, no. 166; no. 167 sends a similar message to Becket, and is the occasion of John's outbursts (see below).

[66] Knowles, *Episcopal Colleagues*, p. 121; *Letters*, ii, no. 174, pp. 138–41.

[67] Horace, *Epistolae*, i, 17, line 62.

[68] *Letters*, ii, no. 174 was addressed to Bartholomew, bishop of Exeter; and to Exeter were also addressed several others of his most thunderous epistles. No close student of John's letters has ever believed, I think, that they were literary exercises, not actually sent; the amount of minor gossip in most of them seems conclusive against this view – and the curious confusion over the addresses of some of the letters to Exeter (noted in *Letters*, ii, p. liv) is most readily explained if it reflects the actual condition of the packets of letters sent.

how much we can really learn of the state of philosophical study in John's age from the *Metalogicon*.[69] Let me simply say that I have consumed as many years in editing his letters as John spent in writing them, and my friendship with him (not without its ambiguities, as you can imagine) is based upon them. Even from the letters I could follow many intellectual themes, including a revelation of a much deeper biblical learning – based partly on contacts with Jewish scholars – than he is usually accorded from his famous letter on the canon of scripture to the count of Champagne. On that, to my pleasure, Professor Saltman has put me right;[70] and there are many more learned in the *Policraticus* and the *Metalogicon* than I.

Editing the letters has been one of the toughest tasks of my academic life. At first it was made easy by all that the late Father Millor did in his splendid thesis, and by all that Sir Roger Mynors, and a host of others, had done;[71] and at all points I was helped by many other scholars. My chief task was to revise H. E. Butler's translation of the early letters and to translate the later ones myself; and to introduce and annotate the whole collection – that is, to explain John's meaning and put it in its setting. The translation was vital to the edition: useless to edit such a collection without really enquiring what it means; impossible to discover what it means unless one tries to express it in one's own tongue. But those kind critics who have helped and castigated my efforts – Roger Mynors, Michael Winterbottom, Diana Greenway – have had to tell me in their various ways that my mind is not up to John's. In some ways I am glad of this: for his mind was immensely complex, subtle, ironical; he loved to write at several levels simultaneously. Even his most forceful rhetoric gets tripped in the complexities of his irony. His more personal letters can be like a labyrinth without a chart. The two I have selected, however, are relatively plain.

In the autumn of 1160 it was clear that Archbishop Theobald, John's master, was dying.[72] His special wish was to see his most brilliant protégé, also his archdeacon, Thomas Becket, before he died; and this wish was very

[69] See studies discussed by D. E. Luscombe, 'John of Salisbury in Recent Scholarship' (n. 1), pp. 22–24.

[70] See Luscombe, 'John of Salisbury in Recent Scholarship', pp. 21–22, 34–35; Avrom Saltman, 'John of Salisbury and the World of the Old Testament', in *The World of John of Salisbury*, pp. 343–63, especially pp. 357–63.

[71] The edition was based on the London thesis by W. J. Millor, revised by Sir Roger Mynors; the translation to *Letters*, i, was by H. E. Butler; the whole was revised and annotated (with much help from Millor's thesis), and the translation of *Letters*, ii, provided, by myself, with the help of many scholars named in the preface to volume two, especially Sir Roger Mynors, Professor Michael Winterbottom and Professor Diana Greenway.

[72] For what follows see *Letters*, i, pp. xxxvii–xxxviii, 266–67; M. G. Cheney, 'The Recognition of Pope Alexander III', *EHR*, 84 (1969), pp. 474–97; Saltman, *Theobald* (n. 6), pp. 54–55.

likely sharpened by his own desire to see Becket his successor. Meanwhile Becket was not only archdeacon of Canterbury and nominal head of Theobald's administration; he was also royal chancellor and active head of King Henry II's. This post he had achieved at the very outset of Henry's reign (probably at the beginning of 1155) at Theobald's suggestion. He was the king's inseparable companion in France; and so it was difficult for him to get leave to visit his old master. It has often been said, in imitation of Becket's contemporary biographers, that in 1155 a good cleric was turned into the perfect royal servant, and in 1162, by a conversion equally dramatic, a worldly, royal servant was converted into an ascetic, intransigent archbishop; and although many explanations, some charitable, some very uncharitable, have been found for these transformations, the basic paradox remains.[73] One of John's early letters seems to me among the most significant documents for the whole course of Becket's career. John and Thomas were close personal friends: they had served Theobald together since the 1140s, and in the late 1150s John's two major works were dedicated to the chancellor; in the 1160s John and Thomas were to be exiles in a common cause, even though they lived apart. Thus John to Thomas in the autumn of 1160:

In accordance with your command, my dear friend, I had drafted my lord's letters to our lord the king and to yourself in such austere terms that the necessity of your speedy return might be impressed upon you, unless you should prefer to be charged with disobedience and to suffer the penalty of my lord's anathema and the loss of all the possessions which the church of Canterbury has conferred upon you. But since the unexpected arrival of Hugh of Dover with the king's request coupled with promises and cajolements, I have been compelled by the urgent instructions of my lord to temper the rigour of my language and to make some concessions to necessities of state. If the statements of persons returning from overseas are true, as I pray that they may be, the king and all his court are so dependent on your counsel that there is not a hope of peace in the near future, unless your wisdom pave the way for it. This has made my lord to be at times perplexed as to the reason why our lord the king and yourself from time to time make contradictory demands and give different reasons in your letters for hastening or postponing your return, seeing that common report and rumour seems to indicate that you are so strongly of one heart and mind, that in view of such intimate friendship your desires and dislikes must coincide. He has also sometimes asked whether there may not be some collusion between you in this matter. But I think I have an inkling of the truth, and realise almost as vividly as if I were

[73] For a statement by one of the major authorities, see D. Knowles, *Thomas Becket* (London, 1970); Knowles, *The Historian and Character and Other Essays* (Cambridge, 1963), ch. 6. For a less favourable view, W. L. Warren, *Henry II* (London, 1973), ch. 13. See now F. Barlow, *Thomas Becket* (London, 1986).

on the spot what your situation is in the midst of your labours in a distant land. And so when I was compelled to cancel the letters I had already drafted, I began to doubt whether it would not be better to keep back my messenger rather than send him at once. Because he had already received the licence, which we had contrived to get in advance, and was on the point of setting out, I at length decided to explore your feelings; and I have managed to send letters which I have made as urgent as I could, though they make some concession to the king's will, both to yourself and him.[74]

Thomas was the king's man and the archbishop's man. He was caught in a spider's web of patronage;[75] a kind of trap. The dual authority of the spiritual and the temporal, of king and pope, of church and state, made this a very common kind of trap, and it was frequently to torment John himself. What this letter expresses with unique clarity is Thomas's dilemma throughout his later years: the dual allegiance made him the favourite servant of both his masters, but exposed him to potential suspicion. Theobald was mildly and tolerantly suspicious; Henry was a man of intense, mercurial temperament who could shift in a moment from sunshine to thunder.[76] Even as chancellor, it was Becket's central problem to convince both his masters that he was still loyal to them; for patronage carries this unavoidable concomitant with it, the need to exhibit loyalty, the fear, on both sides, of the consequences of suspicion of its opposite. When Becket was archbishop, the king viewed his independence and his stand against the king as mere treachery.[77] I have no wish to pass judgement now on Becket's manner of stating his independence: no two modern witnesses will ever agree on that.[78] But it is quite clear that, whatever Becket did, the long years of ambiguity must have made his position intensely difficult; and when the king denounced him as a traitor, *proditor ille*, a deep feeling of resentment, made harsher by the growing gap between the learned clerk and the secular warrior noble, was bound to stir angry and dangerous feelings. On 29 December 1170 these feelings were expressed in a fearful drama in Canterbury cathedral. Soon after, John wrote to his old friend John of Canterbury, bishop of

[74] *Letters*, i, no. 128, pp. 221–22.

[75] The nature and significance of this in twelfth-century England has never been fully explored: for various aspects of it, see esp. Southern, *Medieval Humanism* (n. 29), ch. 11; J. Lally, 'Secular Patronage at the Court of King Henry II', *Bulletin of the Institute of Historical Research*, 49 (1976), pp. 159–84.

[76] Warren, *Henry II*, ch. 5, esp. pp. 207–17, lays out and discusses the contemporary attitudes to Henry II. See also Knowles, *Thomas Becket*, pp. 33–37, 156–59; John's *Letters*, ii, nos 168, 174–76 (esp. pp. 156–59), 288.

[77] See esp. Knowles, *Historian and Character*, pp. 112–13.

[78] See n. 73.

Poitiers,[79] 'Quite unexpectedly, quite in passing, but by God's mercy, I have just learned that the bearer was on his way across the sea to you', and he seized with pleasure and relief the heaven-sent opportunity to pour out the story of the most famous of his letters. First, he expounded the nature of the deed, then the events of the murder. As the four barons broke into the Cathedral, in the confusion and hubbub, Thomas Becket stood firm, waiting for his end, and with him William FitzStephen and a few others, the more stalwart of his entourage; but most fled, including John himself: let those of us who are convinced we would not have been with him condemn him for it. John's writings reveal a man full of the ordinary human emotions of fear and sensitivity: he was not of heroic mould; yet equally not lacking in moral courage when he saw a principle or a cause clear before him. Thus this letter, though the earliest and one of the most moving, is not an eyewitness account of the murder.[80] But of the aftermath it is. As the murderers left they ordered that the corpse

should not be buried among the holy archbishops, but thrown into a vile marsh or hung on a gibbet. Hence the good men who were there feared that force was being invoked against them, and buried him in the crypt, before the altar of St John the Baptist and St Augustine, apostle of the English, in a marble tomb, before Satan's servants had answered the summons to this sacrilege. And there many mighty wonders are performed, to God's glory: great throngs of people gather to feel in themselves and witness in others the power and mercy of Him who always shows His wonder and His glory in His saints. In the place where Thomas suffered, and where he lay the night through, before the high altar, awaiting burial, and where he was buried at last, the palsied are cured, the blind see, the deaf hear, the dumb speak, the lame walk, folk suffering from fevers are cured, the lepers are cleansed, those possessed of a devil are freed, and the sick are made whole from all manner of disease, blasphemers taken over by the devil are put to confusion: God works all this and more, which would take long to describe; He who alone and over all is blessed for ever, and chose those to be the sharers in His glory whom He meant to cause to triumph over the enemies of truth and faith by true loyalty, zeal for justice, the virtue of confession, and perseverance in steadfastness unconquerable. I should not have dreamt to write such words on any account had not my eyes been witness to the certainty of this.

[79] *Letters*, ii, no. 305. The letter evidently circulated as a narrative of the murder; but there is no reason to doubt that it was originally written as a personal letter to John of Canterbury, bishop of Poitiers, early in 1171, and an extended version sent to Peter of Celle, abbot of Saint-Rémi – see ibid., pp. 724–25 n. 1.

[80] For eyewitnesses, see Knowles, *Historian and Character*, pp. 123–28, and *Thomas Becket*, pp. 172–73; and Barlow, *Thomas Becket*, ch. 11. For what follows, *Letters*, ii, no. 305, pp. 734–37.

For some years more John remained in England, carrying on his work at Canterbury, serving his friends the bishops of Worcester and Exeter in handling appeals to the curia; a dignified elder statesman.[81] When king and pope had been formally reconciled, and the bishoprics were filled, no bishopric came John's way; and notoriously, it was the king's men, not Becket's clerks, who filled the majority of them.[82] They included some of John's friends, Reginald son of Jocelin bishop of Salisbury, who became bishop of Bath, and Richard of Ilchester, the great financier, who went to Winchester, in particular. John seemed to have reached the limit of his career, when the noble leader of the French church, William of the White Hands, bishop of Chartres and archbishop of Sens, suggested to his brother-in-law the Most Christian King Louis that he give up Chartres to their friend and protégé, Master John of Salisbury, in honour of the martyr by whose prayers both hoped to win their way to heaven.[83] The king and the canons of Chartres acquiesced, and King Henry released him. What Henry really thought I should dearly like to know: perhaps it confirmed his suspicions of John's loyalty; in any case it provided a fitting and dignified end to John's career. Hastily putting together the materials he had been collecting (much too slowly) for a magisterial life and letters of St Thomas, he sailed for France, leaving the materials in Canterbury for others to complete.[84] He ended his days in Chartres in 1180. But when I contemplate the royal portal – all that is left of the cathedral at Chartres as John knew it – or when I reread his letters and hear his familiar voice, it is impossible to believe that he has been parted from us so long. For he lives in his writings as do few of his world.

[81] See *Letters*, ii, pp. xliv–xlvi; for other evidence see *English Episcopal Acta*, 8, ed. M. J. Franklin (London, 1993), nos 140–41, 166, 171; *English Episcopal Acta*, 12, ed. F. Barlow (London, 1996), index, p. 344, under Salisbury, John of.

[82] See *Councils and Synods*, i, ed. D. Whitelock, M. Brett and C. N. L. Brooke (Oxford, 1981), 2, pp. 956–65; R. Foreville, *L'église et la royauté en Angleterre sous Henri II Plantagenêt* (Paris, 1943), pp. 373–84; H. Mayr-Harting, 'Henry II and the Papacy, 1170–1189', in *Journal of Ecclesiastical History*, 16 (1965), pp. 39–53, at pp. 50–51.

[83] See *Letters*, ii, pp. xlvi–xlvii; Ralph de Diceto, *Opera historica*, ed. W. Stubbs, RS (London, 1876), i, pp. 410–12.

[84] *Letters*, ii, pp. lviii–lxiii; see especially A. Duggan, *Thomas Becket: A Textual History of his Letters* (Oxford, 1980), esp. pp. 94–98. On the doubts whether John was a successful bishop, see Luscombe, 'John of Salisbury in Recent Scholarship', pp. 35–36.

15

St Clare

with Rosalind Brooke

St Clare died on 11 August 1253, and the celebration of her seventh centenary in 1953 was accompanied by a revival of scholarly interest in her life and work scarcely to be paralleled since the Bollandists passed through August. Grau established the canon of her writings and published an annotated German translation. Hardick fixed the chronology of her life – born in 1193–94, received into the religious life at the age of eighteen in 1212; from 1212 to 1253 head and leader (from 1216 abbess) of the community in San Damiano.[1] Much else has occurred besides since 1953 in scholarly publication, and little perhaps remains to be discovered about her life and works. Yet something can still be said of the relation of Clare and her movement

From *Medieval Women: Dedicated and Presented to Professor Rosalind M. T. Hill on the Occasion of her Seventieth Birthday*, ed. D. Baker, *Studies in Church History*, Subsidia 1 (Oxford, 1978), pp. 275–87.

[1] For a general view of Clare and the early history of her Order, see J. R. H. Moorman, *The Franciscan Order from its Origins to the year 1517* (Oxford, 1968), pp. 32–39, 205–15; M. Robson, *St Francis of Assisi* (London, 1997), ch. 7. On the wider context, see the classic study of H. Grundmann, *Religious Movements in the Middle Ages* (English translation by S. Rowan, Notre Dame, 1995): chs. 3–6 deal specifically with the religious movements among women and the *Frauenfrage*; ch. 5, pt. 3, with the early Franciscan sisters, including Clare herself; ch. 5, pt, 4, on the relations of the mendicant orders and their female communities. See also B. Bolton, '*Mulieres sanctae*', *Studies In Church History* 10 (1973), pp. 77–95; *Chiara di Assisi* (Spoleto, 1993); J. Dalarun, *Francesco: un passaggio* (Rome, 1994).

The main products of 1953 were: *S. Chiara d'Assisi, 1253–1953; Studi e Cronaca del VII Centenario* (Assisi, 1954); E. Grau and L. Hardick, *Leben und Schriften der heiligen Klara von Assisi* (1st edn, actually 1952; 3rd edn, Werl, 1960) and the English version *The legend and writings of St Clare* (St Bonaventure, New York, 1953), including a revised version of P. Robinson's translation – Hardick's study of Clare also appeared in French translation in *Spiritualité de Sainte Claire* (Paris, 1961); A. Fortini, 'Nuove notizie intorno a S. Chiara di Assisi'; *Archivum Franciscanum Historicum*, 46 (1953), pp. 3–43; *Franziskanische Studien*, 35 (1953), esp. L. Hardick, 'Zur Chronologie im Leben der hl. Klara', pp. 174–210, and E. Grau, 'Die Regel der hl. Klara (1253) in ihrer Abhängigkeit von der Regel der Minderbrüder (1223)', pp. 211–73. For the rules, her writings and other early sources see nn. 3–5.

to the wider issues of female involvement in the religious movements of
the twelfth and thirteenth centuries, and her own record leaves many puzzles.
In the modern world there are roughly three women in a religious order
to every man; in the twelfth century, though our evidence is even more
approximate, we can be sure that the men vastly outnumbered the women,
and the balance was only redressed in the thirteenth century, and then only
in Germany and the Low Countries.[2] Part of the reason was a deliberate
constriction or restriction of female initiative, and of this Clare is an
exceptionally interesting witness. Her life was outwardly stable and peaceful,
save for the occasion when she is said to have routed some Saracen troops
of the Emperor Frederick II.[3] But the popes and the cardinal protectors
found it necessary to provide her own and her sister communities with no
less than six rules between 1219 and 1263,[4] which does not suggest that all
was peaceful within. Indeed it is commonly assumed that between Clare

[2] See Grundmann, *Religious Movements* (as n. 1); Bolton, '*Mulieres Sanctae*'. Cf.
C. N. L. Brooke and W. Swaan, *The Monastic World* (London, 1974), pp. 177–78, 254 (ch. 11,
n. 2). For the very rapid growth of Cistercian houses of nuns in Germany in the thirteenth
century see maps and index to F. Van der Meer, *Atlas de l'Ordre Cistercien* (Amsterdam-
Brussels, 1965); for corrections, see above, p. 197 n. 8. On Cistercian nuns see also n. 13.

[3] Canonisation process, ed. Z. Lazzeri, 'Il processo di canonizzazione di S. Chiara d'Assisi',
Archivum Franciscanum Historicum, 13 (1920), pp. 403–507, esp. pp. 451–52, 455–56, 471; *Legenda
Sanctae Clarae*, ed. F. Pennacchi (Assisi, 1910), cc. 21–22, pp. 30–31. These are the chief sources
for Clare's life. The process was also edited (modern Italian) by N. Vian, *Il processo di S. Chiara
d'Assisi* (Milan, 1962). For editions of *Legenda S. Clarae*, see n. 1: *Legenda*, pp. xiii ff. discusses
the attribution to Thomas of Celano and produces verbal parallels to his lives of Francis on
pp. xviii–xxvi: see also on the sources M. Fasslinder, 'Untersuchungen über die Quelle zum
Leben der hl. Klara von Assisi', *Franziskanische Studien* 23 (1936), pp. 296–335. Celano's
authorship has been generally accepted in recent studies, though it is far from certain. Modern
lives are legion: there is still useful material in E. Gilliat-Smith, *St Clare of Assisi* (London/To-
ronto, 1914) and relevant chapters of the lives of St Francis by Paul Sabatier and Father
Cuthbert; among biographies F. Casolini, *Chiara d'Assisi* (Assisi, 1953, 3rd edn 1954) is the
best documented we have seen of those produced in 1953; there is a useful brief summary
and bibliography by L. Hardick in *New Catholic Encyclopedia* iii (1967), p. 913; and see n. 1.

[4] See excellent summary in Moorman, *The Franciscan Order*, pp. 211–15; the most important
are edited from the original bulls in *Bullarii Franciscani Epitome*, ed. C. Eubel (Quaracchi,
1908), pp. 234–37 (Gregory IX, reissuing in 1239 in revised form his own earlier, lost, rule),
pp. 241–46 (Innocent IV, 1247), pp. 251–57 (Innocent IV's confirmation of St Clare's rule, 1253),
pp. 269–75 (Urban IV, 1263) – we have made up the number six by adding Urban IV's
confirmation in 1263 of the 'Isabelline' rule of 1252 to the two of Hugolino and Gregory, two
of Innocent IV and one of Urban IV listed here; but the computation is somewhat arbitrary
since there were presumably only minor differences between the first two, and certainly no
more between 1239 and 1247. On the rules see esp. F. Oliger, 'De origine regularum Ordinis
S. Clarae', *Archivum Franciscanum Historicum* 5 (1912), pp. 181–209, 413–47 (esp. on the rule
of 1218–19, pp. 193 ff.); M. Fasslinder, 'Untersuchungen über die Quelle', *Franziskanische Studien* 23 (1936), pp. 306–19.

and the curia, and within her own mind and soul, there was considerable friction and conflict. Perhaps it is possible to see this in a slightly plainer light than hitherto by setting the story of her life and rules in firmer juxtaposition to some other movements of female religious.

Anyone wishing to penetrate to the heart of St Francis's intentions and inspirations naturally starts with his *Testament*; and so it must be with St Clare. We immediately encounter the difficulty that until the 1980s Clare's *Testament* was only known to survive in a transcript from an ancient manuscript in Wadding's *Annales*, from which later editors have copied it.[5] Early in this century several scholars expressed doubts of its authenticity, but these seem mostly to have been resolved. The edition published in *Sources chrétiennes* in 1985 brought to light four manuscripts, gave it a critical text and underpinned its authenticity. There are no evident anachronisms; and, above all, it bears the kind of relation to the text of her rule that could reasonably be expected. The authenticity of Clare's own rule is guaranteed by the original text of the papal bull of confirmation which quotes it verbatim and was issued two days before her death. In its heart lies a crucial passage with strong echoes of Francis's *Testament* in its style and some of its words; and this passage is almost identical with the central core of Clare's *Testament*.[6] The differences are such as we should expect: Clare's *Testament* is more autobiographical, and summarises two of Francis's letters to her; the rule is terser and yet quotes the letters at length. It is natural to suppose that both represent Clare's own attempt to complete her life's work, as Francis had, by providing her own rule and *Testament*, and it would be unreasonable seriously to question the *Testament*'s authenticity. Nonetheless, one is bound to accord a respect for the words of her *Rule* slightly greater than that one gives to her *Testament* – even if one

---

[5] L. Wadding, *Annales Minorum*, ii (Lyon, 1628), pp. 46–49 (= 1253), c. v), whence *Acta Sanctorum*, August, ii, pp. 747–48, *Seraphicae legislationis textus originales* (Quaracchi, 1897), pp. 273–80. Her writings were edited by M.-F. Becker, J.-F. Godet and T. Matura in Claire d'Assise, *Écrits*, Sources Chrétiennes, 325 (Paris, 1985), with commentary. For earlier studies of the *Testament*'s authenticity see P. Robinson in *Archivum Franciscanum Historicum*, 3 (1910), pp. 442–46, citing also a fifteenth-century French and a sixteenth-century Italian version; *S. Chiara d'Assisi 1253–1953*, pp. 519–20. Apart from the *Rule* and *Testament*, Clare's only substantial surviving writings are her letters to Agnes of Bohemia, in Claire d'Assise, *Écrits*, pp. 82–119; also in *Archivum Franciscanum Historicum*, 17 (1924), pp. 509–19; *S. Chiara d'Assisi 1253–1953*, pp. 132–43, with Italian translation. For an English translation of her writings, see *Francis and Clare: The Complete Works*, trans. R. J. Armstrong and I. C. Brady (London, 1982).

[6] Rule of St Clare, c. vi (33), in Claire d'Assise, *Écrits*, pp. 142–44; ed. C. Eubel, *Bullarii Francescani Epitome* (Quaracchi, 1908), pp. 254–55.

bears in mind that the papal chancery may have tidied up Clare's Latin, as it is likely that they tidied Francis's.[7]

The common core of the two documents deals with the basis of Clare's way of life: she had promised obedience to Francis, and to lead a life of poverty and imitation of Christ and His Mother. Directly before it in the *Testament* Clare describes how Francis, immediately after his conversion, and before he had brothers or companions, laboured to rebuild the church of San Damiano, where he had been inspired to leave the world. 'Climbing then on the church's wall, he spoke in a loud voice in French (*lingua francigena*) to a group of poor folk standing round: "Come and help me in my work on the monastery of San Damiano, since there will one day be ladies there, and by their celebrated, holy way of life Our Father in Heaven will be glorified in all His Holy Church".'[8] The substance of this story is happily confirmed in an earlier source, the *Vita secunda* of Thomas of Celano, with such differences as make clear that our two witnesses are independent. Clare very likely knew the version in Celano, but if so she supplemented or possibly corrected it. In the early days after his conversion Francis was begging oil for the lamps in San Damiano, but drew back feeling suddenly shy from a throng of men amusing themselves round the door of a house he wanted to enter. Then he took courage and spoke up fervently *lingua gallica* urging all those present to help with the fabric of San Damiano, saying in the hearing of all that there would be a monastery there of holy virgins of Christ.[9] If we accept the authenticity of Clare's *Testament*, she is an exceptionally reliable source for earlier Assisi tradition, though she might well have had a prejudice in favour of such a tale. Celano's stories mostly came from the saint's companions, and this (though not otherwise recorded) has a distinct flavour of early tradition about it,[10] since no one is likely to have invented stories about Francis hesitating to beg, and the reference to the holy ladies is quite incidental to the point of the story. There seems thus to be exceptionally reliable early evidence that Francis had in mind at the outset of his adventures to provide a home for a community of women. This is consistent with the evidence that the

---

[7] There is a notable absence of grammatical error in the *Regula Bullata*. Minor errors can be discerned in Francis's autograph and it was alleged that he deliberately allowed errors to appear in his Latin.

[8] Claire d'Assise, *Écrits*, p. 168; Wadding, *Annales*, ii, p. 47.

[9] Thomas of Celano, *Vita Secunda*, in *Analecta Franciscana*, x, pp. 127–268, c. 13.

[10] For the known sources of Celano's *Vita Secunda*, see *Scripta Leonis, Rufini et Angeli, sociorum S. Francisci*, ed. and trans. R. B. Brooke, OMT (Oxford, 1970, corr. repr. 1990), introduction, esp. pp. 73–76; J. R. H. Moorman, *The Sources for the Life of S. Francis of Assisi* (Manchester, 1940, repr. Farnborough 1966), esp. pp. 90 ff., 110–27.

initiative for Clare's conversion came from him rather than from her. It would be relatively easy to imagine a sequence of events starting with an impulsive girl insisting on joining Francis and his companions, insisting on his providing her with a way and means of life – thus facing him from the start with a problem already showing some of the embarrassing ambiguities which many have discerned in later events. But for such a reconstruction there is no evidence. Several witnesses in the canonisation process stated fairly plainly that she changed her way of life on his advice – 'sancti viri monitis ad Deum conversa' as Celano has it in the *Vita prima*; and the *Legenda S. Clarae* tells of many secret meetings in which Francis's burning words convinced her.[11] The last account may be a little coloured, but the drift of all the evidence is the same: Francis took the initiative in seeking a female companion or supporter, and may well have envisaged at the outset a religious institute in which men and women collaborated.

Most of the new movements and orders of the twelfth and thirteenth centuries had followers of both sexes. One can divide them, with no great precision, into orders in which the women played a part from the start and were welcomed by the founders, and those whose leaders refused to acknowledge the women religious claiming to be their disciples. Robert of Arbrissel, in whose life every impulse of the religious movements of the late eleventh and early twelfth centuries may be discerned, ended by founding the order of Fontevrault in which women played a predominant role.[12] St Gilbert of Sempringham founded a double order of canons and nuns strictly segregated. The Cistercian fathers buried their heads in the sand, ostrich-like, and for two generations or more seem to have claimed, against all the evidence, that there were no Cistercian women.[13] St Norbert inspired a very large number of both sexes to join his order in early days; but his women suffered the fate of the lay brothers in the Franciscan order a century later. There were alleged by Norbert's biographer to be over ten thousand Premonstratensian women in the middle of the twelfth century,[14] but presently recruiting was forbidden and the female communities died of attrition.

[11] Z. Lazzeri, 'Il processo di canonizzazione', *Archivum Franciscanum Historicum*, 13 (1920), pp. 452, 459, 464, 480, 488, 489 (speaks of secret meetings), 493; *Legenda S. Clarae*, cc. 5–6, pp. 8–10; Thomas of Celano, *Vita Prima* (*Analecta Francescana*, x, pp. 1–117), c. 18 echoed in *Scripta Leonis* no. 109, p. 280.

[12] Grundmann, *Religious Movements* (n. 1), pp. 18–21; R. B. Brooke, *Coming of the Friars* (London, 1975), pp. 57–58 and refs.; J. von Walter, *Die ersten Wanderprediger Frankreichs*, i (Leipzig, 1903).

[13] Our own knowledge of this subject owes much to the work of Dr Sally Thompson (see above, p. 218 n. 19).

[14] R. B. Brooke, *Coming of the Friars*, pp. 58–59, esp. p. 59 and n. 1 and refs.; *Monumenta Germaniae Historica, Scriptores*, 12, pp. 657, 659; Grundmann, p. 21 and p. 267, n. 79.

St Dominic fostered a house of nuns at Prouille before he founded his own order, and he himself was sometimes looked after in his middle years by some of his holy female disciples, as they gave witness in his canonisation process.[15] But when the order began to form, the Dominican nuns were always kept at a distance, semi-detached at least, even though friars and nuns could sometimes still be on terms of remarkable spiritual intimacy as the correspondence of Jordan of Saxony and Diana Dandolo reveals.[16]

Francis's story has something in common with Dominic's, but more perhaps, in the end, with Norbert's. The indications are that in early days Friars Minor and Poor Sisters worked hand in hand, that Francis and Clare were much on the terms of Dominic and his sisters. But by about 1218 a Cistercian monk was visitor to the houses inspired by San Damiano,[17] and although relations with the friars were presently restored, the order (if such it can be called) was formally placed under the rule of St Benedict in 1219;[18] Clare herself lived out her later years cloistered and enclosed in San Damiano. Visits from Francis were relatively rare, though there was one famous occasion when he was nursed at San Damiano in a serious illness and composed the *Canticle of Brother Sun*;[19] and Clare survived his death for almost twenty-seven years, nearly a whole generation, which witnessed many vicissitudes in her relations with his order.

What are the indications of a closer bond in early days? There is a famous story in the *Actus-Fioretti* which, if true, belongs to the very early years of Clare's conversion, of how Francis sent Brother Masseo to consult her and Brother Silvester as to his own true vocation – to serve the world by preaching or to become a contemplative; and how both advised him that Jesus' will was that he should serve many, not himself alone, and preach.[20] The *Actus* is a late and unreliable source; but both this and its neighbour story of how Clare was greatly comforted by a visit to Francis, and how the sisters in San Damiano lived in fear that he would send her

---

[15] Ed. A. Walz, *Monumenta Ordinis Praedicatorum Historica*, 16 (Paris, 1935), pp. 89–194 (text pp. 123 ff.; see esp. pp. 181–82, Toulouse depositions, cc. 15–17, on women's evidence); compare Brooke, *Coming of the Friars*, pp. 102, 177–83.

[16] *Beati Iordani de Saxonia Epistulae*, ed. A. Walz, *Monumenta Ordinis Praedicatorum Historica*, 23 (1951).

[17] Father Cuthbert, *Life of St Francis of Assisi* (2nd edn, London, 1913), p. 172 and n.

[18] In Hugolino's rule, for which see n. 4. On Hugolino's relations with Clare see below at nn. 35–8 and his letter of 1218–19 in *Analecta Franciscana* 3 (1910), p. 183 (cf. *The Legend and Writings of St Clare*, pp. 111–13).

[19] *Scripta Leonis*, nos. 42–43 and 45, pp. 162–67, 170–71; cf. P. Sabatier, *Vie de S. François d'Assise* (Paris, 1893–4), c. 18; Cuthbert, *Life of St Francis*, pp. 418–25.

[20] *Actus b. Francisci et sociorum eius*, ed. P. Sabatier (Paris, 1902), c. 16, pp. 55–59 (= *Fioretti* c. 16); cf. the neighbour story c. 15, *Actus*, pp. 52–54.

away to another house, as Agnes, her sister, had been sent to Florence, have
a hint of early tradition about them unusual in this book; and it is evident
that Francis needed periods of refreshment in a hermitage, and was tempted
to make the Carceri and Fonte Colombo his home;[21] and likely enough
that in early years Clare might have been one of his confidantes.

The other indication is more securely based. The earliest evidence about
the Poor Sisters is in the well-known passage in Jacques de Vitry's letter
written in October 1216 as he lay in the harbour of Genoa preparing to sail
to Acre.[22] It has often been cited, but has still something to tell us. Jacques
de Vitry was one of the great enthusiasts of his age, a fervent preacher, an
ardent crusader, and yet a man who reveals his thoughts in a straightforward,
attractive manner in his letters. He had lived in the diocese of Liège as a
canon regular, and fallen under the influence of St Marie d'Oignies, one
of the notable female religious leaders of the Low Countries; the *Frauenfrage*
and the rising power of the women in the religious movements of the age
were therefore familiar to him. He came south in 1216 to be consecrated
bishop of Acre, and gives in this letter (among other details) his impression
of Milan, *fovea ... hereticorum*, and of the papal curia in Perugia, obsessed
with worldly business. In each city he found a consolation. In Milan hardly
anyone resisted the heretics, save certain 'holy men and religious women',
whose enemies maliciously called *Patareni*, but whom the pope has called
Humiliati and licenced to preach and resist the heretics. They live of the
labour of their own hands, and have so prospered in the diocese of Milan
that there were one hundred and fifty 'congregationes conventuales, virorum
ex una parte, mulierum ex altera' ... established by them, apart from those
who have stayed in their own houses. In the region of Perugia he found
one consolation too: many of both sexes have left the world, called *fratres
minores et sorores minores*. They are revered by pope and cardinals, but have
no care for temporal things, labouring for the cure of souls.

They live according to the pattern of the primitive church ... By day they enter

---

[21] See esp. F. C. Burkitt, 'Fonte Colombo and its Traditions', in Burkitt and others, *Franciscan
Essays*, ii (British Society of Franciscan Studies, 1932), pp. 41–55. Compare *Scripta Leonis*,
pp. 110–11 and pp. 111 n. 1, 134–7, 186–9, 284–7 (cf. pp. 60 ff.).

[22] For what follows see *Lettres de Jacques de Vitry*, ed. R. B. C. Huygens (Leiden, 1960), no.
1, pp. 71–78 (on Humiliati, pp. 72–73; on the Franciscans, pp. 75–76; on the date, p. 52). For
later comments on Francis and his order see no. 6, pp. 131–33 (1220); Jacques de Vitry, *Historia
Occidentalis*, ed. J. F. Hinnebusch, *Spicilegium Friburgense* 17 (Fribourg, 1972), pp. 158–63. On
the Humiliati, see Grundmann, *Religious Movements* (n. 1), pp. 32–40; B. Bolton, 'Innocent
III's treatment of the *Humiliati*', *Studies In Church History*, 8 (1972, pp. 73–82; and 'Sources
for the Early History of the *Humiliati*', *Studies In Church History*, 11 (1975), pp. 125–33 (p. 125
for bibliography, p. 129 for Jacques de Vitry).

cities and towns, giving practical help that they may benefit some; by night they
return to a hermitage or lonely houses, devoting themselves to contemplation.
The women live together near the cities in separate hostels; they receive nothing,
but live by the toil of their hands, and are greatly upset and troubled because
they are honoured by clergy and laity more than they wish.

And he goes on to describe the annual chapter of the order and the
promulgation of *institutiones sanctas et a domino papa confirmatas.*

Doubtless Jacques de Vitry was influenced by the experience of his
homeland, and by his recent meeting with the *Humiliati.* Yet he was a
contemporary witness, and a shrewd one, perfectly capable of distinguishing
one religious system from another; his later letter about St Francis's visit
to the east shows a penetrating mixture of respect and critical reflection on
the Franciscan way of life. His evidence is entirely consistent with the
indications that Francis originally intended women to play as central a part
in his activities as men, and that their role was at first not so different as
it later became.

Yet this makes all the more curious the well-known puzzle: in his later
life he very rarely visited the sisters himself, and he altogether prevented
the kind of cooperation which Jacques de Vitry seems to be describing. His
companions were at pains to emphasise that he rejected all familiarity with
women and forbade his brothers to visit the sisters save when specially
instructed. In Thomas of Celano's second Life there are two striking passages,
which doubtless came from those close to Francis, even though no precise
sources are known, expressing the saint's attitude to women. Chapters 112–14
warn sternly against any mingling with women, and in chapter 112 the saint
is made to say that he never looked them in the face, and only knew two
by sight. They are not named, but it has always been assumed that the
reference is to St Clare and the Lady Jacoba dei Settesoli.[23] In chapters
204–7 Francis is shown instructing by precept and example how the friars are
to treat the sisters: they are to visit them indeed, but rarely and unwillingly.
When he was at San Damiano being nursed in his sickness the 'vicar'
(presumably Elias) frequently admonished him to preach the word of God
to the ladies; eventually he did so, but by an acted parable only: he formed
a circle of cinders and prayed and did penance in their midst. Celano tells
us that they were mightily edified; but doubtless they were disappointed
too, for this was a far cry from the collaboration of earlier days.

Celano spells out that Francis's purpose was to teach the friars by example
that they should visit the sisters indeed, but reluctantly and occasionally,

---

[23] Cuthbert, *Life of St Francis* (n. 17), p. 161 and n. 2. But compare Sabatier, *Vie de S. François*
(n. 19), p. 150 and n. 1, who simply disbelieves Celano.

and thus avoid the snares of female companionship. Doubtless his expla-nation was basically correct: Francis projected himself, especially in his later years, as an example; he became increasingly aware that what he said and did was noted and followed, and he deliberately fostered this attitude to enforce what he reckoned essential lessons. For a large order trying to establish its respectability before the hierarchy at large in the 1220s – and the 1240s when Celano was writing – it was doubtless essential to avoid the suspicion of excessive familiarity even with holy women. But in what measure can we penetrate to the root of the separation of Francis and Clare, and understand how it began?

We may probably discern two stages in the story. The *Legenda S. Clarae* has a highly coloured account of the efforts of St Clare family's to fetch her back, and their even sterner efforts to recover her sister Agnes.[24] The witnesses at the canonisation process told a calmer story, but as several of them were evidently old family friends, doubtless they were not inclined to show Clare's relatives in too harsh a light.[25] In the event their attitude must have had serious consequences for Francis's plans. At first both he and Clare were rebels, dropouts from their social order. The son of the rich merchant Pietro Bernardone had made a public renunciation of his father and his worldly goods,[26] and his presence in Assisi was a constant challenge to the values of his parents' society. Yet in the long run this ceased to be so; the outcast became respectable. Paradoxically, the merchant's son turned rebel found himself, however unwillingly, a guest of honour in the houses of bishops and cardinals and the pope himself; and he had great difficulty in Rome in reconciling the hospitality of the curia and the life of abject poverty he demanded of his followers.[27] He moved in circles his father could never have entered. It is true that this was strictly a spiritual not a social respectability, but that made it precious, or at least necessary to him. In his *Testament* he was to lay great emphasis on his relation to priests and to the pope;[28] it was this which enabled his order to survive and prosper while the *Humiliati* remained a local order of declining repu-tation. The story is a very complex one, and many stages in it are imperfectly

[24] *Legenda Sanctae Clarae*, cc. 9–10, 24–26 (esp. cc. 25–6), pp. 14–16, 33–37 (esp. 35–37).

[25] Z. Lazzeri, 'Il processo di canonizzazione', *Archivum Franciscanum Historicum*, 13 (1920), pp. 487–88, 491–93.

[26] Celano, *Vita Prima*, cc. 12–15; *Legenda trium sociorum*, c. 6 (20), ed. T. Desbonnets, 'Legenda Trium Sociorum: édition critique', *Archivum Franciscanum Historicum*, 67 (1974), pp. 38–144, at p. 105.

[27] Cf. *Scripta Leonis*, no. 92, pp. 248–53; C. Brooke, *Medieval Church and Society* (London, 1971), p. 205.

[28] Esser, *Opuscula*, pp. 438–39.

known. Francis must early have become aware that recognition came relatively easily to him, but while Clare remained his colleague and in a sense his companion, it could never come to her. So much is plain; the rest is conjecture. But it is also likely that Clare's background added to the difficulties. Several of the witnesses in the canonisation process emphasise that she came of noble stock,[29] that is to say was Francis's social superior. This is quite in the tradition of the *Humiliati,* whose communities contained a substantial element of well-to-do, and highly-born, men and women parading their denial of the material values of their world;[30] and Francis may well have been encouraged in his persuasions to Clare by the effect such an example would have in Assisi. Evidently her family were both pious and conventional: as one witness observed, when she fell under Francis's influence she was of marriageable age (about seventeen) and good-looking, and her parents thought it high time she was married.[31] Her mother had been on long pilgrimages and was noted for her good works.[32] A reaction against such a home was less excusable in a woman than a man; and it may be that some measure of conformity to social prejudice became necessary to Francis and Clare from a fairly early stage.

The other element in the story is the patronage of Cardinal Hugolino and the search for a rule. The draconian decree of the fourth Lateran council of 1215 against new orders – or against new rules, as it was interpreted – brought notorious difficulties to all the religious leaders Innocent III had formerly helped.[33] After a pause St Dominic returned to the curia claiming the rule of St Augustine as his foundation deed; Francis himself firmly relied on Innocent's verbal approval of his first rule in 1210 – though some kind of recognition of his rule in 1215 is recorded.[34] As the years passed and he came to enjoy more and more the help and patronage of Hugolino, pressure was brought to bear – from within the order, if we may believe the *Verba S. Francisci,* but via the cardinal – on Francis to accept an existing rule.[35] This he steadfastly refused, but it was not until 1223, eight years after

---

[29] Z. Lazzeri, 'Il processo di canonizzazione', *Archivum Franciscanum Historicum,* 13 (1920), pp. 443, 487, 491–92; compare *Legenda Sanctae Clarae,* c. 1, pp. 4–5.

[30] B. Bolton, 'Sources for the Early History of the *Humiliati',* *Studies in Church History,* 11, esp. pp. 131–32; compare Grundmann, *Religious Movements,* pp. 158–69.

[31] Lazzeri, 'Il processo', *Archivum Franciscanum Historicum,* 13 (1920), p. 490.

[32] Ibid., p. 443; *Legenda Sanctae Clarae,* c. 1, pp. 4–5.

[33] R. B. Brooke, *Coming of the Friars,* pp. 86–8, 160–1 and refs.; *Sacrorum Conciliorum nova et amplissima collectio,* ed. J. D. Mansi, 53 vols. (Florence etc., 1759–1927), xxii, cols. 998–99, 1002–3.

[34] *Scripta Leonis,* c. 67, pp. 204–5; cf. Grundmann, *Religious Movements,* pp. 62–63, 292–93.

[35] *Scripta Leonis,* no. 114, pp. 286–89 (cf. pp. 59–60); R. B. Brooke, *Early Franciscan Government* (Cambridge, 1959), pp. 72–3, 286 ff.

the council and only three before his death, that the final version of his *Rule* received formal papal approval. Meanwhile, long before, Hugolino himself had been using San Damiano as a recruiting ground for superiors for his own foundations when he was legate in Lombardy and Tuscany;[36] and in a general way giving encouragement to communities inspired by St Clare and her disciples. These needed a rule, and Hugolino provided a rule himself, in 1219, intended for the whole group of houses.[37] We know its text from his own reissue, when he was pope Gregory IX, in 1239; and we have his own word for it that the texts were essentially the same. At its base lies subjection to the rule of St Benedict, strict enclosure and the right to communal property, for Hugolino evidently reckoned total poverty incompatible with an effectively enclosed life.[38] It has the strange provision which seems to limit the novitiate to a few days;[39] but is otherwise quite a clear, straightforward rule for a strict, austere, utterly retired life, much influenced by Cistercian customs. In all probability Clare had accepted by this date the need for enclosure; and Hugolino's rule was accompanied by a slight renewal of Franciscan contacts, since a Franciscan replaced a Cistercian visitor about the same time.[40] But there can be little doubt that she resisted from the first any suggestion that she was not bound to the rule of St Francis and to poverty.[41] It took Francis eight years to obtain confirmation of his rule, and Clare had to wait another thirty for hers. Her life ended in a quiet but dramatic triumph. Innocent IV, not the pope most noted for sympathy with Franciscan poverty in its more extreme forms, came and settled for a while in Perugia, and he and his cardinals visited the dying abbess, now a figure of great prestige, generally and widely

[36] On Hugolino as legate, R. B. Brooke, *Early Franciscan Government*, pp. 59 ff. esp. pp. 62–67, 286; E. Brem, *Papst Gregor IX bis zum Beginn seines Pontifikats* (Heidelberg, 1911), esp. pp. 26 ff., 111 ff.

[37] See n. 4.

[38] Eubel, *Bullarii Franciscani Epitome*, pp. 234–37; cf. p. 234, n. 1 and refs.

[39] Eubel, *Epitome*, p. 234; see refs. in n. 4 for commentary.

[40] See n. 17; brother Philip was visitor for a while in and after 1219, but was removed after Francis's return from the east in 1221 for acting beyond his instructions; he was, however, visitor for a long period in later years – *Analecta Franciscana*, x, p. 21, n. 12 (note to Celano, *Vita Prima*, c. 25), and refs.; Moorman, *The Franciscan Order* (n. 1), pp. 13, 32, 38n.

[41] This is implicit in her *Rule* – explicit indeed in her claim in the *Testament* to have had the privilege of poverty from Innocent III as well as Innocent IV. On this much of the discussion of the authenticity of the *Testament* has turned; we need not doubt that Clare believed she had this privilege from Innocent III, just as we cannot doubt Francis believed that the same pope had confirmed his *Rule*. Gregory IX also confirmed the privilege, for San Damiano alone.

admired.[42] Two days before her death the pope at last confirmed her own version of her own rule.[43] It enshrined the privilege of poverty, which she claimed to have had from Innocent III and which Innocent IV had already confirmed to her; it laid less emphasis than Gregory on enclosure, though the nuns were only allowed to go out in case of necessity; it said nothing of St Benedict; and it was closely modelled on the rule of St Francis and has many echoes and quotations from it.[44] It was a personal privilege for Clare and her community: long since, her own fixed enclosure and her resistance to the implications of Hugolino's rule had made it impossible for her to be in any sense an administrative head of her order. She was its inspiration and its link with Francis; and in both these senses, it seems clear, Hugolino as cardinal and as Pope Gregory IX had accepted her position. In 1253 she was free to make her own *Testament* and the confession in her rule:[45] 'postquam altissimus pater caelestis per gratiam suam cor meum dignatus est illustrare ... After the most high heavenly Father by his grace deigned to illuminate my heart, so that I might do penance by the example and teaching of our most blessed father Francis, a short while after his conversion, together with my sisters I willingly promised obedience to him' – an obedience, be it noted, which subjected her to Francis's rule, not to Benedict's.

> The blessed father expected us to have no fear of poverty, toil, tribulation, reviling and the world's scorn, but rather to hold them highly delectable things; and so he was moved by *pietas* and wrote for us a pattern of living – *formam vivendi* – in this fashion: 'By God's inspiration you have made yourselves daughters and slaves of the most high, supreme king, the heavenly Father, and have wedded yourselves to the Holy Spirit by choosing to live according to the perfection of the Holy Gospel; and so I will and promise, on my own account and my brothers', always to have such diligent care of you as of ourselves,[46] and a particular responsibility.' While he lived he diligently fulfilled his promise, and willed his brothers always to fulfil it. Also, to prevent us from anywhere falling off from the most holy poverty on which we had entered – or any of our sisters yet to

---

[42] *Legenda Sanctae Clarae*, cc. 40–42, pp. 56–60, esp. pp. 56–57, c. 44, pp. 61–62; for her death and funeral, conducted by the pope and cardinals, *Legenda Sanctae Clarae*, cc. 45–48, pp. 62–72.

[43] *Solet annuere*, 9 August 1253, Eubel, *Bullarii Franciscani Epitome*, pp. 251–57; this was also for San Damiano alone.

[44] See E. Grau, 'Die Regel der hl. Klara (1253) in ihrer Abhängigkeit von der Regel der Minderbrüder (1223)', *Franziskanische Studien*, 35 (1953), pp. 211–73; the *Rule* of St Clare and its main sources are conveniently laid out in Gilliat-Smith, *Clare of Assisi* (n. 3), pp. 287–305.

[45] What follows is the version in the *Rule*, Claire d'Assise, *Écrits*, pp. 142–5; also in Eubel, *Bullarii Franciscani Epitome*, pp. 254–55; for the closely parallel passage in the *Testament*, Claire, *Écrits*, pp. 170–73; Wadding, *Annales*, ii, pp. 46–49 (= 1253, c. v). See above, p. 277

[46] *Curam diligentem*, which could mean 'loving care'.

come – a little before his death he wrote to us his final will, saying: "I, little brother Francis, wish to follow the life and poverty of our most high Lord Jesus Christ and his most holy mother, and to persevere in it to the end. And I ask you all, my ladies, and I give you counsel that you always live in this most holy way of life and poverty. And take much care not to draw back from it at all, on any man's teaching or advice, for ever." And thus I was ever anxious with my sisters to preserve the holy poverty which we promised to God and the blessed Francis; and thus the abbesses who succeed me in this office, and all the sisters, are bound to observe it unbroken to the end – that is, in not receiving or holding any possession or property by themselves or through any intermediary, nor anything which can reasonably be called property, save only as much land as necessity demands for decent provision of the monastery and its separation from the world; and that land shall not be worked except for a garden to service their own needs.

Francis was ready to obey Hugolino and the pope so long as they demanded nothing incompatible with his own revelation – 'no man showed me what I ought to do, but the most high himself revealed to me that I ought to live according to the pattern of the holy gospel'.[47] So also Clare: she would obey Francis so long as he demanded nothing incompatible with his own instruction to poverty; and in the end she would obey no cardinal or pope who made her renounce obedience to Francis and his instructions. What passed between her and Gregory IX is a puzzle and a mystery, just as is much of what passed between Francis and Hugolino between 1215 and 1223.[48] But the essence of the matter was that Francis instructed her to poverty, and doubtless to a life of contemplation; and copious witnesses at the canonisation process confirmed that this kind of life was congenial to her, both because she was by nature a contemplative and because she was obedient to Francis.[49] This betokened, however, a marked change in the attitude both of Francis and of Clare to her vocation between 1212 and 1219; how much this owed to changes in him and in her, how much to social and ecclesiastical pressure, is quite obscure. Yet surely we may conclude that – whether or not Francis owed his own decision to lead an active life to her advice – she owed her own, contrary, decision to him.

[47] Francis's *Testament*, Esser, *Opuscula*, p. 439.
[48] See esp. R. B. Brooke, *Early Franciscan Government*, pp. 59–76 and *Scripta Leonis*, pp. 59–60; also the refs. cited in nn. 18, 35 above, and *Archivum Franciscanum Historicum*, 13 (1920), p. 452.
[49] *Archivum Franciscanum Historicum*, 13 (1920), pp. 403–507 passim; compare *Legenda Sanctae Clarae*, esp. cc. 19–20, pp. 27–29.

16

Chaucer's Parson and Edmund Gonville: Contrasting Roles of Fourteenth Century Incumbents

When I first studied the fourteenth-century church I was struck by the ambiguity and ambivalence of much that I saw.[1] I wrote in 1957:

> The fourteenth century was a period of extraordinary spiritual vitality. The century which produced the *Cloud of Unknowing* and *Piers Plowman* would need no further advertisement; but the wealth of religious literature which fills our older libraries and has ... been revealed to us in W. A. Pantin's admirable survey is astounding. There is a mass of semi-popular theological and legal literature, intended for the instruction of the rank-and-file clergy; the specifically mystical writings of Richard Rolle and the author of the *Cloud*; and a multitude of vernacular works of devotion written for and sometimes by the literate layman. There is a weight of evidence for ordinary devotion and genuine pastoral care by men as diverse as Archbishop Thoresby of York and Chaucer's poor parson. The better fourteenth-century bishops made efforts to improve the education even of the lower clergy, and not merely of their *familia* and the diocesan administrators. It was possible for Edmund Gonville, founder of Gonville Hall in Cambridge and at least two other religious houses besides, to combine high finance with the pastoral care of a resident country rector. Gonville was a

First printed in *Studies in Clergy and Ministry in Medieval England*, Purvis Seminar Studies, ed. D. M. Smith, Borthwick Studies in History, 1 (York, 1991), pp. 1–19.

[1] I opened this lecture with a warm word of thanks to the University of York and to David Smith for their generous invitation to the first Purvis Seminar – and of appreciation of the late Canon Purvis. In revising this paper I had kind help from several members of the seminar and in particular from Jonathan Hughes. I knew Canon Purvis a little and recall him as a kindly elder citizen at gatherings of ecclesiastical historians; as the revered founder of the Borthwick Institute; as one deeply engaged in the York Mystery plays, and so a 'man of mystery and drama'.

phenomenon even in the fourteenth century; but he can be fitted into his own century as easily as into any other.[2]

At the same time I reckoned that Mammon had his grip on the English church in a quite spectacular fashion. It was then that it became a normal practice to translate bishops from see to see, mounting the economic scale as they went. It was then that the practice of chopping churches first catches our eye – of what seems to have been a well-established stock exchange in benefices by which the impecunious could barter his living for one less well paid, and in return the broker would pay his debts; by the same token the more prosperous could move into a better living after paying a suitable premium. 'The gravest charge against the fourteenth century church', said I – for I was young and bold in those days, 'is that it allowed its revenues to be diverted [from men of spiritual vision like William Langland, living in squalor in his 'cot on Cornhill'] to usurers like [David] Wollore and land-agents like the Pellegrini'.[3]

I still think these examples reflect in some sense the special character of the fourteenth-century church; but I see nothing unusual now in its ambivalence. That seems to be a mark of the English church in every century. In the mid-eleventh century R. R. Darlington and Frank Barlow alike have found fervour and reform; few pastoral bishops have come near St Wulfstan of Worcester.[4] But they had a little difficulty with Stigand, who was not only the most remarkable pluralist in recorded history before Thomas Wolsey, but archbishop of Canterbury to boot.[5] I have lived long in the twelfth century and naturally regard it as the golden age of the medieval church; but to it we owe the model of the medieval archdeacon, whose

[2] C. Brooke, 'The Middle Ages', in *A History of St Paul's Cathedral*, ed. W. R. Matthews and W. M. Atkins (London, 1957), pp. 1–99, 361–65, at p. 84. My account of the fourteenth century was, and is, much indebted to W. A. Pantin, *The English Church in the Fourteenth Century* (Cambridge, 1955).

[3] Brooke, 'The Middle Ages', p. 85; for Wollore and Pellegrini see ibid., pp. 40, 48, 64. For fourteenth-century pluralists see the returns to the papal enquiry of 1366 in *Registrum Simonis Langham*, ed. A. C. Wood (Canterbury and York Society, 1956), pp. 5–111; *Registrum Simonis de Sudbiria* (London), ed. R. C. Fowler et al., 2 (Canterbury and York Soc., 1938), pp. 148–82; and commentary by A. Hamilton Thompson, 'Pluralism in the Mediaeval Church: With Notes on Pluralists in the Diocese of Lincoln, 1366', *Associated Architectural Societies' Reports and Papers*, 33 (1915–16), pp. 35–73; 34 (1917–18), pp. 1–26; 35 (1919–20), pp. 87–108, 199–242; 36 (1921–2), pp. 1–41.

[4] R. R. Darlington, 'Ecclesiastical Reform in the Late Old English Period', *EHR*, 51 (1936), pp. 385–428; F. Barlow, *The English Church 1000–1066* (2nd edn, London, 1979). See now Emma Mason, *St Wulfstan of Worcester* (Oxford, 1990).

[5] Stigand was archbishop of Canterbury and bishop of Winchester and enjoyed revenues from several abbeys: see e.g. evidence cited in *Heads*, pp. 45, 65–66.

eternal destiny was as doubtful then as in the nineteenth century, and who was already commonly an absentee or a pluralist or both.[6] We cannot find a Stigand; but we can find Henry of Blois, who combined one of the richest sees with one of the richest abbeys in the land – and who was nonetheless made something of a hero by David Knowles, not without reason.[7] Henry reflects the ambivalence of the twelfth century in a single frame. In the reigns of Henry VII and Henry VIII – to take a great leap forward – we may contemplate John Colet and St John Fisher with admiration or Cardinal Wolsey with envy. But we must allow that Henry VII, who made Fisher a bishop, also 'virtually set apart the bishopric of Worcester to maintain a diplomatic agent at the Roman Court.'[8] Likewise Henry VII, a conventionally devout man surrounded by goodly clerks, helped his favourite diplomat Christopher Urswick to five archdeaconries (which I believe to be the record), and the deanery of York for good measure; and set Richard Fox in the see of Winchester.[9] Now Fox was a great political prelate, but also the patron of John Fisher, who loved him dearly, and the founder of Corpus Christi College, Oxford; and he raised a splendid chantry at the end of his life in Winchester cathedral as close to his patron St Swithun as was reasonably possible. For later centuries let Sir Thomas Bertram alone suffice: at the turn of the eighteenth and nineteenth centuries this austere man who expected a high level of conduct from his clergy as well as his daughters, was prepared nonetheless to sell the living of Mansfield to Dr Grant to pay his son's debts; he was ashamed, but chiefly because it prevented him from presenting his second son to the living – until Jane Austen, with a peremptory wave of her wand, sent Dr Grant to apoplexy and death after three good dinners in one week, and so provided for the newly-wed Edmund Bertram at the end.[10]

It is high time I returned to the fourteenth century, from lofty generalisations covering many centuries, to case studies within the frontiers of one.

[6] Above, pp. 118, 128; John of Salisbury, *Letters*, ii, pp. 24–27, no. 140.

[7] D. Knowles, *Monastic Order in England, 940–1216* (2nd edn, Cambridge, 1963), pp. 286–93; Knowles, *The Episcopal Colleagues of Archbishop Thomas Becket* (Cambridge, 1951), pp. 34–37, 109–11.

[8] F. R. H. Du Boulay in *The English Church and the Papacy in the Middle Ages*, ed. C. H. Lawrence (London, 1965), p. 222.

[9] Cf. C. N. L. Brooke, 'The University Chancellor', in *Humanism, Reform and the Reformation: The Career of Bishop John Fisher*, ed. B. Bradshaw and E. Duffy (Cambridge, 1989), pp. 47–66, at pp. 55–56, 64–65, nn. 44, 51; A. B. Emden, *A Biographical Register of the University of Cambridge to 1500* (Cambridge, 1963), pp. 239–41, 605–6. On Fox and Fisher, see Bradshaw in *Humanism, Reform and the Reformation*, p. 3; Brooke, 'The University Chancellor', pp. 49, 62 n. 13.

[10] *Mansfield Park*, i, ch. 3; iii, ch. 17.

The sources provide much rich material on the structure of the church, on its learning and unlearning, its law and custom, on its prosopography; but they offer very lean fare when we seek a menu of intimate sketches from clerical life. If we ask, what did a fourteenth-century parson actually do? How did he pass his life? We ask a question our evidence is peculiarly ill-fitted to answer. I have chosen two of the best documented fourteenth-century parsons; but I must own at once that there is a difficulty which some might think fatal in both. For Gonville the evidence is mostly circumstantial: it delineates for us a character deeply devoted both to mammon and to God, but we have to speculate how he made his money, and conjecture the nature of his religious sentiment. Chaucer's parson is in an even worse case. He did not exist at all. Yet I hope something can be made of them.

Edmund Gonville came of a rising gentry family of French extraction, recently settled in Norfolk: his brother Nicholas married the heiress of the manor of Larling and thus his father became lord of the manor.[11] This remarkable arrangement strongly suggests that the family was already engaged in land management and money-lending. Edmund was evidently involved in the family inheritance, and one of his foundations, the college of chantry priests at Rushford, was formed out of a family holding. He was also a man of considerable substance: he had a hand in founding three religious houses, of Dominicans at Thetford in 1335, of chantry priests at Rushford (very close to Thetford) in 1342, and of scholars in Cambridge in 1348; and he was able to make a loan of 300 marks to Edward III, which was perhaps his douceur for the licence in mortmain to found Gonville Hall, without going bankrupt.[12] His success as a founder clearly points to hidden sources of wealth and patronage. Yet he himself was never a pluralist, never held more than one living at a time. He was rector of Thelnetham in Suffolk (1320–26), and of Rushford or Rushworth and Terrington St Clement in Norfolk (1326–42, 1343–51).[13] That is all.

Francis Blomefield, the eighteenth-century Norfolk antiquary, was a Caian, and naturally took a special interest in Edmund Gonville, first founder of his

[11] On Gonville and his family see Brooke, *History of Gonville and Caius College* (Woodbridge, 1985; corr. repr. 1996), pp. 2–3, 7–12 and refs in p. 2 n. 4; E. K. Bennet, *Historical Memorials of the College of St John Evangelist, Rushworth or Rushford, Co. Norfolk* (Norwich, 1887, repr. from *Norfolk Archaeology*, 10 (1888, *sic*), pp. 50–64, 77–382), pp. 8–18, 63–71; J. Venn, *Biographical History of Gonville and Caius College*, iii (Cambridge, 1901), pp. 1–4; C. Norton in Norton, D. Park and P. Binski, *Dominican Painting in East Anglia* (Woodbridge, 1987), pp. 87–88 and n. 22.

[12] See n. 11; T. Rymer, *Foedera*, iii, 1 (edn of London, 1825), p. 69.

[13] Brooke, *History of Gonville and Caius College*, p. 2 and n. 4.

college. In his account of the origin of the house of Dominican Friars at Thetford, founded in or about 1335, he describes Gonville as agent of the earls of Surrey and Lancaster for their East Anglian estates.[14] No earlier source has been found for this statement and Gonville does not figure in Sir Robert Somerville's great study of the early history of the duchy of Lancaster.[15] Recently, furthermore, Christopher Norton has shown that Blomefield and everyone else, myself included, has misunderstood the process which lay behind the foundation of the Thetford house.[16] But the effect of his enquiry is very much to strengthen the impression that Gonville was a land agent on a substantial scale . The friary was founded on land held in 1335 by John de Warenne, earl of Surrey. But Warenne's estate had been passing like a shut-tlecock between Warenne and the earls of Lancaster and others for nearly twenty years before this event. From 1327 Warenne had a life interest in the estate, which was to pass to Henry of Lancaster on his death. When Warenne died in 1347 Henry was already dead and it was his son, later the first duke, who succeeded to Warenne's estate.[17] There is no doubt that Gonville was in some sense the agent of Warenne in the foundation; and it is a reasonable inference that he had already won the approval of Lancaster for it. As so often with Gonville, a little speculation leads one to a scheme of daring imagination. All Gonville's foundations have a pastoral element in them, and Thetford was the one major town of East Anglia lacking a Dominican convent from which well-trained preachers could help cure the souls of the borderland of Norfolk and Suffolk.[18] Gonville could offer a simple plan to Warenne and Lancaster – to Warenne, a gift which could do no harm to his heirs, since he had only a life interest in it; to Lancaster, a gift which could do no harm to him, since Warenne had it for life and was still hale and hearty. To both he could offer a scheme which involved no trouble, since Gonville himself would see to it. This is one of many indications that Gonville was a man of affairs, who made his way by acting as agent for the great in the regions of East Anglia where he lived and worked. He even acted on occasion for the king and was honoured with the title king's clerk.[19]

[14] F. Blomefield, *An Essay towards a Topographical History of the County of Norfolk*, i (Fers-field, 1739), p. 427.

[15] R. Somerville, *History of the Duchy of Lancaster*, i (London, 1953).

[16] Norton, Park and Binski, *Dominican Painting*, pp. 87–88 n. 22.

[17] Ibid.

[18] Norton in Norton, Park and Binski, *Dominican Painting*, pp. 83–87; cf. D. Knowles and R. N. Hadcock, *Medieval Religious Houses: England and Wales* (2nd edn, London, 1971), pp. 213–20, and map of 'The Friars in England and Wales'; W. A. Hinnebusch, *The Early English Friars Preachers* (Rome, 1951), esp. map p. 57.

[19] Gonville is 'clerico nostro' in the royal licence in mortmain for the foundation of Gonville Hall, Venn, *Biographical History*, iii, p. 325; cf. *Calendar of Patent Rolls, 1345–48*, pp. 19–20.

When the economic history of late twentieth-century England comes to be written, our descendants will learn how our affairs were managed not by industrialists or landlords, as in Victorian England, but by accountants and consultants, who created nothing but piles of paper, and yet made large fortunes by fructifying (as their contemporaries supposed) the economy. The key to how the fourteenth-century economy worked must lie in the profession of land agents, and agents of various kinds. Vast estates were held by rentier, absentee landlords, and their management must have involved immense and complex problems. Let us inspect one remarkable estate of special interest, the prebend of Masham in York minster. It comprised many acres in Masham and Kirkby Malzeard, and the rectorial tithes of both churches.[20] It was extremely valuable and so its holder was rarely if ever in the later middle ages resident in York or Masham. Thus in 1447 it was given to the young George Neville, who was fourteen and shortly to become an undergraduate at Balliol – and with unprecedented rapidity chancellor of Oxford.[21] In the 1360s (not for the first time) it had been held by two cardinals, one of them a Benedictine monk vowed to a life of personal poverty in a palace in Avignon.[22] These characters evidently never visited Masham; it was attractive to them because it was a rich plurality, and its revenues could be managed by a reliable agent. We know something of the stewards and bailiffs of great estates; but of the men who farmed the glebe and the tithes of rectories past counting we know almost nothing. By good fortune I worked on the chapter of St Paul's while Roger Highfield was studying the relations of England and Avignon;[23] and we were able to compare notes on Raymond Pellegrini, a Gascon from the see of Cahors, 'who had probably first come to England in the 1320s, and had risen to be a papal collector and papal ambassador in the 1340s and 1350s, was a member of a family which made a profession out of Anglo-papal relations, and specialized in managing the English properties of the Avignon

[20] On the prebend and prebendaries of Masham, see C. T. Clay, ed., *York Minster Fasti*, Yorkshire Archaeological Society Record Series, 123–24 (1958–59), i, pp. 80–84, ii, pp. 51–55; *Fasti 1300–1541*, vi, pp. 66–68. On medieval estate management, see esp. D. Oschinsky, *Walter of Henley* (Oxford, 1971).

[21] Brooke, 'The University Chancellor', in *Humanism, Reform and the Reformation* (n. 9), pp. 52–53, 63 n. 35, based on G. Keir, 'The Ecclesiastical Career of George Neville, 1432–1476' (unpublished B.Litt. thesis, University of Oxford, 1970); A. B. Emden, *A Biographical Register of the University of Oxford to 1500*, 3 vols (Oxford, 1957–59), ii, pp. 1347–49.

[22] *Fasti, 1300–1541*, vi, pp. 66–67.

[23] J. R. L. Highfield, 'The Relations between the Church and the English Crown, 1348–78' (unpublished D.Phil. thesis, University of Oxford, 1950).

cardinals. St Paul's churchyard was a highly convenient business centre, and so Raymond purchased for himself a stagiaryship [a resident canonry], and added to his store of properties some of the manors of St Paul's.'[24] The details of the business operations of these agents are totally obscure, and we rarely know their names. Yet they played a crucial role in English society and in the church international.

It seems abundantly clear that Edmund Gonville was an agent who dealt both in secular estates and clerical; and a diplomat who knew how to manipulate his friendship network to further his purposes. We may conjecture that this helped in his business career; we can be certain that it helped him in his pious foundations. His role in founding the house of Dominican friars in Thetford is incomprehensible unless he enjoyed the confidence of Warenne and the two Lancasters, father and son. When he founded his second house, the college of chantry priests at Rushford, he depended much more on the support of his family in whose patrimony it was set, and of the bishop of Norwich, Anthony Bek the younger, with whose aid he appropriated and converted Rushford from a rectory into a college.[25] With Bek's successor, William Bateman, another star of the papal curia, he was to be even more closely linked.[26] In 1342 Gonville gathered a group of local notables to witness his foundation charter at Rushford.[27] The function of the college was to provide a group ministry for the parish and sing masses daily for the founder and his family. Five masses a day were to help the passage of Gonville's soul to heaven in perpetuity – or anyway until the days of Henry VIII. Doubtless precedents can be found for this arrangement; the one most familiar to me is the church of St Michael in Cambridge – now in the heart of Gonville's College, though this is the product of later events after Gonville's death. St Michael's was rebuilt by Hervey de Stanton, chancellor of the exchequer in Edward II's later years, to be college chapel and parish church combined; and he made the fellows of his college – all of whom were to be priests – the joint rectors of the parishes.[28]

[24] Brooke, 'The Middle Ages', p. 64, cf. p. xxiii.
[25] Bek the younger (Norwich, 1337–43) to distinguish him from the bishop of Durham (1284–1311).
[26] On Bateman, see C. N. L. Brooke, *A History of Gonville and Caius College* (Woodbridge, 1985; corr. repr. 1996), pp. 5–6, 13–18, and refs. in p. 5 n. 7, esp. to A. Hamilton Thompson, 'William Bateman, Bishop of Norwich, 1344–1355', *Norfolk Archaeology*, 25 (1935), pp. 102–37.
[27] Bennet, *Rushworth*, pp. 37–43, incorporating Gonville's statutes.
[28] R. Willis and J. W. Clark, *The Architectural History of the University of Cambridge and of the Colleges of Cambridge and Eton* (Cambridge, 1886; repr. 1988), iii, pp. 489–92, 521–22; C. Brooke, 'The Churches of Medieval Cambridge', in *History, Society and the Churches: Essays in Honour of Owen Chadwick*, ed. D. Beales and G. Best (Cambridge, 1985), pp. 49–76, esp. p. 72; cf. A. E. Stamp, *Michaelhouse* (Cambridge, 1924).

Gonville's third foundation was one of a flurry of small colleges founded in Cambridge in the mid fourteenth century – Pembroke, Gonville Hall, Trinity Hall and Corpus.[29] They all reflect Gonville's network of friends. In the founding of Pembroke Gonville acted as the countess of Pembroke's man of affairs in Cambridge. Trinity Hall was founded by his bishop, William Bateman – who took over Gonville Hall itself after its founder's death – and Corpus by two guilds one of which was nominally headed by Henry of Lancaster.[30] Bateman may have been inspired by Gonville to his own foundation; he was certainly ready to set Gonville Hall on its feet. Gonville's relation with Duke Henry is entirely speculative, and this is all the more tantalising since Henry was to write one of the most remarkable exercises in lay piety of the century, the *Livre des seyntz medicines*, in 1354, three years after Gonville's death, two years after the founding of Corpus.[31] Among Henry's close associates was the successful soldier from Hainault, Walter de Manny or Mauny. Manny is named on the letters patent granting the licence in mortmain for the foundation of Gonville Hall as Gonville's agent in the royal court.[32] Gonville Hall was dedicated to the Annunciation of the Blessed Virgin and founded in 1348; in 1349 Manny established a cemetery and chapel in the city of London for victims of the plague, also dedicated to the Annunciation; and many years later he converted it into the Charterhouse.[33] These glimpses of the founders of Cambridge colleges, of lay piety, and of the patronage of the Carthusians, bring into view in an intriguing way much of the avant-garde in fourteenth-century religious sentiment.

To this we may add the most spectacular and the most speculative item of all. In 1987 Christopher Norton, David Park and Paul Binski published their brilliant study of the Thornham Parva retable and the closely similar

[29] Brooke, *History of Gonville and Caius*, pp. 9–18; C. Brooke, R. Highfield and W. Swaan, *Oxford and Cambridge* (Cambridge, 1988), pp. 92–100; D. R. Leader, *A History of the University of Cambridge*, i (Cambridge, 1989), pp. 78–88.

[30] On Pembroke, see J. Ringrose, 'The Foundress and her College', in *Pembroke College Cambridge: A Celebration*, ed. A. V. Grimstone (Cambridge, 1997), pp. 1–12, esp. p. 5; C. Brooke, 'What Happened in 1348', *The Caian* (1998), pp. 29–32, esp. pp. 29–30. On Trinity Hall, see C. Crawley, *Trinity Hall* (Cambridge, 1976), pp. 1–15; on Corpus, C. R. Cheney, 'The Gilds of the Blessed Virgin Mary and of Corpus Christi', *Letter of the Corpus Association*, no. 63 (1984), pp. 24–35; C. P. Hall, 'The Gild of Corpus Christi and the Foundation of Corpus Christi College', in *Medieval Cambridge*, ed. P. Zutshi (Woodbridge, 1993), pp. 65–91.

[31] Pantin, *The English Church*, pp. 231–33.

[32] Venn, *Biographical History*, iii, p. 325; Brooke, *History of Gonville and Caius College*, p. 1 and n. 1.

[33] D. Knowles and W. F. Grimes, *Charterhouse* (London, 1954).

altar frontal in the Musée de Cluny in Paris – and argued that they formed a single scheme of adornment intended for the high altar of the Dominican church in Thetford, prepared for its foundation in or soon after 1335.[34] The whole composition was an exquisite work of a fine school of local craftsmen, possibly working in Thetford itself; with reasonable assurance East Anglian – and one may suppose that its making was supervised by the man of affairs who organised the more mundane aspects of the foundation, Edmund Gonville. The retable portrays a gallery of eight saints with a crucifixion in their midst.[35] They are in pairs – two apostles, Peter and Paul, two assorted martyrs, John the Baptist and Edmund, two favourite virgin martyrs, Catherine and Margaret, two Dominicans, Dominic himself and Peter Martyr. The odd pair are Edmund and John, and the authors have pointed out how appropriate the choice of saints would have been to a Dominican convent founded by Edmund Gonville and John de Warenne.[36] The frontal shows scenes from the life of the Virgin; but one is missing – the known parallels make it almost certain that it was the Annunciation; we are again reminded that this was a special devotion of Gonville's.[37] The frontispiece of this splendid book brings us very near the taste and sentiment of a remarkable man; but the Annunciation is missing, as if to remind us that we are in a world of speculation.

In contrast, the most secure revelation of Gonville's mind survives in his statutes for the college of chantry priests at Rushford.[38] This was a foundation for five chaplains, of whom one was to be master, freely elected by his brothers – subject to confirmation by the bishop – and for life unless they fell into crime. The first duty of one and all was to celebrate mass daily for the founder, his family and all the faithful departed; and responsibility for pastoral care of Rushford lay with the master – to 'minister sacraments and sacramentals, as the care of souls enjoined upon him demands and requires' – though he might delegate it to one of the chaplains.[39] All were bound to perpetual residence. For this small community of humble devout chaplains, dedicated

[34] Norton, Park and Binski, *Dominican Painting* (n. 11), esp. for what follows, pp. 82–101; and for Gonville's role, pp. 87–88, 91. Doubts were expressed by Pamela Tudor-Craig (Lady Wedgwood) in her review in *Antiquaries Journal*, 68 (1988), pp. 367–68. Her chief ground was the suggestion that the retable was earlier in date than Norton, Park and Binski had argued. Paul Binski has kindly informed me that dendrochronology now establishes that it cannot be as early as Lady Wedgwood suggested and confirms their dating.
[35] Norton, Park and Binski, *Dominican Painting*, frontispiece, pp. 90–91.
[36] C. Norton in Norton, D. Park and P. Binski, *Dominican Painting*, p. 91.
[37] Ibid., pp. 43–44, 91 n. 28, 100.
[38] Bennet, *Rushworth*, pp. 37–43.
[39] Bennet, *Rushworth*, p. 41.

to the common life, to a round of prayer and masses, and to the care of the souls of the village, he built a substantial house.[40] These statutes lucidly reflect what an experienced parish priest and man of affairs reckoned was necessary for the safety of his soul and his parishioners – and to provide a decent manner of life for what we should call a group ministry.

In contrast the draft statutes he left in Gonville Hall tell us almost nothing of the religious duties of the fellows.[41] Since his stated aim was to provide for poor scholars and to do honour to God and the church and the health of his soul, we may presume that he would have expected the fellows to pray for him, even though he was already well provided with masses. Presumably such provision would have been added in a final version. But Gonville died before this was composed, and William Bateman totally ignored Gonville's draft.[42] The instruction he gave his scribe when he first dictated the college's statutes comprised a very elaborate list of prayers and masses for founders and benefactors; and for the rest, to copy the statutes of Trinity Hall. Gonville had intended his college to serve arts men completing their course and turning into theologians (though other disciplines were not excluded); Bateman nearly made it a college of lawyers. But evidently when he gave the document to the master and fellows, they protested that he had forgotten to provide for their stipends and that Gonville meant them to study theology. So the margin of this extraordinary document is filled with details of their income, and into the clause detailing the studies they might pursue has been added 'or theology'. Bateman lived just long enough to tidy these inadvertent statutes up;[43] meanwhile this first version illustrates how remote the most benevolent of founders might be – how much they needed men of affairs on the spot to set their plans in frame.

This was the function Edmund Gonville had performed as land agent, tithe agent, commissioner of marshland, founder, benefactor and parish priest.[44] But if we ask, at the end of the day, what he did as parish priest,

---

[40] Bennet, *Rushworth*, facing p. 28.

[41] Venn, *Biographical History*, iii, pp. 341–45.

[42] Brooke, *A History of Gonville and Caius College* (Woodbridge, 1985, corr. repr. 1996), pp. 14–15.

[43] J. Venn, *Biographical History*, iii, pp. 345–52.

[44] References to Gonville were gathered in Bennet, *Historical Memorials* and Venn, *Biographical History*, iii, pp. 1–4; cf. Brooke, *A History of Gonville and Caius College*, ch. 1; Brooke in *Dictionnaire d'histoire et de géographie ecclésiastiques*, s. v. Gonville. Cf. *Historical Manuscripts Commission, Twelfth Report*, appendix ix (1891), p. 376, and A. Gibbons, *Ely Episcopal Records* (Lincoln, 1891), p. 91n. (bishop of Ely, bailiff's accounts, showing Gonville as commissioner of Marshland sending letters); *Calendar of Close Rolls, 1330–33*, p. 342 (owing debt); *1333–37*,

we cannot say. We know he cared deeply for the church's sacraments and pastoral care, and for all his great connections and expertise in handling tithes and advowsons, he was never a pluralist.[45] Since his raison d'être as a man of affairs was his local influence, the jobs he could do because he was on the spot, we may reckon that he often was resident, and the charter for Rushford was duly sealed at Rushford while he was still its rector.[46] But when the bishop of Ely's accountant noted payments for the carriage of letters from Gonville as commissioner of Marshland, he was at Rushford even though now rector of Terrington – though Terrington itself is in the Marshland and helps to explain his office.[47] It could be argued that a man so obviously conscientious and caring, who enjoined perpetual residence on his priests at Rushford, must have resided himself. But conscience does not work so. I am reminded of John Fisher (no less) laying down similar rules of residence for the fellows of St John's College, Cambridge, although he himself, as bishop of Rochester, had been for many years a non-resident chancellor of the university and had actually appointed his own archdeacon as master of the college.[48] Perhaps the most likely answer is that Gonville was partially resident – that he divided his last years between Terrington, Rushford, Cambridge and the other places in East Anglia where his interest lay. But this is even more speculative than his patronage of the retable and frontal. None the less the remarkable galaxy of fragments of evidence which gathers round Edmund Gonville shows us a man deeply interested in and devoted to the affairs both of mammon and of God.

p. 56 (advowson business); *1343–46*, p. 552 (advowson and land); *Calendar of Patent Rolls, 1334–38*, p. 158 (foundation of Thetford), pp. 141–42, 439 (on commission of oyer and terminer, 1335, 1337); *1340–43*, p. 188 (Rushford); *1343–45*, p. 337 (a feoffee of land and advowsons); *1345–48*, p. 176 (appointed commissioner 'de walliis et fossatis' in Marshland); *1348–50*, pp. 19–20, 77 (one of a commission to arrest persons prosecuting appeals, evidently in defiance of Praemunire); *Year Books of Edward II*, xvii, *8 Edward II*, ed. W. C. Bolland, Selden Society, p. 72; *18–19 Edward III*, ed. L. O. Pike, RS (London, 1905), pp. 341–42n. (both show him active, presumably trading, in advowsons); *Calendar of Inquisitions Post Mortem*, viii, p. 482 (involved in land transactions); *Calendar of Papal Letters*, iii (1897), p. 369: indult to choose a confessor for plenary remission on death, dated 22 June 1350.

[45] At least, no other benefices held by him have come to light.

[46] Bennet, *Historical Memorials*, pp. 37–43.

[47] See n. 44.

[48] M. Underwood, 'John Fisher and the Promotion of Learning', and C. N. L. Brooke, 'The University Chancellor', in *Humanism, Reform and the Reformation* (n. 9), pp. 26, 36, 40, 56–59.

Geoffrey Chaucer was likewise a successful man of affairs, evidently involved in mammon; his attitude to God is more problematic.[49] It is a very remarkable coincidence that the two most distinguished poets of the Middle English world, Langland and Chaucer, should have been so nearly of an age – all the more striking because they are so far apart in idiom and sentiment.[50] A few things they had in common. Both were connected with the city of London and both idealised ploughmen. Langland made of Piers or Peter the plough-man the symbol of Christ Himself; and in the Prologue to the Canterbury Tales, amid as choice a collection of rogues as one could wish to meet on a pilgrimage, saintliness is only found in the ploughman and his brother. He is a real ploughman

> That hadde ylad of dong ful many a fother;
> A trewe swynkere and a good was he,
> Lyvynge in pees and parfit charitee.
> God loved he best with al his hoole herte
> At alle tymes, thogh him gamed or smerte,
> And thanne his neighebor right as hymselve.
> He wolde thresshe, and therto dyke and delve,
> For Cristes sake, for every povre wight,
> Withouten hire, if it lay in his myght.
> His tithes payde he ful faire and wel,
> Bothe of his propre swynk and his catel.
> In a tabard he rood upon a mere.[51]

The ploughman accompanies his brother, 'a povre persoun of a toun' – but rich in holy thought and work; and Chaucer proceeds to his celebrated portrait of the perfect parish priest. What could be more edifying, more straightforward, more simple? Yet one does not have to read far in Chaucer to discover that nothing is simple or straightforward in his company.[52] A historian who talks about Chaucer puts his head in a noose. I do not pretend to have studied him deeply; but I have gone far enough to have a very deep respect for one of the most brilliant minds and one of the most mordant and unpredictable pens the student of the middle ages can

[49] For his life, see *Chaucer Life Records*, ed. M. M. Crow and C. C. Olson (Oxford, 1966); summary in *The Riverside Chaucer*, ed. L. D. Benson (Oxford, 1987), pp. xi–xxii: all the quotations below are taken from this edition.

[50] I assume in this passage that all the versions of *Piers Plowman* were written by one man, called William Langland, which was a desperate heresy twenty years ago, but now seems once again to be widely held.

[51] *Prologue*, lines 530–41, p. 32.

[52] See comment and references in Brooke, *The Medieval Idea of Marriage* (Oxford, 1989), ch. 8 – and cf. ibid., ch. 9 on Shakespeare.

encounter. The only thing I am certain of is that Chaucer, like Shakespeare, was a great deal more clever than most – perhaps all – his critics.

Most of the portraits of clergy or religious in the Prologue are harsh or unkind to our ears. Jill Mann, in an admirable book, has shown how much of the portraits was drawn from contemporary literature – from the current stereotype.[53] They are types – but with many individual features; and years ago J. M. Manly in a less admirable book showed a great deal of often misplaced ingenuity in identifying the men who sat for some of the portraits.[54] Chaucer's subtle mingling of the individual and the general helps to give a sharp edge to his satire. Chaucer's monk is any religious – and a good fellow; a manly man, to be an abbot able.[55] True, he pays little attention to the rules of St Benedict and St Augustine; but fair enough; why should he? – 'Lat Austyn have his swynk to hym reserved!' As for the portrait of the friar, the prize beggar, the ladies' man, the hypocrite, the reputation of the medieval friars was darkened by it for ever – or at least until hundreds of wills had been combed to show that the impression Chaucer's friar makes on us was not the impression the orders four made on the community as a whole. Nor could it have been or they would not have had to wait for Thomas Cromwell to go out of business.

My favourite is the prioress, gentle, kindly, sentimental, of perfect manners (after a fashion), entirely worldly, with many features taken from a conventional romance, including her 'brooch of gold ful sheene,

> On which ther was first write a crowned A,
> And after *Amor vincit omnia*.'[56]

The piling up of satire and affection makes this portrait a perfect miniature of Chaucer's art. In *Troilus and Criseyde* he lavished 8000 lines on a similar portrait of a dear, kind, good, beautiful, creature who swore eternal fidelity to her lover – but when she was compelled by her tyrannical father, and the decree of Priam's parliament, to go over to the camp of the Greeks, she very quickly became Diomed's girl; what else could she do?[57] The mingling of warmth and cynicism is brilliantly contrived; though naturally it did not deceive Shakespeare, who took over the cynicism and left the warmth behind. Naturally, say I, since I take it this kind of ambivalence is a central characteristic of both poets.

[53] J. Mann, *Chaucer and Medieval Estates Satire* (Cambridge, 1973), esp. chs 2–3.

[54] J. M. Manly, *Some New Light on Chaucer* (London, 1926).

[55] Mann, *Chaucer and Medieval Estates Satire*, pp. 17–37; above, pp. 214–15. For what follows, see *Prologue*, lines 165–269, esp. 188, pp. 26–27.

[56] *Prologue*, lines 160–62, p. 26.

[57] Brooke, *Marriage*, pp. 220–27.

The *Canterbury Tales* were never finished, and their textual history is strange and full of hazards.[58] There is no agreement among the best witnesses as to the order of the Tales, though I take it the *Prologue* (whenever it was actually written) must be intended to come first; and the retraction, and the *Parson's Tale* which precedes and seems inextricably attached to it (whenever they were written), must be intended to come at the end. By the same token, it has often been observed that not all the tales fit the tellers to perfection. The Wife of Bath, for example, seems more learned in Jerome's invective against Jovinian than one might expect.[59] Whatever may be the truth of this, there are at least two tales which give the impression of perfectly fitting their teller's character as revealed in the *Prologue*, and those are the *Parson's Tale* and the *Prioress's Tale*.

After a prologue of moving conventional piety, the prioress proceeds in the sweetest, gentlest tones, to tell the story of little Hugh of Lincoln – she pretends the story is set among Christian folk far far away, in Asia; but she brings it home to Lincoln in the end.[60] Into this charming idyll she suddenly intrudes an extremely precise account of the brutal murder of the small child by a Jewish assassin, followed by the even more brutal punishment of the Jew by the local Christian provost.[61] Then the martyr dies a most edifying death in the local abbey proclaiming his love of the Blessed Virgin, and a marble tomb is made for him, as for young Hugh of Lincoln. Commenting on the repugnant antisemitism of the story, a modern commentator has written 'we are forced to recognise that Chaucer was a man of his time, sharing its faults as well as its virtues'.[62] I do not doubt that Chaucer was a man of his time; but a man of exceptional penetration and depth of insight. And he has told us that very conventional story in such a way as to make the contrast between the prioress' sentimental tones and the harsh brutality of the central scene deeply shocking. To my way of thinking the commentator was not sufficiently shocked: he can look back and say – he was only a medieval layman, after all. Maybe; but Chaucer has used every trick of his art to make the contrast as horrifying as possible; and that is a game he plays often in his *Tales*. I am reminded less of the prejudices of the fourteenth century than of the *Merchant of Venice*. There again a Jew is punished for sins proverbially (however unjustly) attached

---

[58] See esp. J. H. Fisher, 'Animadversions on the Text of Chaucer, 1988', *Speculum*, 63 (1988), pp. 779–93.

[59] *Wife of Bath's Prologue*, lines 673–75, p. 114.

[60] *Prioress's Tale*, esp. lines 488–89, 684, pp. 209–12.

[61] *Prioress's Tale*, lines 565–634, pp. 210–11.

[62] *Riverside Chaucer*, p. 16.

to his race. But his punishment is palpably unjust and the Christians certainly don't escape without a whipping.

The *Parson's Tale* is an extremely sombre sermon – or rather a vernacular treatise on penance and the seven deadly sins.[63] It was evidently composed by Chaucer himself from well-known sources, though doubtless it drew some inspiration from fine preachers he had encountered. It is full of vigour and life – austere, puritanical, conventional in its theology; but vivid and terrifying, though avoiding the preacher's stories and *exempla*. Here he is on adultery:

> This synne, as seith the prophete, bireveth man and womman hir goode fame and al hire honour, and it is ful plesaunt to the devel, for therby wynneth he the mooste partie of this world. And right as a marchant deliteth hym moost in chaffare that he hath moost avantage of, right so deliteth the fend in this ordure.[64]

And of married folk:

> many man weneth that he may nat synne for no likerousnesse [lecherousness] that he dooth with his wyf, certes, that opinion is fals. God woot, a man may sleen hymself with his owene knyf, and make hymselve dronken of his owene tonne [barrel]. Certes, be it wyf, be it child, or any worldly thyng that he loveth biforn God, it is his mawmet [his idol], and he is an ydolastre. Man sholde loven hys wyf by discrecioun, paciently and atemprely, and thanne is she as though it were his suster.[65]

And he makes married love for the sake of fleshly desires alone a sort of adultery. There are glimpses of kinder things – of a loftier view of marriage, for example, though he is very firm that the wife should be subject to the husband – there is no quarter given to the feminism of the Wife of Bath. But at the very end, and very briefly, we learn

> what is the fruyt of penaunce; and, after the word of Jhesu Crist, it is the endelees blisse of hevene, ther joye hath no contrarioustee of wo ne grevaunce; ther alle harmes been passed of this present lyf; ther as is the sikernesse fro the peyne of helle; ther as is the blisful compaignye that rejoysen hem everemo, everich [one] of otheres joye ... This blisful regne maye men purchace by poverte espiritueel,

---

[63] See commentary and references in *Riverside Chaucer*, pp. 956–65. On its sources see S. Wenzel, 'The Source for the *Remedia* of the Parson's Tale', *Traditio*, 27 (1971), pp. 433–53; Wenzel notes Chaucer's errors and the toning down of traditional pessimism about women and marriage (pp. 451–53); the sources and errors are set in perspective in L. W. Patterson's fundamental study of the tale as a coherent manual on sin and confession. 'The *Parson's Tale* and the quitting of the Canterbury Tales', *Traditio*, 34 (1978), pp. 331–80; cf. A. Hudson, *The Premature Reformation* (Oxford, 1988), p. 390 n. 2.

[64] *Parson's Tale*, lines 850–51, p. 318.

[65] *Parson's Tale*, lines 859–61, p. 318.

and the glorie by lowenesse, the plentee of joye by hunger and thurst, and the reste by travaille, and the lyf by deeth and mortificacion of synne.[66]

And without more ado we are launched into Chaucer's little prayer to his reader, and his retraction, in accordance with the teaching on penance he has just unfolded or hearkened to, of all his worldly books, including 'the tales of Caunterbury, thilke that sownen into synne'; and begs forgiveness for them.[67] He thanks Christ and his blissful Mother for his devout and moral works, beseeching them that until his life's end they send him grace to bewail his sins and study the salvation of his soul; and to grant him grace of true penitence, confession and satisfaction – 'so that I may been oon of hem at the day of doom that shulle be saved'.[68]

This startling conclusion has sent some critics scuttling for shelter. He is cheating us again, say some: with brilliant imagination showing the consequence of listening to too eloquent a sermon. It is not by Chaucer at all, say others. Now we might imagine Thomas Chaucer, the poet's son, who may well have presided over the copying and dissemination of his father's masterpiece, feeling anxiety about old Geoffrey's salvation at the end and putting a little penitence into his mouth.[69] But if he wanted his father to retract the bulk of the book, he should not have allowed it to circulate. So other critics reckon that it is very hard to make sense of any explanation except the simplest and most obvious: that this was truly Chaucer's own final reflection on his work and his destiny.

The Merchant of Prato, a generation younger than Chaucer, ended his life a convinced anticlerical – at least to the extent of agreeing with his fervently pious and anticlerical attorney in not leaving his vast charitable bequests in the hands of the church.[70] But when his end was near, he summoned five Franciscan friars to help him on his way.[71] When we read the Prologue to the Canterbury Tales, we go far astray if we seek Chaucer's own views and attitudes: he is holding up society's views of itself to its own mirror. But he does nothing in his handling of monk, friar, summoner or pardoner at least to counter the conventional anticlericalism of his day. The clerk does rather better, the parson is in a different world. Yet there is nothing here to make

---

[66] *Parson's Tale*, lines 1076–80, p. 327.

[67] *Retraction*, line 1086, p. 328.

[68] *Retraction*, line 1092, p. 328.

[69] On his possible role in the textual transmission, see J. H. Fisher, 'Animadversions on the Text of Chaucer, 1988' in *Speculum*, 63 (1988), p. 789; *Chaucer Life Records* (n. 49), p. 603 (index s. v. Chaucer, Thomas) citing M. B. Rudd, *Thomas Chaucer* (Ann Arbor, Michigan, 1926).

[70] C. Brooke, *Medieval Church and Society* (London, 1971), pp. 233–47, at p. 244; based on I. Origo, *The Merchant of Prato* (Harmondsworth, 1963), pp. 326–28, 342ff, 379–80.

[71] Brooke, *Medieval Church and Society*, p. 245; Origo, *Merchant of Prato*, p. 341.

us suppose that Geoffrey Chaucer as a member of parliament would have voted against Provisors or Praemunire, or the proposal to disendow the church; and he allowed the Host to jest that the parson was a Lollard.[72] Yet it seems that he summoned a poor parish priest to his deathbed to instruct him and purge his sins: in imagination, that is, he entered the mind of such a man, and explored it to its depths.

Jill Mann points out very justly that time and again in the Prologue we are offered the character's own assessments of themselves – it is a part of that mingling of affection and satire of which I have spoken.[73] Chaucer speaks as if he approves what he is merely presenting as a part of his satire. We do violence to his method, therefore, as she points out, to assume that every word he utters about his ideal characters, the parson and the plough-man, should be taken as the poet's own. The friar may shock us while he reminds us of our own prejudices; the parson administers a shock of surprise, that in that anticlerical world one of the humble, despised rank-and-file clergy should emerge in such glory. Perhaps it is not a great shock: and much of the account of him is devoted to denouncing priests less worthy than he. The central point is that bad priests are worse than useless – for they corrupt. Chaucer's retraction does not suggest to me that the parson was in any precise sense a priest he knew – if so, he might have retracted rather earlier in life. But the tale and the retraction together show brilliant insight into the mind of such a man; and in that sense Chaucer is describing a real priest who could actually have existed; not just a type, but an ideal; and yet in his imagination an ideal which might be realised. To that extent he is as real as Edmund Gonville – though equally rare. As we listen to Chaucer's description of him, let us beware the sting in the tail.[74]

---

[72] On Provisors and Praemunire, see esp. Pantin, *The English Church*, pp. 84–93; on the proposal for disendowment, A. Hudson, *The Premature Reformation* (Oxford, 1988), pp. 113–16, 337–42. The Host's 'I smelle a Lollere in the wynd' (*Epilogue of the Man of Law's Tale*, line 1173, p. 104) is set admirably in its context by Anne Hudson, *The Premature Reformation*, pp. 390–94. She shows that Chaucer was acquainted with 'some of the characteristic language used by and about the Wycliffites' (ibid., p. 391), and suggests that it is significant that Chaucer in the *Prologue* makes no mention of mass or confession; there may have been a sniff of Lollardy in the priest. She emphasises, however, that this does not apply to the *Parson's Tale*, which is monumentally orthodox and makes confession its centre. Chaucer or his audience may well have enjoyed the notion of Lollard sympathies as a stick to beat the higher clergy with – but I doubt if it is right, in the parson's case, to drive any deep wedge between *Prologue* and *Tale*. None the less, her essential point, that Chaucer enjoyed offering reminiscences of Lollardy, is surely right; and also that this did not imply any overt commitment to a condemned heresy at the time that Chaucer was writing (see esp. ibid., pp. 393–94).

[73] Mann, *Chaucer and Medieval Estates Satire*, esp. on the parson, pp. 66–67.

[74] *Prologue*, lines 477–528, pp. 31–32.

A good man was ther of religioun,
And was a povre Persoun of a Toun,
But riche he was of hooly thoght and werk.
He was also a lerned man, a clerk,
That Cristes gospel trewely wolde preche;
His parisshens devoutly wolde he teche.
Benygne he was, and wonder diligent,
And in adversitee ful pacient,
And swich he was ypreved ofte sithes.
Ful looth were hym to cursen for his tithes,
But rather wolde he yeven, out of doute,
Unto his povre parisshens aboute
Of his offryng and eek of his substaunce.
He koude in litel thyng have suffisaunce.
Wyd was his parisshe, and houses fer asonder,
But he ne lefte nat, for reyn ne thonder,
In siknesse nor in meschief to visite
The ferreste in his parisshe, muche and lite,
Upon his feet, and in his hand a staf.
This noble ensample to his sheep he yaf,
That first he wroghte, and afterward he taughte.
Out of the gospel he tho wordes caughte,
And this figure he added eek therto,
That if gold ruste, what shal iren do?
For if a preest be foul, on whom we truste,
No wonder is a lewed man to ruste;
And shame it is, if a prest take keep,
A shiten [defiled] shepherde and a clene sheep.
Wel oghte a preest ensample for to yive,
By his clennesse, how that his sheep sholde lyve.
He sette nat his benefice to hyre
And leet his sheep encombred in the myre
And ran to Londoun unto Seinte Poules
To seken hym a chaunterie for soules,
Or with a bretherhed to been withholde;
But dwelte at hoom, and kepte wel his folde,
So that the wolf ne made it nat myscarie;
He was a shepherde and noght a mercenarie.
And though he hooly were and vertuous,
He was to synful men nat despitous,
Ne of his speche daungerous ne digne,
But in his techyng discreet and benygne.
To drawen folk to hevene by fairnesse,
By good ensample, this was his bisynesse.

But it were any persone obstinat,
What so he were, of heigh or lough estat,
Hym wolde he snybben sharply for the nonys.
A bettre preest I trowe that nowher noon ys.
He waited after no pompe and reverence,
Ne maked him a spiced conscience,
But Cristes loore and his apostles twelve
He taughte; but first he folwed it hymselve.

Index

Figures in bold refer to illustrations.